Martyn Turner's

GREATEST HITS

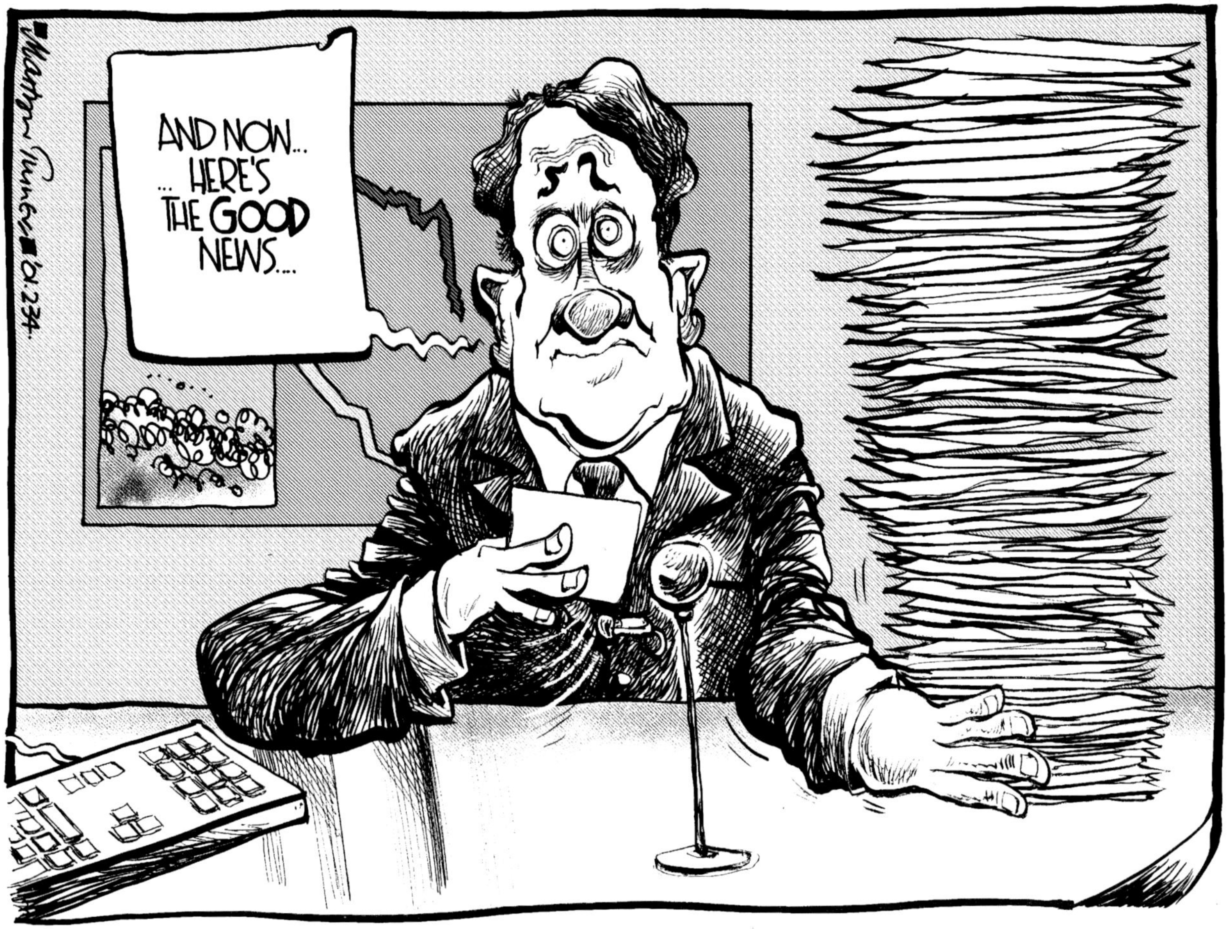
AND NOW...
... HERE'S
THE GOOD
NEWS....

Martyn Turner's

GREATEST HITS

GILL & MACMILLAN

Gill & Macmillan Ltd
Hume Avenue, Park West, Dublin 12
with associated companies throughout the world
www.gillmacmillan.ie
© Martyn Turner 2003
0 7171 3573 X

Design and print origination by O'K Graphic Design, Dublin
Printed in Malaysia

The paper used in this book comes from the wood pulp of managed forests.
For every tree felled, at least one tree is planted, thereby renewing natural resources.

A CIP catalogue record for this book is available from the British Library.

1 3 5 4 2

Also by Martyn Turner

The Book (political cartoons 1973–83), Irish Times Books, Dublin, 1983.

Illuminations – 101 Drawings From Early Irish History, Boethius Press, Kilkenny, 1986.

A Fistful of Dáilers (political cartoons 1983–87), Gill and Macmillan, Dublin 1987.

Not Viking Likely, Irish Life Viking Adventure, Dublin, 1988.

Heavy Weather, Gill and Macmillan, Dublin, 1989.

The Guy Who Won The Tour De France (political cartoons 1987–91), Gill and Macmillan, Dublin, 1991.

The Long Goodbye (a cartoon history of the career of Charles J. Haughey), Irish Times Books, Dublin, 1992.

Politics Et Al (political cartoons 1991–92), Irish Times Books, Dublin, 1992.

The Odd Couple (political cartoons 1992–94), Irish Times Books, Dublin, 1994.

Pack Up Your Troubles: 25 Years of Northern Ireland Cartoons, Blackstaff Press, Belfast, 1995.

The Noble Art of Politics (political cartoons 1994–96), Blackstaff Press, Belfast, 1996.

Brace Yourself, Bridge It (political cartoons 1996–98), Blackstaff Press, Belfast, 1998.

The Golfer's Guide to World History, Blackstaff Press, Belfast, 1999.

Railings (political cartoons 1998–2000), Blackstaff Press, Belfast, 2000.

Edited by Martyn Turner

Thin Black Lines (political cartoons and development education), co-edited with Dr Colm Regan and Scott Sinclair, Development Education Centre, Birmingham, 1988.

Columba! A Cartoon History of South America, co-edited with Dr Colm Regan, Potatoe Press, Dublin, 1993.

Thin Black Lines Rides Again (political cartoons and development education), co-edited with Dr Colm Regan and Scott Sinclair, Development Education Centre, Birmingham, 1994.

Contents

Introduction

M*artyn Turner's Greatest Hits* was a working title that never got superseded by anything better. My own efforts at naming the 14 or so books I have produced over the last 30 odd years were usually puns based on other people's efforts; *A Fistful of Dáilers* (which came back from the Hong Kong printers in packets marked 'A Fishful of Dollars'), *The Long Goodbye, Pack Up Your Troubles, The Odd Couple*. I confess that every time I had to think of a title for a collection of political cartoons I was intimidated by the knowledge that Jack Ohman, a cartoonist who operates out of Oregon or thereabouts, had already produced the perfect title for any bunch of political cartoons; 'Do I Have To Draw You A Picture?' Follow that. But this time we have gone for doing exactly what it says on the tin. Except, of course, the 300 or so cartoons herein weren't all hits but then who knows what worked and what didn't. I certainly don't.

Thus the criteria for this selection is pretty much based on what has lasted through the decades rather than what worked at the time. In a Christmas quiz in the *Irish Times* one year they reprinted a cartoon and wrote underneath, 'This cartoon appeared on the front page of the *Irish Times* in February. What news story was it about?' It was one of the questions in that quiz I couldn't answer and yet, clearly, at the time I drew it the *Irish Times* had felt it so pertinent and appropriate that they had printed it on the front page. You won't see it reprinted here — or any others that lost their purpose quicker than a Fianna Fáil election manifesto after polling day.

On the odd occasion I meet what George Bush calls folks and everyone else calls people, I usually get complimented on a recent cartoon (usually one drawn by someone else. I used to explain in detail that I didn't do it and was always told I was wrong so, these days, I just say thank you and take full credit) and then get told that the one they really liked was … 'internment for 14 year-old girls', the Yeltsin bottle, the guy who won the Tour de France, the Patriot … The genuine hits. All four of them. The few that struck a chord right across the board.

The rest are ones I like, ones other people have mentioned, ones that got reprinted widely and ones that have survived 30 years and still, sort of, make sense. I have drawn over 9,000 cartoons in the last three decades. *The Phoenix*, that bastion of right-wing nationalist orthodoxy, tells us that they are all the same, which I actually take, in my dotage, as a great compliment. One of my constant companions on the stereo since the late 1960s has been Neil Young. At a concert he replied to someone shouting names of his songs out from the audience with the line, 'Don't worry, they are all the same song.' Well, as bigoted as any northern politician, my views haven't really changed since my teenage years. Set in stone. These are all the same cartoon; only the people, subject, captions and drawing change. The banging my head against the brick wall of right-wing, nationalistic, narrow-minded politics remains the same. Well if it's good enough for Mr Young…

Martyn Turner

P.S. I would like to thank the following people who over the years haven't interfered and have let me get on with what I want to do, drawing it in the way I wanted to draw it and saying what I want to say: Jean Turner (of course), various editors and deputy editors, production helpmates and comment page editors of the *Irish Times* (especially just retired Pat), and a few editors from across the water who contribute to my pension fund from time to time. Thank you. Without people like you, what is left of press freedom in this neck of the woods would be even thinner on the ground than it is.

CENSORED

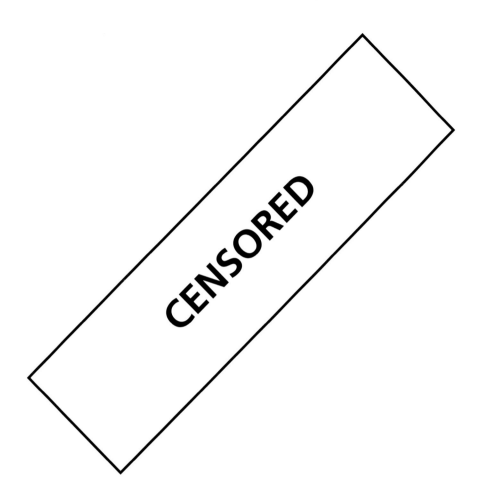

Not wanted...

Here's a few cartoons that didn't get published where they were supposed to be published but, as one man's poison is another man's meat, got befriended by some publication somewhere.

The drawing of Brian Faulkner making a gesture to the minority was rejected by the (now defunct) *Sunday News* in Belfast on grounds of poor taste. It was published by the *Irish Times*.

But it was poor taste that kept the cartoon about Pat Buchanan out of the *Irish Times*. A night editor (now defunct) decreed that *Irish Times* readers didn't want to see 'elephant shit at their breakfast table' and replaced it with a cartoon on the same subject that I had rejected myself. Gloriously, I flogged it to an English Sunday paper for a three-figure sum. They, of course, being English, have no taste at all.

Bishop Casey. Ah, Bishop Casey. The *Irish Times* told me, in a rare display of editorial interference (they are the least interfering of any of the newspapers I have crossed swords with over the years), that it would have to be a very good cartoon indeed for me to get any comment about Bishop Casey into the paper. It was a sensitive subject. I sent them the enclosed and they went into conclave for two days before rejecting it. It became the cover of *Fortnight*.

When Charles J. Haughey announced his imminent retirement, the *Irish Times* decided on a special supplement where they reprinted a few articles and some of my old cartoons and also asked me to do a new one, in colour. I submitted the '35 years of public service...' and it didn't get printed.

'Why?' I asked.

'Because the lawyers said it was libellous.'

'But it's true.'

'That doesn't matter,' they said, 'and even though it is true it would be up to us to prove, in court, the implication that he was living beyond his means.'

Now, of course, it has been proved by McCracken and the

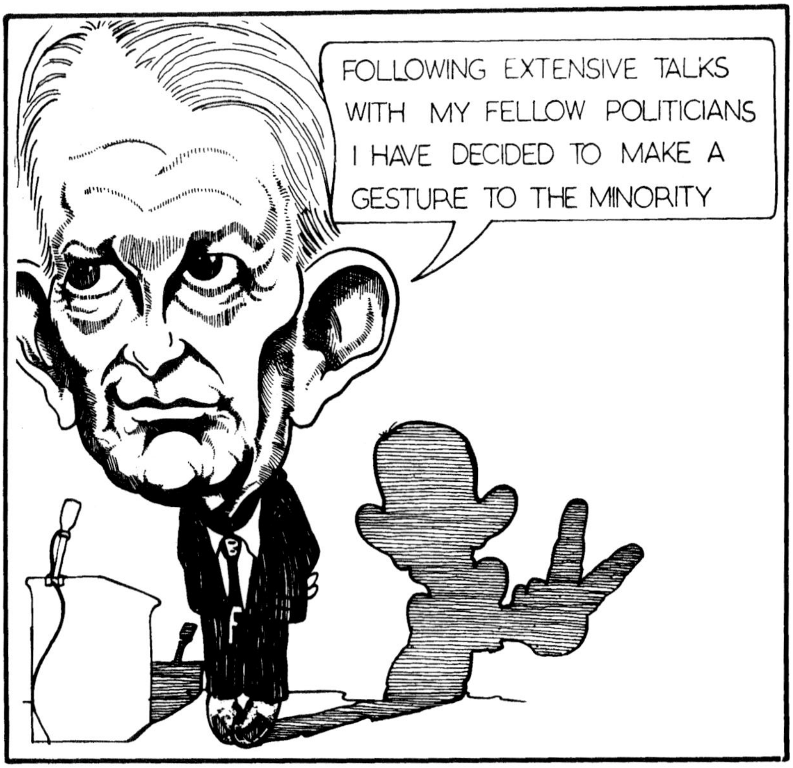
FOLLOWING EXTENSIVE TALKS WITH MY FELLOW POLITICIANS I HAVE DECIDED TO MAKE A GESTURE TO THE MINORITY

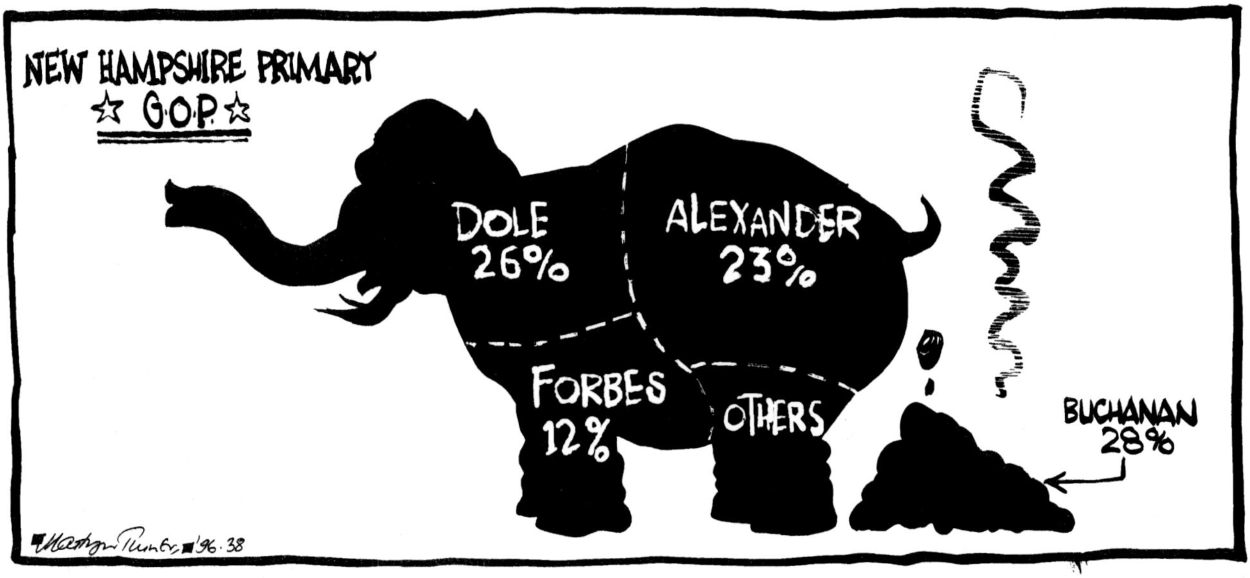
NEW HAMPSHIRE PRIMARY
☆ G.O.P. ☆
DOLE 26%
ALEXANDER 23%
FORBES 12%
OTHERS
BUCHANAN 28%

Revenue Commissioners. But it shows the straightjacket that the press in Ireland operates under. How many of the tribunals we have now would have been necessary if we had a truly free press? A cartoon in this book somewhere is a caricature of Ray Burke, an auctioneer, standing by a 'For Sale' sign. When I drew it, the double entendre hadn't actually occurred to me, but it occurred to the legal eagles of the *Irish Times* and I had to change it. Ray Burke, at the time, hadn't been tribunalised. We didn't know, officially, that he was as much for sale as any of his properties. What, as they say, the dogs in the street knew, wasn't allowed to be known in the public print. We get the country we deserve. We voted in these politicians who legislate their restrictive and self-serving laws. Here endeth the lesson.

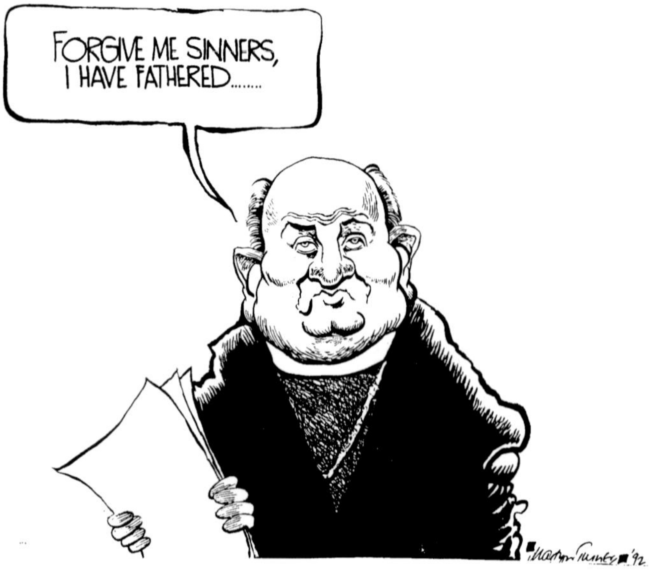
FORGIVE ME SINNERS, I HAVE FATHERED........
Martyn Turner '92

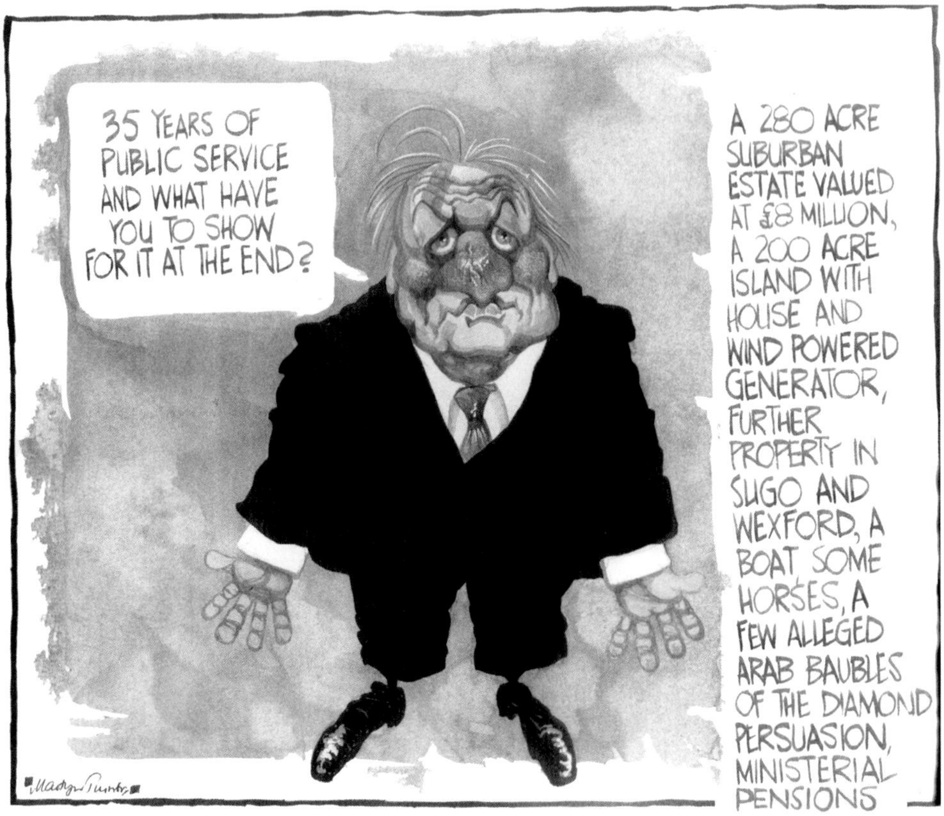
35 YEARS OF PUBLIC SERVICE AND WHAT HAVE YOU TO SHOW FOR IT AT THE END?
A 280 ACRE SUBURBAN ESTATE VALUED AT £8 MILLION, A 200 ACRE ISLAND WITH HOUSE AND WIND POWERED GENERATOR, FURTHER PROPERTY IN SLIGO AND WEXFORD, A BOAT SOME HORSES, A FEW ALLEGED ARAB BAUBLES OF THE DIAMOND PERSUASION, MINISTERIAL PENSIONS
Martyn Turner

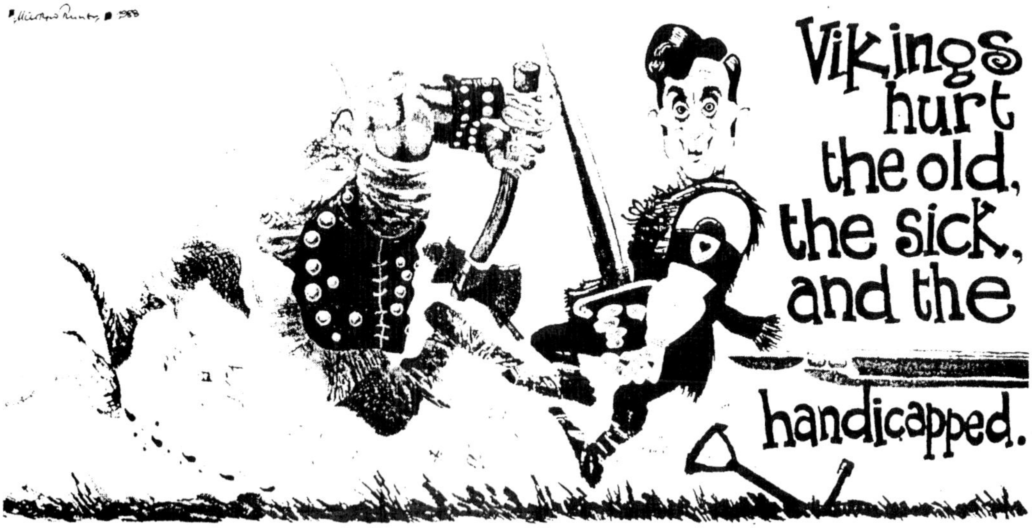
Vikings hurt the old, the sick, and the handicapped.

Manager darts in and removes a Turner

By Renagh Holohan

A POSTER by the political cartoonist Martyn Turner, commissioned for the Art on the DART project, was pasted over on the order of a senior manager in Iarnrod Eireann immediately after the exhibition was opened at Pearse Station, Westland Row, Dublin, yesterday morning.

The 20-foot by 10-foot exhibit entitled "Election poster 988 AD" shows the Taoiseach, Mr Haughey, and the Minister for Finance, Mr MacSharry, dressed as Vikings and carried the caption "Vikings hurt the old, the sick and the handicapped". It was one of eight posters and six exhibits produced by various artists to mark the Dublin Millennium. The remaining seven posters are still on view at Pearse Station and the exhibits can be seen on DART trains.

LET'S be clear. There can be no justification for the withdrawal of a Martyn Turner poster from the Art on the DART exhibition at Pearse Station, Westland Row. To start even considering a justification is to speak the language of the censor. Art, like literature or journalism, has no value unless it is freely expressed. Having a democratic society means living with the consequences of free expression no matter how uncomfortable.

One would hope that other artists will show solidarity with Turner, as happened some years ago when a Ro... Ballagh kite was suppressed by ... Kilkenny Arts Wee...

VIKING CUTS

Sir,—Regarding Martyn Turner's cartoon (November 3rd) commissioned by the clever DART Art Millennium poster display, may I comment that the greatest insult perceived or imagined was to compare the present Fianna Fail leadership to the Vikings. The Vikings were only in the ha'penny place. — Yours, etc.,

MARY McEVOY.
Quinn's Road,
Shankhill,
Co. Dublin.

* * *

Sir,—The removal by Iarnród Eireann of the Haughey-MacSharry cartoon from Pearse Station is to be applauded, for such a cartoon is deeply insulting and grossly offensive to Vikings. — Yours, etc.,

DERMOT P. CURRAN,
176 Sycamores,
Kilkenny.

'FF jibe' ban derails art

By JEROME REILLY

THE CENSORSHIP of a satirical cartoon featuring the Taoiseach Mr. Haughey and Finance Minister Ray MacSharry has led to a major row between Irish Rail and a number of the country's best known artists. The billboard-sized cartoon, from the nib of Martyn Turner, was blanked out last week by Irish Rail within hours of it being exhibited at Pearse Station as part of the "Art on the DART" scheme.

Now seven other artists have decided to withdraw their work which is also on display, in protest at the "blatant" censorship of Martyn Turner's work.

The cartoon itself depicts an axe-wielding Mr. Haughey with Minister MacSharry in Viking garb complete with helmets. The caption says: "Vikings hurt the old, sick and handicapped."

Irish Rail said it was their policy not to permit materials of a political nature to be displayed in their stations or on their premises.

Yesterday the Douglas Hyde Gallery said that, in protest at the move, they had requeted Irish Rail to remove the remaining works from the billboard project.

And last night an Irish Rail spokesman said they would agree to the Gallery's request to have the remaining works pasted over but with much regret.

P.S. The other cartoon was done for 'Art on the DART', one of a series of art posters commissioned for display at railway stations. CIE decided they didn't want to deride their political masters and covered it up. The other artists who had been commissioned withdrew their works in solidarity. Thus, instead of just being seen by commuters from the south side, it made the front page of the *Irish Times* instead. Sometimes banning things is more of a hassle than letting them be.

Governments of the People

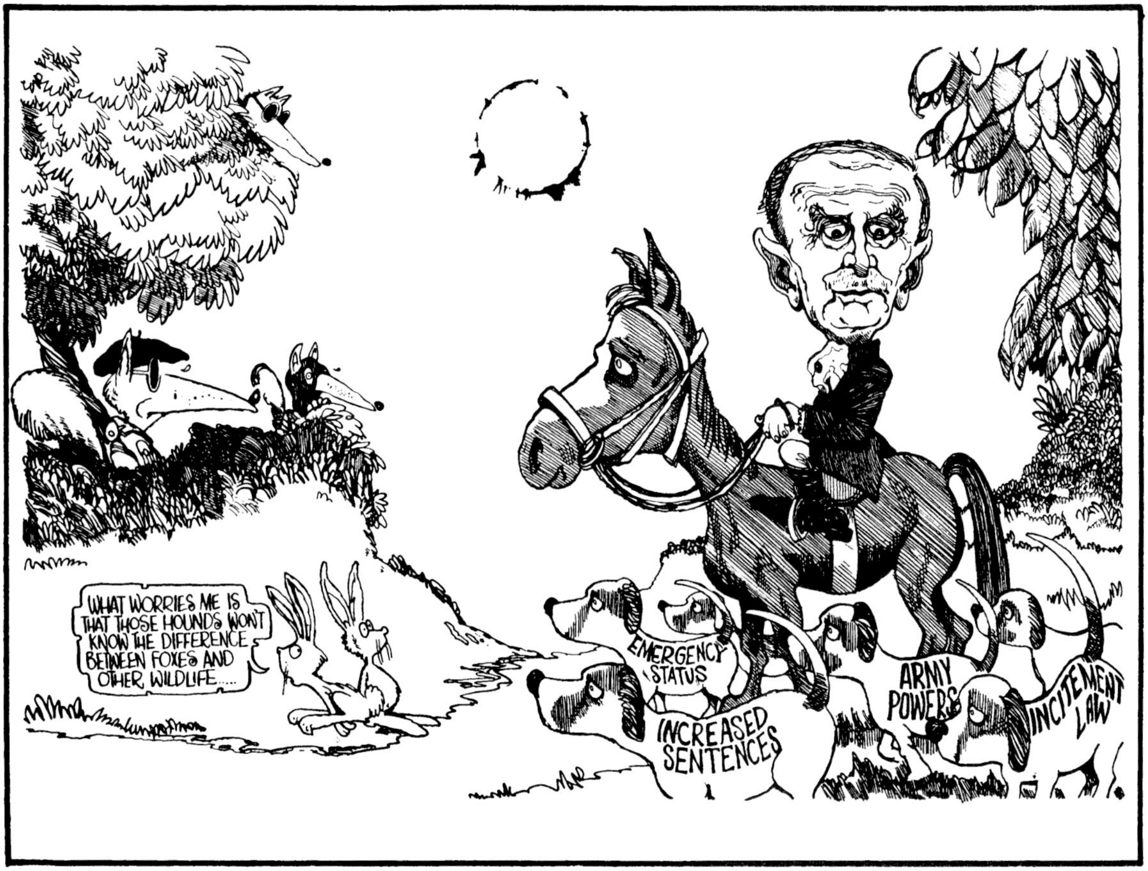
WHAT WORRIES ME IS THAT THOSE HOUNDS WON'T KNOW THE DIFFERENCE BETWEEN FOXES AND OTHER WILDLIFE.....
EMERGENCY STATUS
INCREASED SENTENCES
ARMY POWERS
INCITEMENT LAW

Liam Cosgrave 1973–77

When I moved down from Belfast in 1976 to increase my contributions to the *Irish Times*, the Fine Gael/Labour coalition was coming to the end of its term. But it was there long enough for me to realise how difficult my new job was going to be. How, for example, can one satirise a Taoiseach who votes against his own government's bill, as Liam Cosgrave did? Apart from being opposed to contraception (that was the bill), he was also hot on law and order and had a dislike of 'mongrel foxes'. One of his ministers called the then President a 'thundering disgrace' which led to the limerick printed hereabouts. When I delivered that cartoon, by hand in those days, an editor looked at it and said, 'this is libellous' and, turning to a sub editor added, 'put it on the front page'.

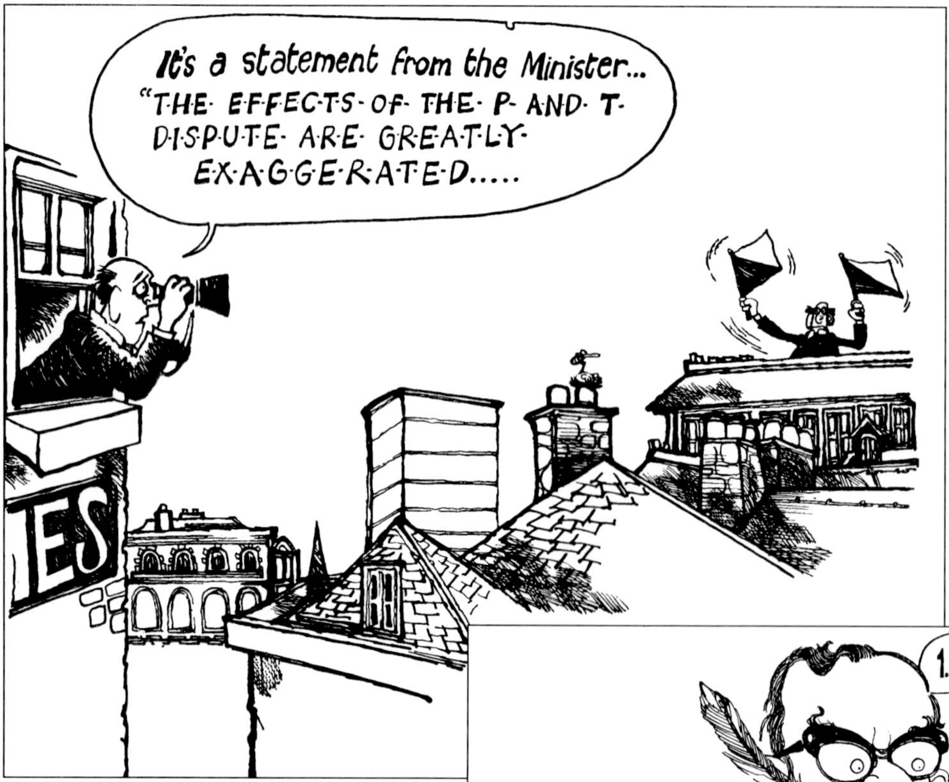
It's a statement from the Minister...
"THE EFFECTS OF THE P AND T DISPUTE ARE GREATLY EXAGGERATED.....
ES

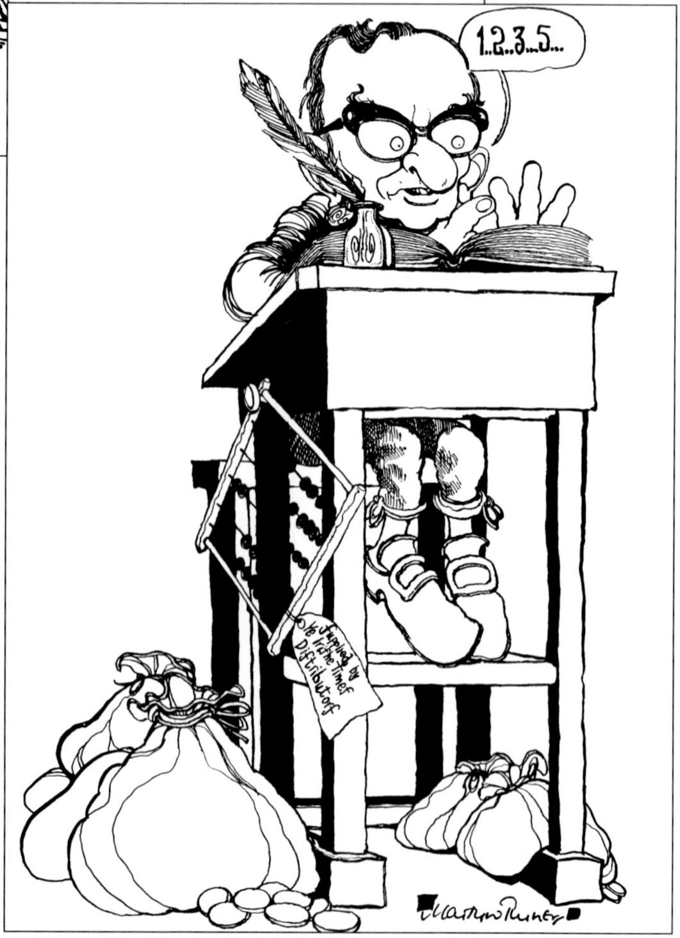
1..2..3..5...
Supplied by ye Irish Times Distributors
Martyn Turner

Richie Ryan

Some lines on the occasion of a
Ministerial speech at Mullingar

While addressing the troops bold and handsome,
His pre-arranged speech overran some,
The T.D. from Louth,
Put his foot in his mouth
And spoke out the back of his transom.

Paddy Donegan

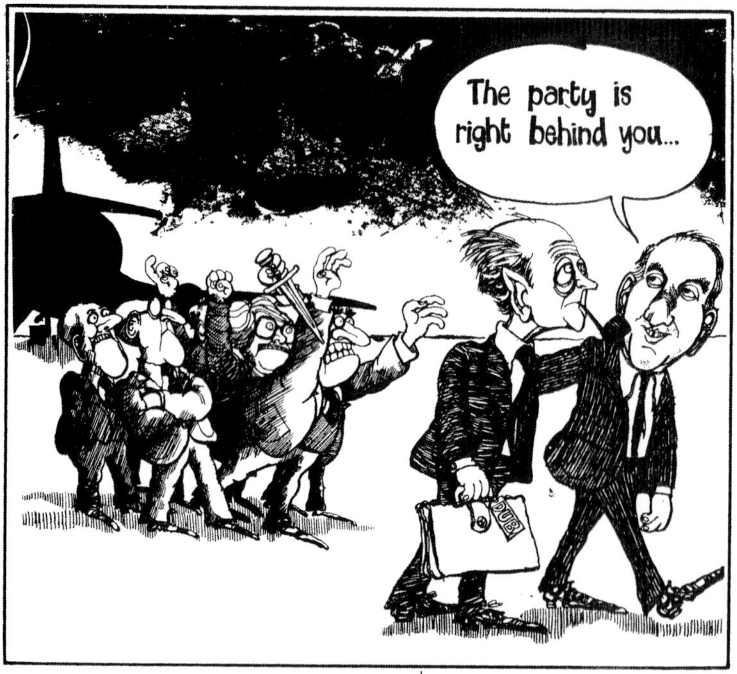
The party is right behind you...

Jack Lynch 1977–79

Jack Lynch's third term of office became the battle-ground for post-Arms-Trial Fianna Fáil. George Colley was Minister for Finance. It was, as they say, a pivotal moment in Irish politics as the shenanigans of Fianna Fáil at this time are still dominating much of our politics today. Who would have thought.

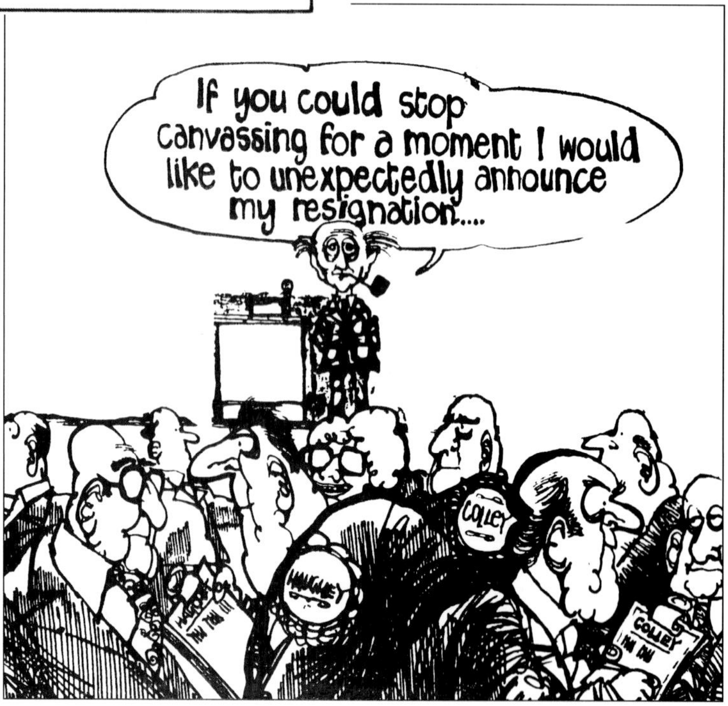
If you could stop canvassing for a moment I would like to unexpectedly announce my resignation....

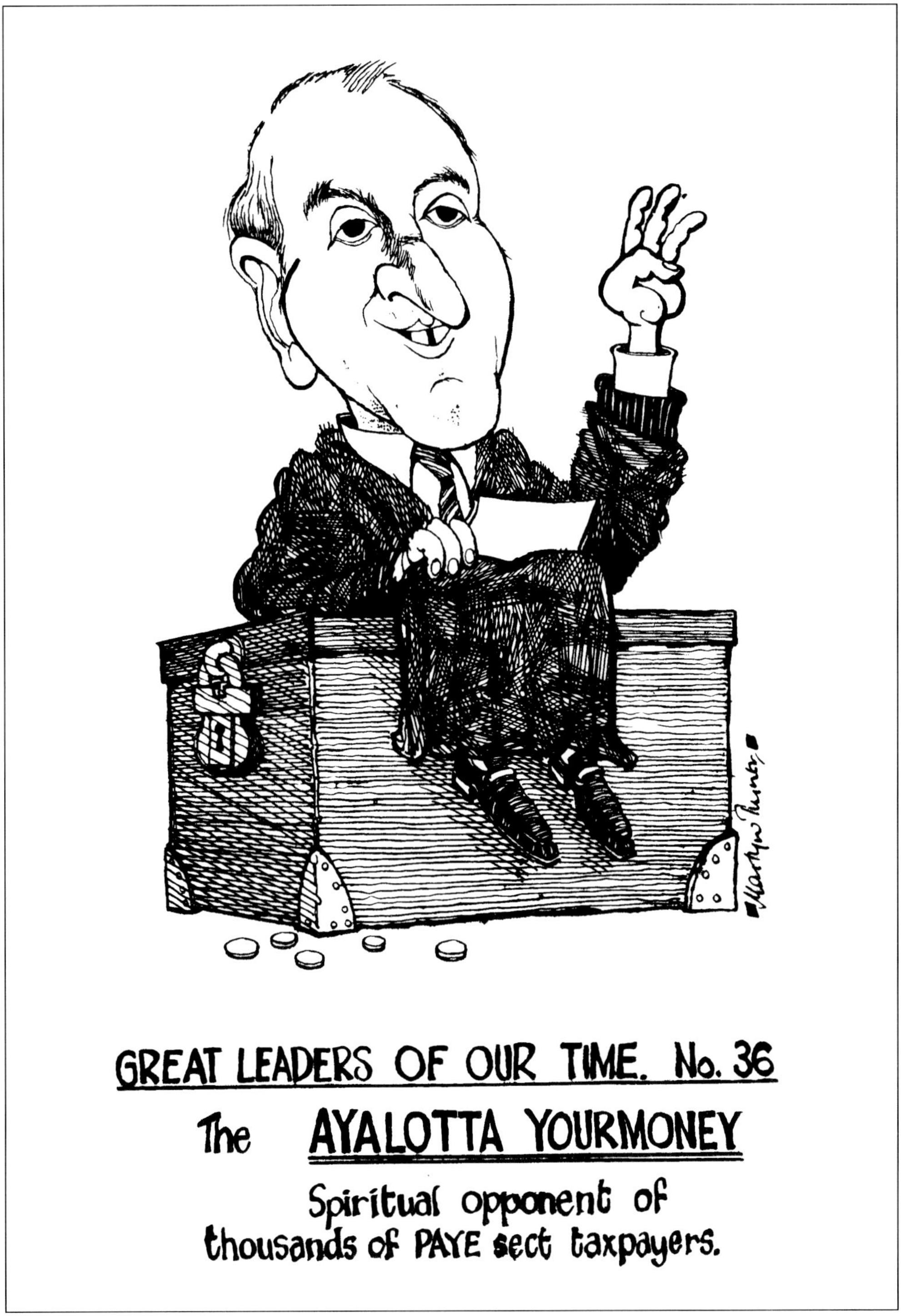
Martyn Turner
GREAT LEADERS OF OUR TIME. No. 36
The AYALOTTA YOURMONEY
Spiritual opponent of
thousands of PAYE sect taxpayers.

George Colley

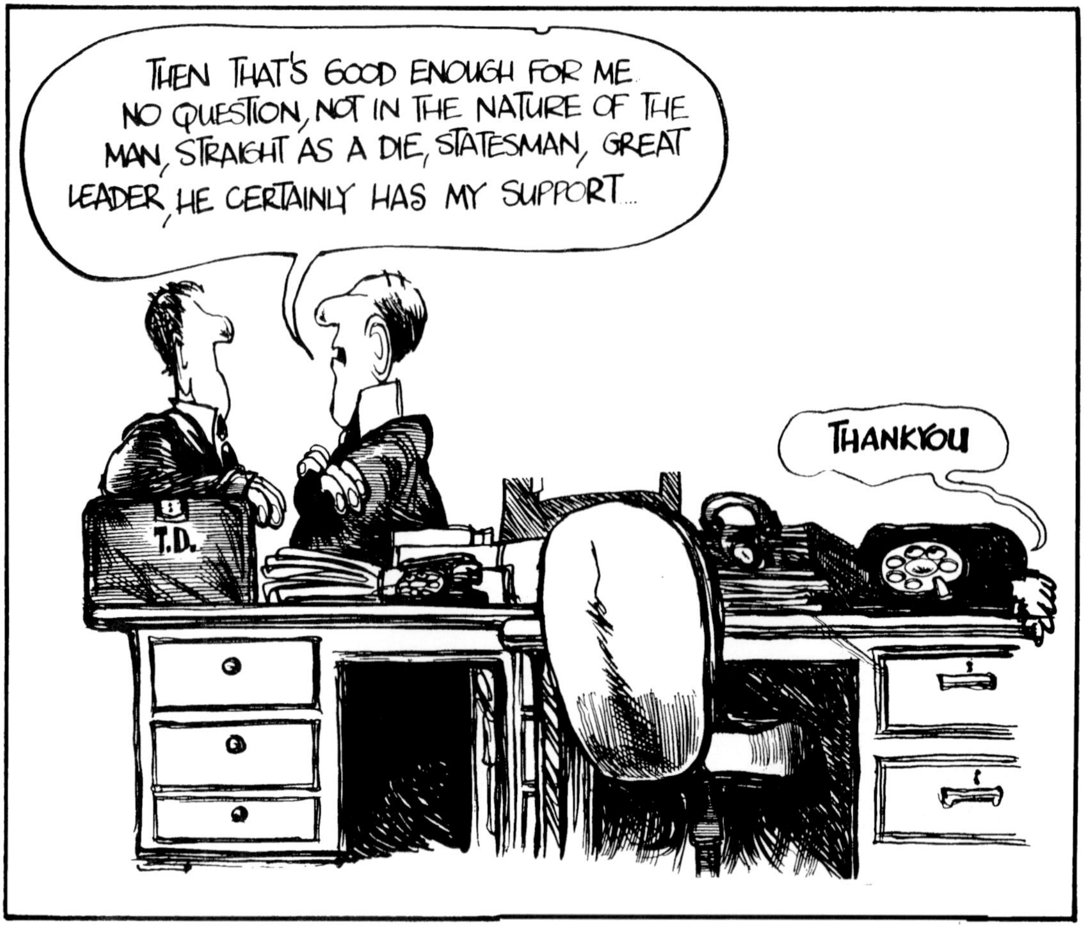
THEN THAT'S GOOD ENOUGH FOR ME. NO QUESTION, NOT IN THE NATURE OF THE MAN, STRAIGHT AS A DIE, STATESMAN, GREAT LEADER, HE CERTAINLY HAS MY SUPPORT...
T.D.
THANKYOU

Charles Haughey 1979–81, February–November 1982, 1987–92

As a taste of things to come there was a minor scandal in CJH's first go at being Supreme Leader when bugs were discovered in the Dáil telephone system. As usual the real culprit was the press who chose to mention it.

In 1982 Fianna Fáil returned to office when the first FitzGerald government collapsed over putting VAT on children's shoes. Surviving with the aid of independent votes, Mr Haughey attempted to rekindle his political love affair with Margaret Thatcher and attempted to quell the backbench discontent that eventually led to the formation of the Progressive Democrats in December 1985.

His third whack at it included a spell governing on Fianna Fáil's own and a spell in conjunction with the PDs, breaking the lifelong FF core value of never going into coalition. It was during this spell that Charlie knocked Stephen Roche off the winner's podium at the Tour de France, visited Belfast, lived beyond his means and, eventually, was dragged from office by the PDs whilst claiming that he would be 'going with dignity'.

Further Fianna Fáil scandals involving telephones also took place under his watch. Journalists' phones were bugged and the Fianna Fáil candidate for the Presidency, Brian Lenihan, was politically damaged because of a phone call he made and a tape-recorded interview he gave. FF and technology just don't go together.

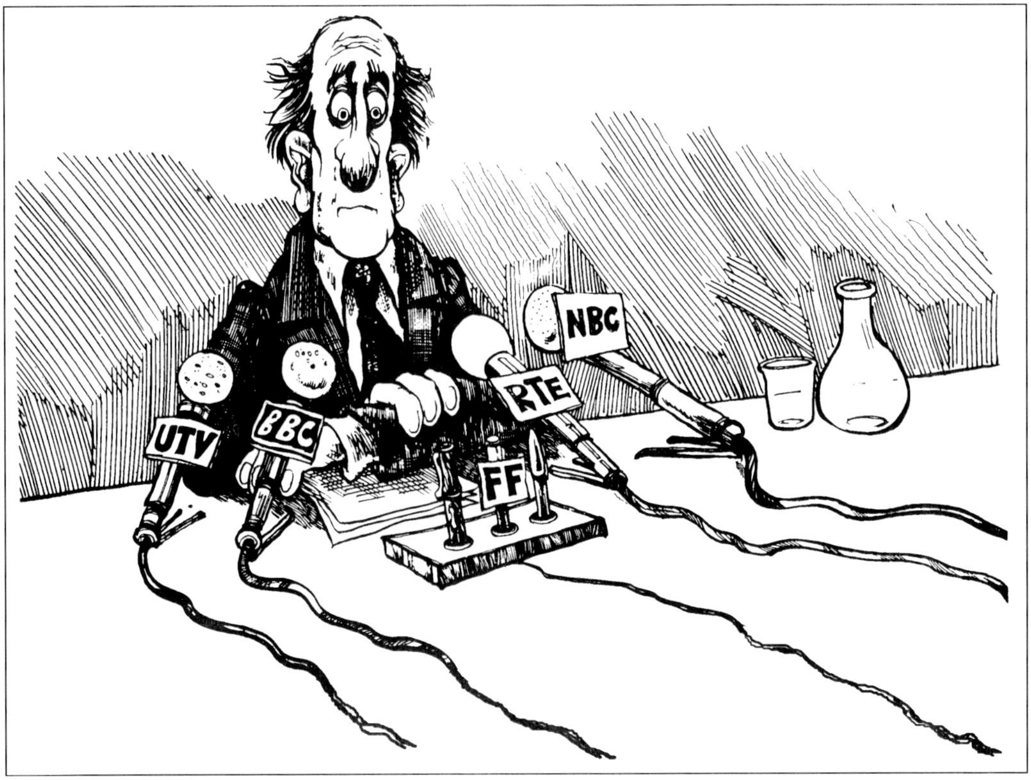
UTV
BBC
FF
RTE
NBC

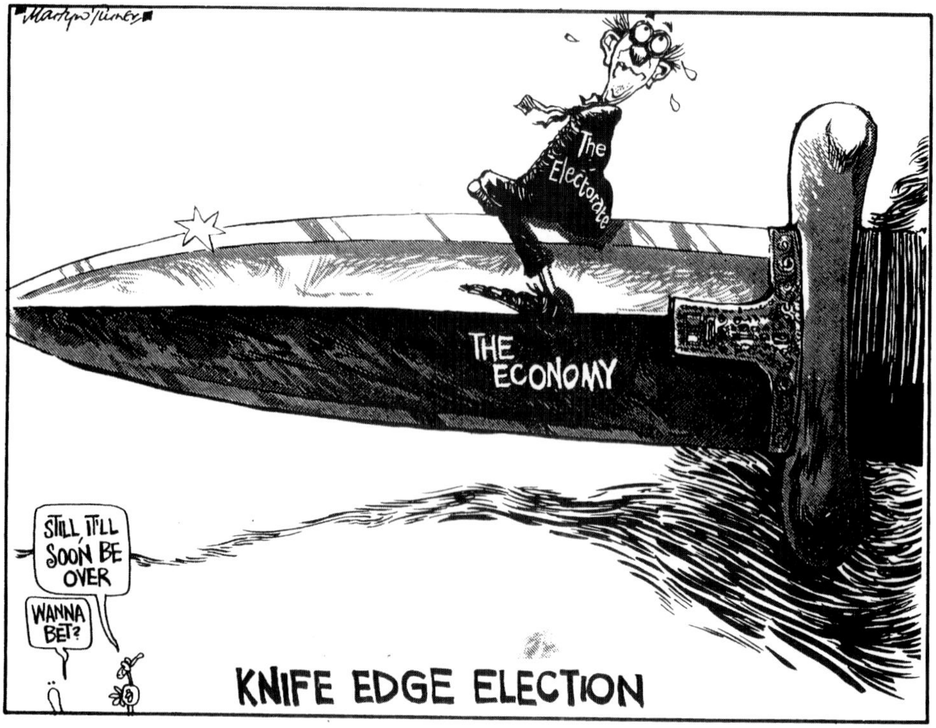
The Electorate
THE ECONOMY
STILL, IT'LL SOON BE OVER
WANNA BET?
KNIFE EDGE ELECTION

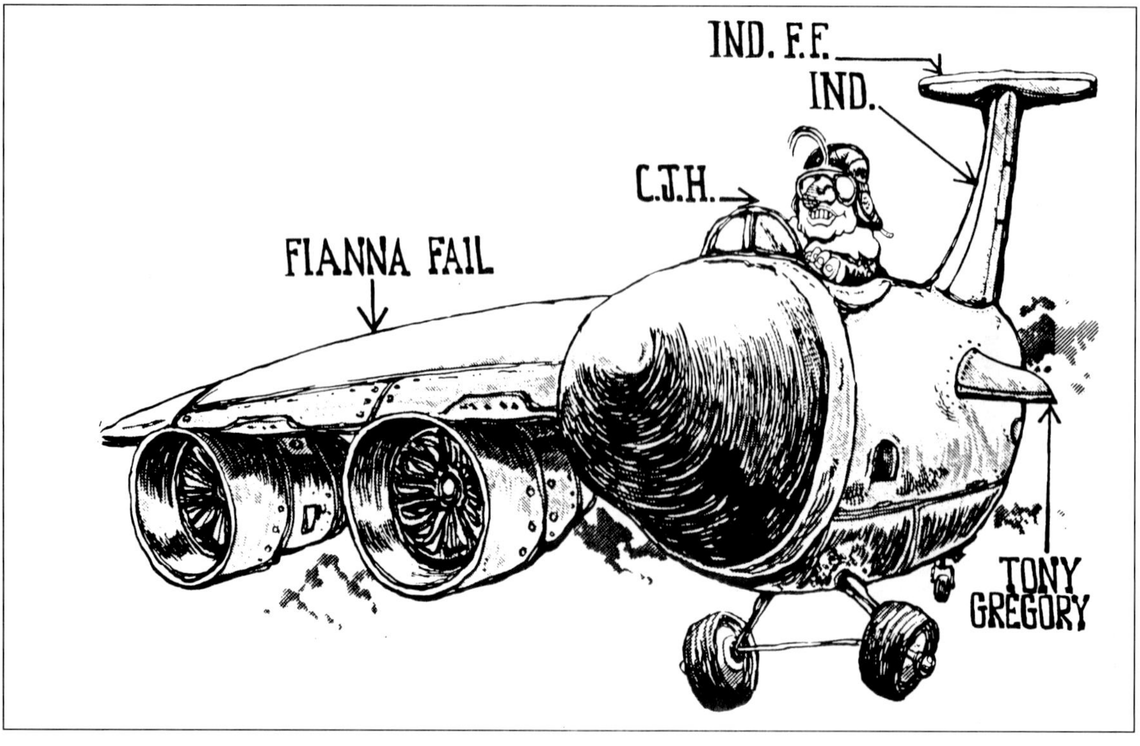
IND. F.F.
IND.
C.J.H.
FIANNA FAIL
TONY GREGORY

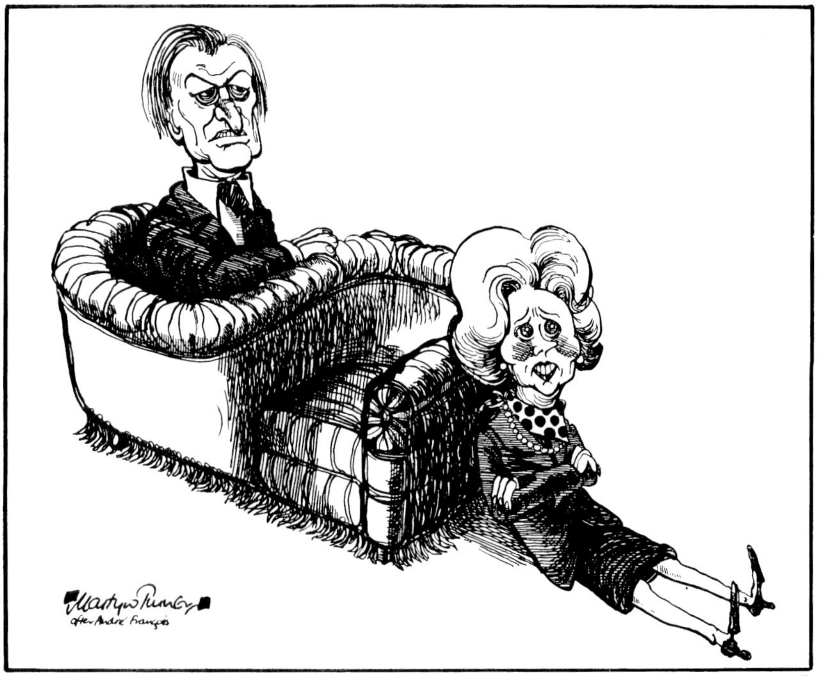
Martyn Turner
after André François

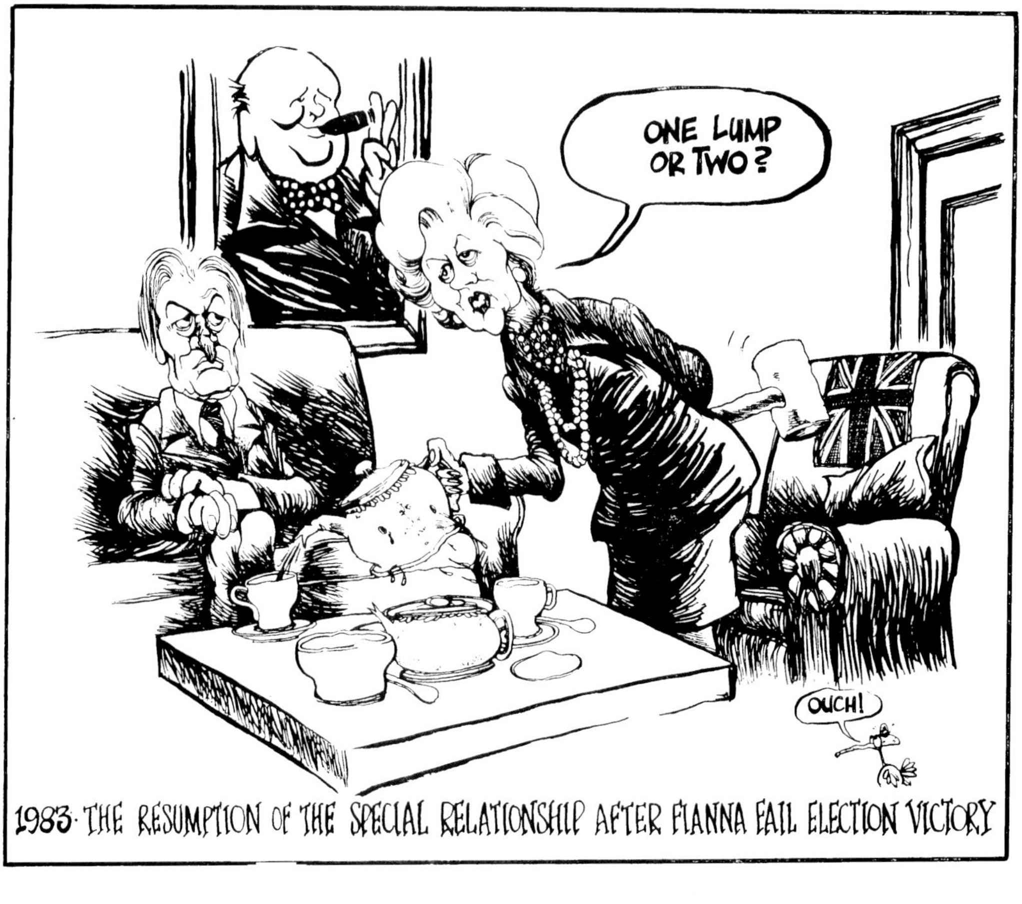
ONE LUMP OR TWO?
OUCH!

1983 · THE RESUMPTION OF THE SPECIAL RELATIONSHIP AFTER FIANNA FAIL ELECTION VICTORY

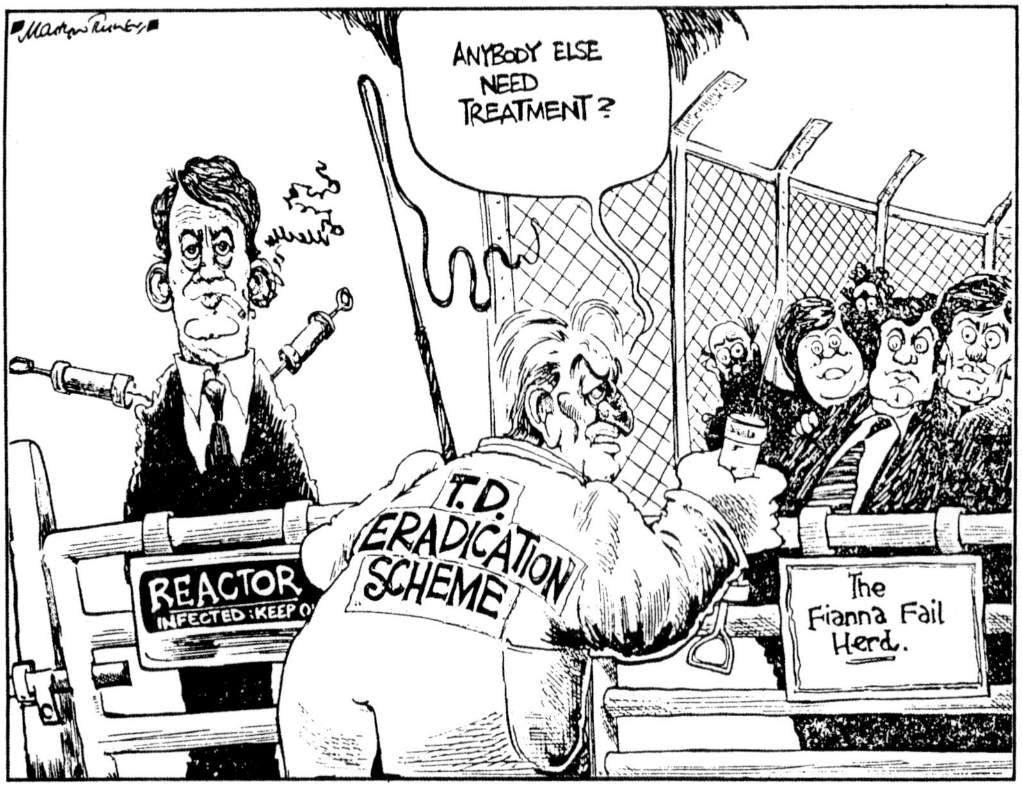
Martyn Turner
ANYBODY ELSE NEED TREATMENT?
REACTOR
INFECTED: KEEP O
T.D. ERADICATION SCHEME
The Fianna Fail Herd.

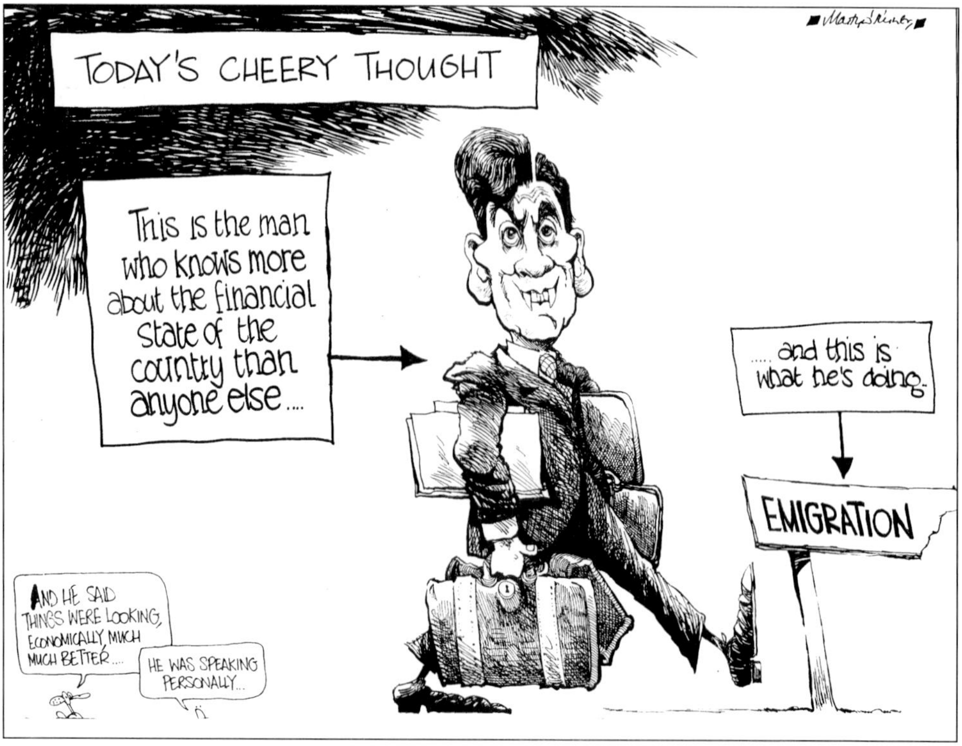
Martyn Turner
TODAY'S CHEERY THOUGHT
This is the man who knows more about the financial state of the country than anyone else....
....and this is what he's doing..
EMIGRATION
AND HE SAID THINGS WERE LOOKING, ECONOMICALLY, MUCH MUCH BETTER....
HE WAS SPEAKING PERSONALLY...

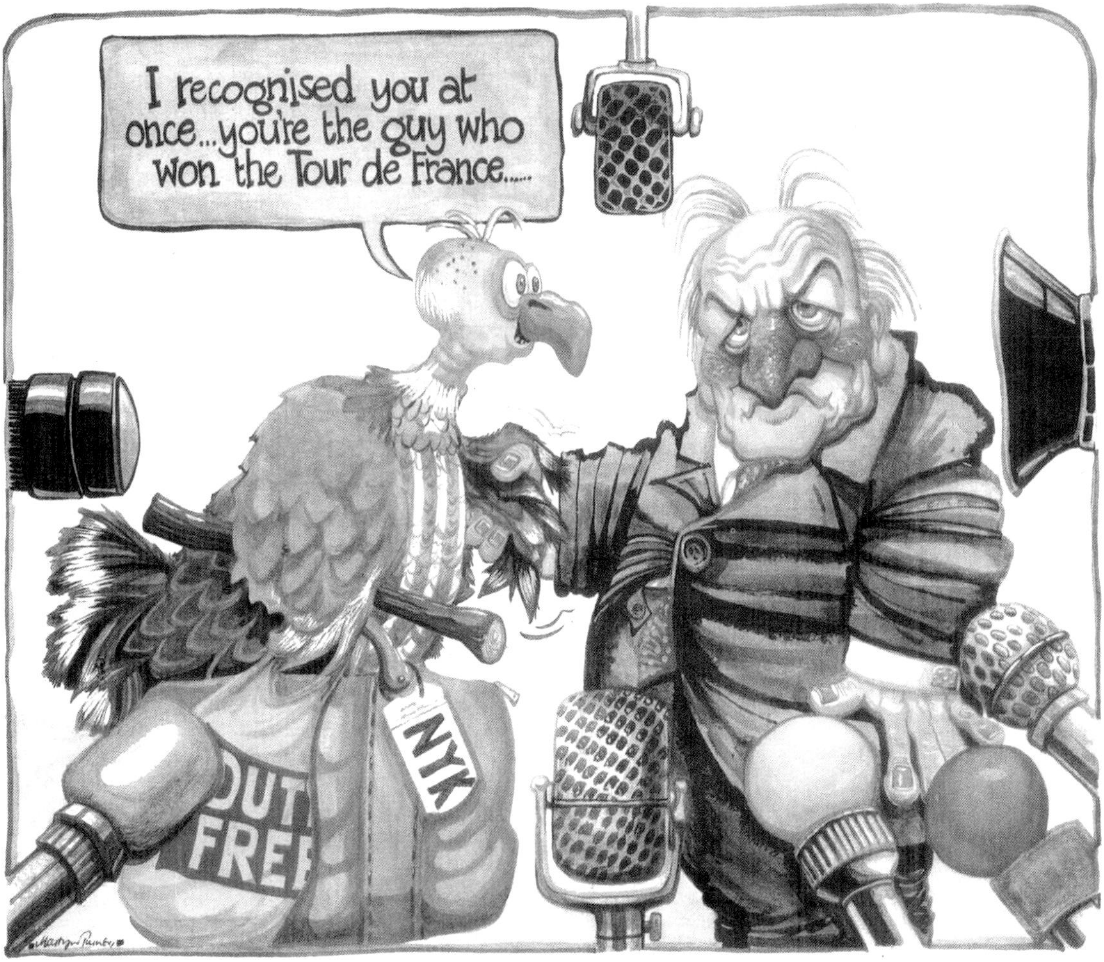
I recognised you at once...you're the guy who won the Tour de France......
NYK
DUTY FREE

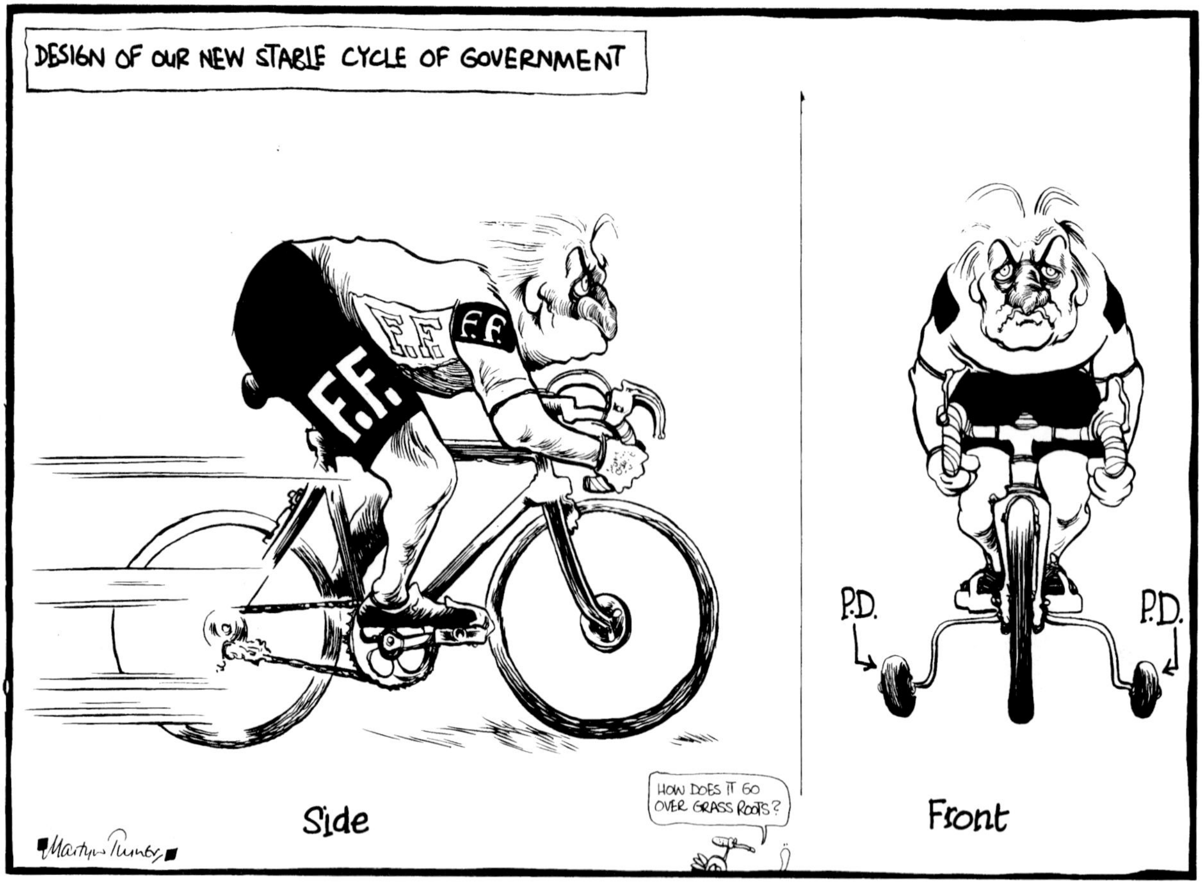
DESIGN OF OUR NEW STABLE CYCLE OF GOVERNMENT
F.F.
F.F.
F.F.
P.D.
P.D.
Side
Front
HOW DOES IT GO OVER GRASS ROOTS?
Martyn Turner

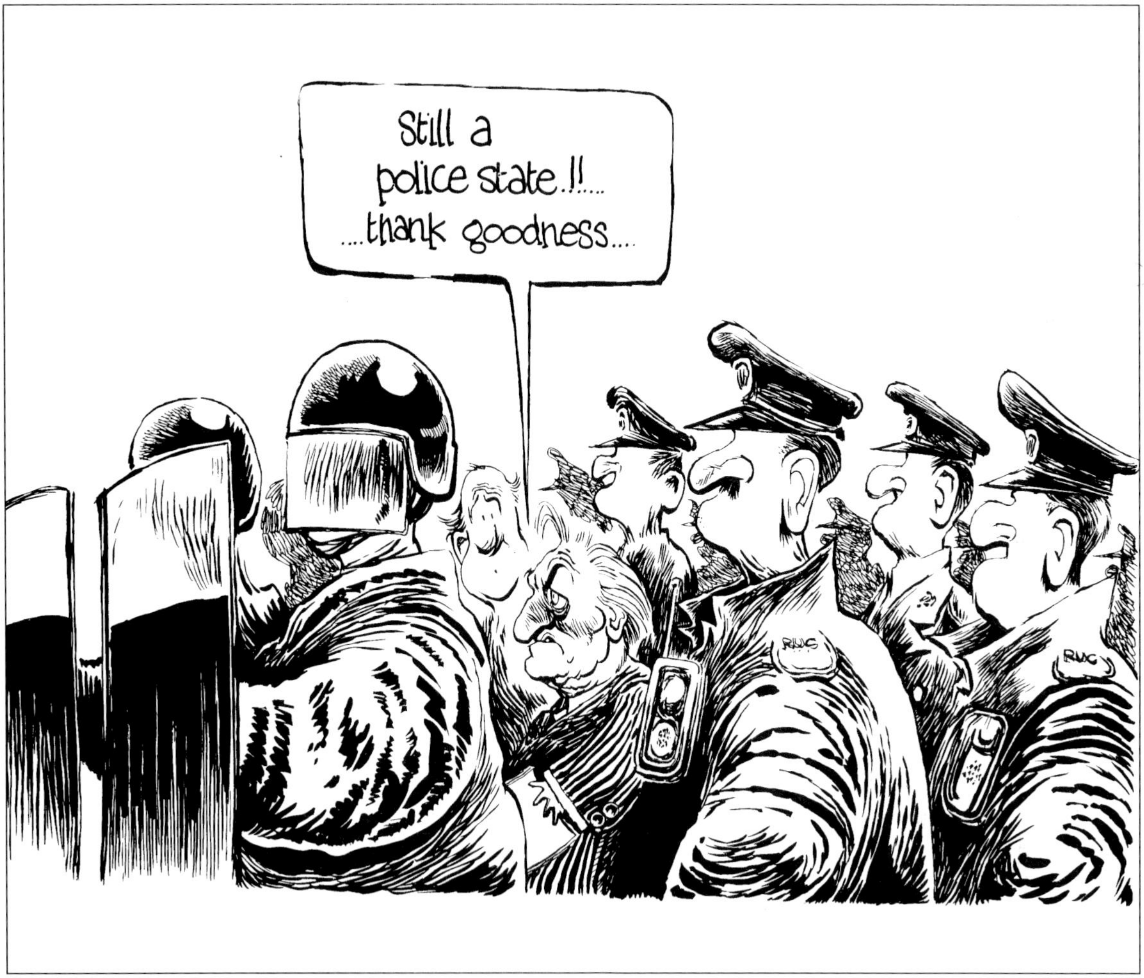
Still a police state !! ....thank goodness....
RUC
RUC

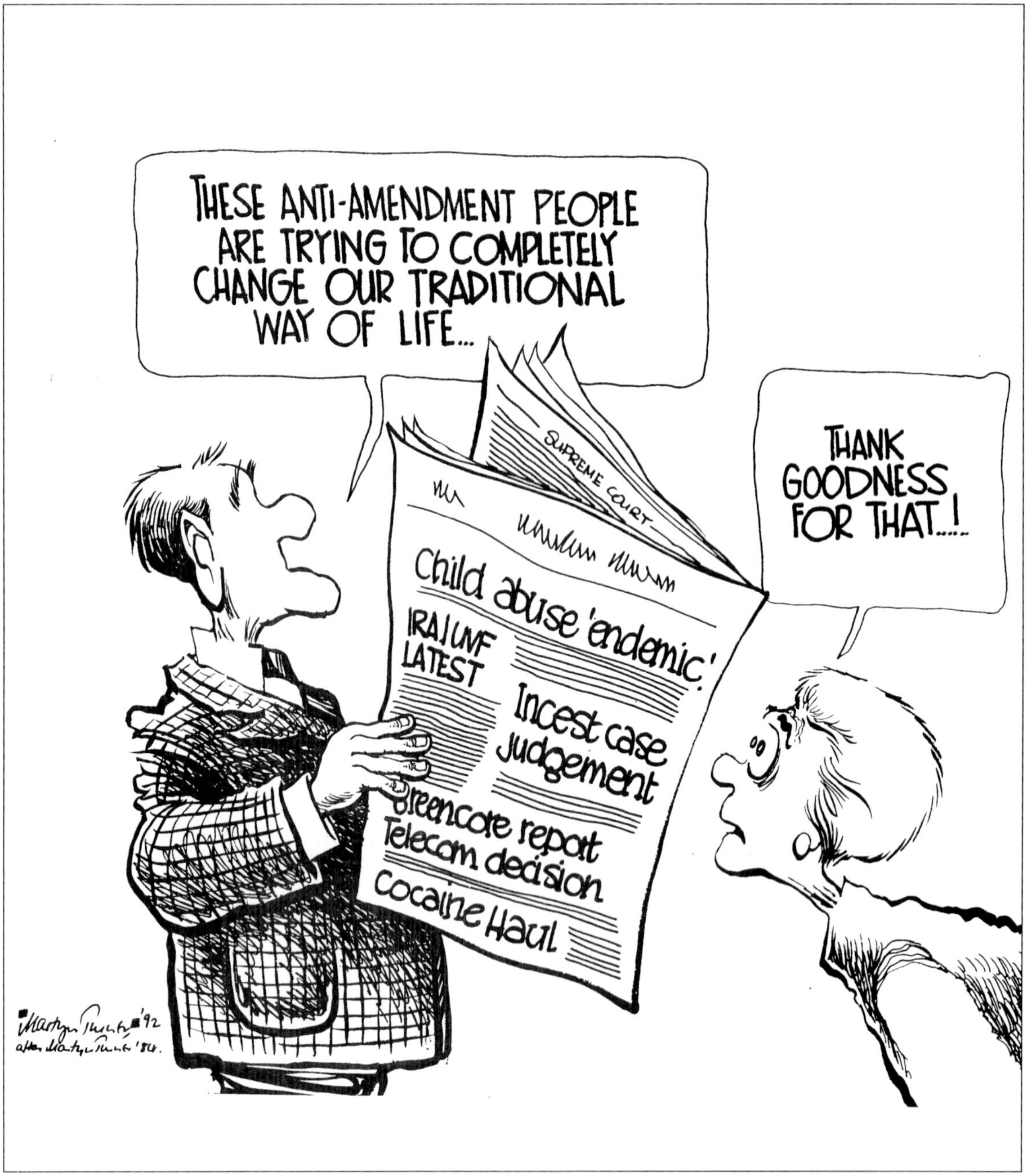
THESE ANTI-AMENDMENT PEOPLE ARE TRYING TO COMPLETELY CHANGE OUR TRADITIONAL WAY OF LIFE...
SUPREME COURT
Child abuse 'endemic'
IRA/UVF LATEST
Incest case judgement
Greencore report
Telecom decision
Cocaine Haul
THANK GOODNESS FOR THAT..!

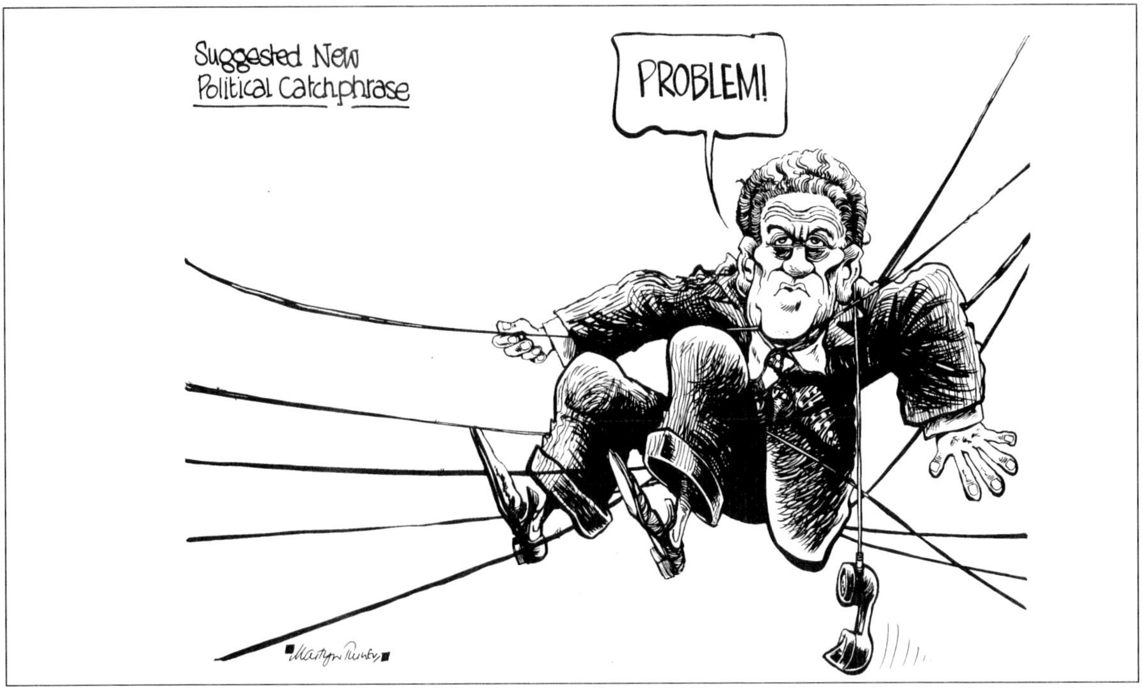
Suggested New
Political Catchphrase
PROBLEM!
Martyn Turner

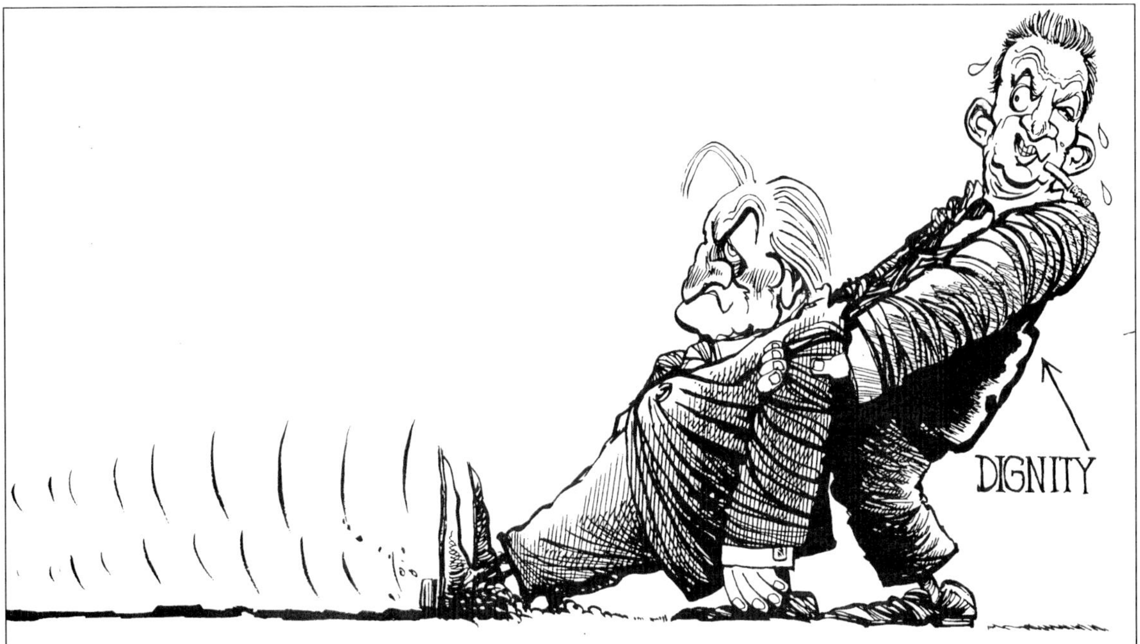
DIGNITY

Taoiseach says he will 'go with dignity'

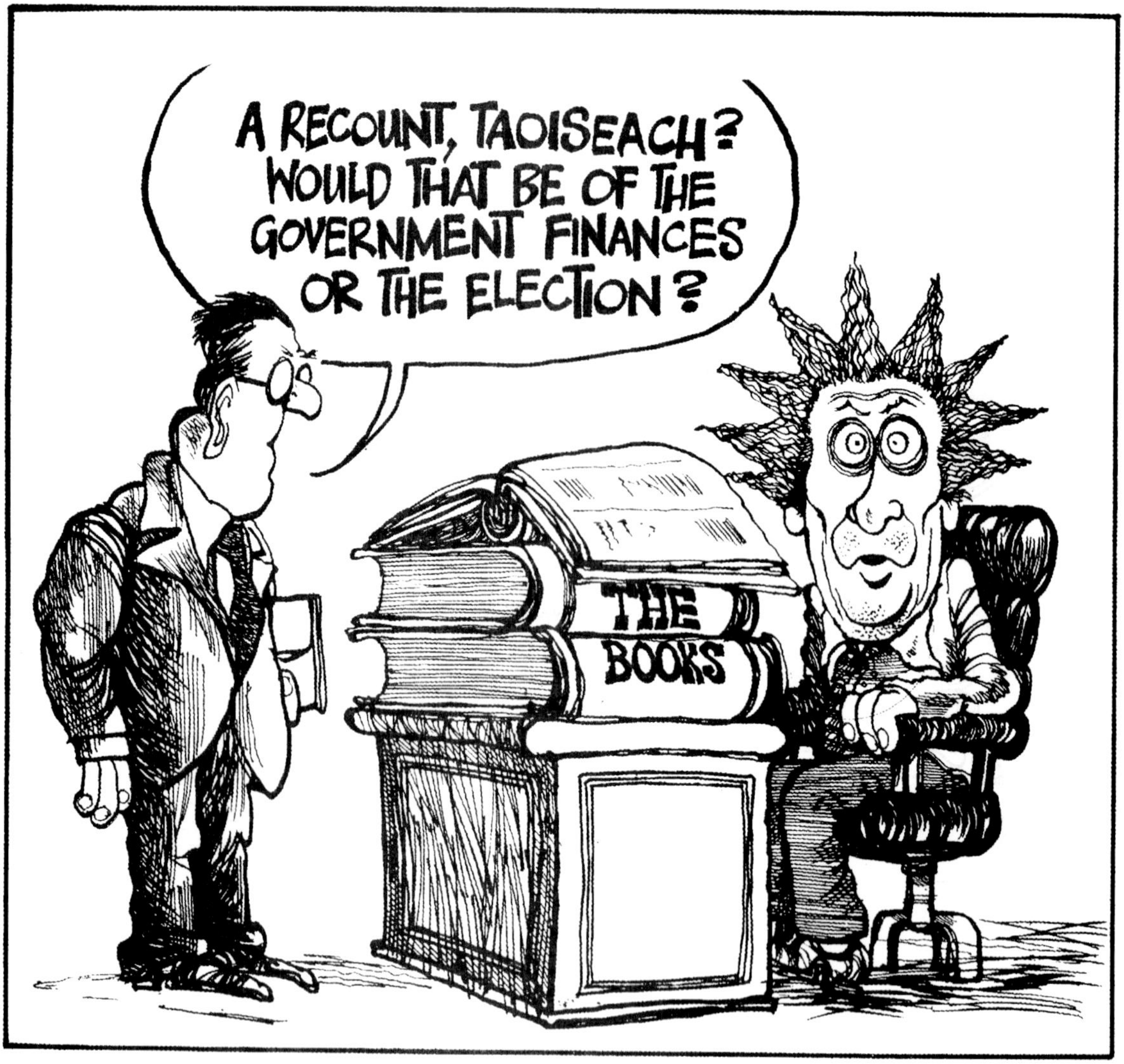
A RECOUNT, TAOISEACH? WOULD THAT BE OF THE GOVERNMENT FINANCES OR THE ELECTION?
THE BOOKS

Garret FitzGerald 1981–82, 1982–87

Despite inheriting a pretty awful economic situation after some Fianna Fáil giveaway electioneering, the two governments of Garret FitzGerald became embroiled in constitutional matters. The interminable wrangling over abortion and divorce became the main feature of the time, which went on and on and on and on. We should be due another referendum sometime soon, shouldn't we? The period also saw the creation of the Progressive Democrats. The coalition with Labour limped on until the general election of 1987 when Fine Gael lost 20 seats and dropped 12 percentage points in the poll.

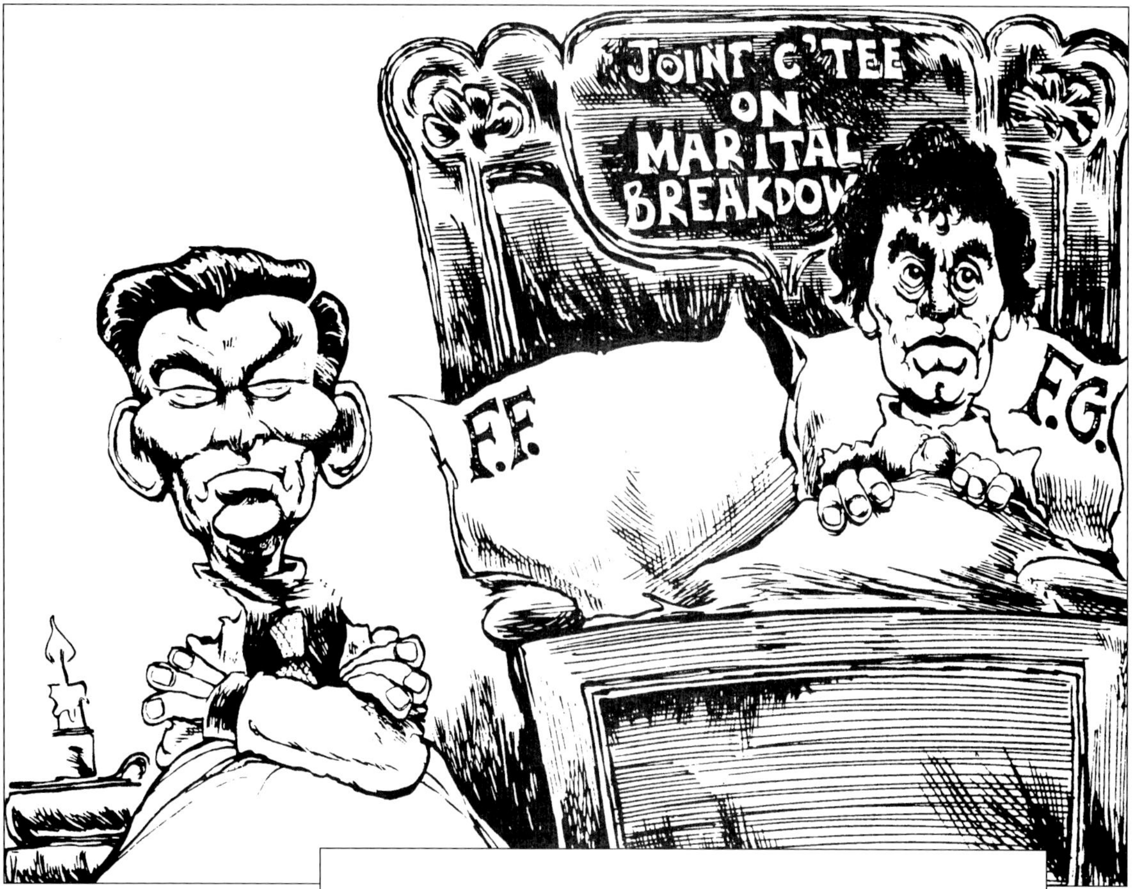
JOINT C'TEE
ON
MARITAL
BREAKDOW
F.F.
F.G.

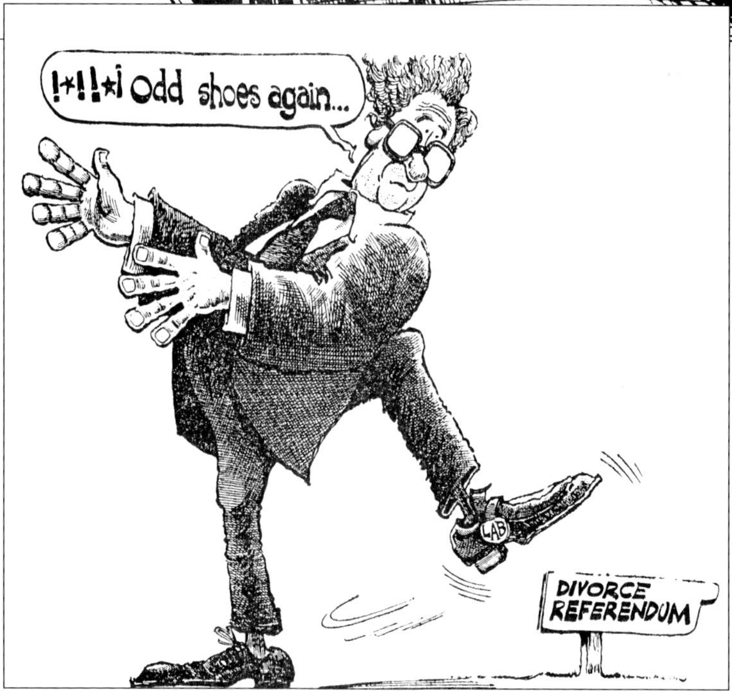
!*!!*¡ odd shoes again...
LAB
DIVORCE
REFERENDUM

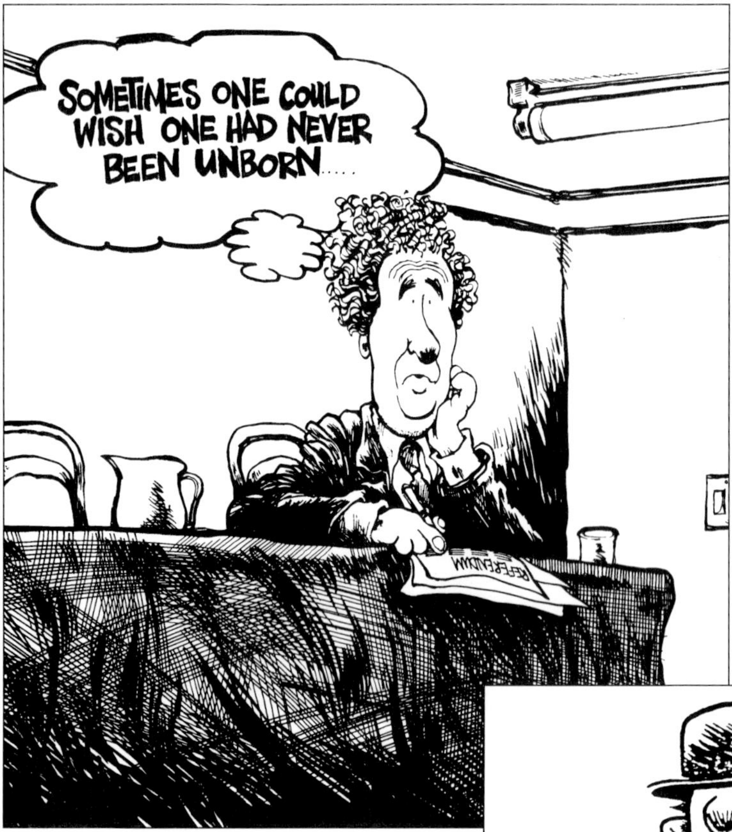
SOMETIMES ONE COULD WISH ONE HAD NEVER BEEN UNBORN.....

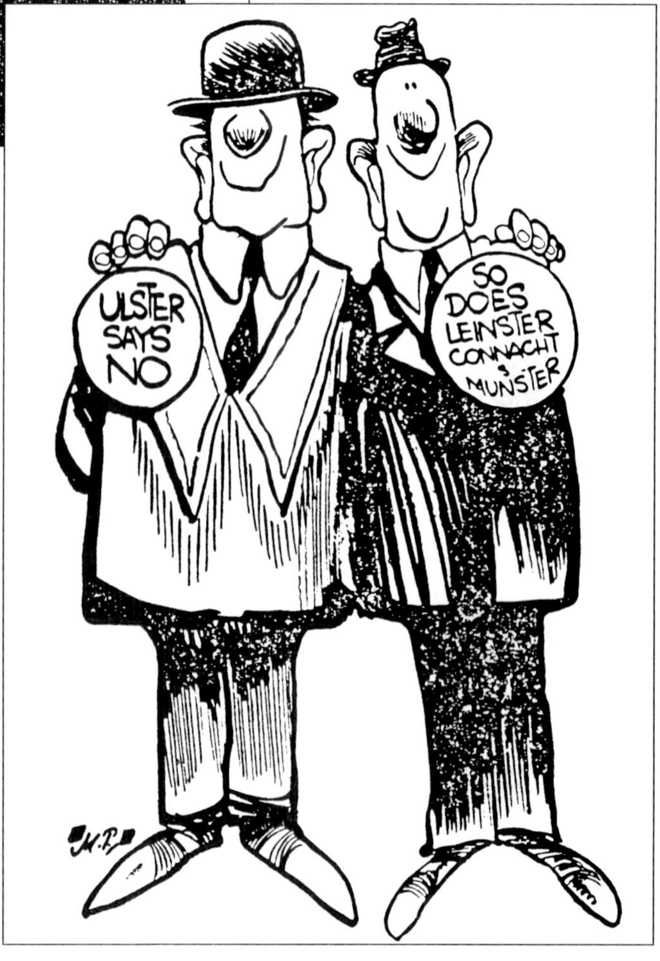
ULSTER SAYS NO
SO DOES LEINSTER CONNACHT & MUNSTER

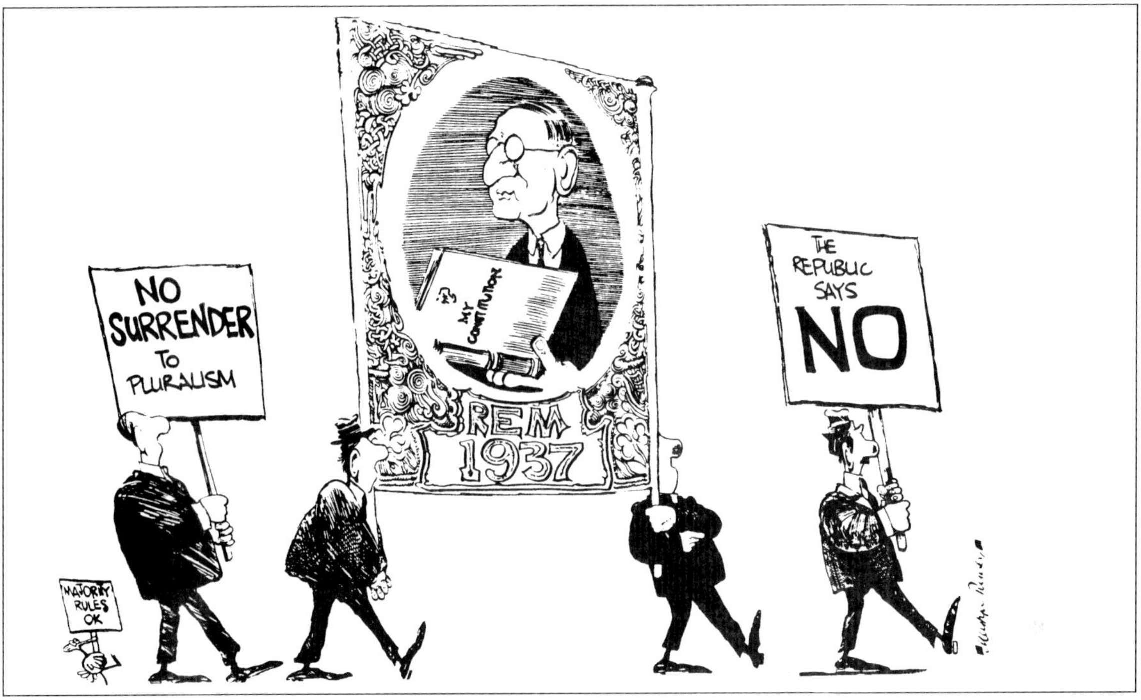
NO SURRENDER TO PLURALISM
REM 1937
MY CONSTITUTION
THE REPUBLIC SAYS NO
MAJORITY RULES OK

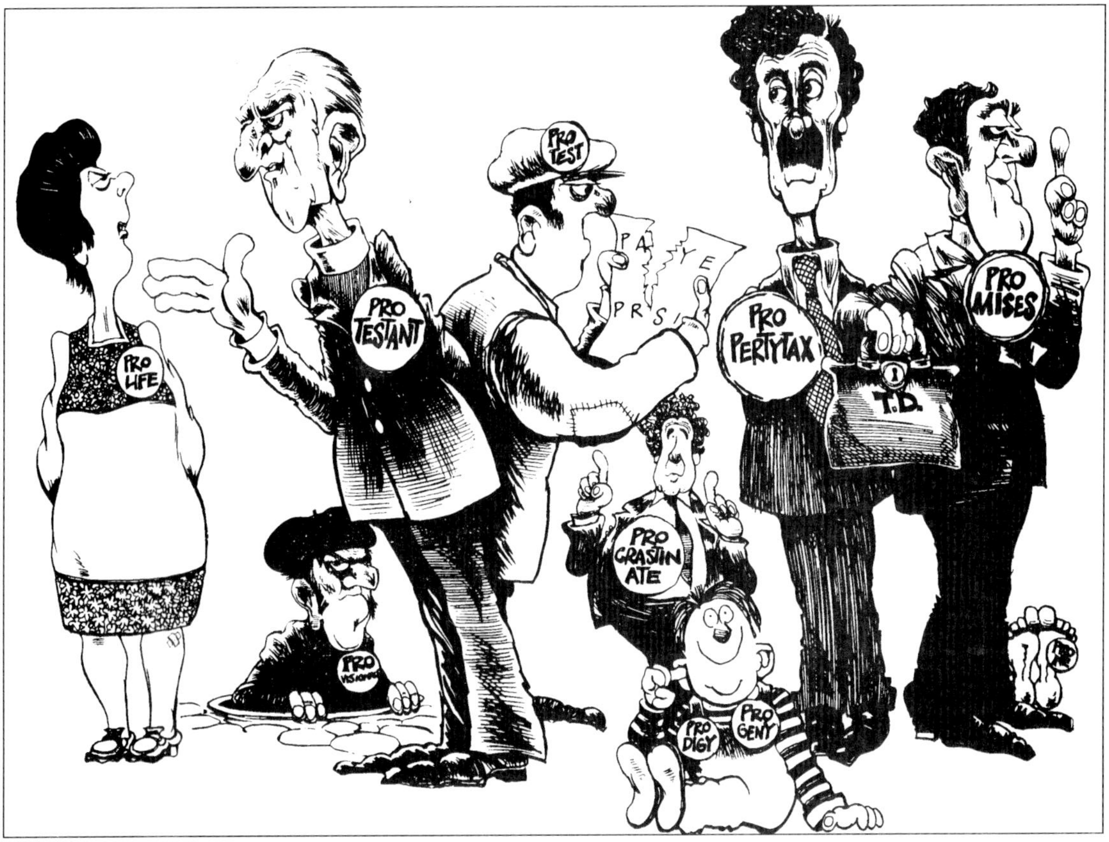
PRO LIFE
PRO TESTANT
PRO TEST
PRO PERTY TAX
PRO MISES
T.D.
PRO GRASTIN ATE
PRO DIGY
PRO GENY

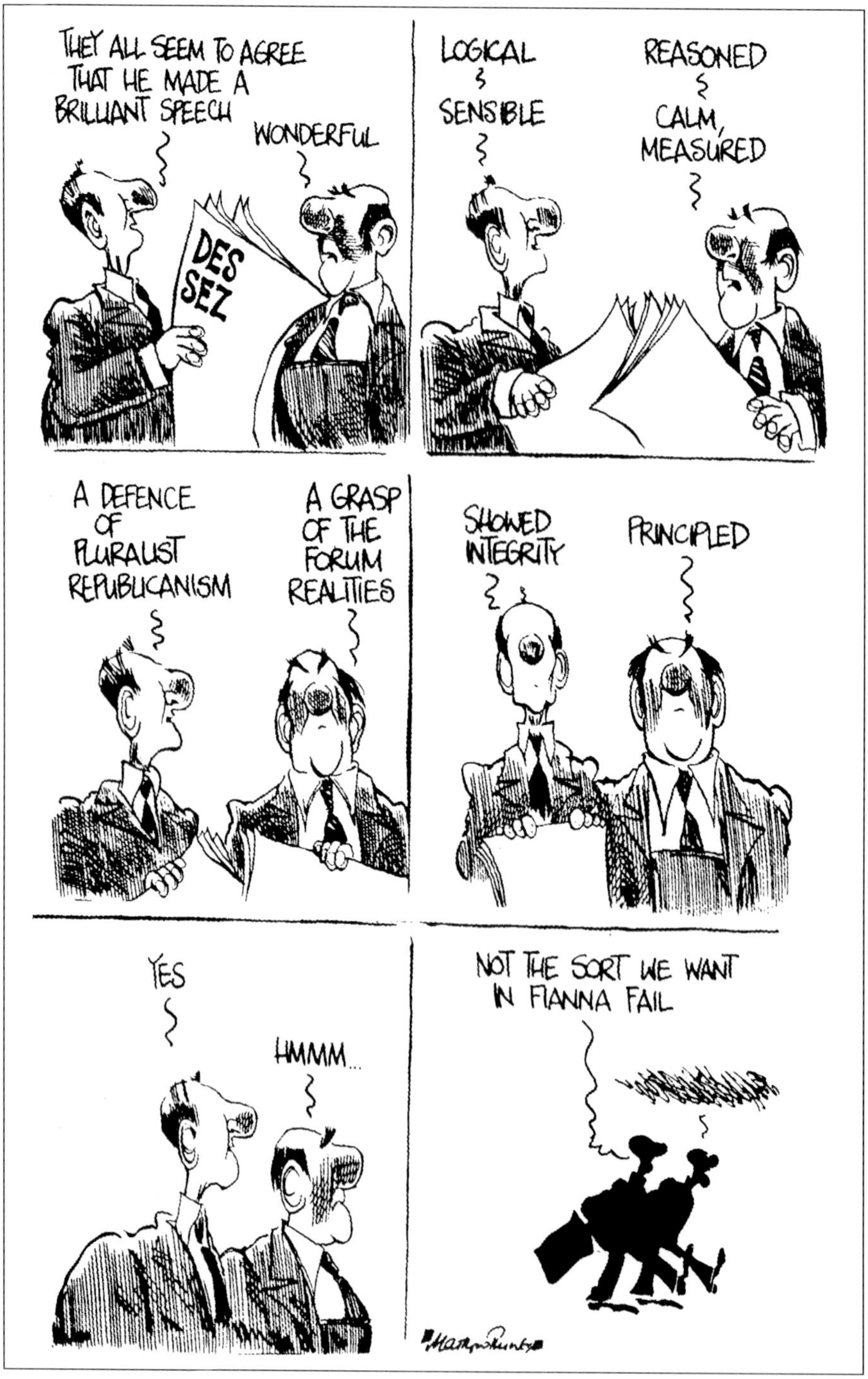
THEY ALL SEEM TO AGREE THAT HE MADE A BRILLIANT SPEECH
WONDERFUL
DES SEZ
LOGICAL
SENSIBLE
REASONED
CALM, MEASURED
A DEFENCE OF PLURALIST REPUBLICANISM
A GRASP OF THE FORUM REALITIES
SHOWED INTEGRITY
PRINCIPLED
YES
HMMM...
NOT THE SORT WE WANT IN FIANNA FAIL

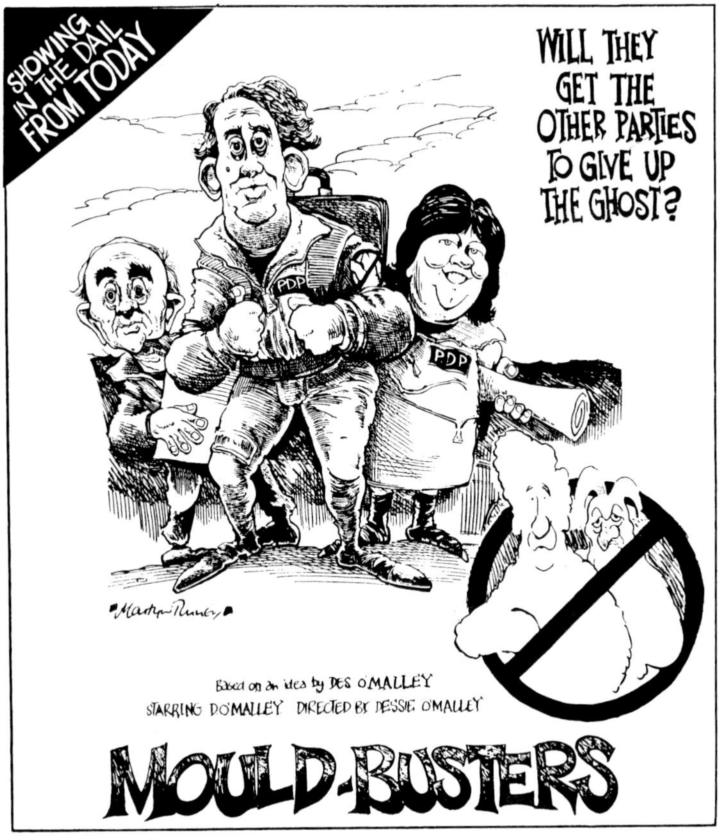
SHOWING IN THE DAIL FROM TODAY
WILL THEY GET THE OTHER PARTIES TO GIVE UP THE GHOST?
PDP
PDP
Martyn Turner
Based on an idea by DES O'MALLEY
STARRING D. O'MALLEY DIRECTED BY DESSIE O'MALLEY
MOULD-BUSTERS

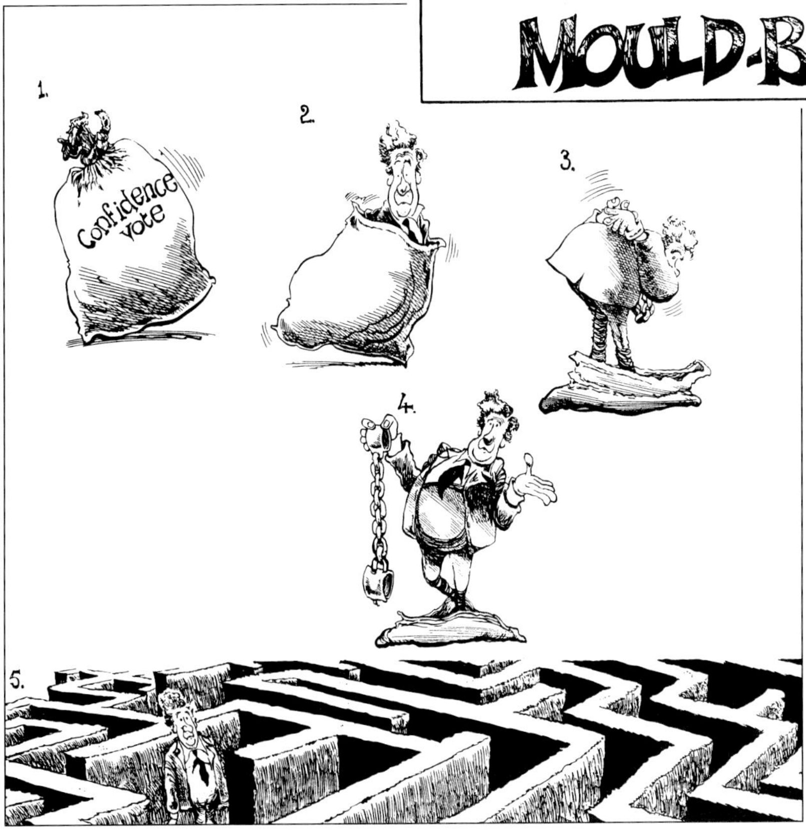
1.
Confidence vote
2.
3.
4.
5.

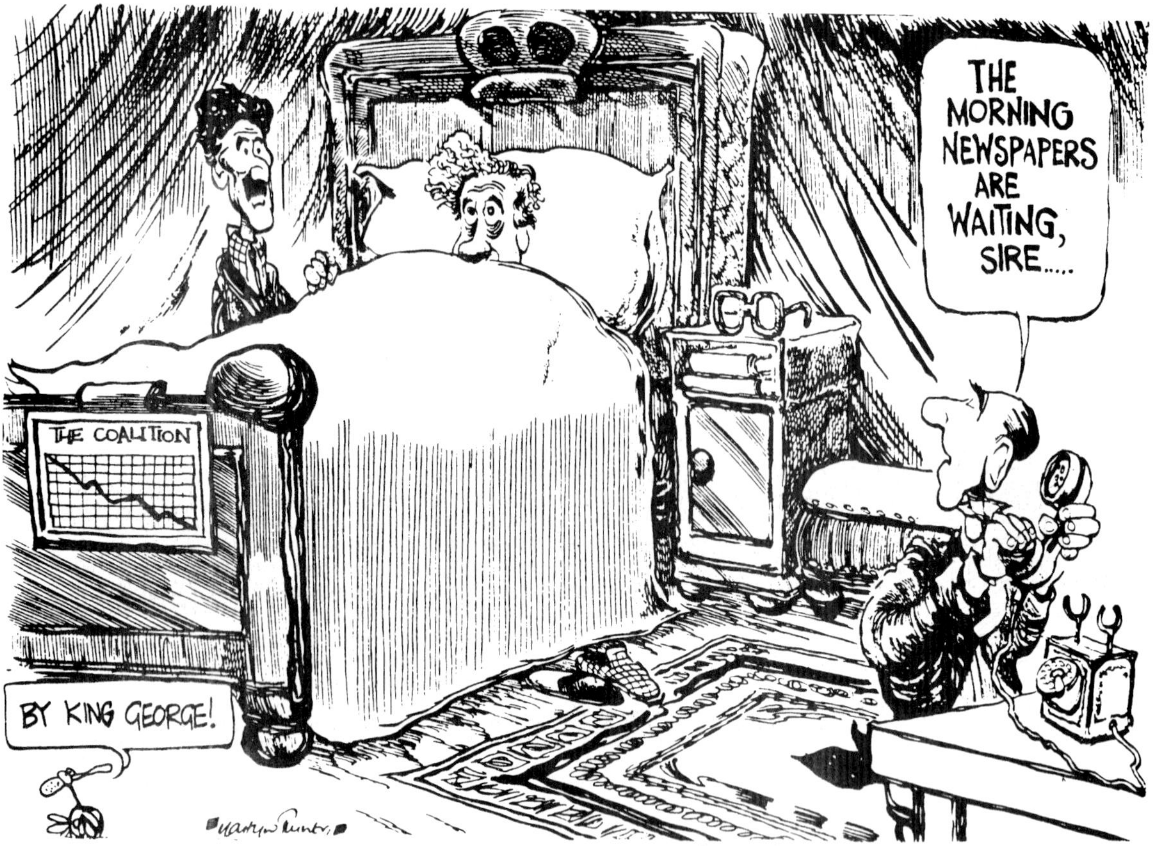
THE MORNING NEWSPAPERS ARE WAITING, SIRE.....
THE COALITION
BY KING GEORGE!

It was revealed that King George's demise was arranged to time with the headlines of the **Morning** papers.

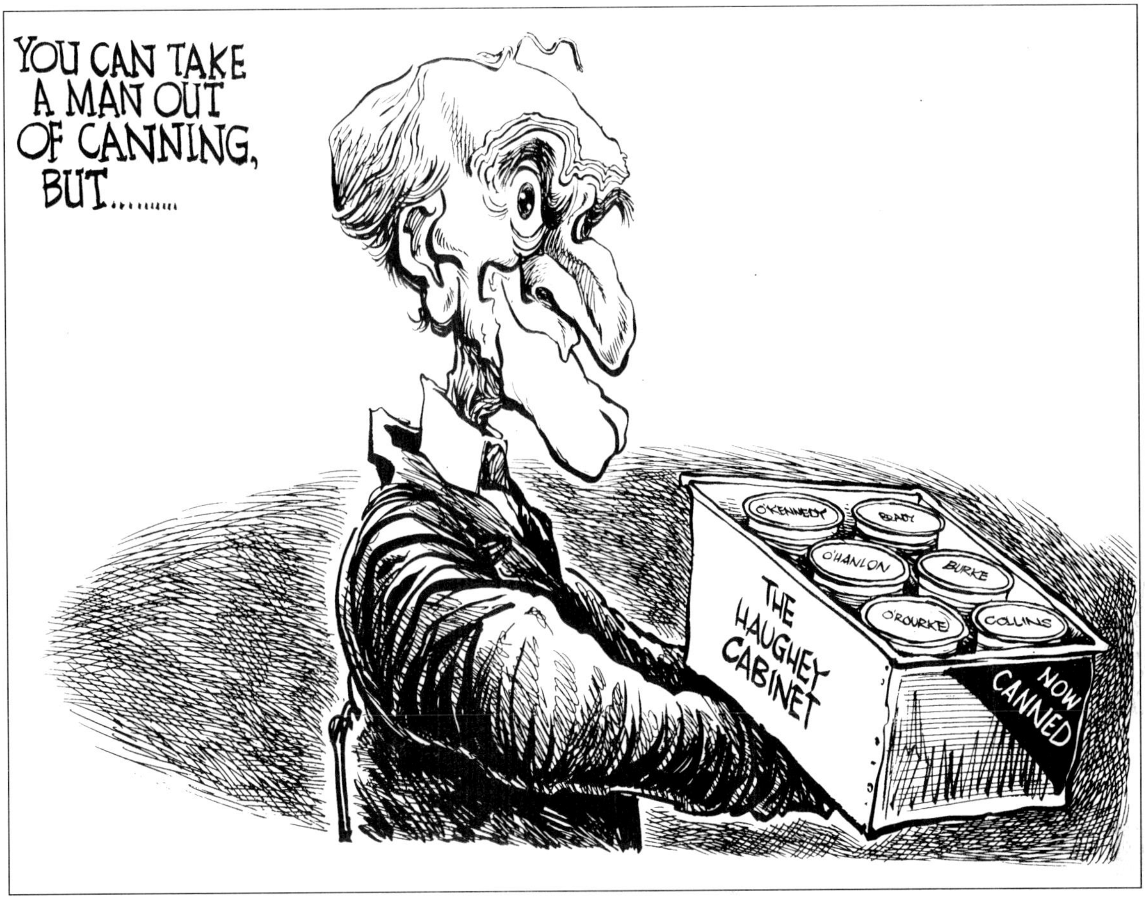
YOU CAN TAKE A MAN OUT OF CANNING, BUT.........
O'KENNEDY
BRADY
O'HANLON
BURKE
O'ROURKE
COLLINS
THE HAUGHEY CABINET
NOW CANNED

Albert Reynolds 1992–94

Albert Reynolds, against whom I would not say a word as he tends to sue, brought a whole new business dynamism to politics. Unfortunately this didn't rest easy with coalition partners and he fell out with the PDs and, eventually, with their replacement, Dick Spring's Labour Party. But he tried to rid FF of Haugheyism, an impossible task, as well as splitting more abortion hairs, playing the poor mouth successfully in Europe, and getting the first hint of the clerical sexual abuse scandals that dominated the headlines latterly. His plan to greet President Yeltsin on the tarmac at Shannon did not go well. There were a few hiccups.

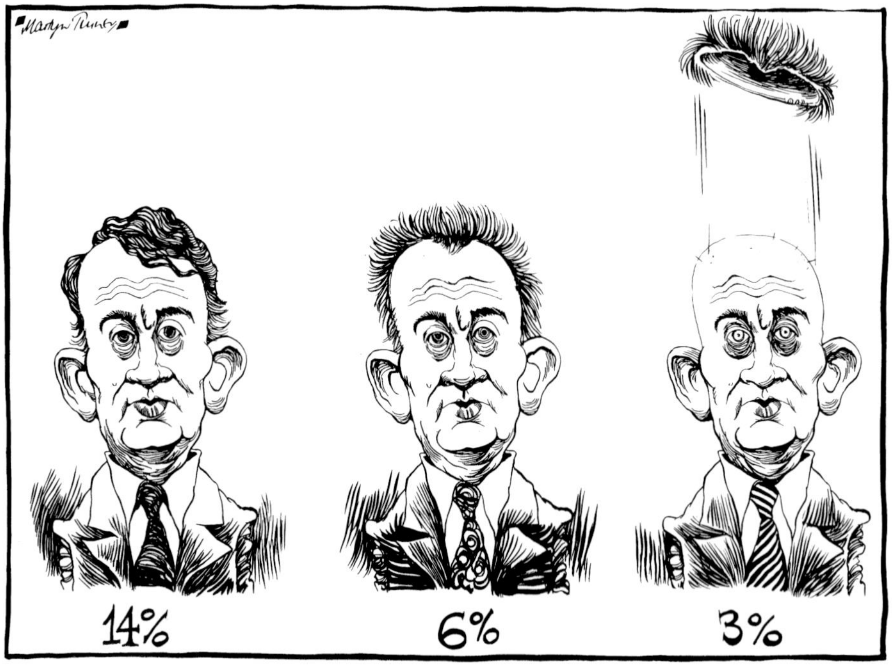
Martyn Turner
14%
6%
3%

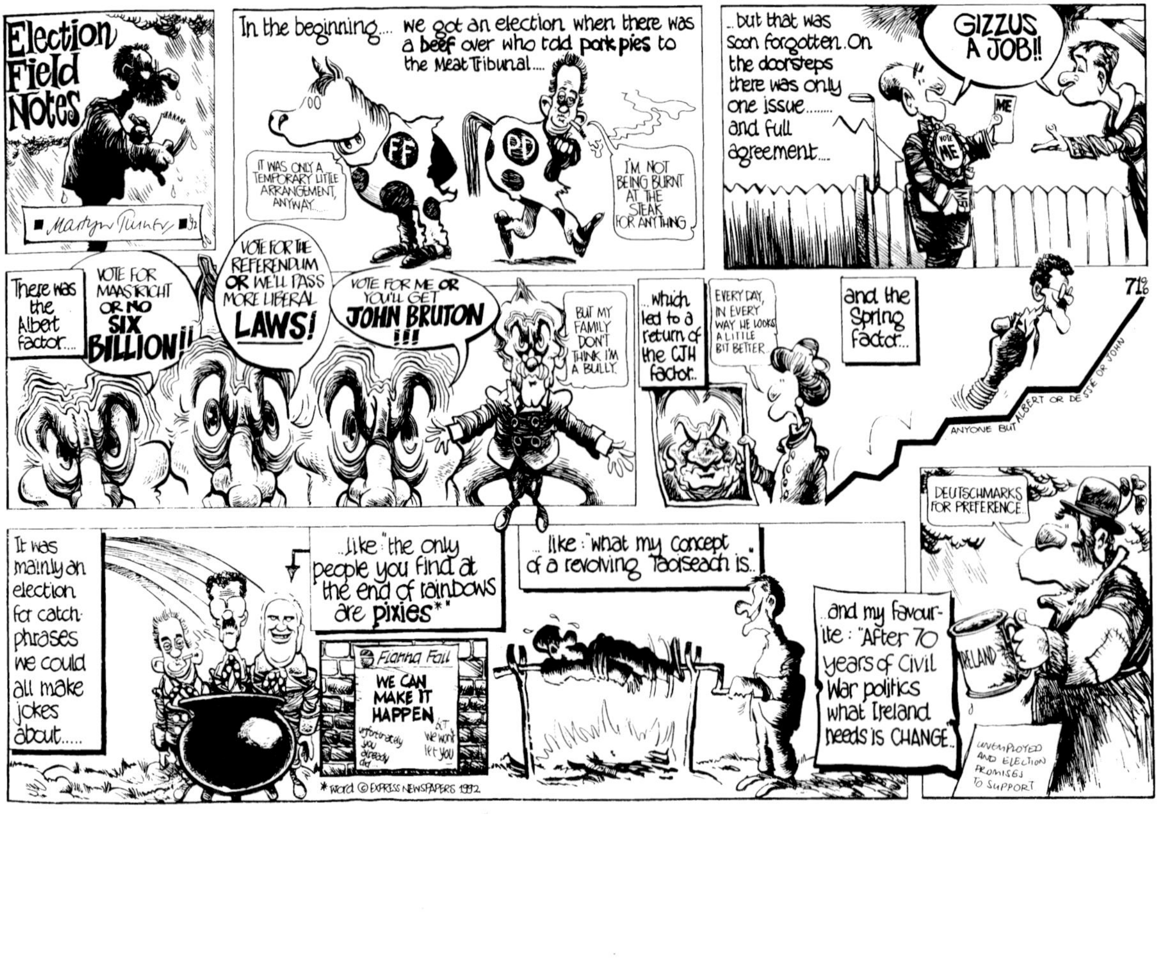
Election Field Notes
Martyn Turner '92
In the beginning.... we got an election when there was a beef over who told pork pies to the Meat Tribunal.....
FF
PD
IT WAS ONLY A TEMPORARY LITTLE ARRANGEMENT, ANYWAY......
I'M NOT BEING BURNT AT THE STEAK FOR ANYTHING
...but that was soon forgotten..On the doorsteps there was only one issue........ and full agreement....
GIZZUS A JOB!!
ME
VOTE ME
There was the Albert factor....
VOTE FOR MAASTRICHT OR NO SIX BILLION!!
VOTE FOR THE REFERENDUM OR WE'LL PASS MORE LIBERAL LAWS!
VOTE FOR ME OR YOU'LL GET JOHN BRUTON !!!
BUT MY FAMILY DON'T THINK I'M A BULLY.
...which led to a return of the CJH factor..
EVERY DAY, IN EVERY WAY HE LOOKS A LITTLE BIT BETTER.
and the Spring factor...
71%
ANYONE BUT
It was mainly an election for catch-phrases we could all make jokes about.....
...like "the only people you find at the end of rainbows are pixies*"
Fianna Fail
WE CAN MAKE IT HAPPEN
... like "what my concept of a revolving Taoiseach is"..
..and my favour-ite : "After 70 years of Civil War politics what Ireland needs is CHANGE"..
DEUTSCHMARKS FOR PREFERENCE..
IRELAND
UNEMPLOYED AND ELECTION PROMISES TO SUPPORT
© EXPRESS NEWSPAPERS 1992

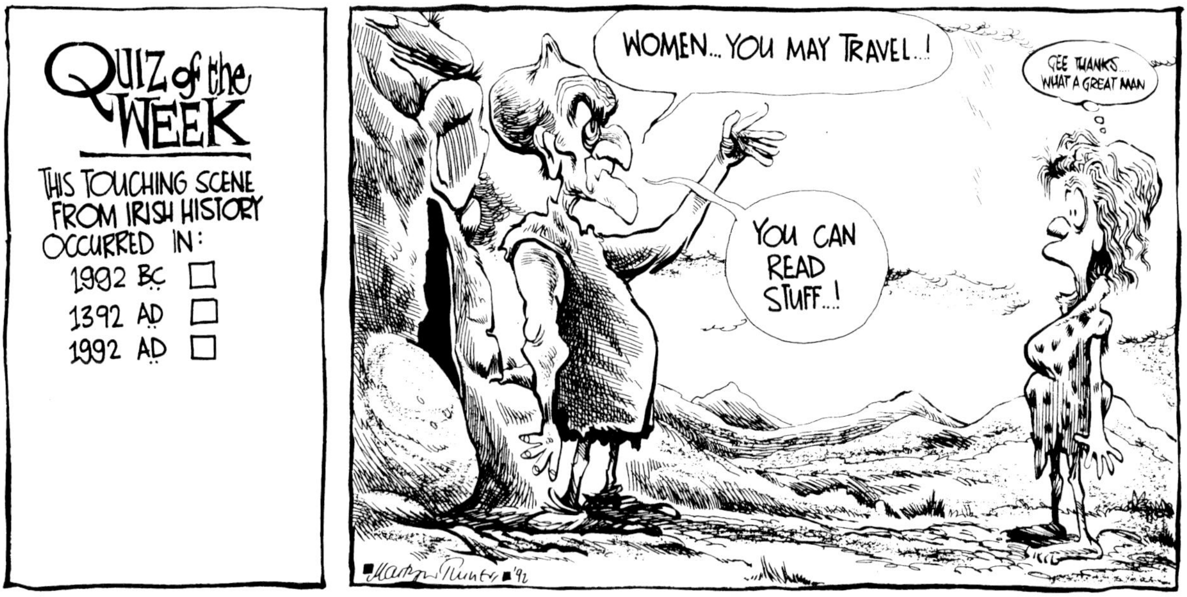
QUIZ of the WEEK
THIS TOUCHING SCENE FROM IRISH HISTORY OCCURRED IN:
1992 BC
1392 AD
1992 AD
WOMEN... YOU MAY TRAVEL..!
YOU CAN READ STUFF...!
GEE THANKS... WHAT A GREAT MAN

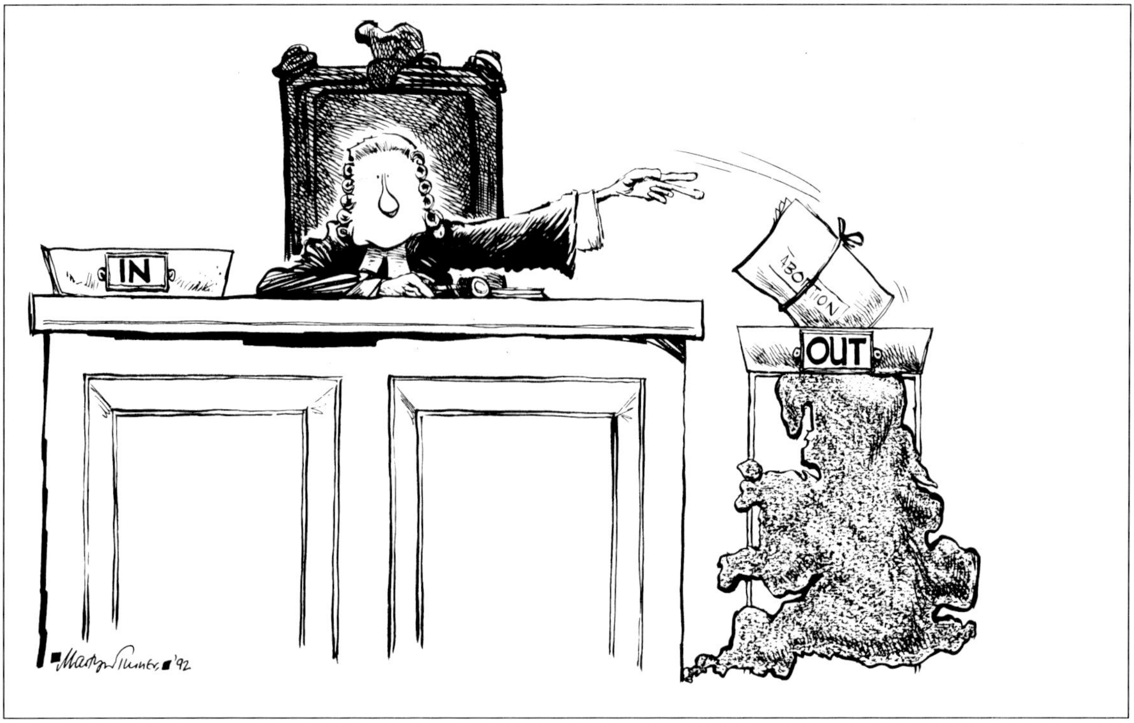
IN
ABORTION
OUT

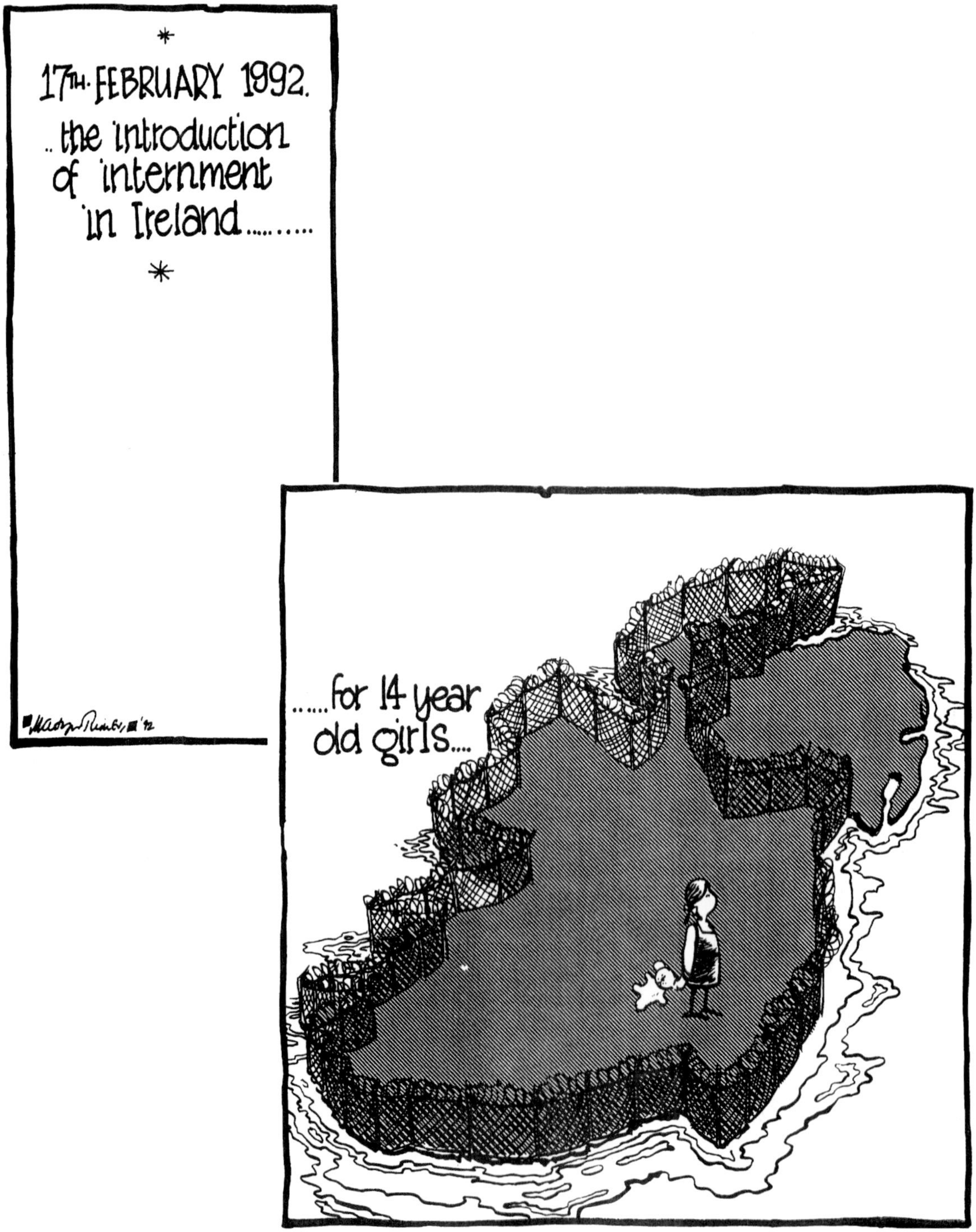
17TH. FEBRUARY 1992.
.. the introduction of internment in Ireland..........
......for 14 year old girls....

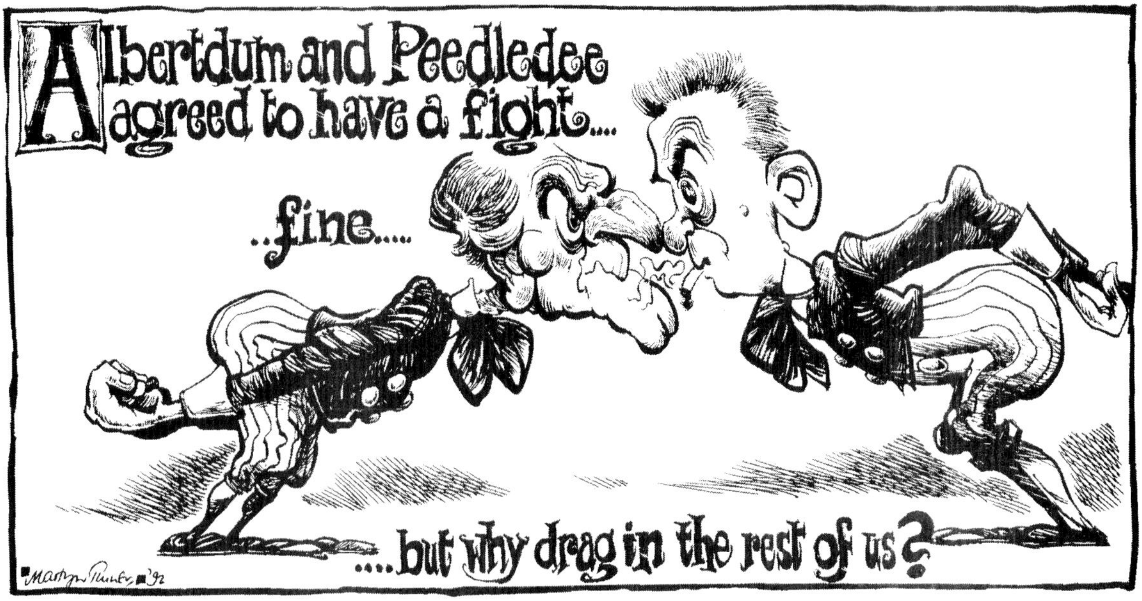
Albertdum and Peedledee agreed to have a fight....
..fine.....
....but why drag in the rest of us?
Martyn Turner '92

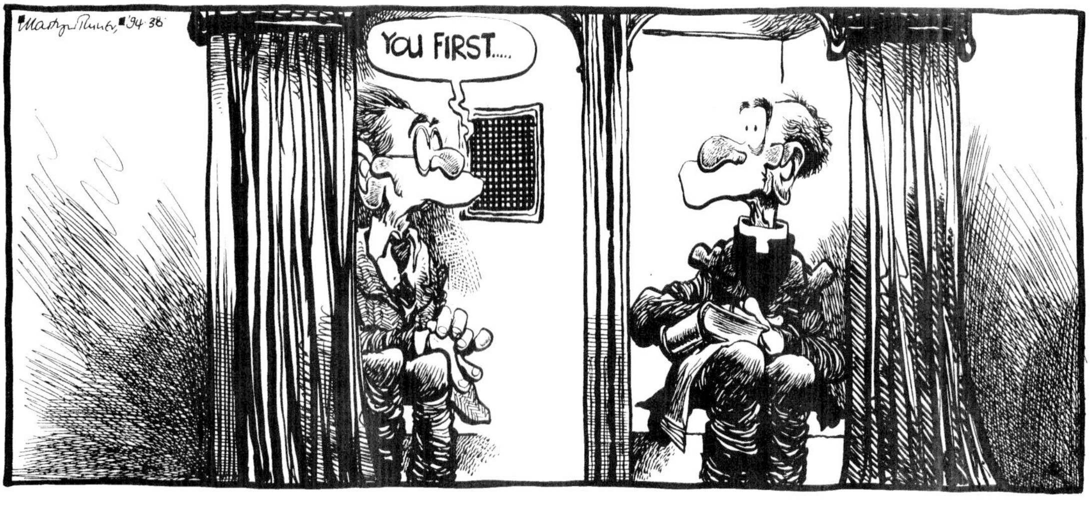
Martyn Turner '94
YOU FIRST.....

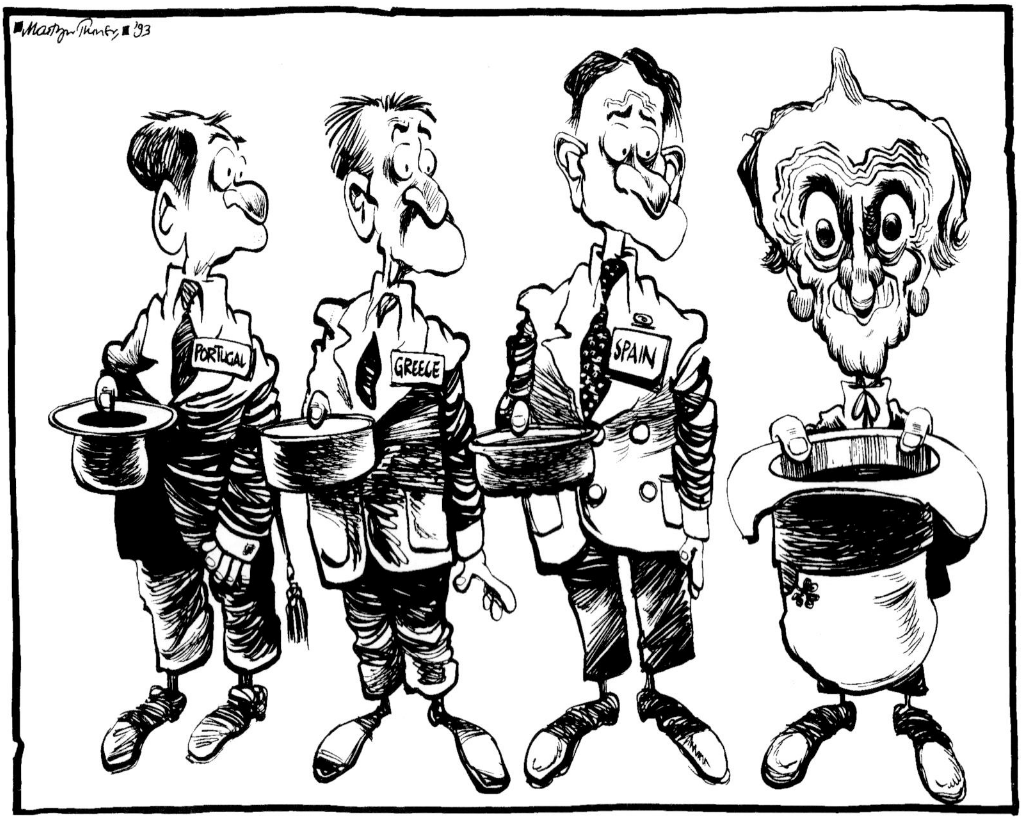
Martyn Turner '93
PORTUGAL
GREECE
SPAIN

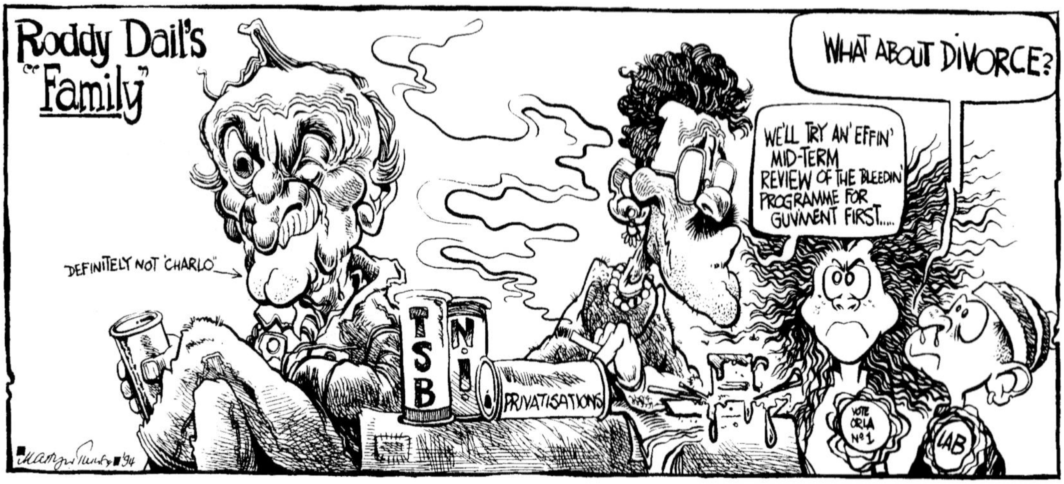
Roddy Dail's "Family"
WHAT ABOUT DIVORCE?
WE'LL TRY AN' EFFIN' MID-TERM REVIEW OF THE BLEEDIN' PROGRAMME FOR GUVMENT FIRST....
DEFINITELY NOT 'CHARLO'
TSB
N!
PRIVATISATIONS
VOTE ORLA No 1
LAB
Martyn Turner '94

QUALIFICATIONS for a ROTATING TAOISEACH
F.F. IS UNREFORMABLE
EVERYBODY OUT...
WE HAVE A DEAL...
CAN NO LONGER SUPPORT...
BEFORE LAST ELECTION
AFTER LAST ELECTION
LAST FRIDAY WEEK.....
LAST WEDNESDAY MORNING...
LUNCHTIME (TO BE CONTD)

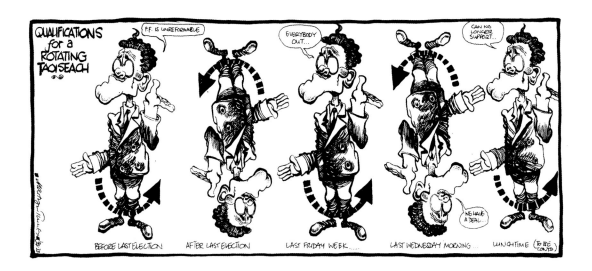

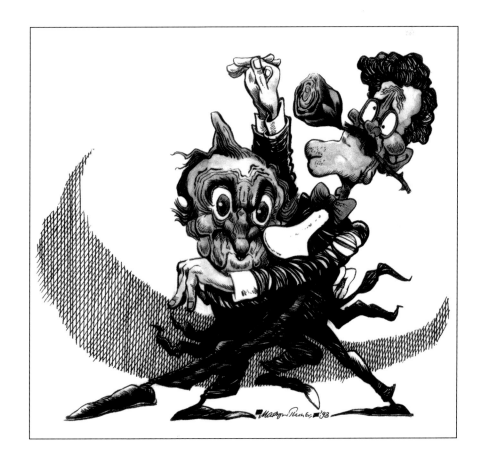

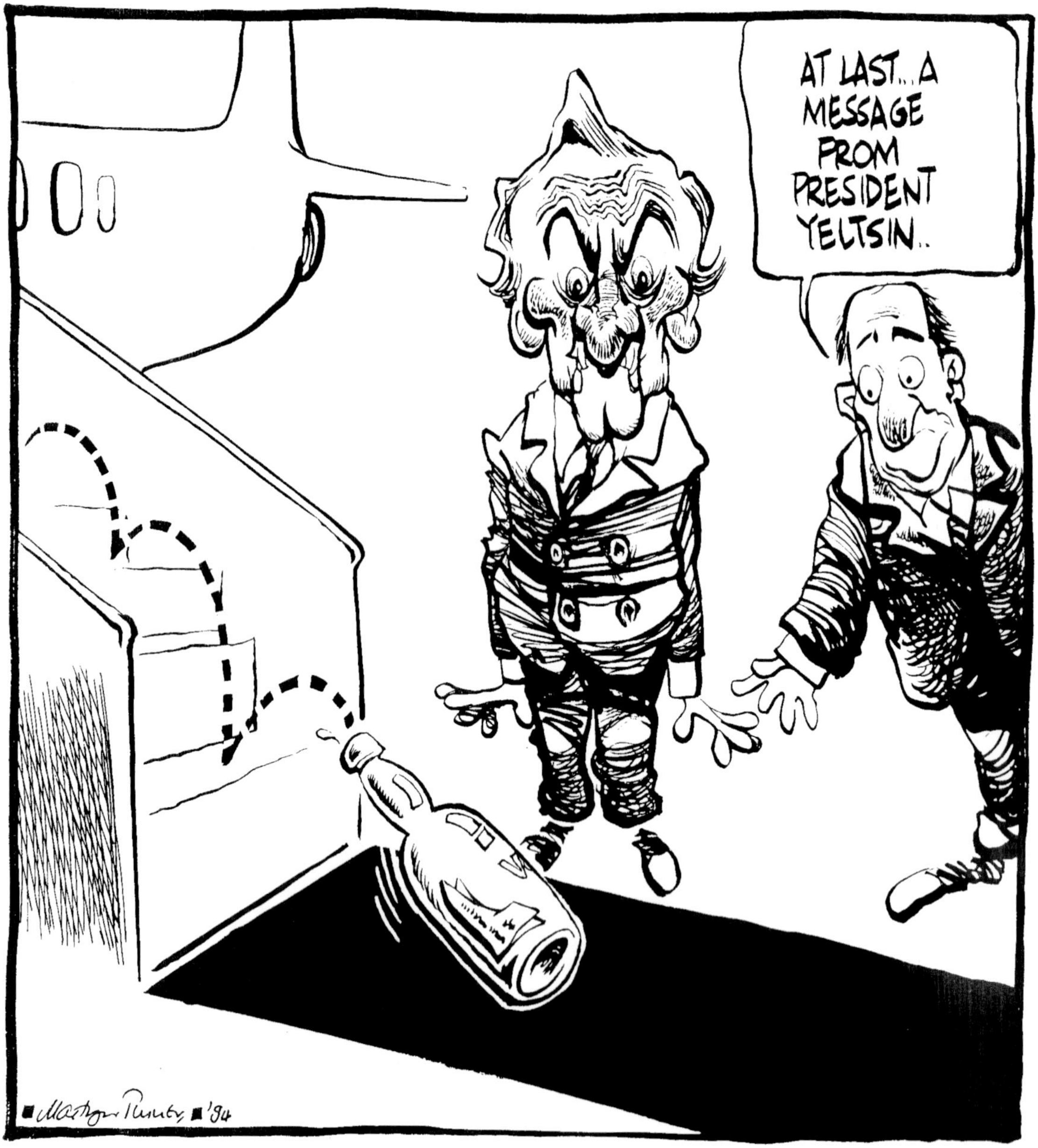
AT LAST...A MESSAGE FROM PRESIDENT YELTSIN..
Martyn Turner '94

John Bruton 1994–97

Taking over when Labour jumped the Fianna Fáil ship, John Bruton introduced transparency into government. His Minister for Agriculture improved on this by introducing bi-location into government by claiming to be in two places at the same time. John Bruton's alleged best friend, Michael Lowry, was caught doing something or other, alleged. Just went to show that Fine Gael were well able to replace Fianna Fáil: given the chance they could be just as dodgy.

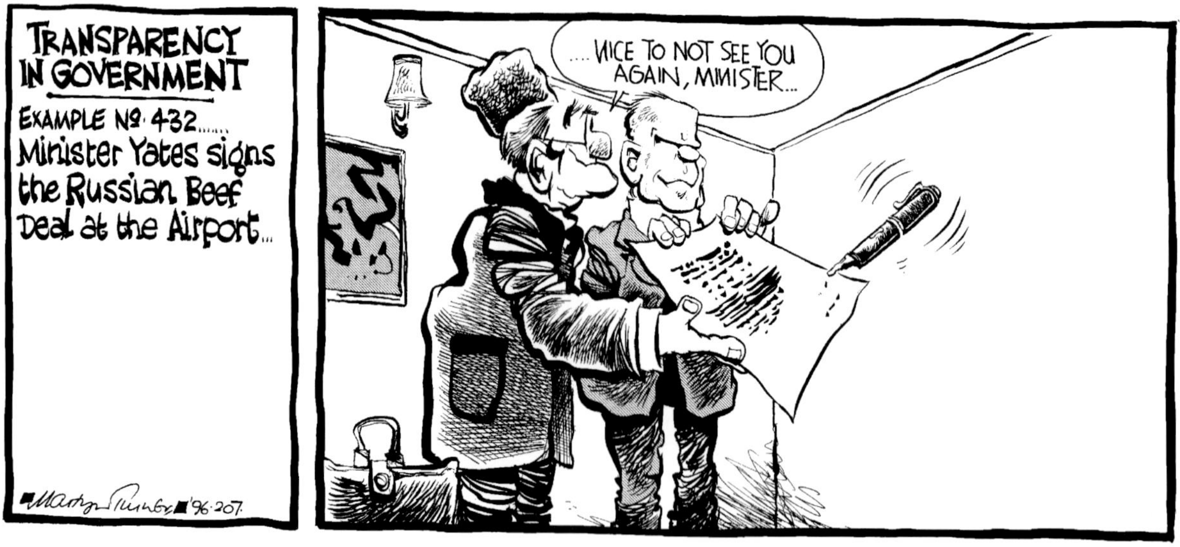
TRANSPARENCY IN GOVERNMENT
EXAMPLE Nº 432......
Minister Yates signs the Russian Beef Deal at the Airport...
....NICE TO NOT SEE YOU AGAIN, MINISTER...
Martyn Turner '96·207·

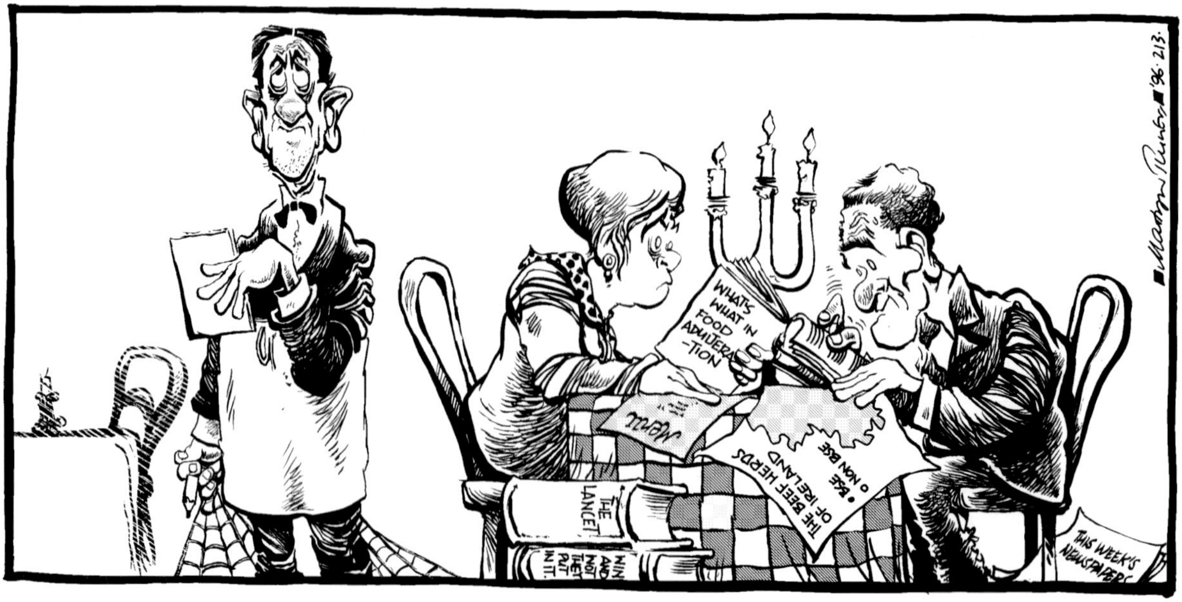
WHAT'S WHAT IN FOOD ADULTERA-TION
Menu
THE BEEF HERDS OF IRELAND
• BSE
• NON BSE
THE LANCET
THIS WEEK'S NEWSPAPERS
Martyn Turner '96·213·

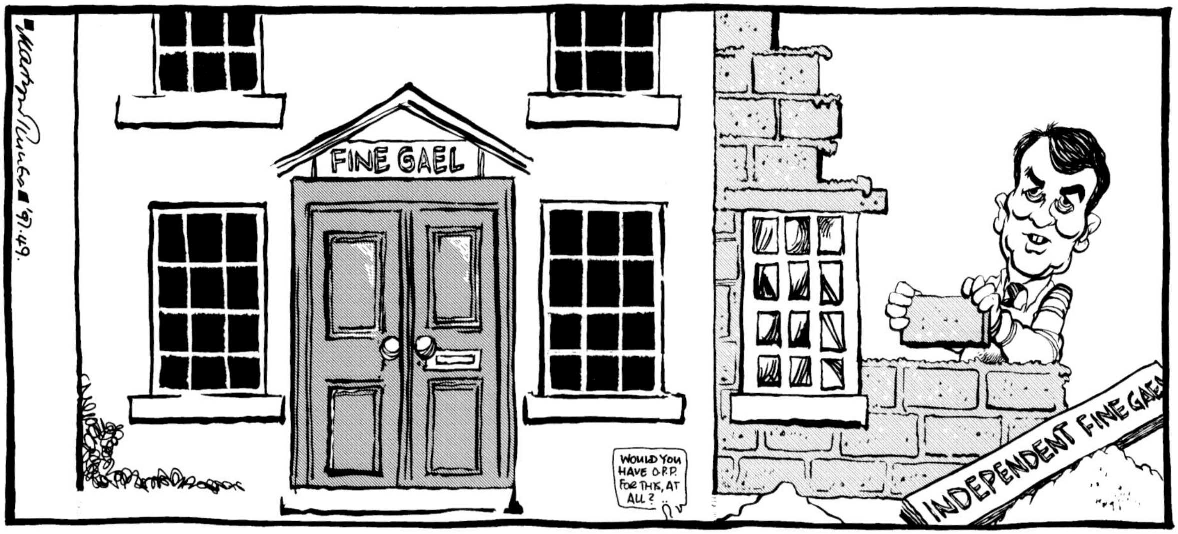
FINE GAEL
WOULD YOU HAVE O.P.P. FOR THIS, AT ALL? ..
INDEPENDENT FINE GAEL
'97.49.

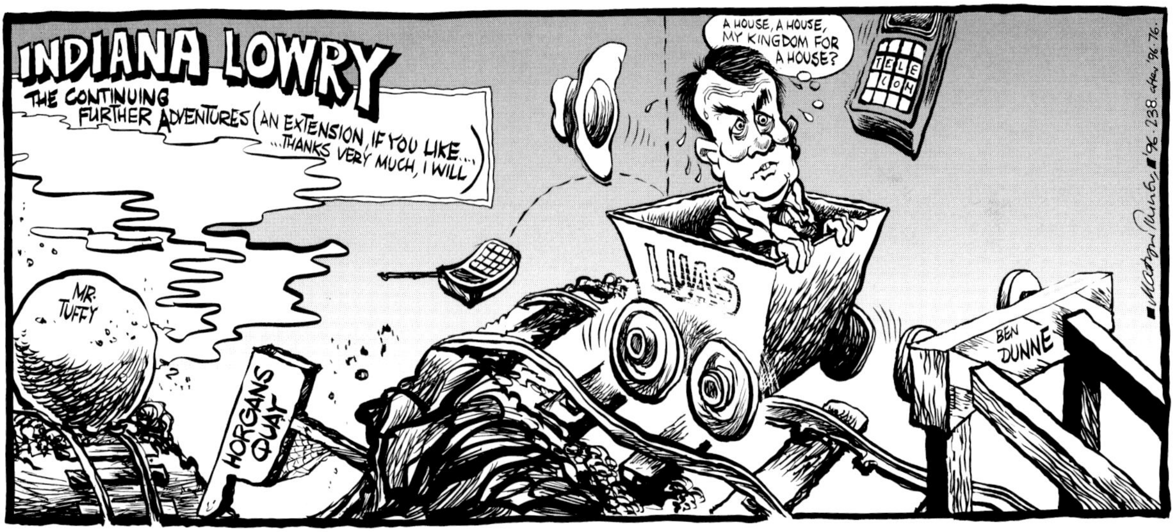
INDIANA LOWRY
THE CONTINUING FURTHER ADVENTURES (AN EXTENSION, IF YOU LIKE... ...THANKS VERY MUCH, I WILL)
A HOUSE, A HOUSE, MY KINGDOM FOR A HOUSE?
TELECOM
LUAS
MR. TUFFY
HORGANS QUAY
BEN DUNNE
'96.238.

Bertie Ahern 1997 – still limping along

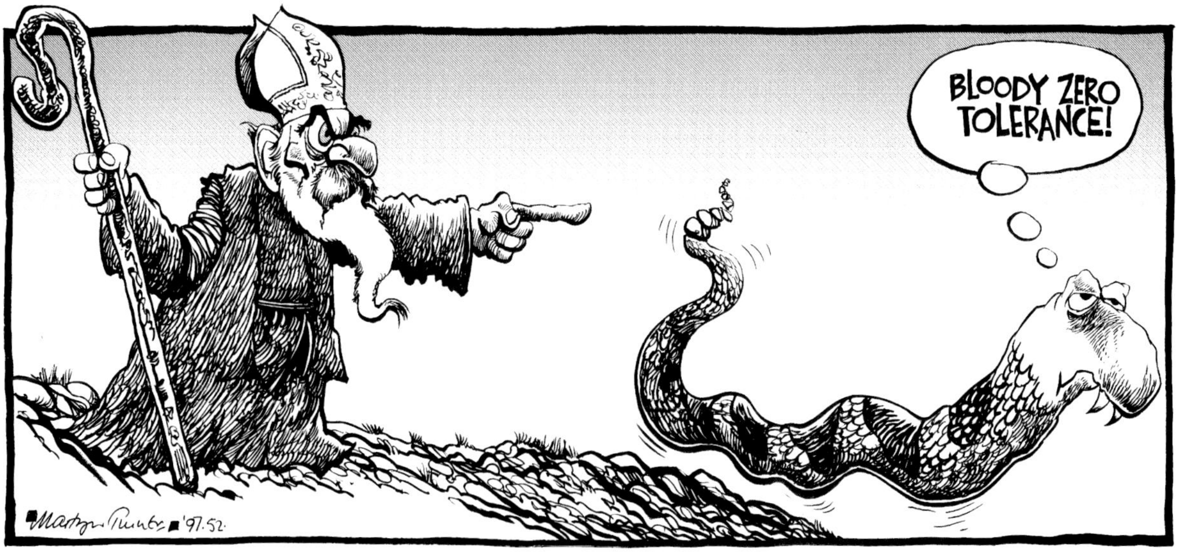
BLOODY ZERO TOLERANCE!

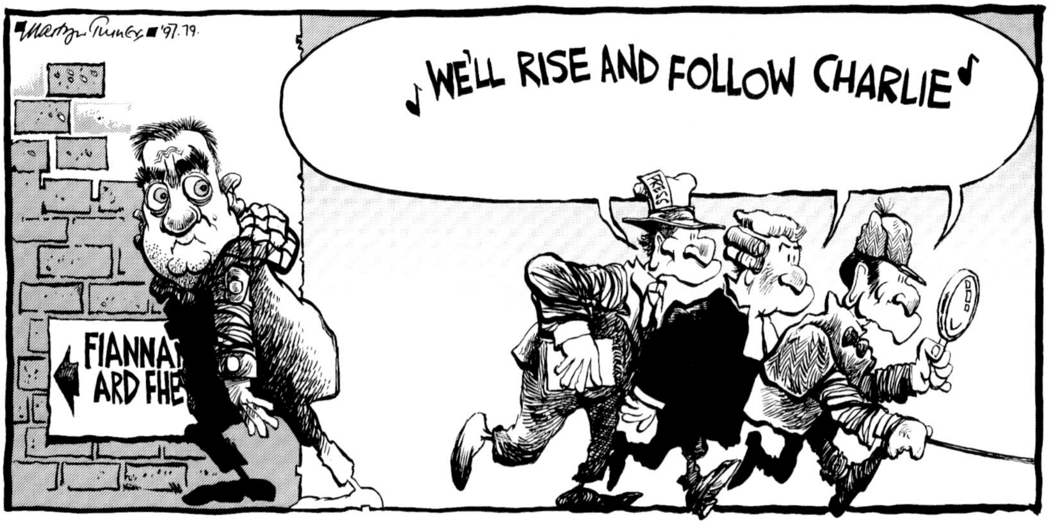
WE'LL RISE AND FOLLOW CHARLIE
FIANNA
ARD FHE
PRESS

There are a lot more cartoons in this section for many reasons. One is that events are so recent that they don't need explanation, I hope. The other is that, with the instigation of the tribunals, the rottenness in the state of Ireland that took place in the last 30 years is now coming into the full light of day.

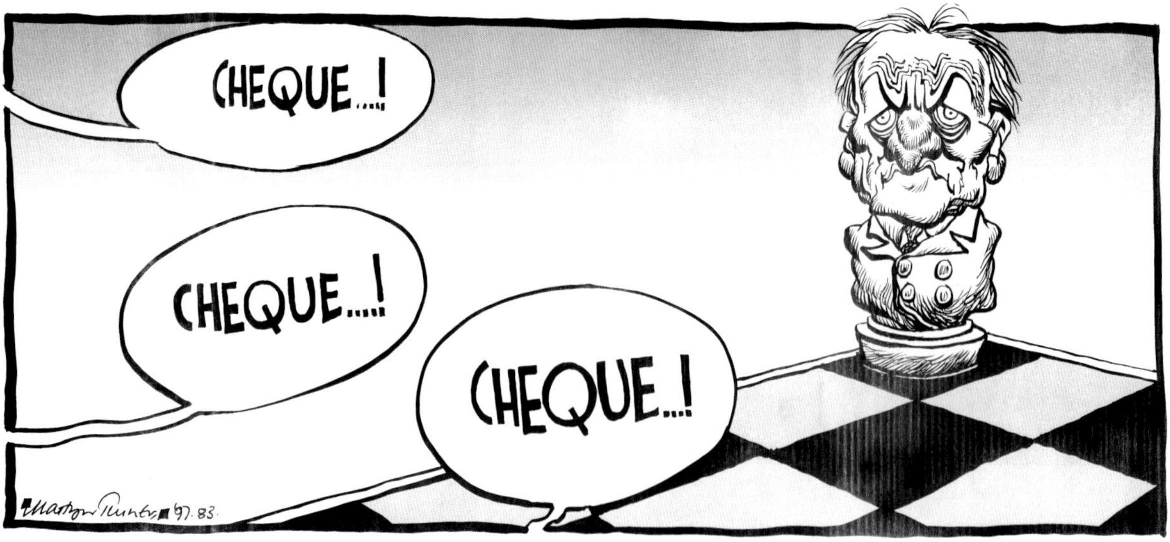
CHEQUE...!
CHEQUE...!
CHEQUE..!
Martyn Turner '97. 83.

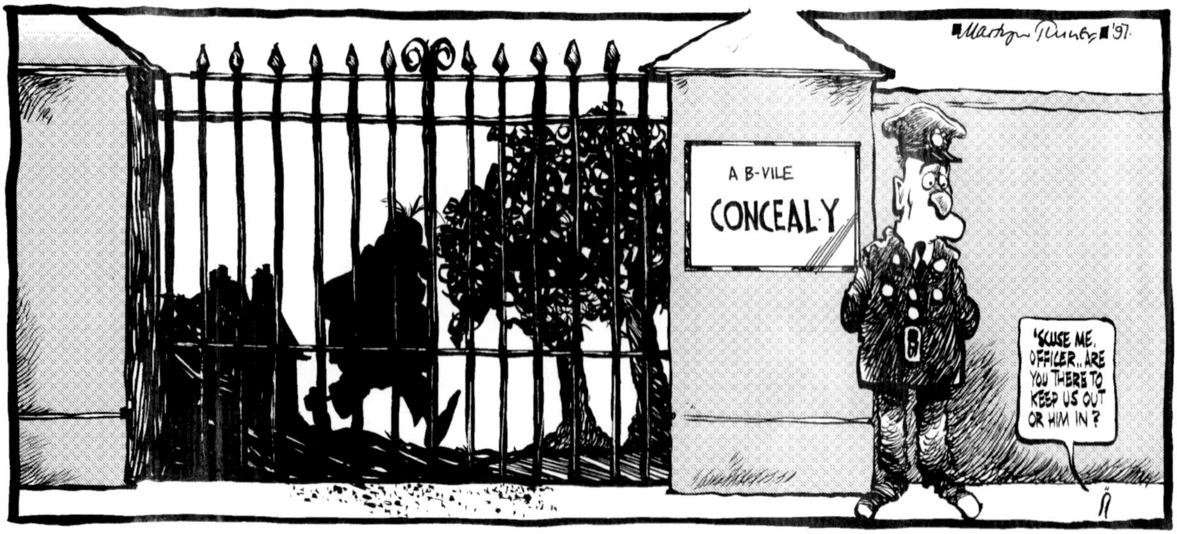
Martyn Turner '97.
A B-VILE
CONCEAL·Y
'SCUSE ME, OFFICER.. ARE YOU THERE TO KEEP US OUT OR HIM IN?

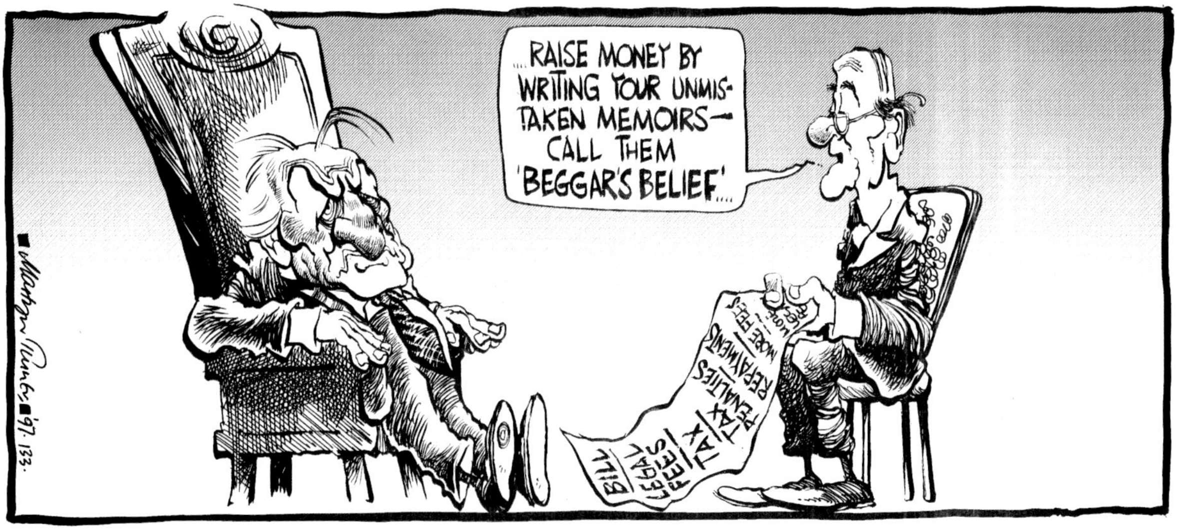
...RAISE MONEY BY WRITING YOUR UNMIS-TAKEN MEMOIRS— CALL THEM 'BEGGAR'S BELIEF'...
BILL
LEGAL FEES
TAX
TAX PENALTIES
REPAYMENTS
MORE FEES

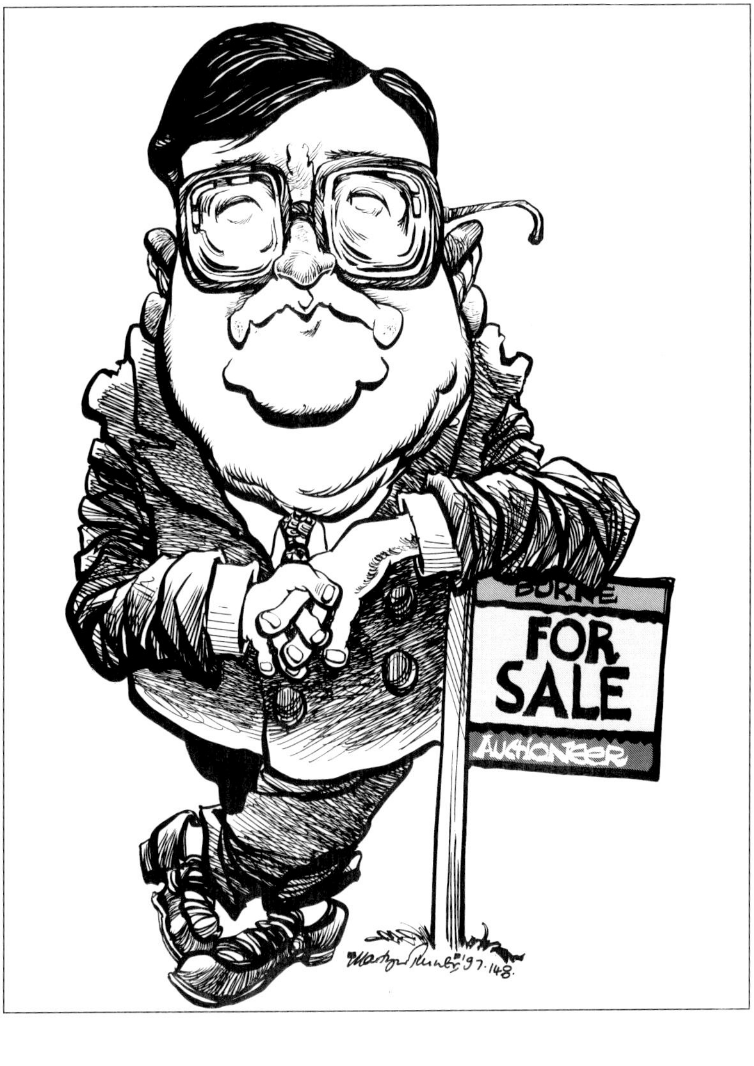
FOR SALE
AUCTIONEER

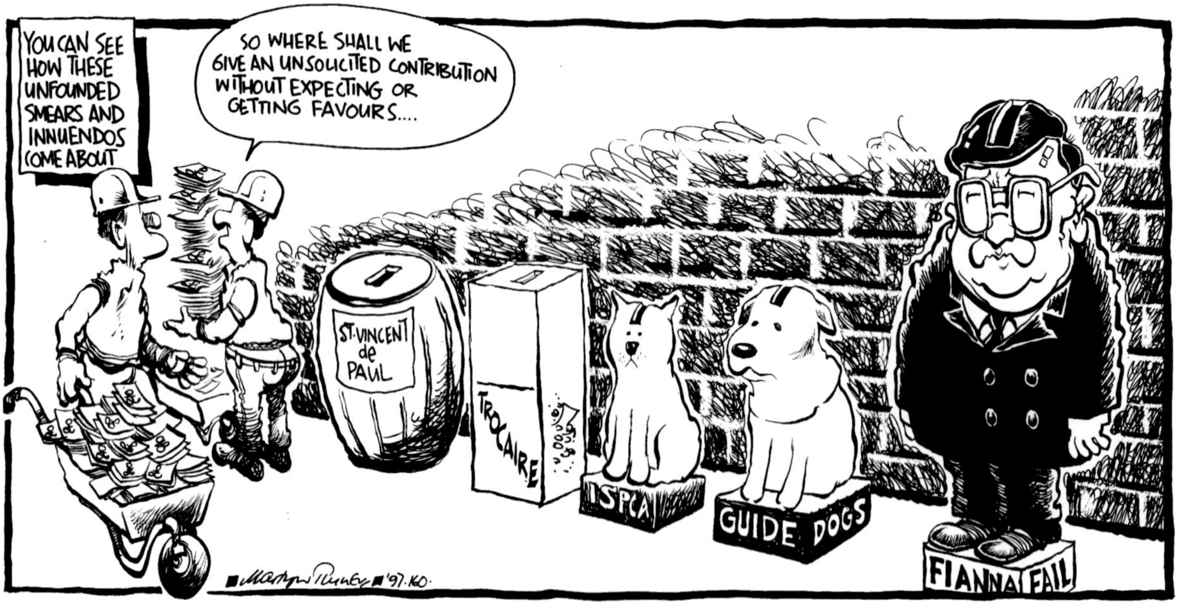
YOU CAN SEE HOW THESE UNFOUNDED SMEARS AND INNUENDOS COME ABOUT
SO WHERE SHALL WE GIVE AN UNSOLICITED CONTRIBUTION WITHOUT EXPECTING OR GETTING FAVOURS....
ST. VINCENT de PAUL
TROCAIRE
ISPCA
GUIDE DOGS
FIANNA FAIL
'97.160.

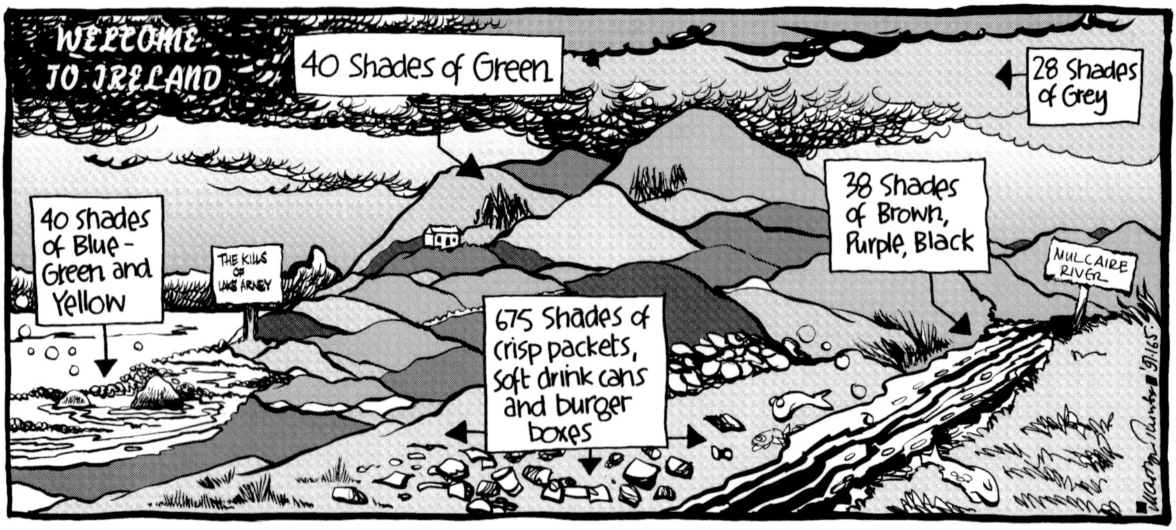
WELCOME TO IRELAND
40 Shades of Green
28 Shades of Grey
40 Shades of Blue-Green and Yellow
THE KILLS OF LAKE ARNEY
38 Shades of Brown, Purple, Black
MULCAIRE RIVER
675 Shades of crisp packets, soft drink cans and burger boxes
'91.165.

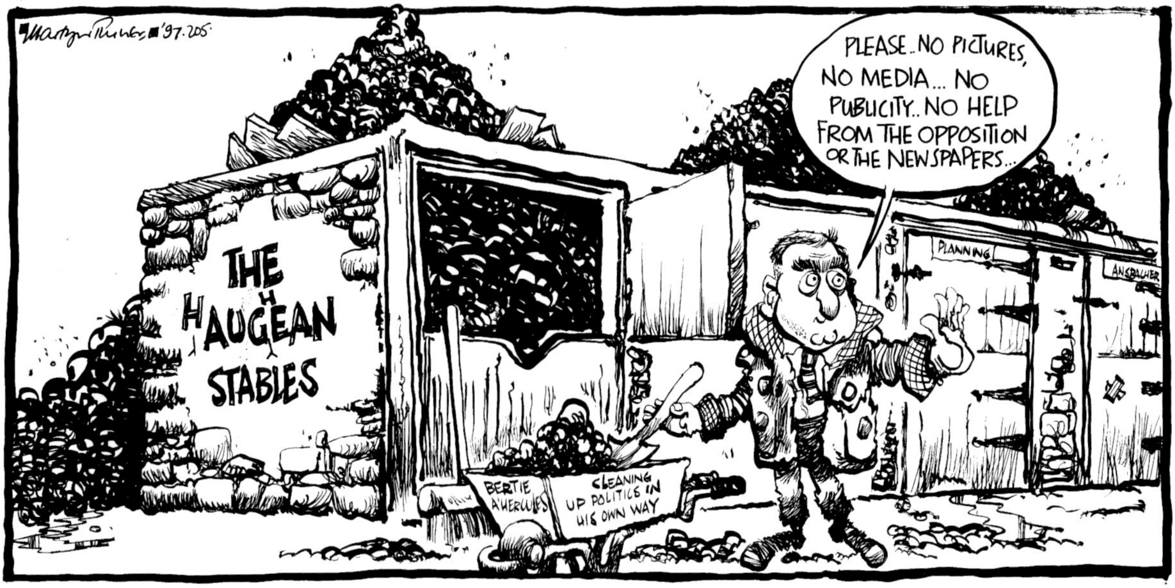
Martyn Turner '97.205
PLEASE..NO PICTURES, NO MEDIA... NO PUBLICITY..NO HELP FROM THE OPPOSITION OR THE NEWSPAPERS...
THE HAUGEAN STABLES
BERTIE A'HERCULES
CLEANING UP POLITICS IN HIS OWN WAY
PLANNING
ANSBACHER

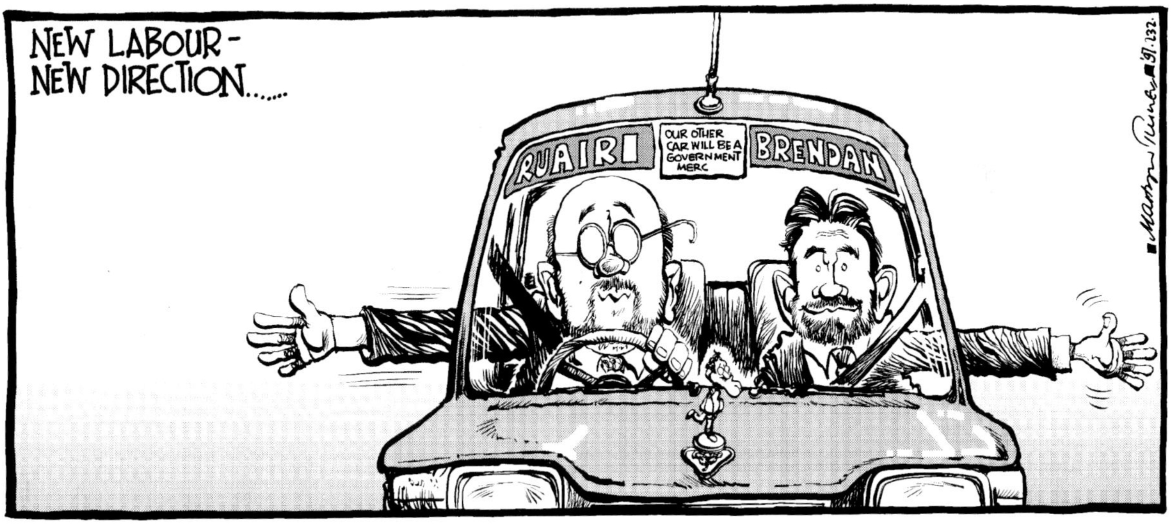
NEW LABOUR - NEW DIRECTION......
Martyn Turner '97.232.
RUAIRI
BRENDAN
OUR OTHER CAR WILL BE A GOVERNMENT MERC

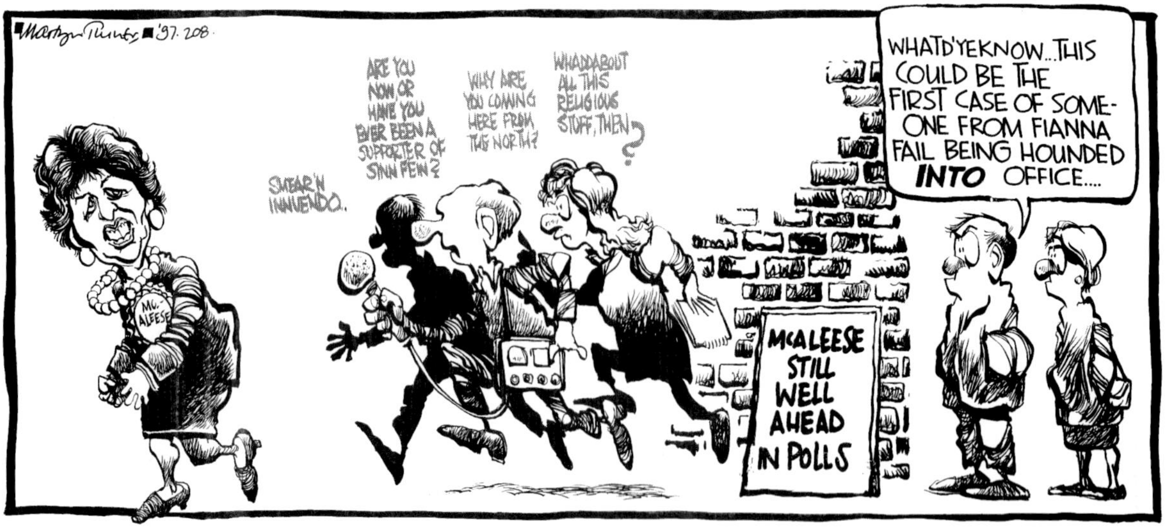

Martyn Turner '97.208
SMEAR 'N INNUENDO.
ARE YOU NOW OR HAVE YOU EVER BEEN A SUPPORTER OF SINN FEIN?
WHY ARE YOU COMING HERE FROM THE NORTH?
WHADDABOUT ALL THIS RELIGIOUS STUFF, THEN?
WHATD'YEKNOW...THIS COULD BE THE FIRST CASE OF SOME-ONE FROM FIANNA FAIL BEING HOUNDED **INTO** OFFICE....
McALEESE STILL WELL AHEAD IN POLLS
MC-ALEESE

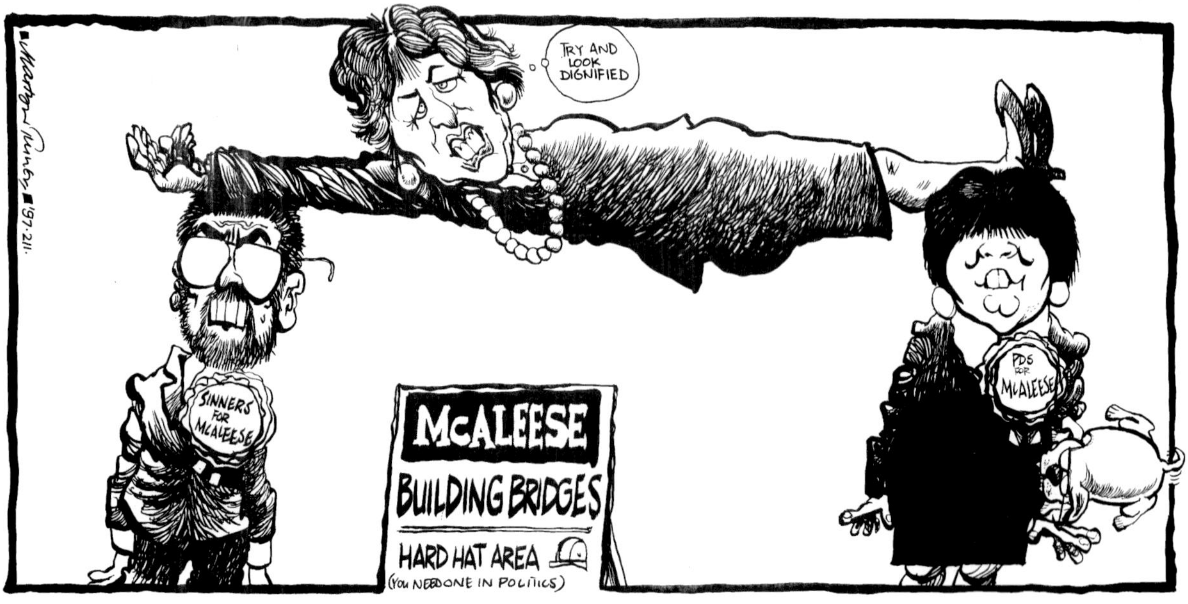

Martyn Turner '97.211.
TRY AND LOOK DIGNIFIED
SINNERS FOR McALEESE
PDS FOR McALEESE
McALEESE
BUILDING BRIDGES
HARD HAT AREA
(YOU NEED ONE IN POLITICS)

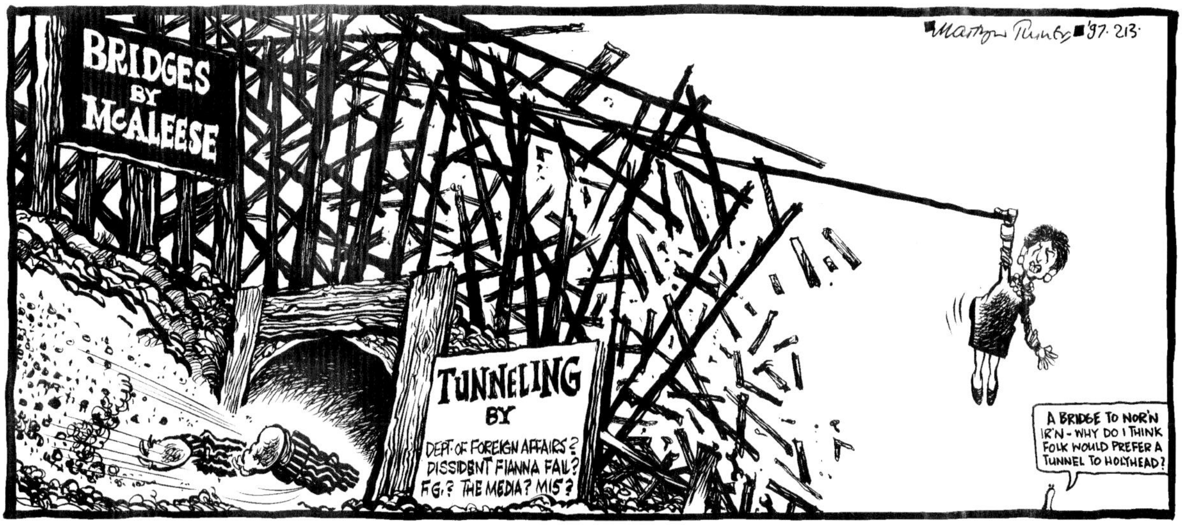
Martyn Turner '97. 213.
BRIDGES BY McALEESE
TUNNELING BY
DEPT. OF FOREIGN AFFAIRS? DISSIDENT FIANNA FAIL? F.G.? THE MEDIA? MI5?
A BRIDGE TO NOR'N IR'N - WHY DO I THINK FOLK WOULD PREFER A TUNNEL TO HOLYHEAD?

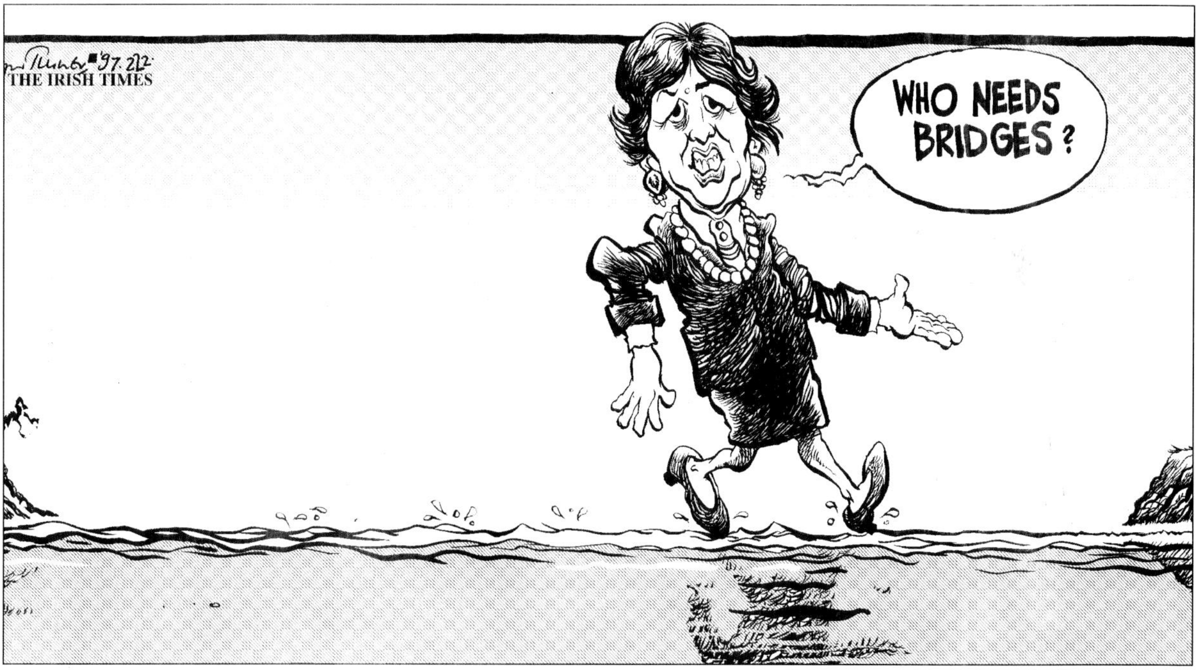
Turner '97. 212.
THE IRISH TIMES
WHO NEEDS BRIDGES?

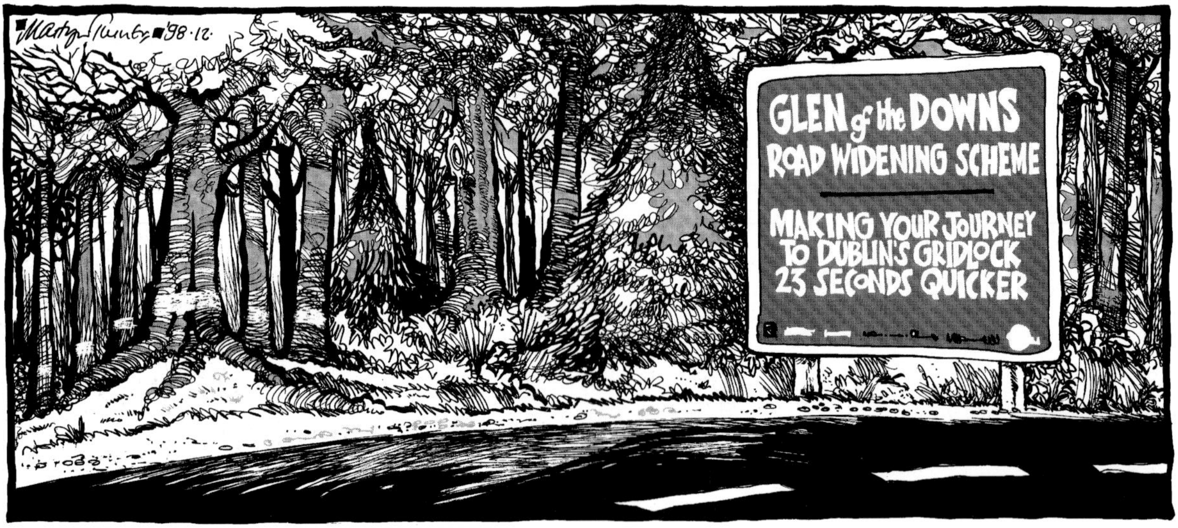
Martyn Turner '98.12.
GLEN of the DOWNS
ROAD WIDENING SCHEME
MAKING YOUR JOURNEY TO DUBLIN'S GRIDLOCK 23 SECONDS QUICKER

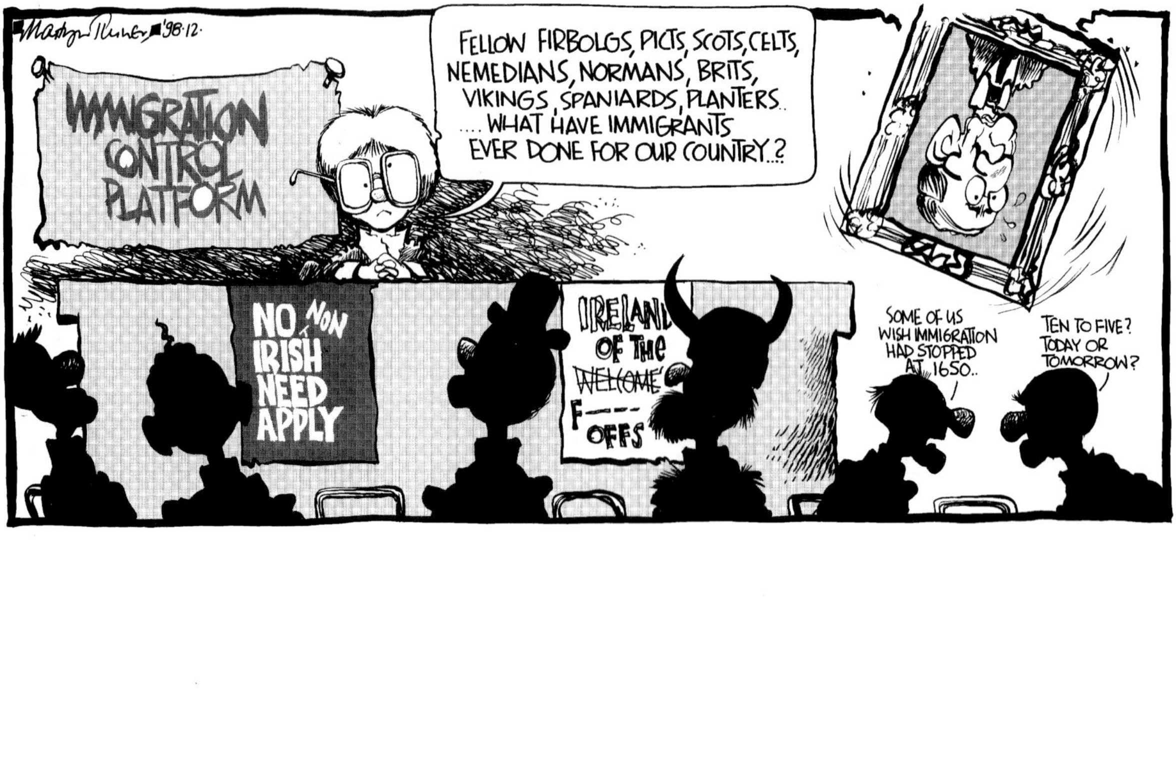
Martyn Turner '98.12.
IMMIGRATION CONTROL PLATFORM
FELLOW FIRBOLGS, PICTS, SCOTS, CELTS, NEMEDIANS, NORMANS, BRITS, VIKINGS, SPANIARDS, PLANTERS.. .... WHAT HAVE IMMIGRANTS EVER DONE FOR OUR COUNTRY..?
NO NON IRISH NEED APPLY
IRELAND OF THE WELCOME F--- OFFS
SOME OF US WISH IMMIGRATION HAD STOPPED AT 1650..
TEN TO FIVE? TODAY OR TOMORROW?

WE ARE GOING TO FIND OUT WHAT HAS BEEN GOING ON IN THIS COUNTRY...
LOOK! THERE IS LIGHT AT THE END OF THE TUNNEL!
TRIBUNALS INTO...
THIS,
THAT,
BUT NOT THE OTHER...
...IT WAS JUST THE GLINT OF GOLD FROM THE LAWYER'S FEES...
Martyn Turner '98.52.

IT'S REALLY GOOD....
...WITH ALL THIS OLD FIANNA FAIL ETHICS STUFF FLYING AROUND....
...FOR YOU TO BE STILL HANGING ON IN WITH US, MARY...
BURKE
POLITICAL OBLIVION
Martyn Turner '98.126.

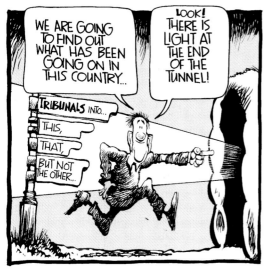

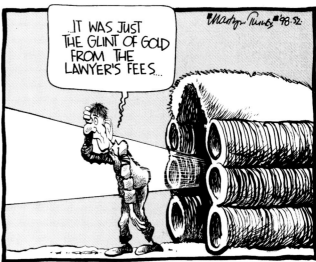

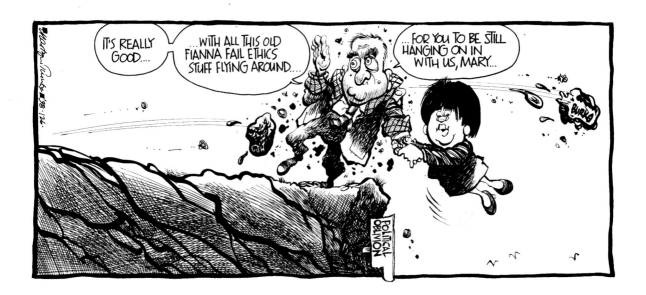

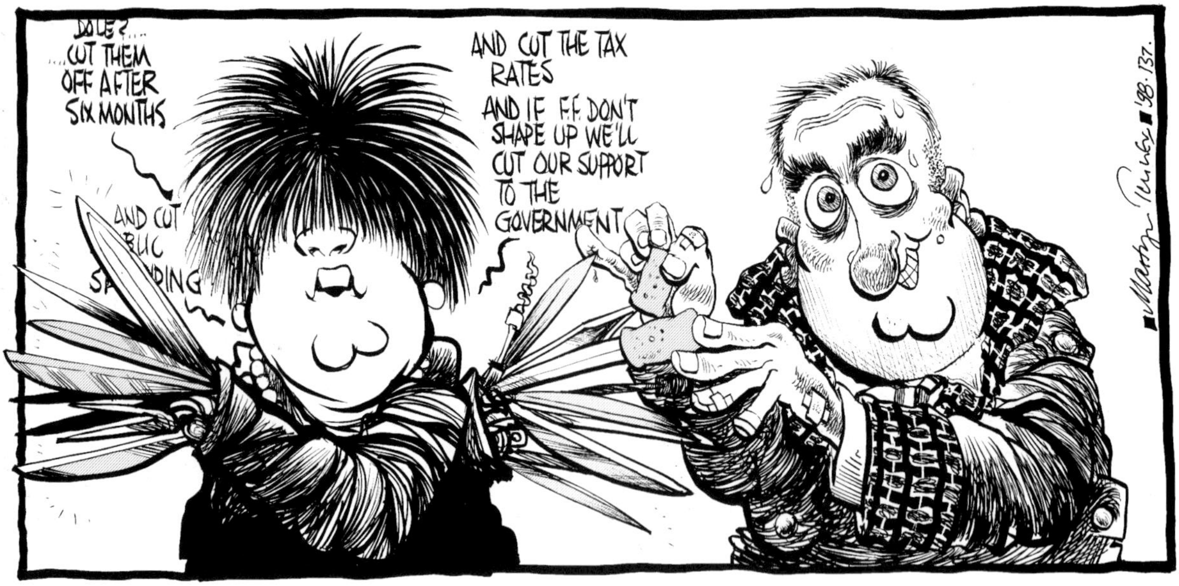
DOLE?... ...CUT THEM OFF AFTER SIX MONTHS
AND CUT
AND CUT THE TAX RATES
AND IF F.F. DON'T SHAPE UP WE'LL CUT OUR SUPPORT TO THE GOVERNMENT
Martyn Turner '98.137.

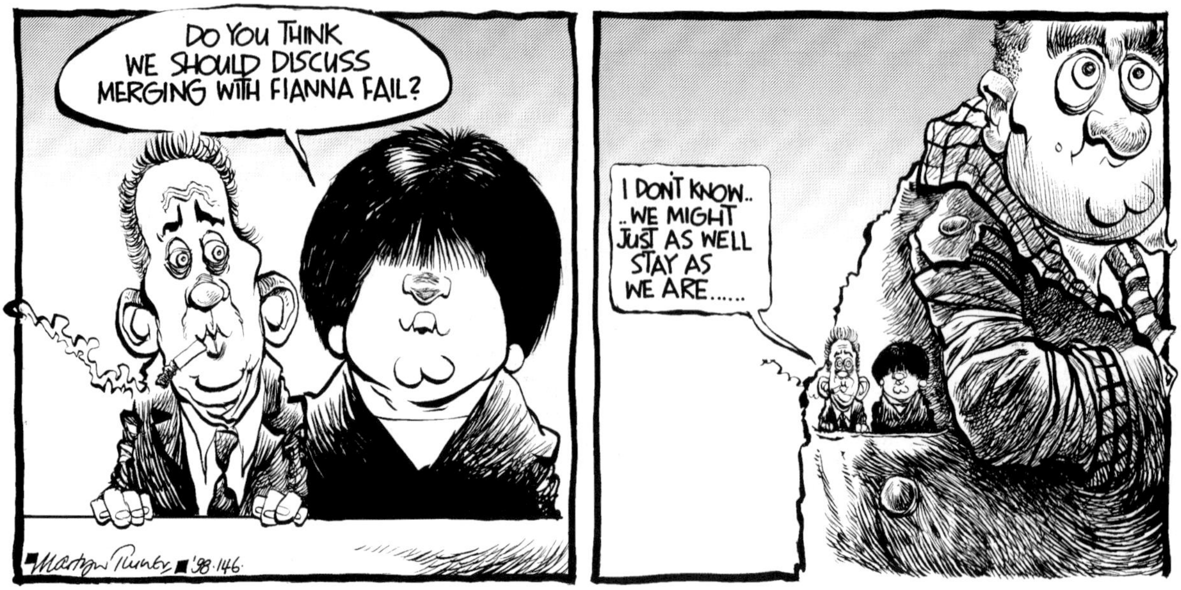
DO YOU THINK WE SHOULD DISCUSS MERGING WITH FIANNA FAIL?
I DON'T KNOW.. ..WE MIGHT JUST AS WELL STAY AS WE ARE......
Martyn Turner '98.146.

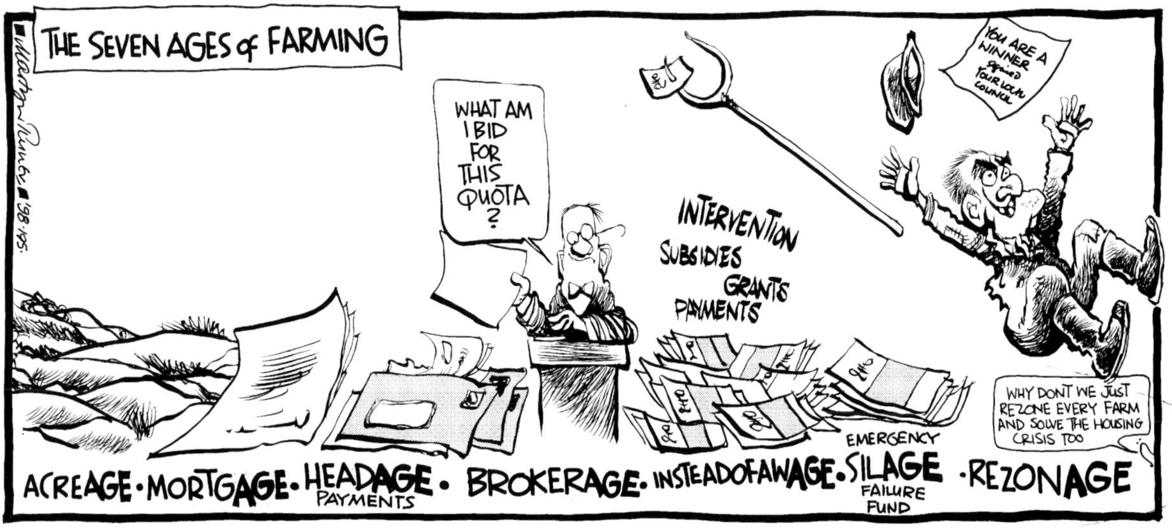
THE SEVEN AGES of FARMING
Martyn Turner '98·195·
WHAT AM I BID FOR THIS QUOTA ?
INTERVENTION
SUBSIDIES
GRANTS
PAYMENTS
YOU ARE A WINNER signed YOUR LOCAL COUNCIL
WHY DONT WE JUST REZONE EVERY FARM AND SOLVE THE HOUSING CRISIS TOO
EMERGENCY
ACREAGE · MORTGAGE · HEADAGE PAYMENTS · BROKERAGE · INSTEADOFAWAGE · SILAGE FAILURE FUND · REZONAGE

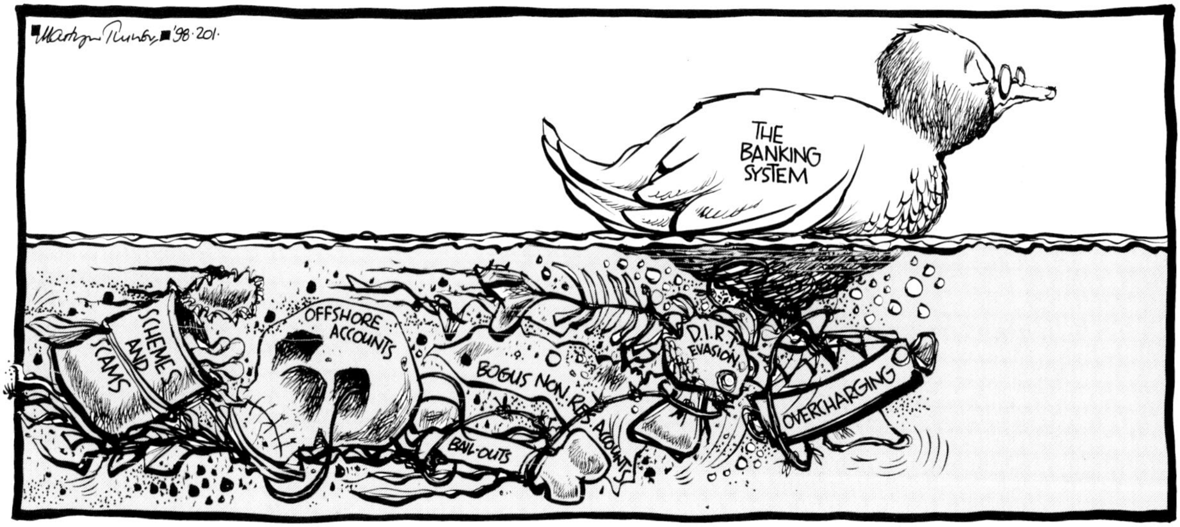
Martyn Turner '98·201·
THE BANKING SYSTEM
SCHEMES AND SCAMS
OFFSHORE ACCOUNTS
BOGUS NON-RES ACCOUNTS
D.I.R.T. EVASION
OVERCHARGING
BAIL-OUTS

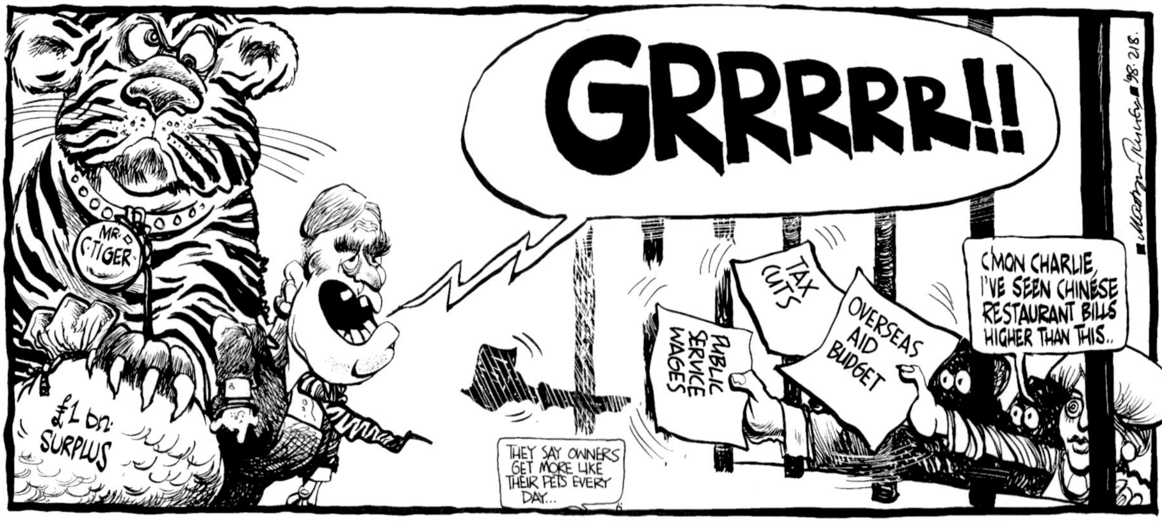
GRRRRR!!
MR. C. TIGER
£1 bn. SURPLUS
PUBLIC SERVICE WAGES
TAX CUTS
OVERSEAS AID BUDGET
C'MON CHARLIE, I'VE SEEN CHINESE RESTAURANT BILLS HIGHER THAN THIS..
THEY SAY OWNERS GET MORE LIKE THEIR PETS EVERY DAY...
Martyn Turner '98 · 218.

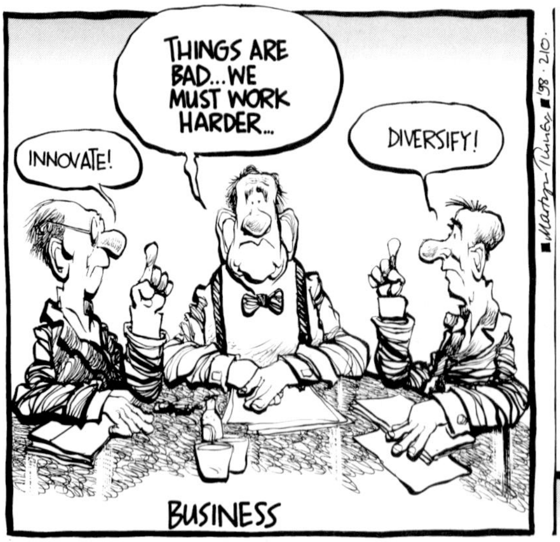
THINGS ARE BAD...WE MUST WORK HARDER...
INNOVATE!
DIVERSIFY!
BUSINESS
Martyn Turner '98 · 210.

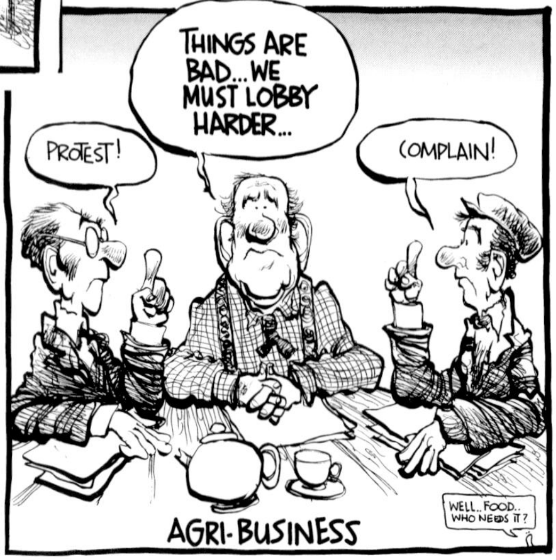
THINGS ARE BAD...WE MUST LOBBY HARDER...
PROTEST!
COMPLAIN!
AGRI-BUSINESS
WELL.. FOOD.. WHO NEEDS IT?

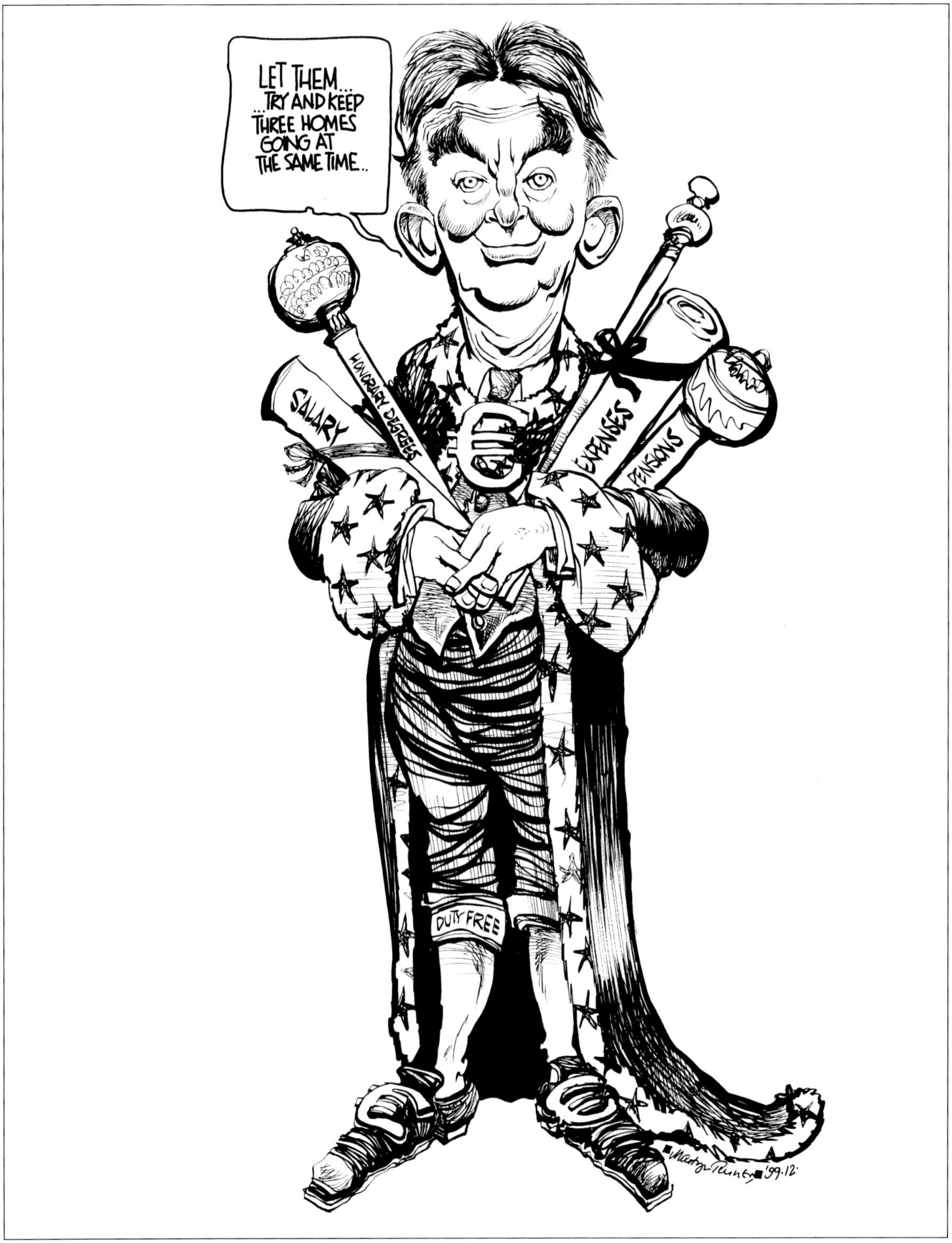
LET THEM...
...TRY AND KEEP
THREE HOMES
GOING AT
THE SAME TIME..
HONORARY DEGREES
SALARY
EXPENSES
PENSIONS
DUTY FREE
Martyn Turner '99.12.

Padraig Flynn

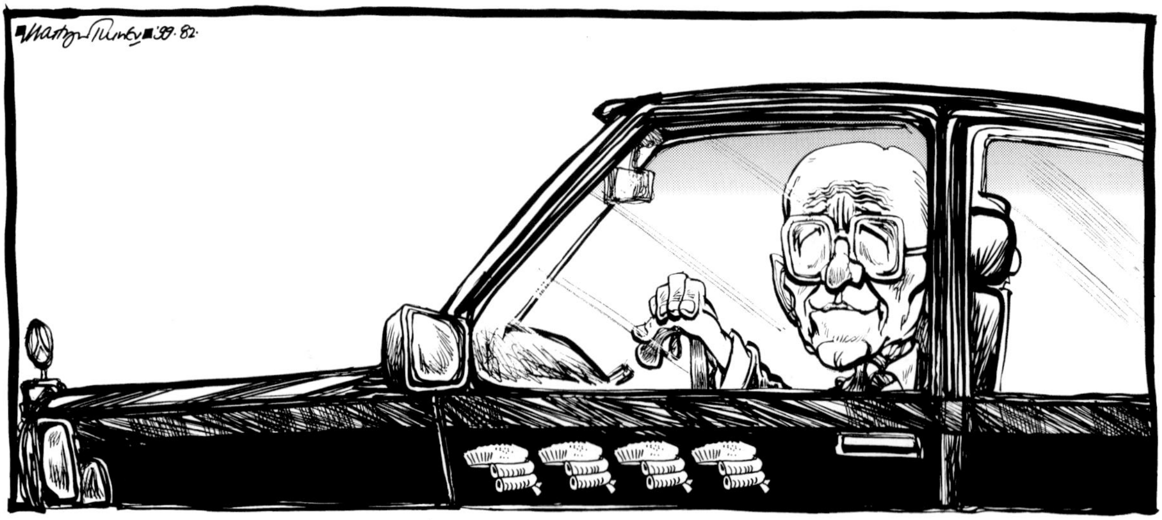

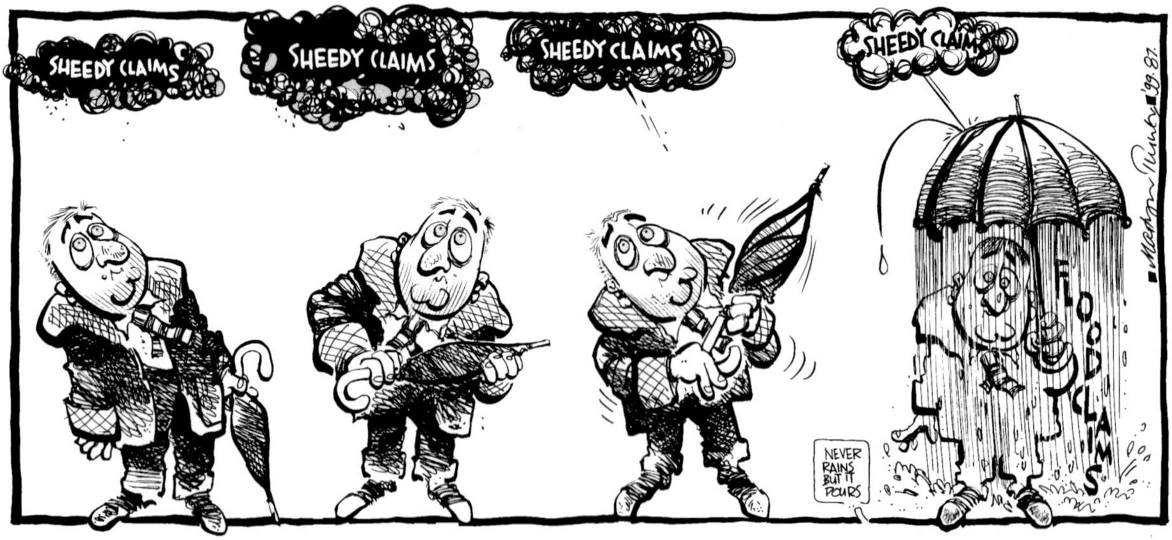
SHEEDY CLAIMS
SHEEDY CLAIMS
SHEEDY CLAIMS
SHEEDY CLAIMS
FLOOD CLAIMS
NEVER RAINS BUT IT POURS

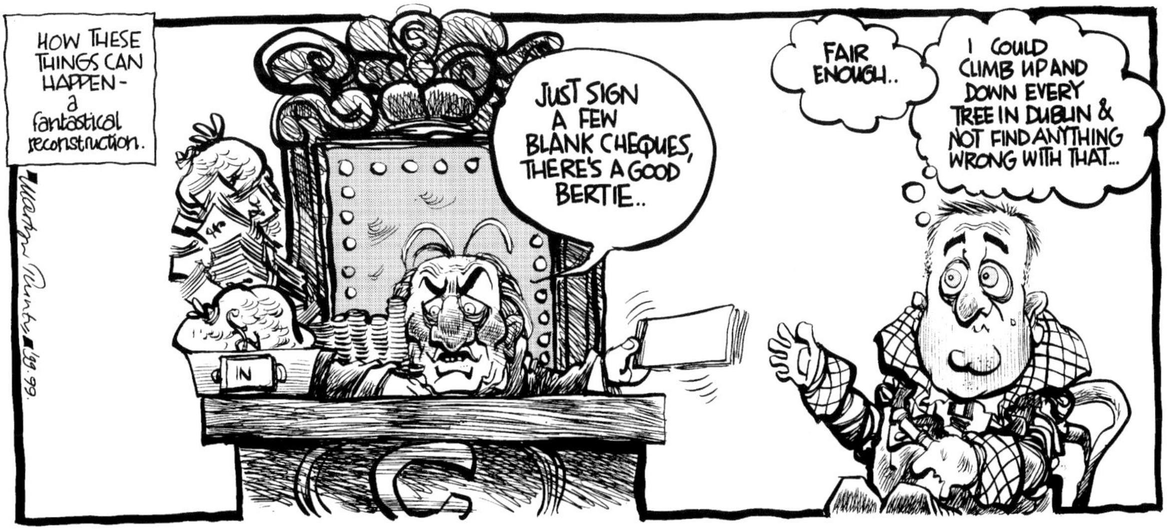
HOW THESE THINGS CAN HAPPEN - a fantastical reconstruction.
JUST SIGN A FEW BLANK CHEQUES, THERE'S A GOOD BERTIE..
FAIR ENOUGH..
I COULD CLIMB UP AND DOWN EVERY TREE IN DUBLIN & NOT FIND ANYTHING WRONG WITH THAT...
IN

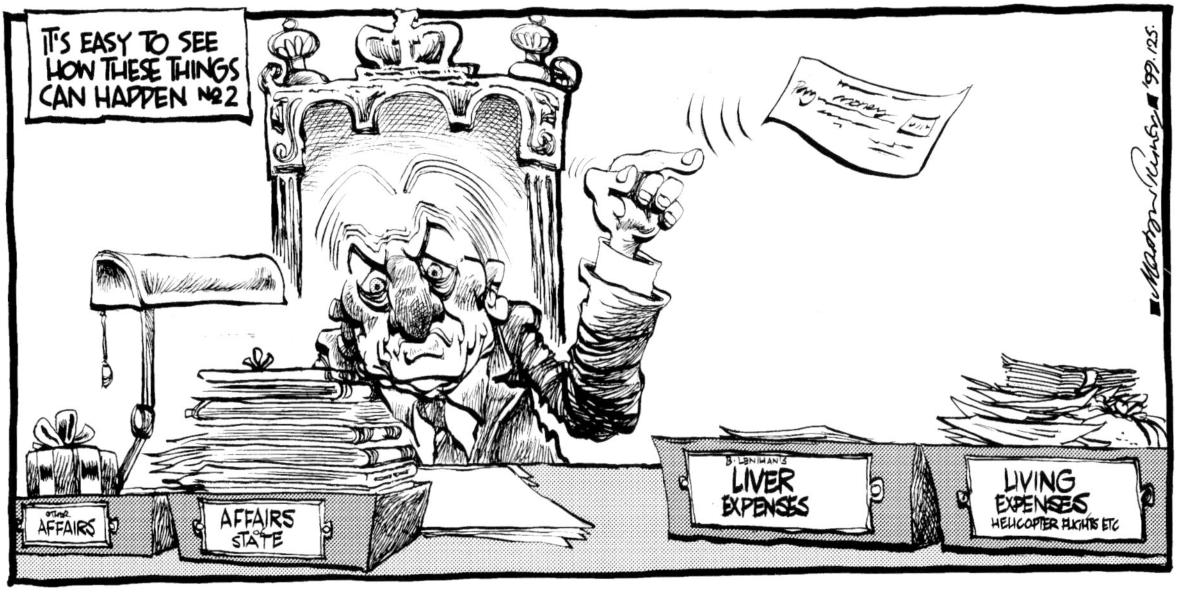
IT'S EASY TO SEE HOW THESE THINGS CAN HAPPEN №2
OTHER AFFAIRS
AFFAIRS OF STATE
B. LENIHAN'S LIVER EXPENSES
LIVING EXPENSES HELICOPTER FLIGHTS ETC

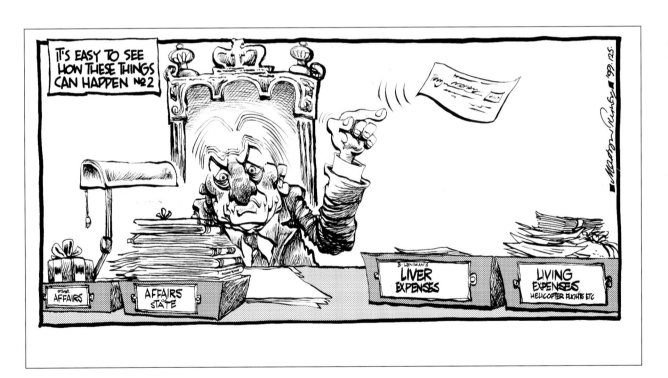

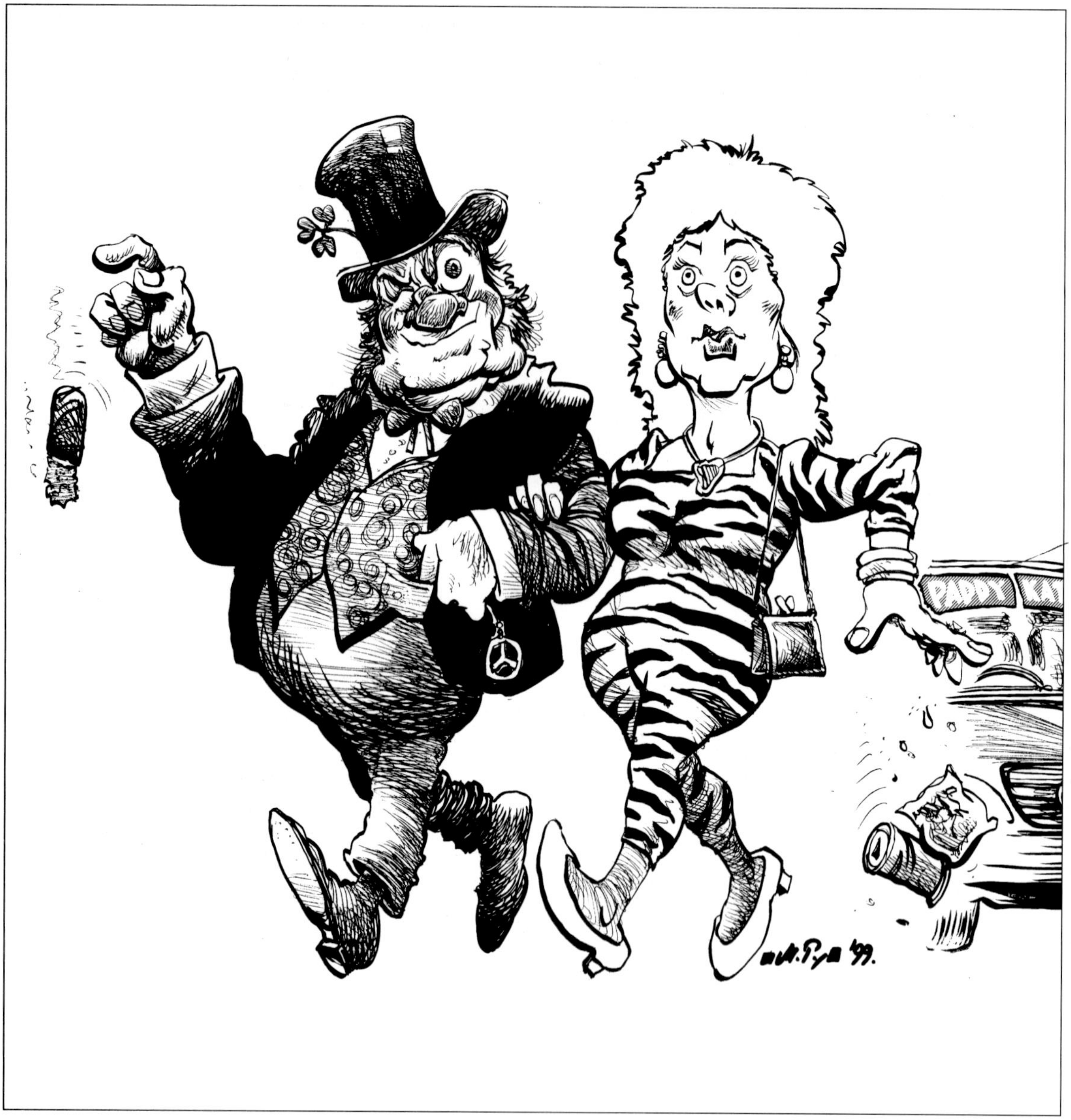
PADDY

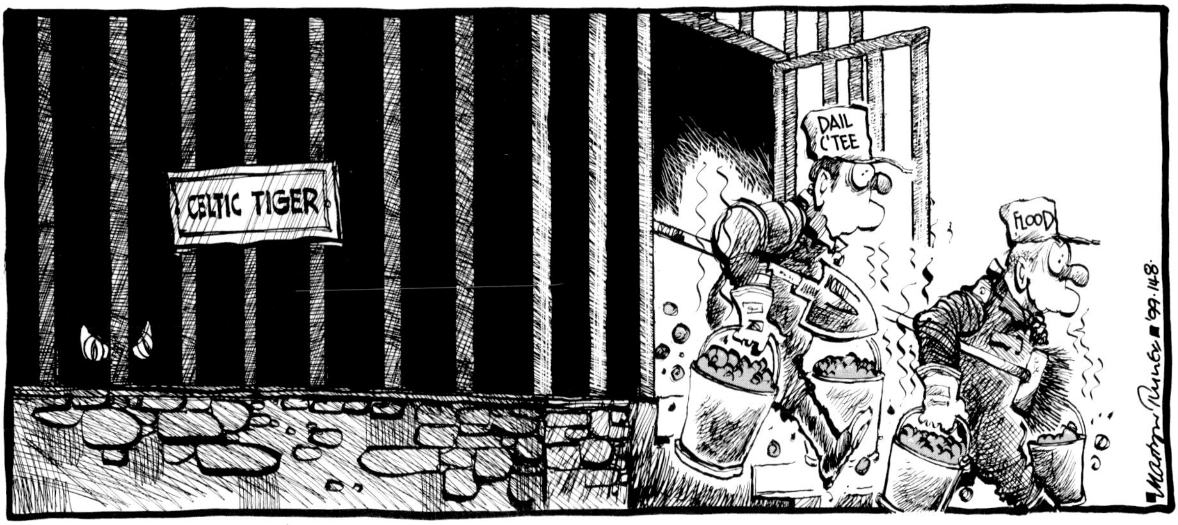

CELTIC TIGER
DAIL C'TEE
FLOOD
Martyn Turner '99.148.

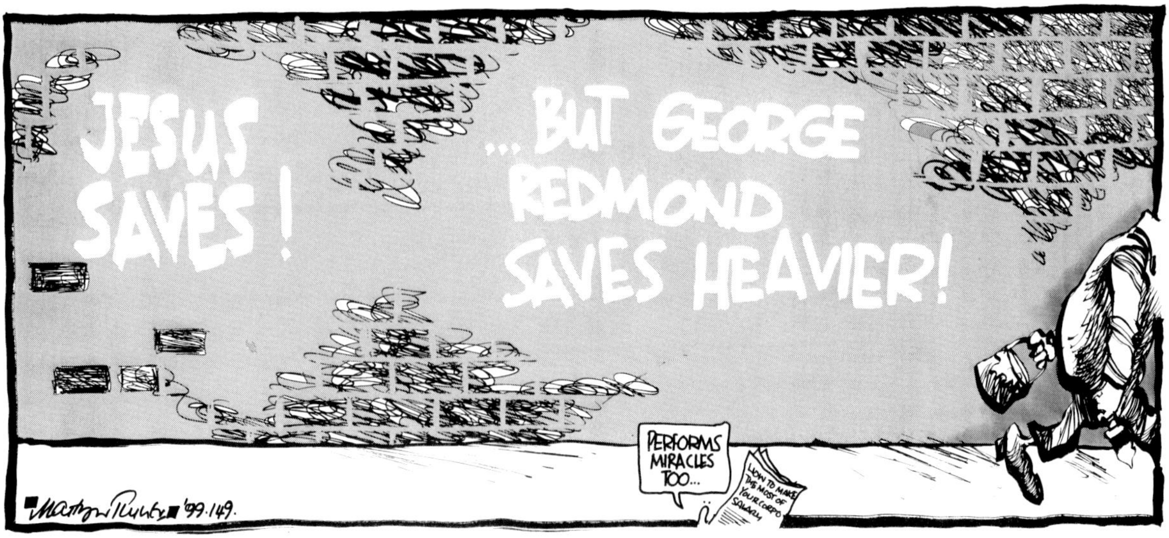

JESUS SAVES!
...BUT GEORGE REDMOND SAVES HEAVIER!
PERFORMS MIRACLES TOO...
HOW TO MAKE THE MOST OF YOUR CORPO SALARY
Martyn Turner '99.149.

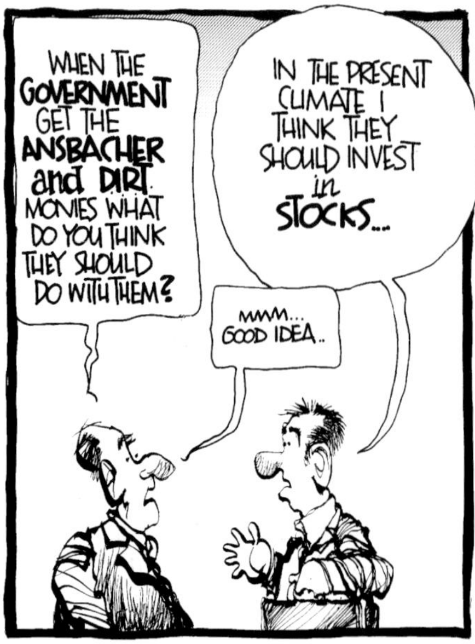
WHEN THE GOVERNMENT GET THE ANSBACHER and DIRT MONIES WHAT DO YOU THINK THEY SHOULD DO WITH THEM?
IN THE PRESENT CLIMATE I THINK THEY SHOULD INVEST in STOCKS...
MMM... GOOD IDEA..

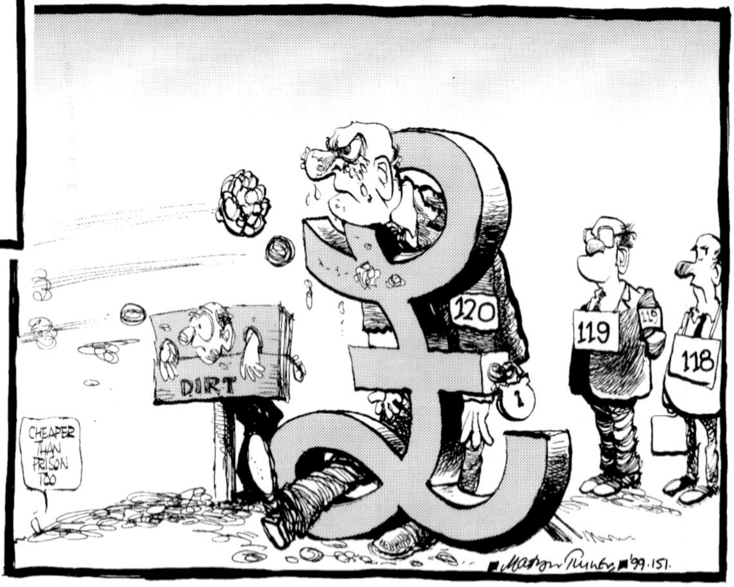
DIRT
120
119
118
CHEAPER THAN PRISON TOO

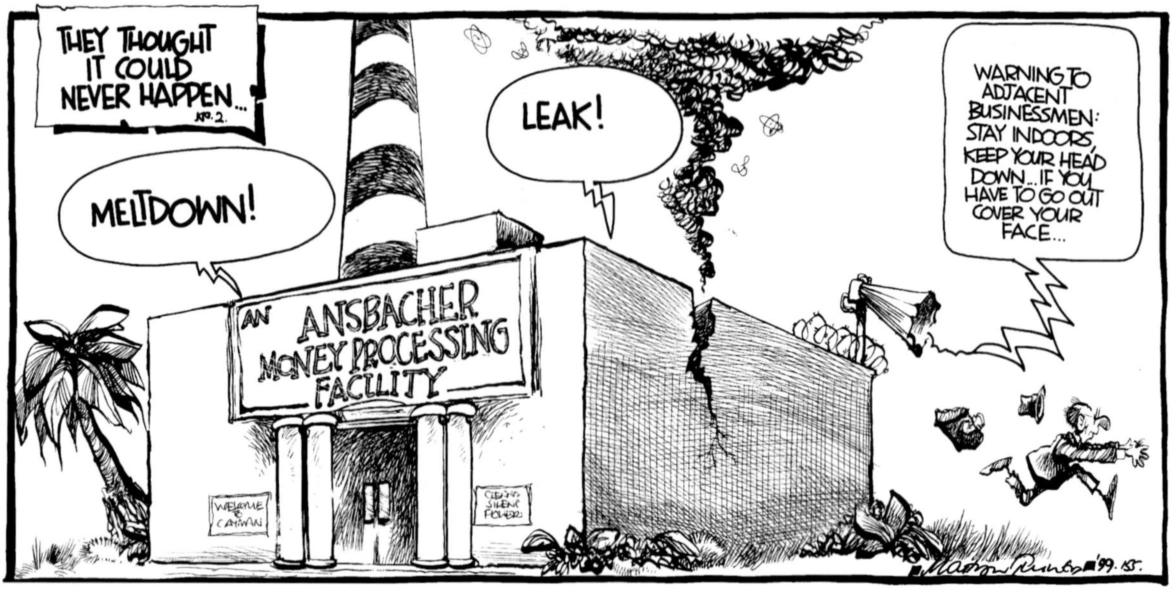
THEY THOUGHT IT COULD NEVER HAPPEN...
MELTDOWN!
LEAK!
WARNING TO ADJACENT BUSINESSMEN: STAY INDOORS, KEEP YOUR HEAD DOWN... IF YOU HAVE TO GO OUT COVER YOUR FACE...
AN ANSBACHER MONEY PROCESSING FACILITY

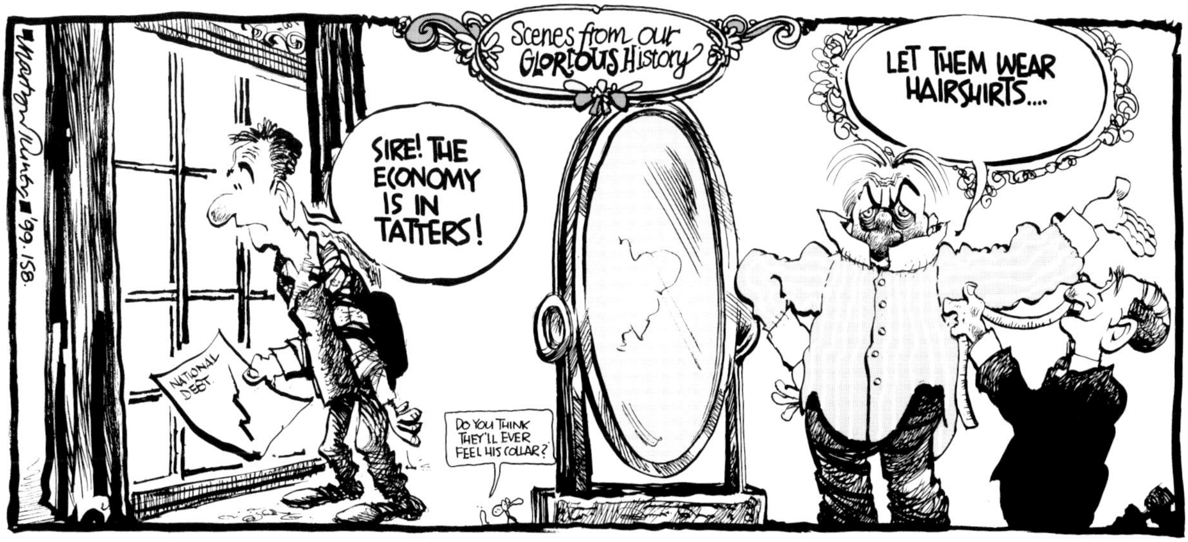
Scenes from our GLORIOUS History
SIRE! THE ECONOMY IS IN TATTERS!
NATIONAL DEBT
LET THEM WEAR HAIRSHIRTS....
DO YOU THINK THEY'LL EVER FEEL HIS COLLAR?

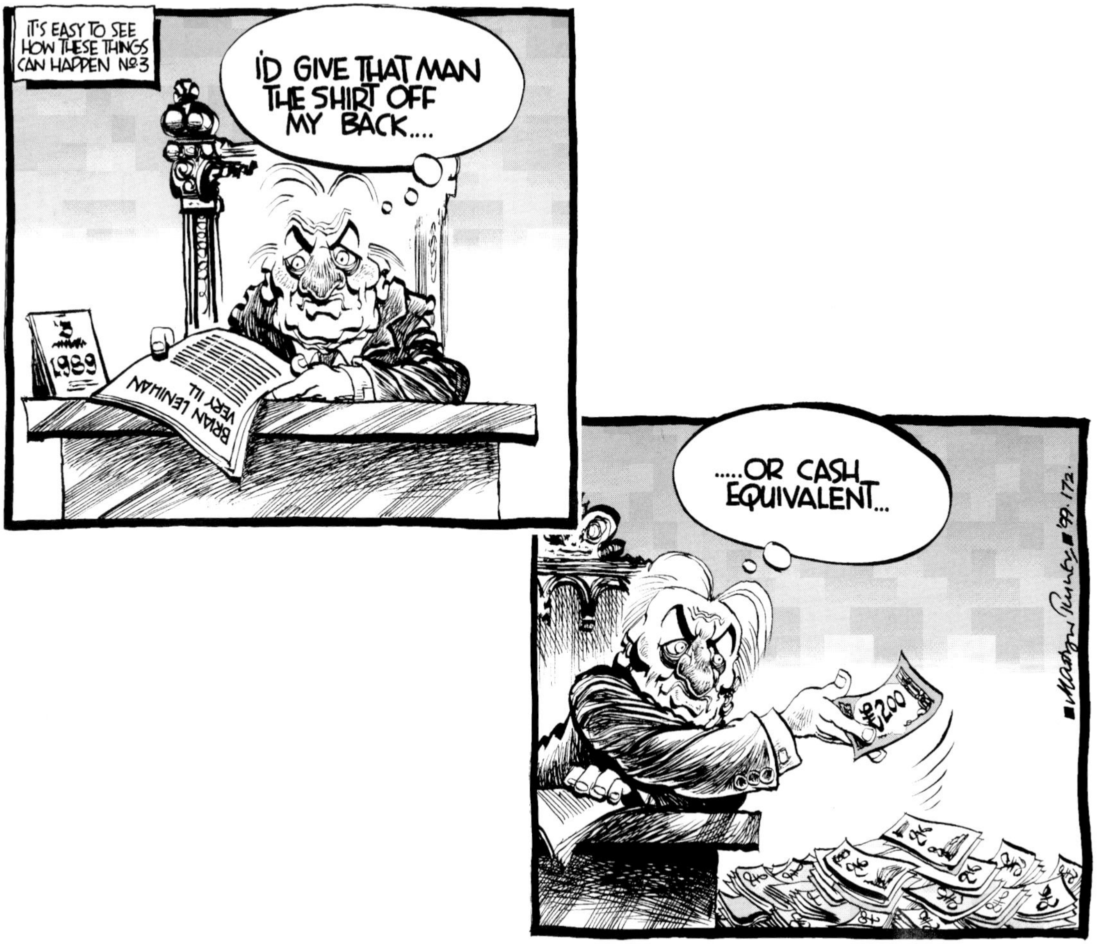
IT'S EASY TO SEE HOW THESE THINGS CAN HAPPEN No. 3
I'D GIVE THAT MAN THE SHIRT OFF MY BACK....
1989
BRIAN LENIHAN VERY ILL
.....OR CASH EQUIVALENT...
£200

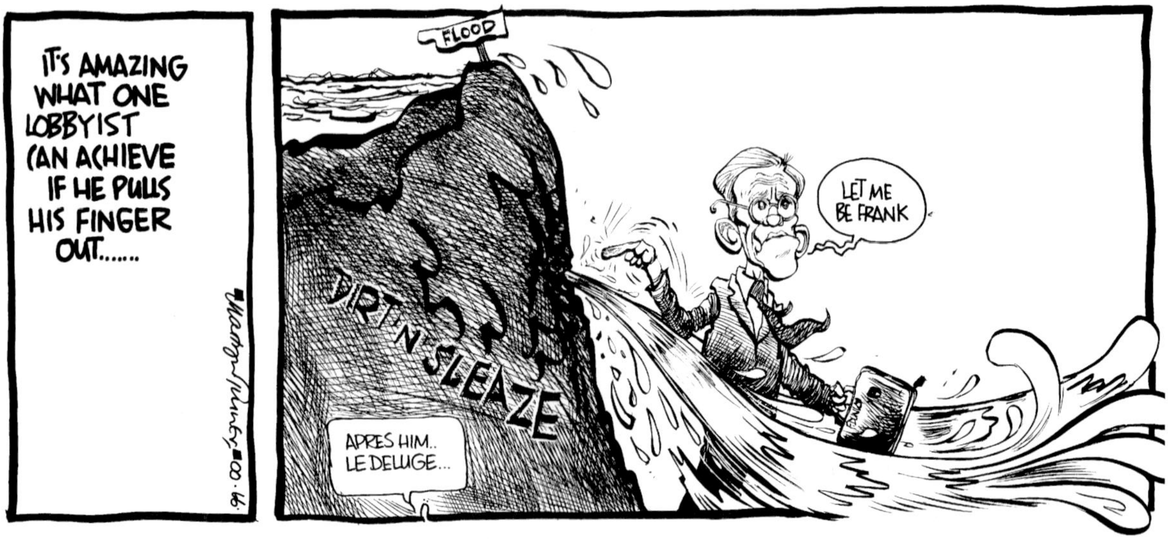
IT'S AMAZING WHAT ONE LOBBYIST CAN ACHIEVE IF HE PULLS HIS FINGER OUT......
FLOOD
DIRT 'N' SLEAZE
APRES HIM.. LE DELUGE...
LET ME BE FRANK
Martyn Turner '00 '86

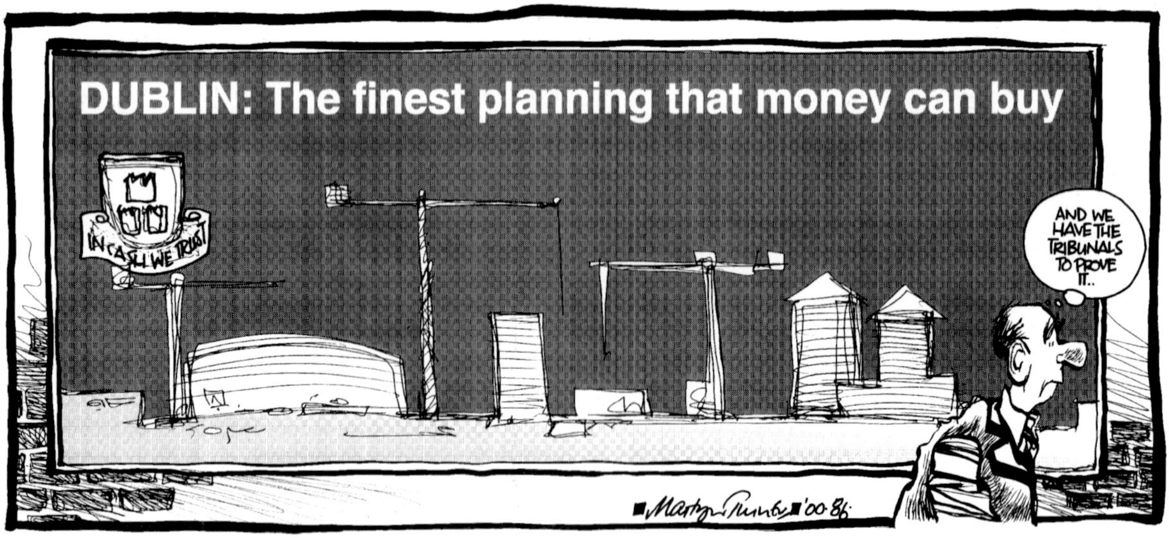
DUBLIN: The finest planning that money can buy
IN CASH WE TRUST
AND WE HAVE THE TRIBUNALS TO PROVE IT..
Martyn Turner '00 '86

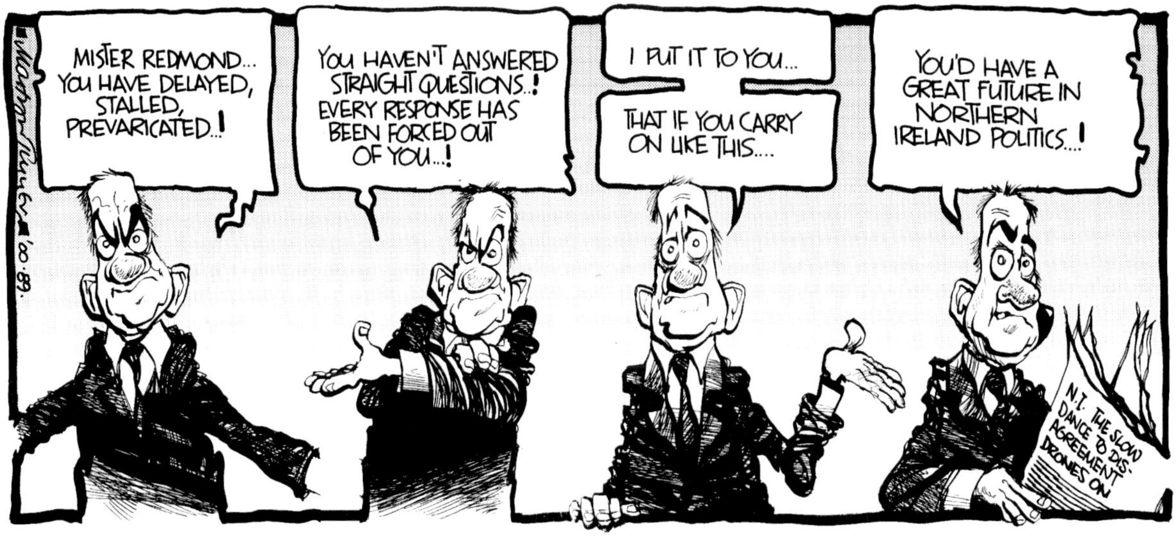
MISTER REDMOND... YOU HAVE DELAYED, STALLED, PREVARICATED..!
YOU HAVEN'T ANSWERED STRAIGHT QUESTIONS..! EVERY RESPONSE HAS BEEN FORCED OUT OF YOU...!
I PUT IT TO YOU...
THAT IF YOU CARRY ON LIKE THIS....
YOU'D HAVE A GREAT FUTURE IN NORTHERN IRELAND POLITICS...!
N.I. THE SLOW DANCE TO DIS-AGREEMENT DRONES ON

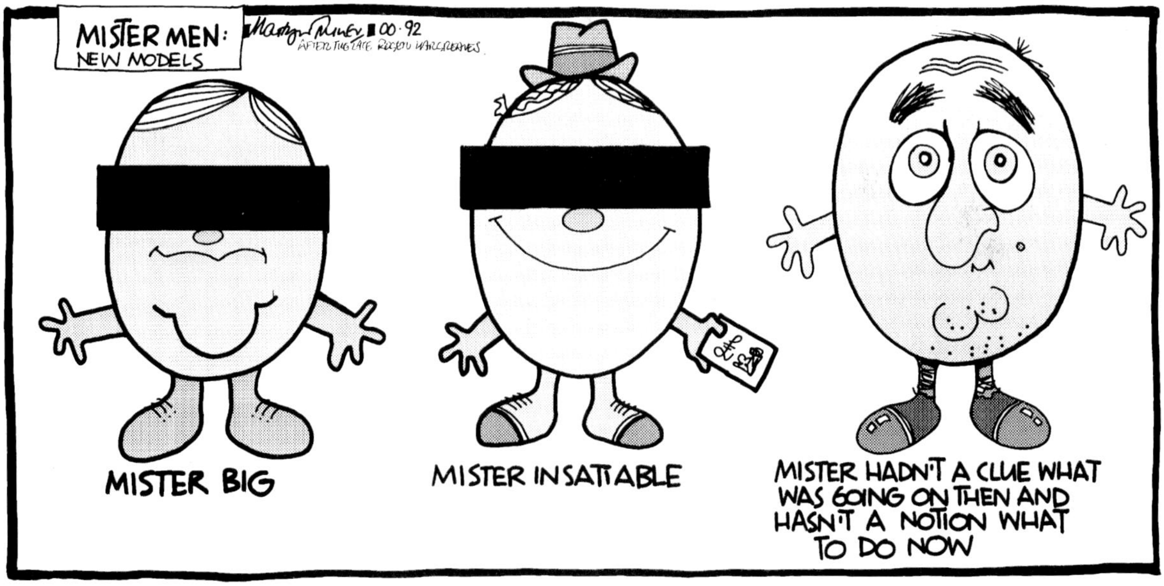
MISTER MEN: NEW MODELS
MISTER BIG
MISTER INSATIABLE
MISTER HADN'T A CLUE WHAT WAS GOING ON THEN AND HASN'T A NOTION WHAT TO DO NOW

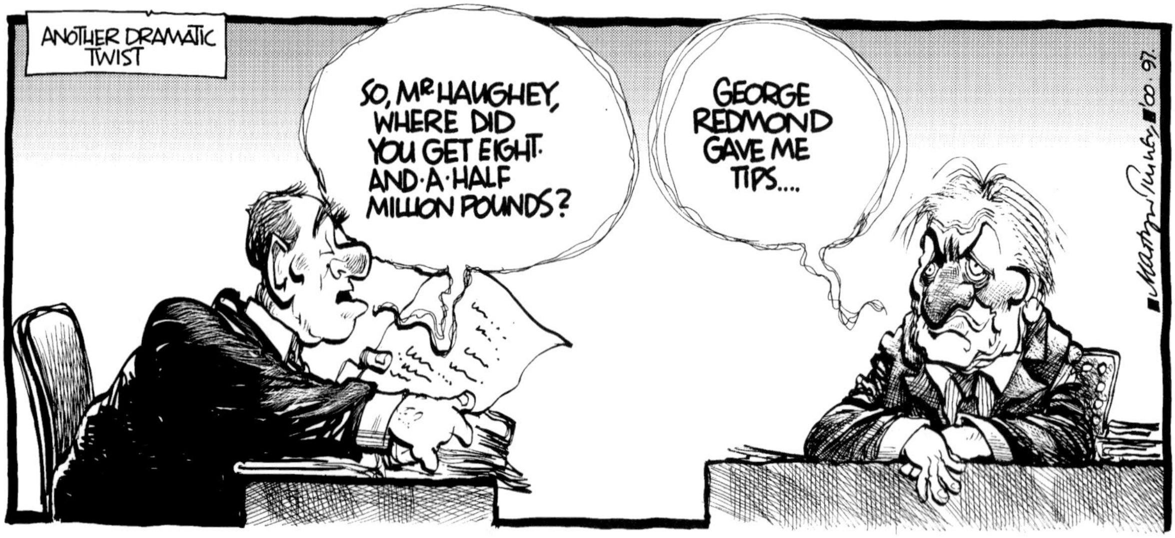
ANOTHER DRAMATIC TWIST
SO, MR HAUGHEY, WHERE DID YOU GET EIGHT-AND-A-HALF MILLION POUNDS?
GEORGE REDMOND GAVE ME TIPS....

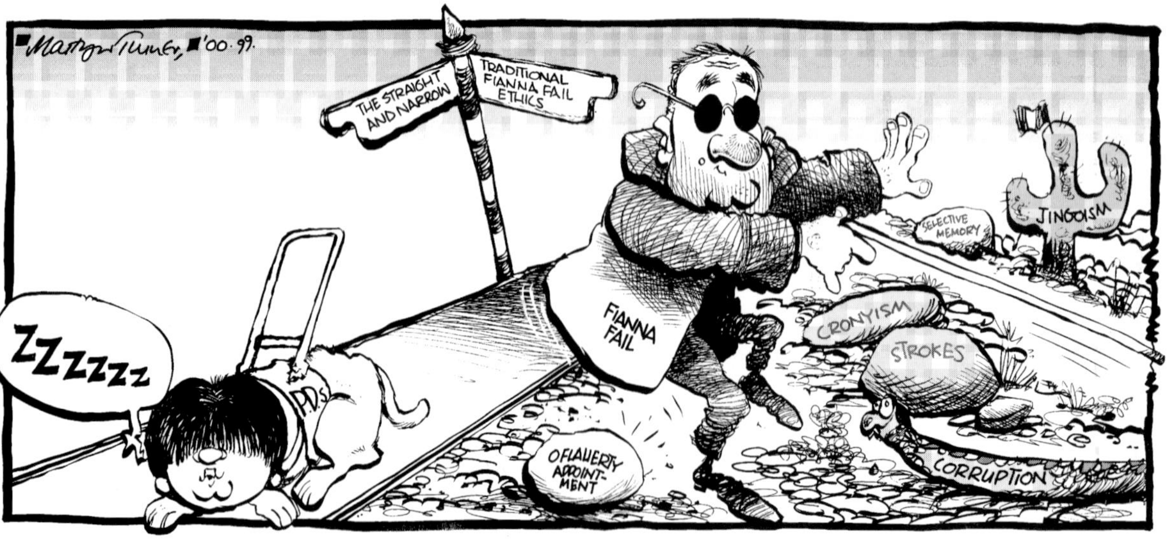
THE STRAIGHT AND NARROW
TRADITIONAL FIANNA FAIL ETHICS
ZZZZZZ
P.D.S
FIANNA FAIL
SELECTIVE MEMORY
JINGOISM
CRONYISM
STROKES
O'FLAHERTY APPOINT-MENT
CORRUPTION

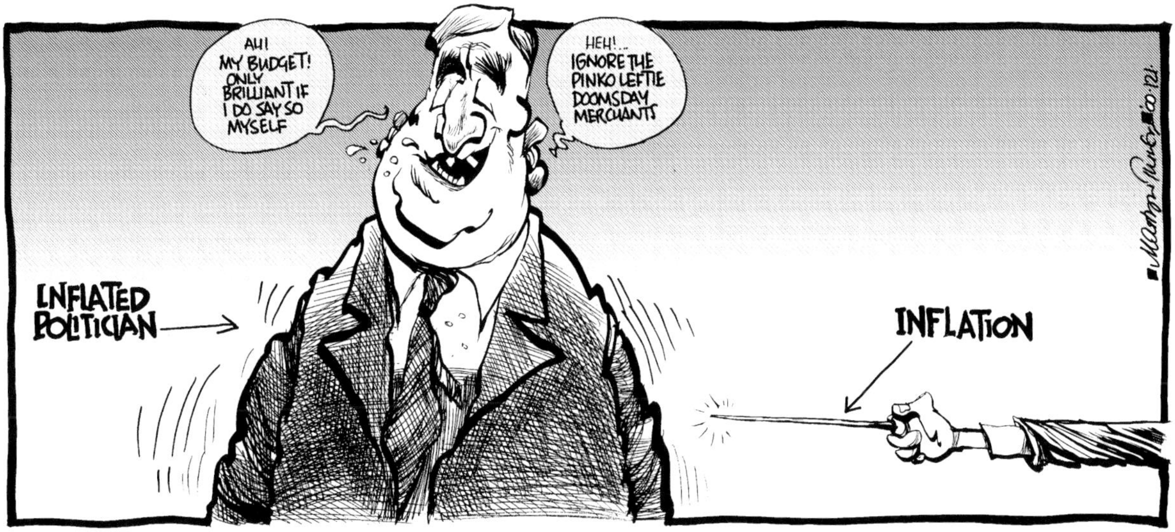
AH! MY BUDGET! ONLY BRILLIANT IF I DO SAY SO MYSELF
HEH!... IGNORE THE PINKO LEFTIE DOOMSDAY MERCHANTS
INFLATED POLITICIAN
INFLATION
Martyn Turner '00.121

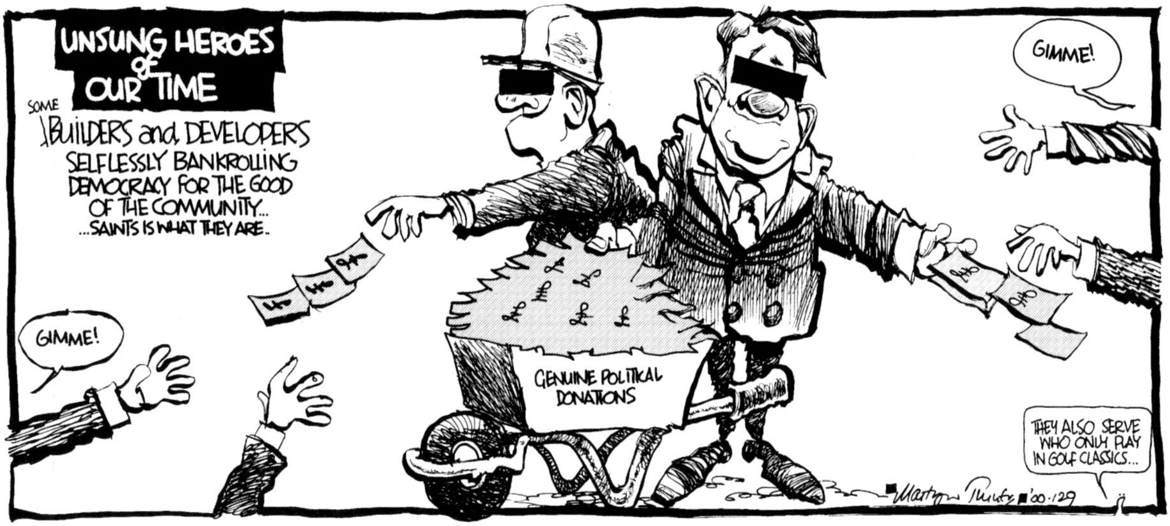
UNSUNG HEROES OF OUR TIME
SOME BUILDERS and DEVELOPERS SELFLESSLY BANKROLLING DEMOCRACY FOR THE GOOD OF THE COMMUNITY...
...SAINTS IS WHAT THEY ARE..
GIMME!
GIMME!
GENUINE POLITICAL DONATIONS
THEY ALSO SERVE WHO ONLY PLAY IN GOLF CLASSICS...
Martyn Turner '00.129

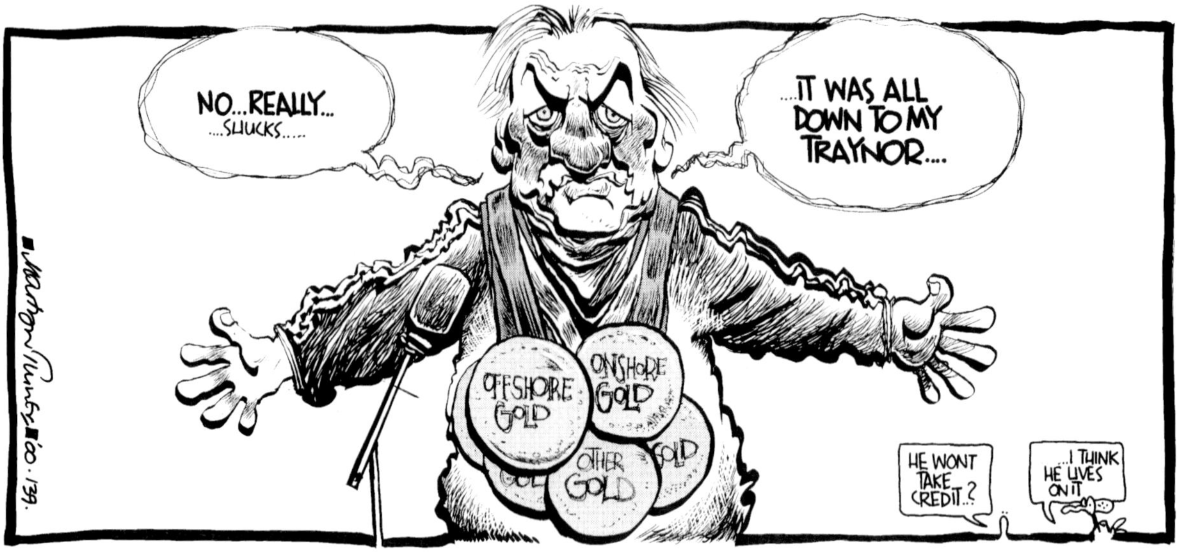
NO...REALLY...
....SHUCKS.....
....IT WAS ALL DOWN TO MY TRAYNOR....
OFFSHORE GOLD
ONSHORE GOLD
OTHER GOLD
GOLD
HE WONT TAKE CREDIT..?
...I THINK HE LIVES ON IT

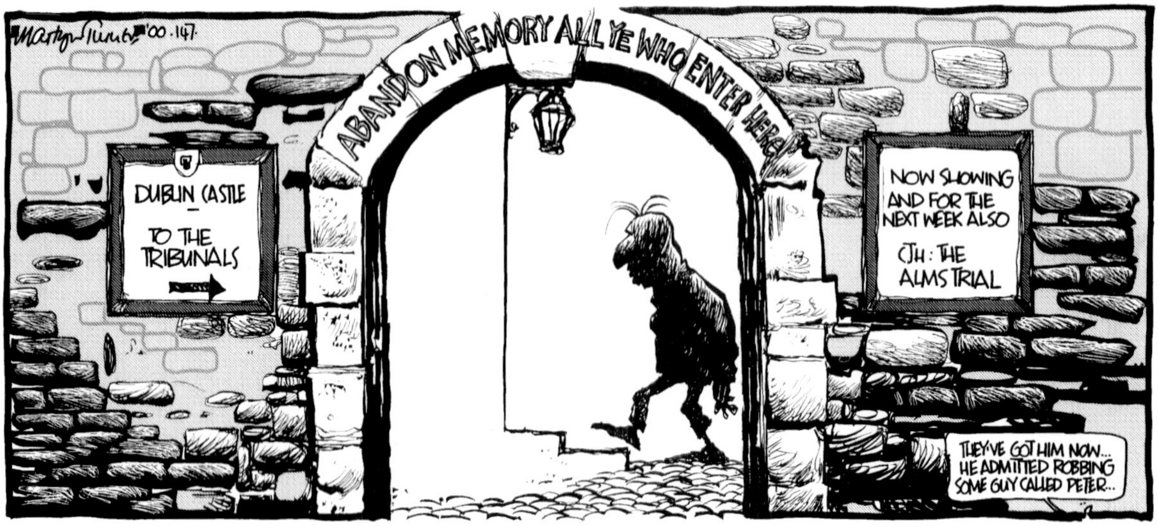
ABANDON MEMORY ALL YE WHO ENTER HERE
DUBLIN CASTLE
TO THE TRIBUNALS
NOW SHOWING AND FOR THE NEXT WEEK ALSO
CJH: THE ALMS TRIAL
THEY'VE GOT HIM NOW... HE ADMITTED ROBBING SOME GUY CALLED PETER...

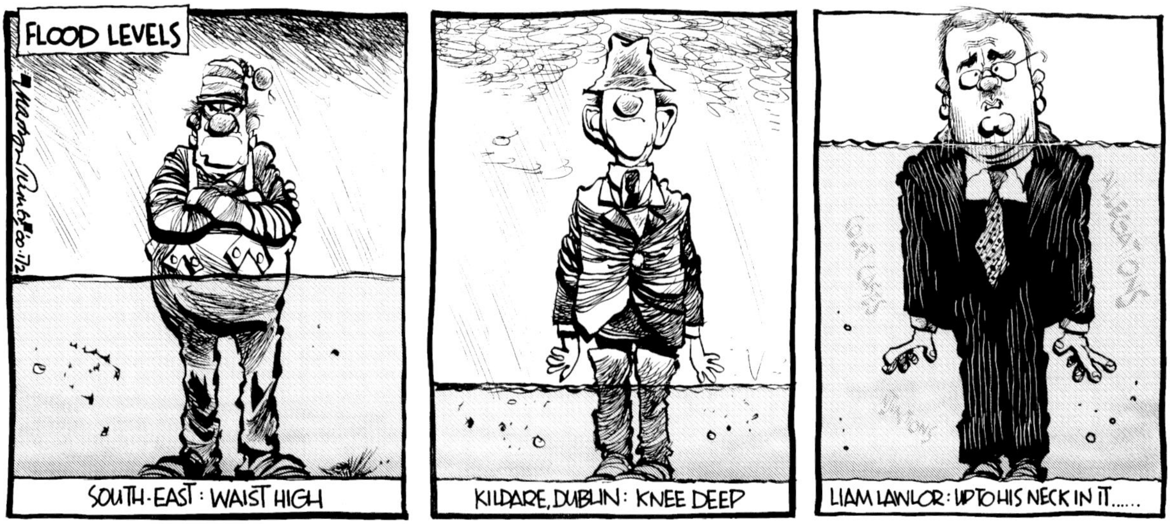
FLOOD LEVELS
SOUTH-EAST: WAIST HIGH
KILDARE, DUBLIN: KNEE DEEP
LIAM LAWLOR: UP TO HIS NECK IN IT......

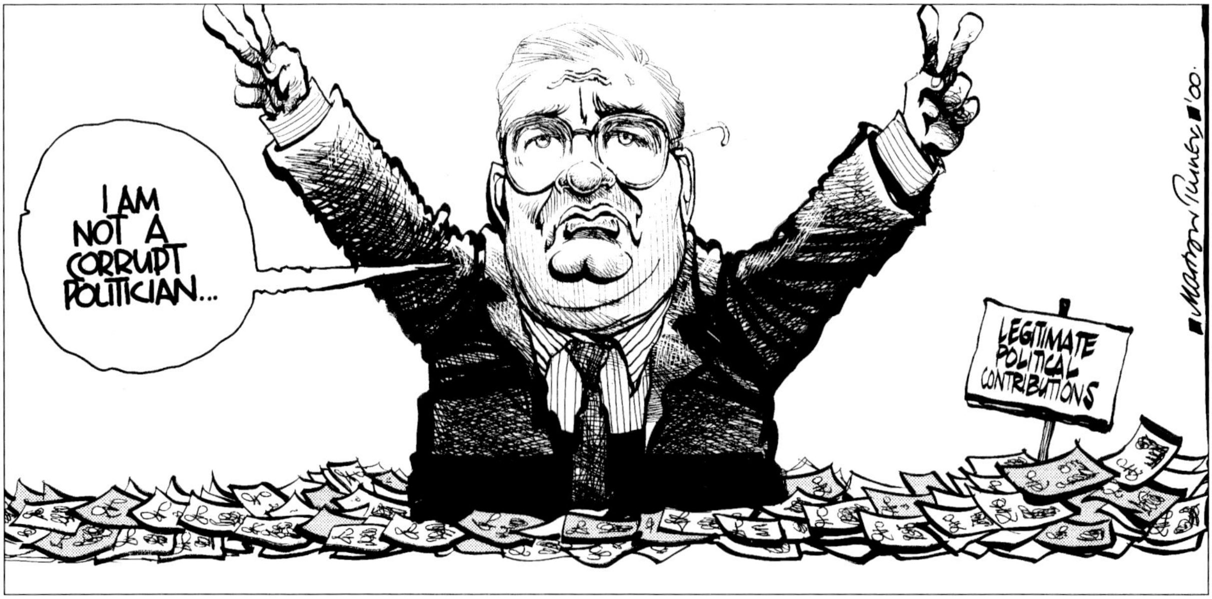
I AM NOT A CORRUPT POLITICIAN...
LEGITIMATE POLITICAL CONTRIBUTIONS

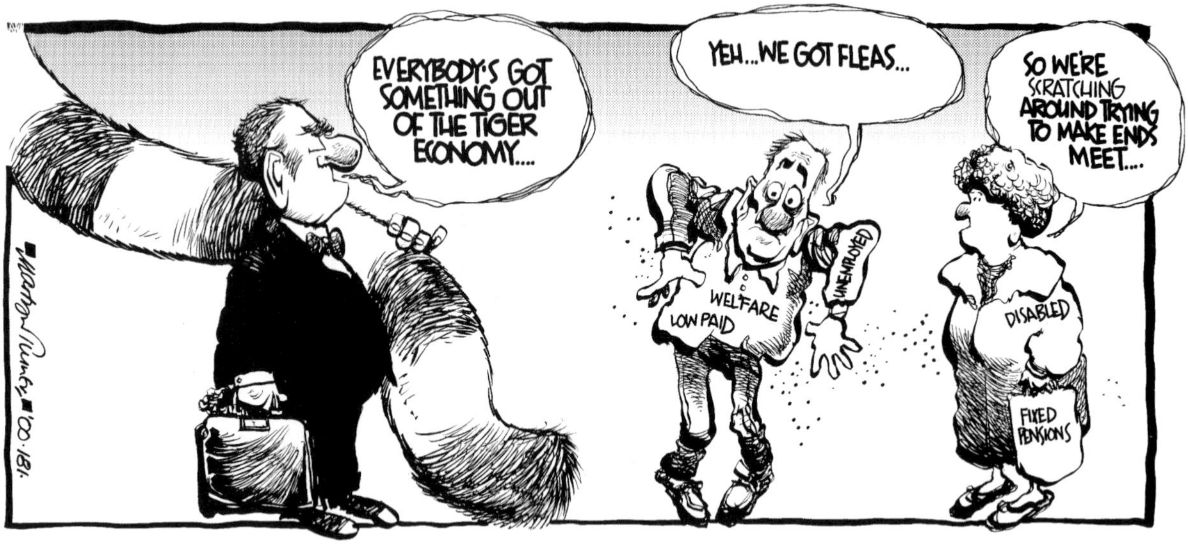
EVERYBODY'S GOT SOMETHING OUT OF THE TIGER ECONOMY....
YEH...WE GOT FLEAS...
SO WE'RE SCRATCHING AROUND TRYING TO MAKE ENDS MEET....
WELFARE
LOW PAID
UNEMPLOYED
DISABLED
FIXED PENSIONS

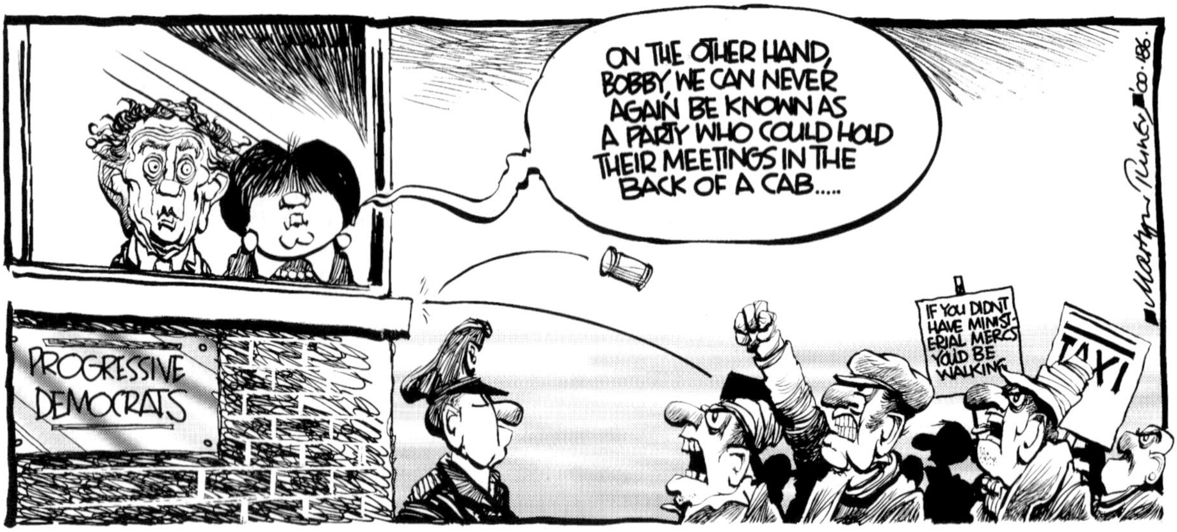
ON THE OTHER HAND, BOBBY, WE CAN NEVER AGAIN BE KNOWN AS A PARTY WHO COULD HOLD THEIR MEETINGS IN THE BACK OF A CAB.....
PROGRESSIVE DEMOCRATS
IF YOU DIDN'T HAVE MINISTERIAL MERCS YOU'D BE WALKING
TAXI

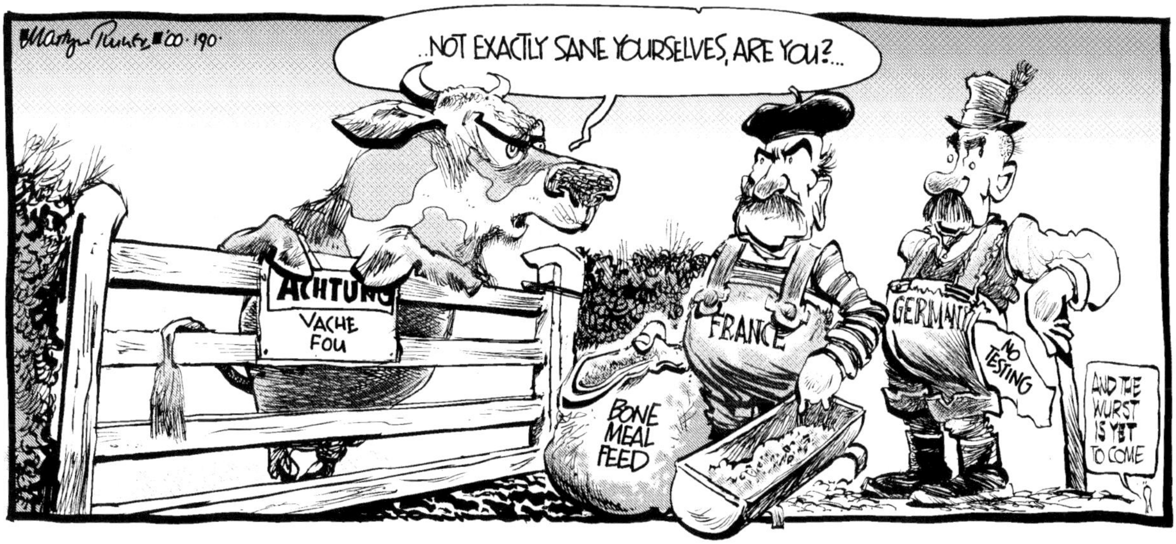
Martyn Turner '00.190.
...NOT EXACTLY SANE YOURSELVES, ARE YOU?...
ACHTUNG
VACHE FOU
BONE MEAL FEED
FRANCE
GERMANY
NO TESTING
AND THE WURST IS YET TO COME

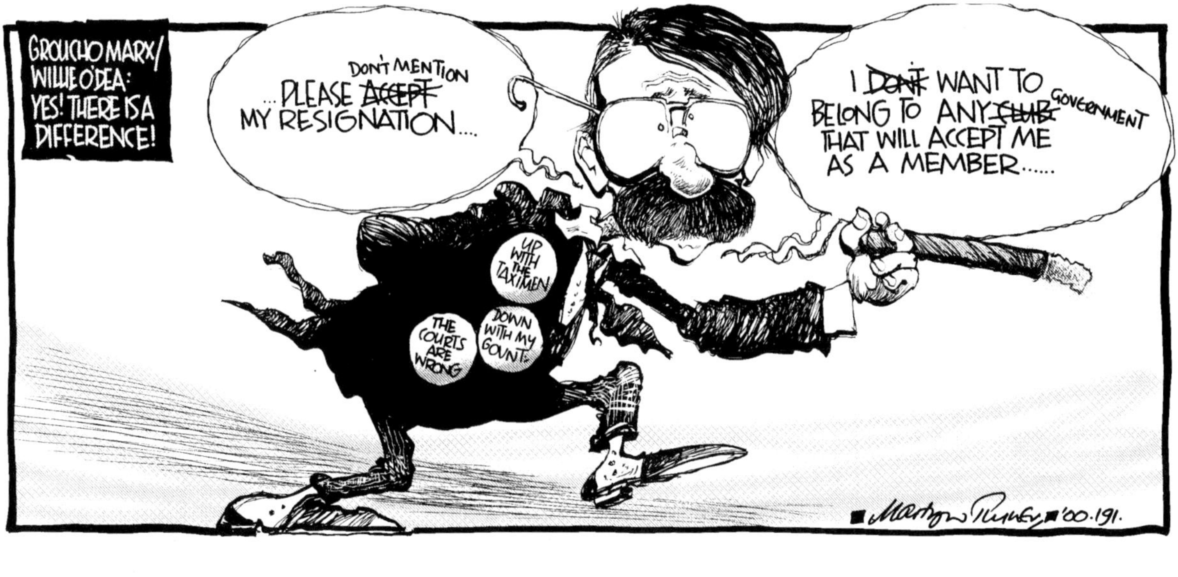
GROUCHO MARX/ WILLIE O'DEA: YES! THERE IS A DIFFERENCE!
...PLEASE ~~ACCEPT~~ DON'T MENTION MY RESIGNATION....
I ~~DON'T~~ WANT TO BELONG TO ANY ~~CLUB~~ GOVERNMENT THAT WILL ACCEPT ME AS A MEMBER......
UP WITH THE TAXIMEN
DOWN WITH MY COUNT
THE COURTS ARE WRONG
Martyn Turner '00.191.

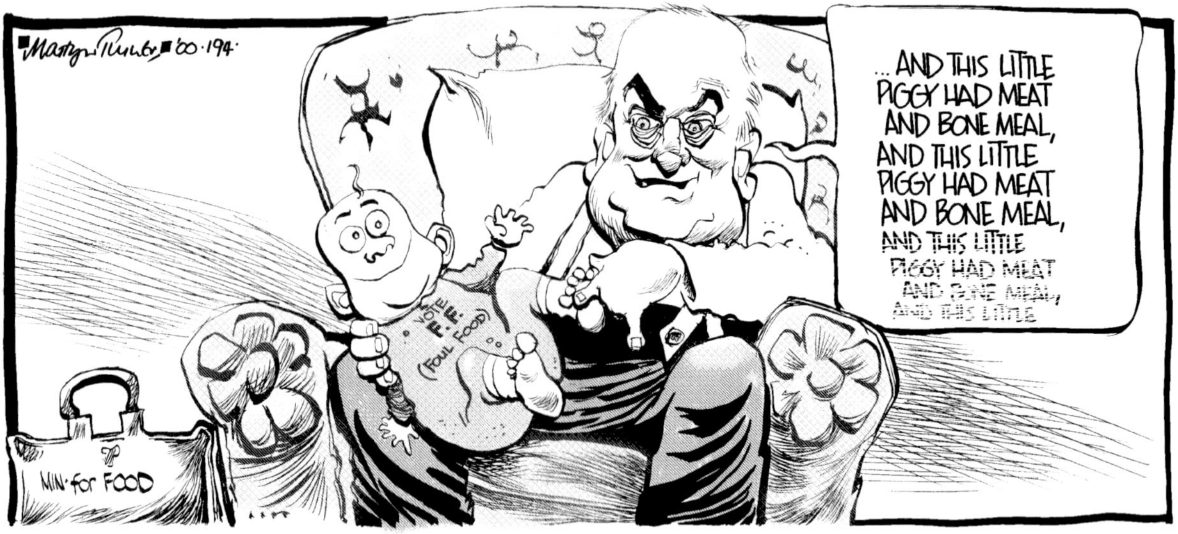
Martyn Turner '00·194·
... AND THIS LITTLE PIGGY HAD MEAT AND BONE MEAL, AND THIS LITTLE PIGGY HAD MEAT AND BONE MEAL, AND THIS LITTLE PIGGY HAD MEAT AND BONE MEAL, AND THIS LITTLE
VOTE F.F. (FOUL FOOD)
MIN·for FOOD

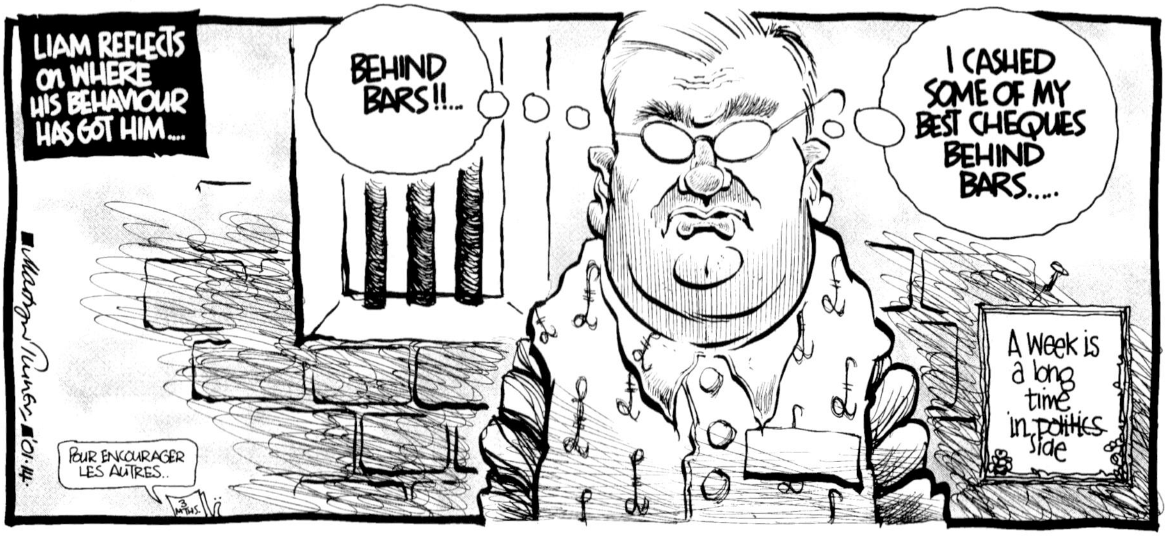
LIAM REFLECTS on WHERE HIS BEHAVIOUR HAS GOT HIM....
BEHIND BARS!!...
I CASHED SOME OF MY BEST CHEQUES BEHIND BARS.....
A week is a long time in politics side
POUR ENCOURAGER LES AUTRES..
3 MTHS.
Martyn Turner '01·14·

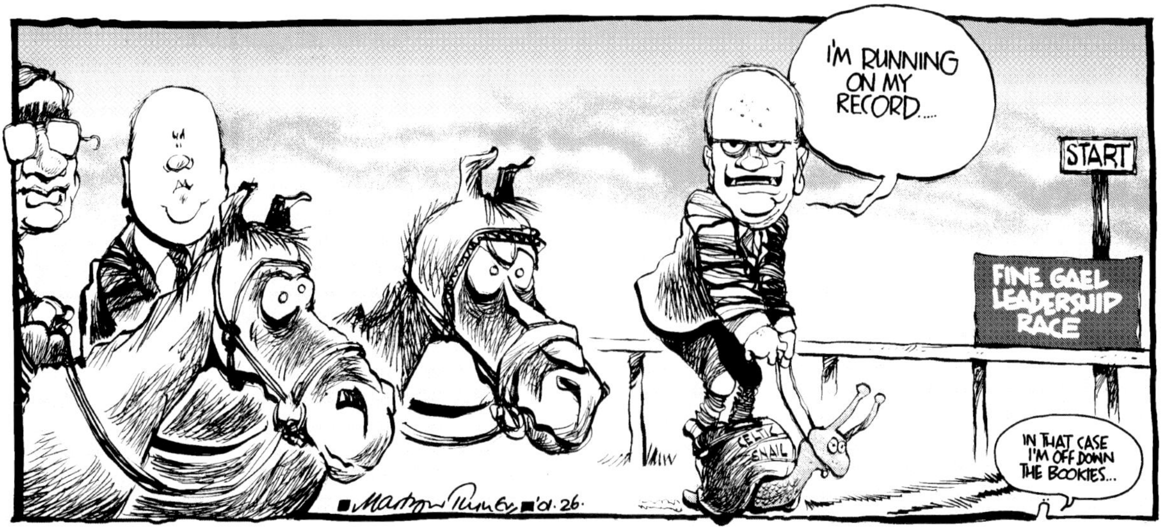
I'M RUNNING ON MY RECORD.....
START
FINE GAEL LEADERSHIP RACE
CELTIC SNAIL
IN THAT CASE I'M OFF DOWN THE BOOKIES...

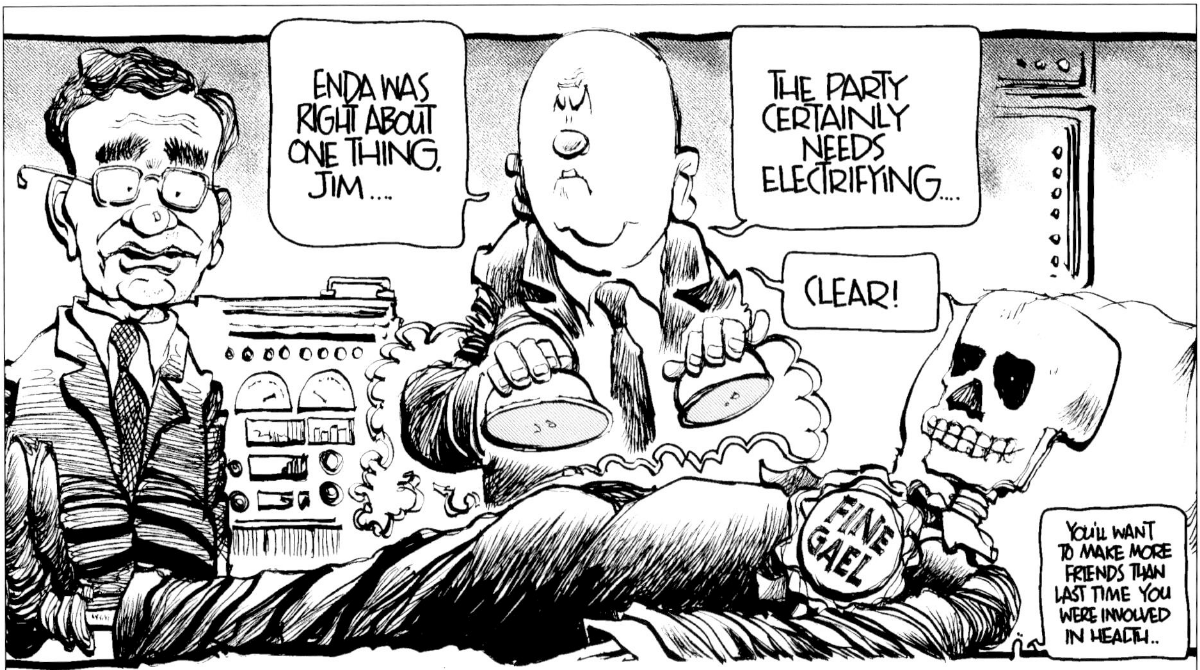
ENDA WAS RIGHT ABOUT ONE THING, JIM....
THE PARTY CERTAINLY NEEDS ELECTRIFYING....
CLEAR!
FINE GAEL
YOU'LL WANT TO MAKE MORE FRIENDS THAN LAST TIME YOU WERE INVOLVED IN HEALTH..

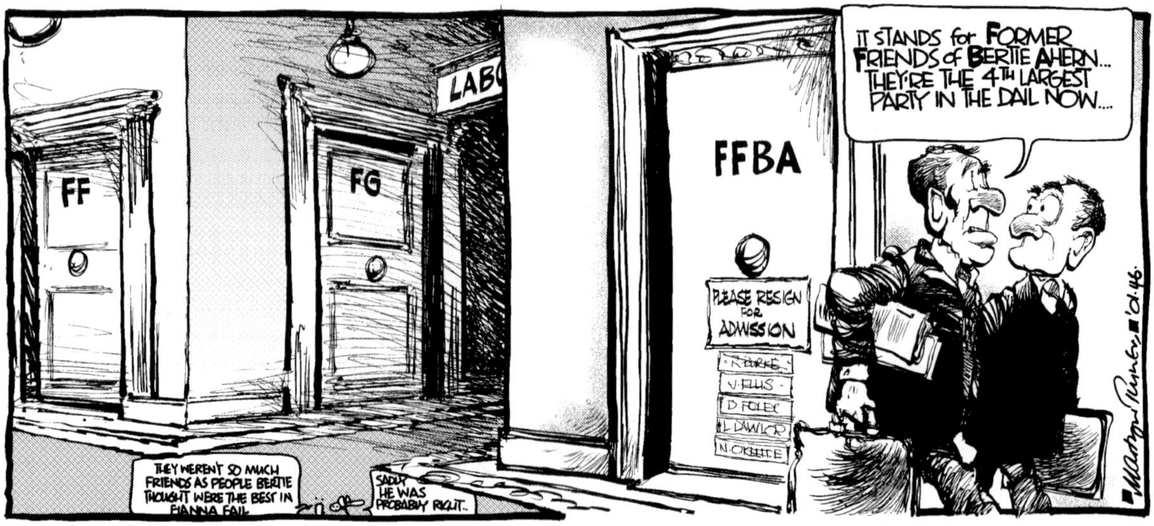
FF
FG
LABO
FFBA
PLEASE RESIGN FOR ADMISSION
R. BURKE
V. ELLIS
D. FOLEY
L. LAWLOR
N. O'KEEFFE
IT STANDS for FORMER FRIENDS of BERTIE AHERN... THEY'RE THE 4TH LARGEST PARTY IN THE DAIL NOW....
THEY WEREN'T SO MUCH FRIENDS AS PEOPLE BERTIE THOUGHT WERE THE BEST IN FIANNA FAIL
SADLY HE WAS PROBABLY RIGHT..
Martyn Turner '01.46.

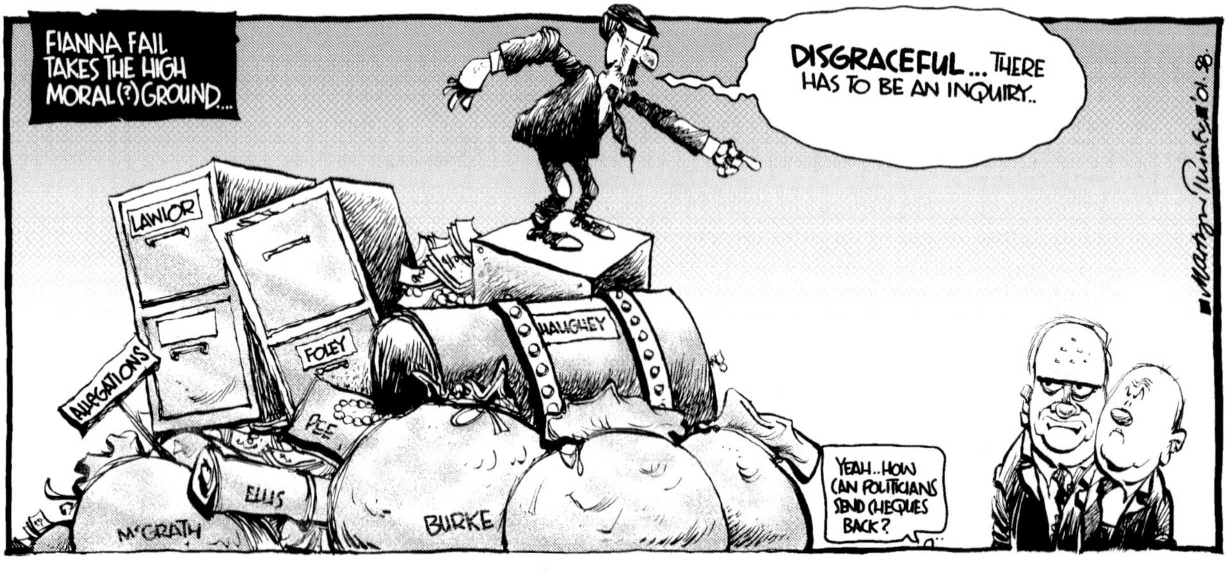
FIANNA FAIL TAKES THE HIGH MORAL(?) GROUND....
DISGRACEFUL... THERE HAS TO BE AN INQUIRY..
LAWLOR
FOLEY
HAUGHEY
ALLEGATIONS
FEE
ELLIS
BURKE
M'GRATH
YEAH.. HOW CAN POLITICIANS SEND CHEQUES BACK?
Martyn Turner '01.38.

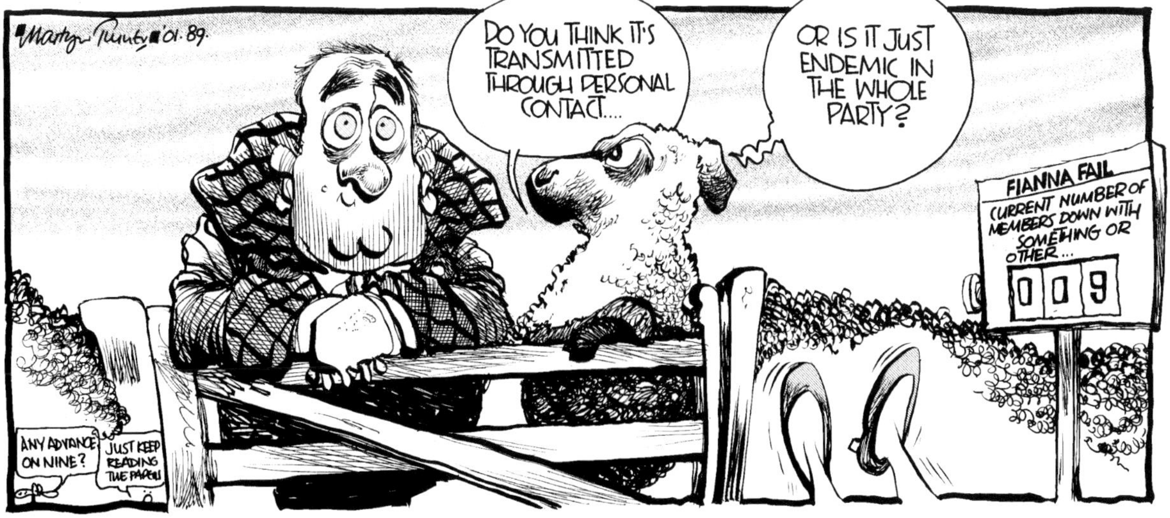
Martyn Turner '01.89.
DO YOU THINK IT'S TRANSMITTED THROUGH PERSONAL CONTACT....
OR IS IT JUST ENDEMIC IN THE WHOLE PARTY?
FIANNA FAIL
CURRENT NUMBER OF MEMBERS DOWN WITH SOMETHING OR OTHER...
0 0 9
ANY ADVANCE ON NINE?
JUST KEEP READING THE PAPER

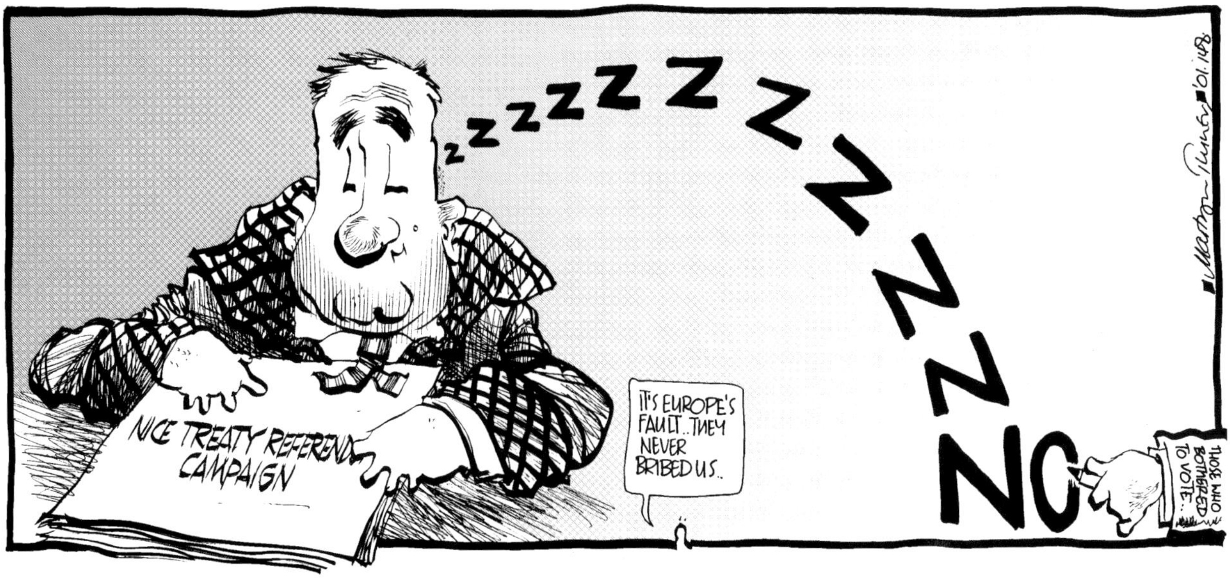
Martyn Turner '01.148.
zzzzzzZZZZZZZZ
NICE TREATY REFEREND CAMPAIGN
IT'S EUROPE'S FAULT.. THEY NEVER BRIBED US..
NO
THOSE WHO BOTHERED TO VOTE..

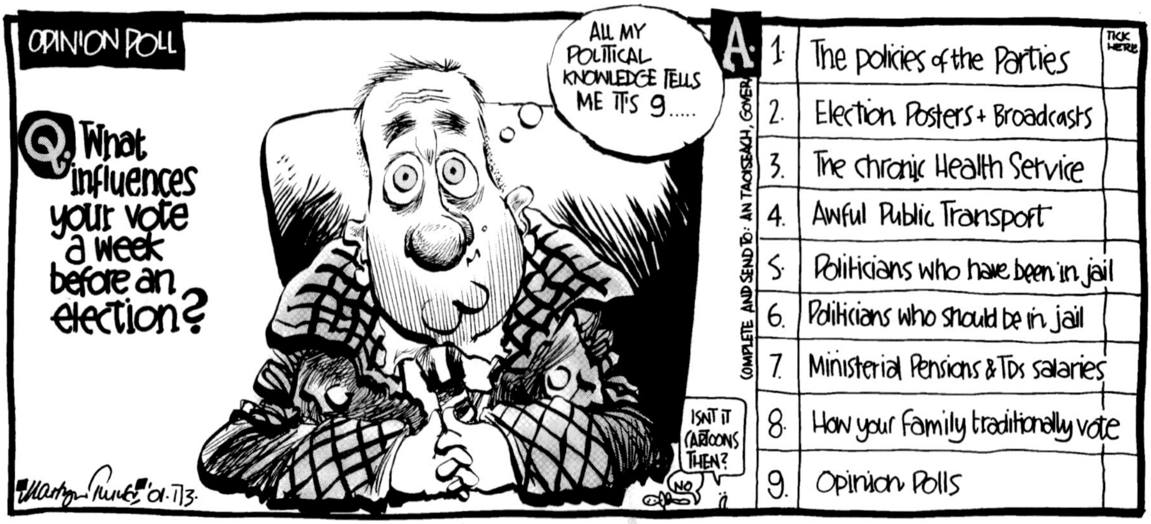
OPINION POLL
Q. What influences your vote a week before an election?
ALL MY POLITICAL KNOWLEDGE TELLS ME IT'S 9.....
A.
COMPLETE AND SEND TO: AN TAOISEACH, GOVER
TICK HERE
1. The policies of the Parties
2. Election Posters + Broadcasts
3. The chronic Health Service
4. Awful Public Transport
5. Politicians who have been in jail
6. Politicians who should be in jail
7. Ministerial Pensions & TDs salaries
8. How your Family traditionally vote
9. Opinion Polls
ISN'T IT CARTOONS THEN?
NO
Martyn Turner '01.7.13.

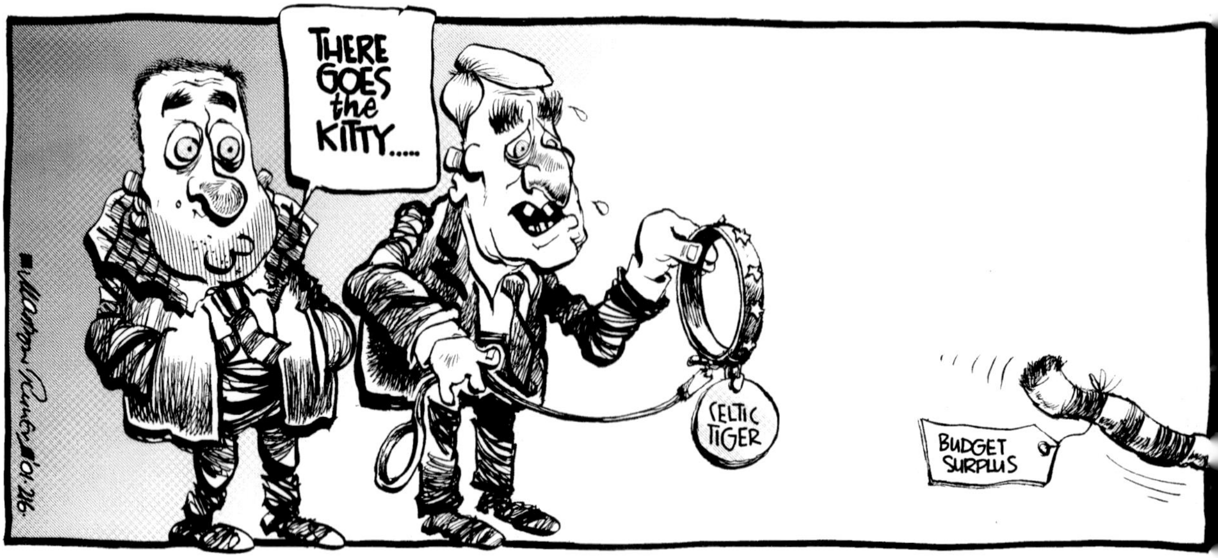
THERE GOES the KITTY.....
CELTIC TIGER
BUDGET SURPLUS
Martyn Turner '01.2.6.

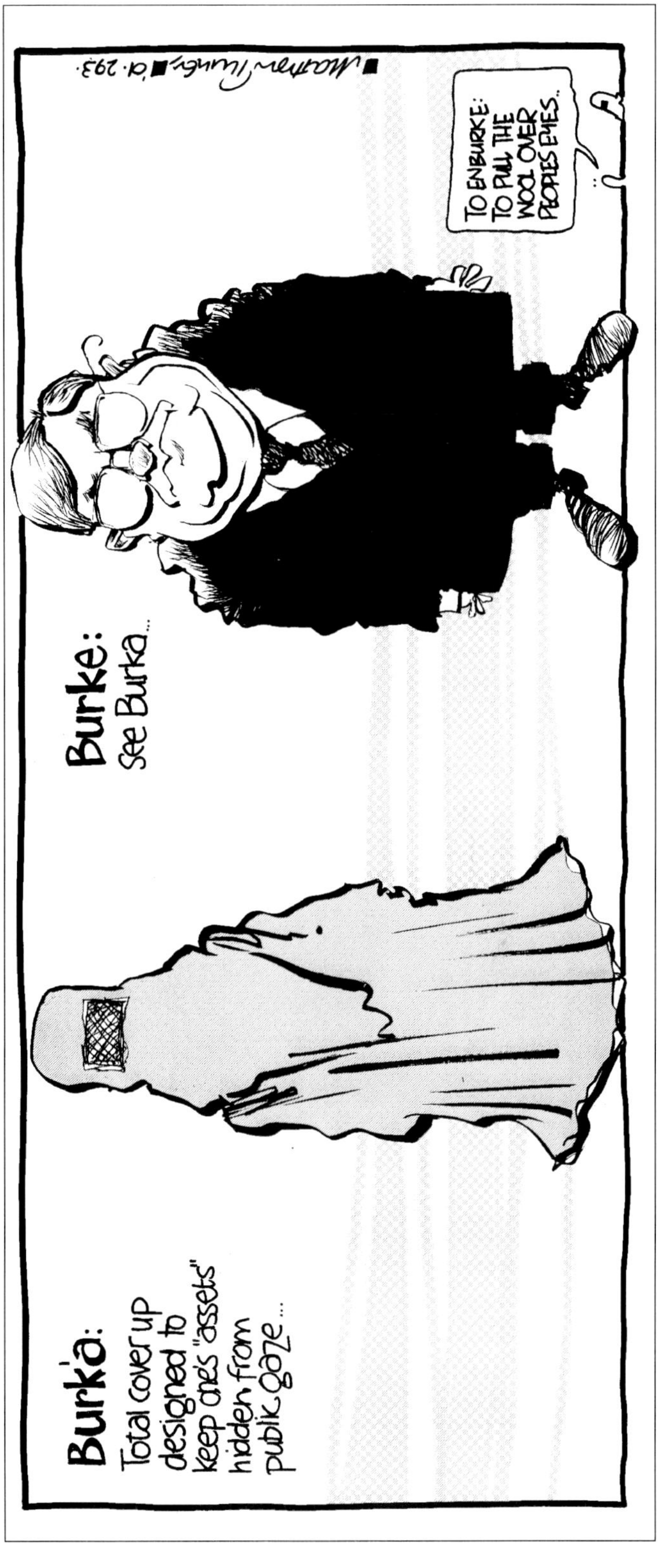
Burka:
Total cover up designed to keep one's "assets" hidden from pubik gaze...
Burke:
see Burka...
TO ENBURKE: TO PULL THE WOOL OVER PEOPLES EYES...

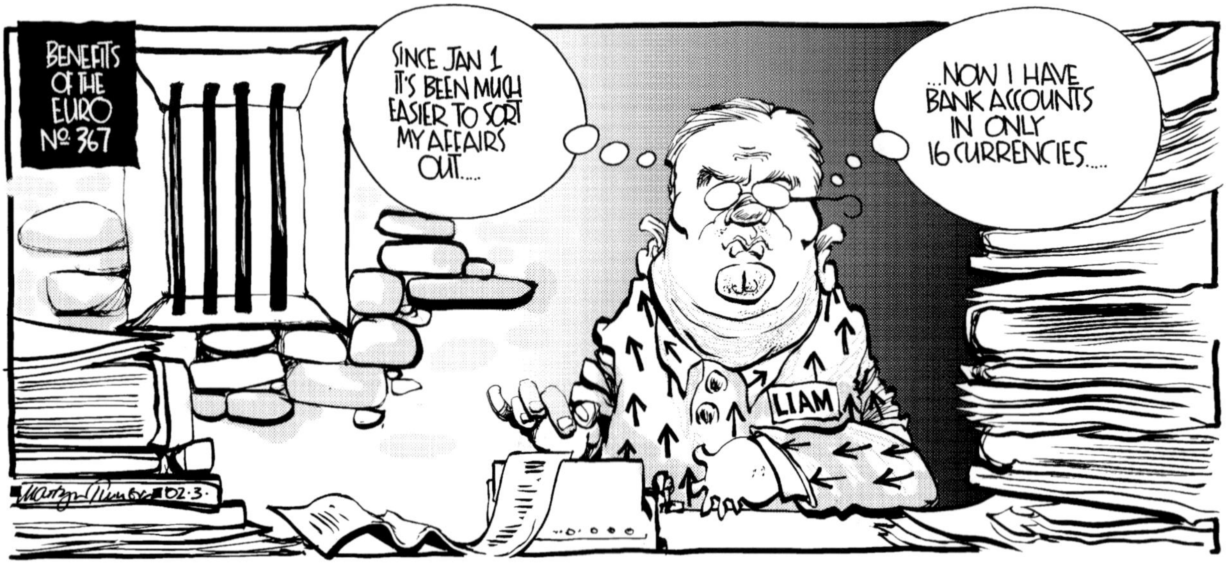
BENEFITS OF THE EURO No 367
SINCE JAN 1 IT'S BEEN MUCH EASIER TO SORT MY AFFAIRS OUT.....
...NOW I HAVE BANK ACCOUNTS IN ONLY 16 CURRENCIES.....
LIAM
'02.3.

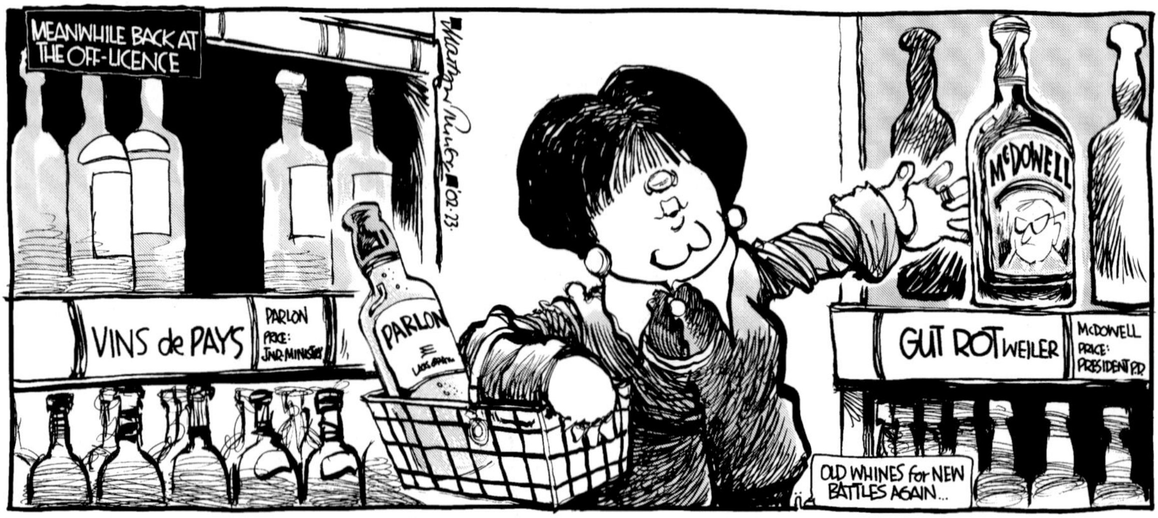
MEANWHILE BACK AT THE OFF-LICENCE
VINS de PAYS
PARLON PRICE: JNR MINISTER
PARLON
GUT ROT WEILER
McDOWELL PRICE: PRESIDENT PD
McDOWELL
OLD WHINES for NEW BATTLES AGAIN...
'02.23.

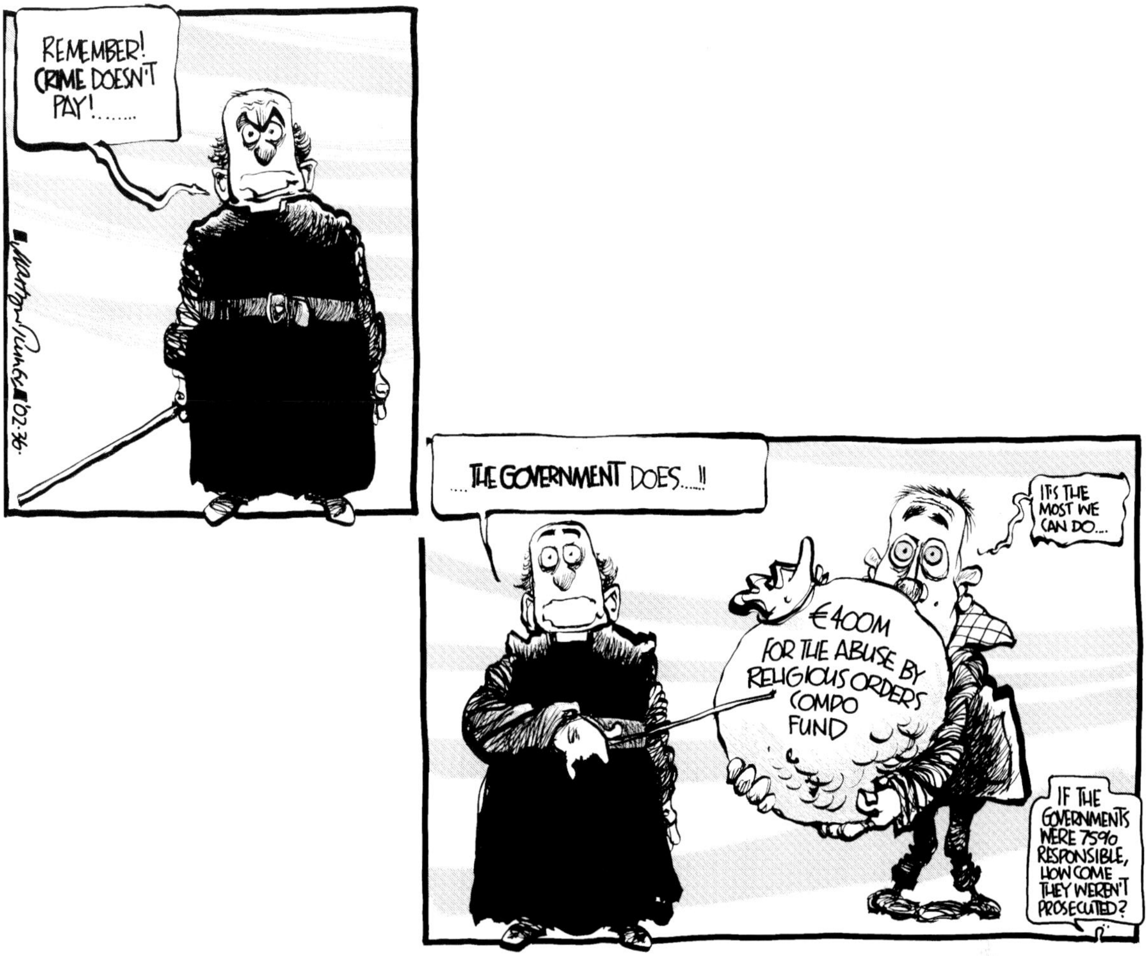
REMEMBER! CRIME DOESN'T PAY!........
....THE GOVERNMENT DOES....!!
IT'S THE MOST WE CAN DO....
€400M FOR THE ABUSE BY RELIGIOUS ORDERS COMPO FUND
IF THE GOVERNMENTS WERE 75% RESPONSIBLE, HOW COME THEY WEREN'T PROSECUTED?

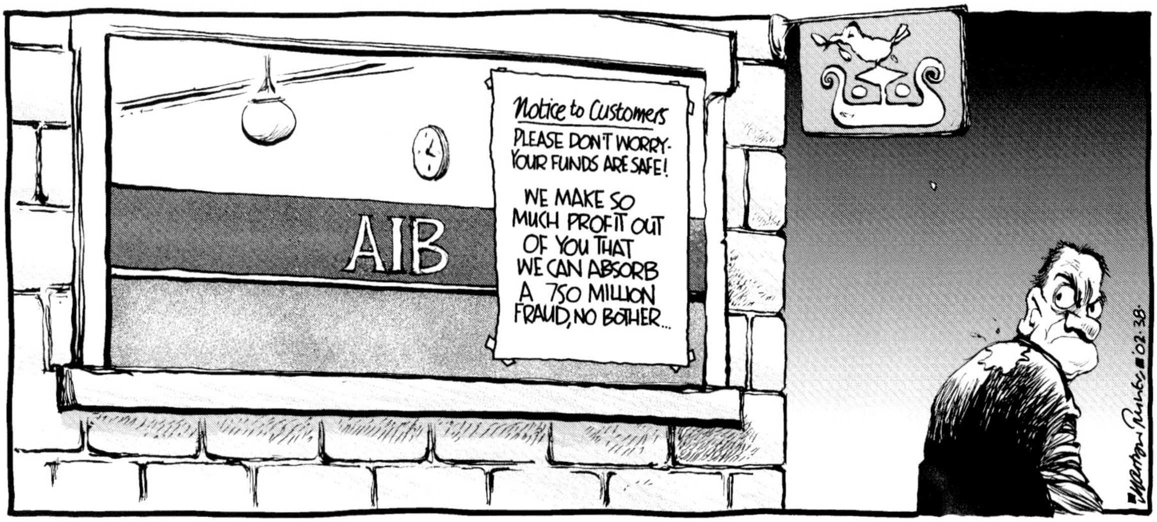
AIB
Notice to Customers
PLEASE DON'T WORRY-
YOUR FUNDS ARE SAFE!
WE MAKE SO MUCH PROFIT OUT OF YOU THAT WE CAN ABSORB A 750 MILLION FRAUD, NO BOTHER...

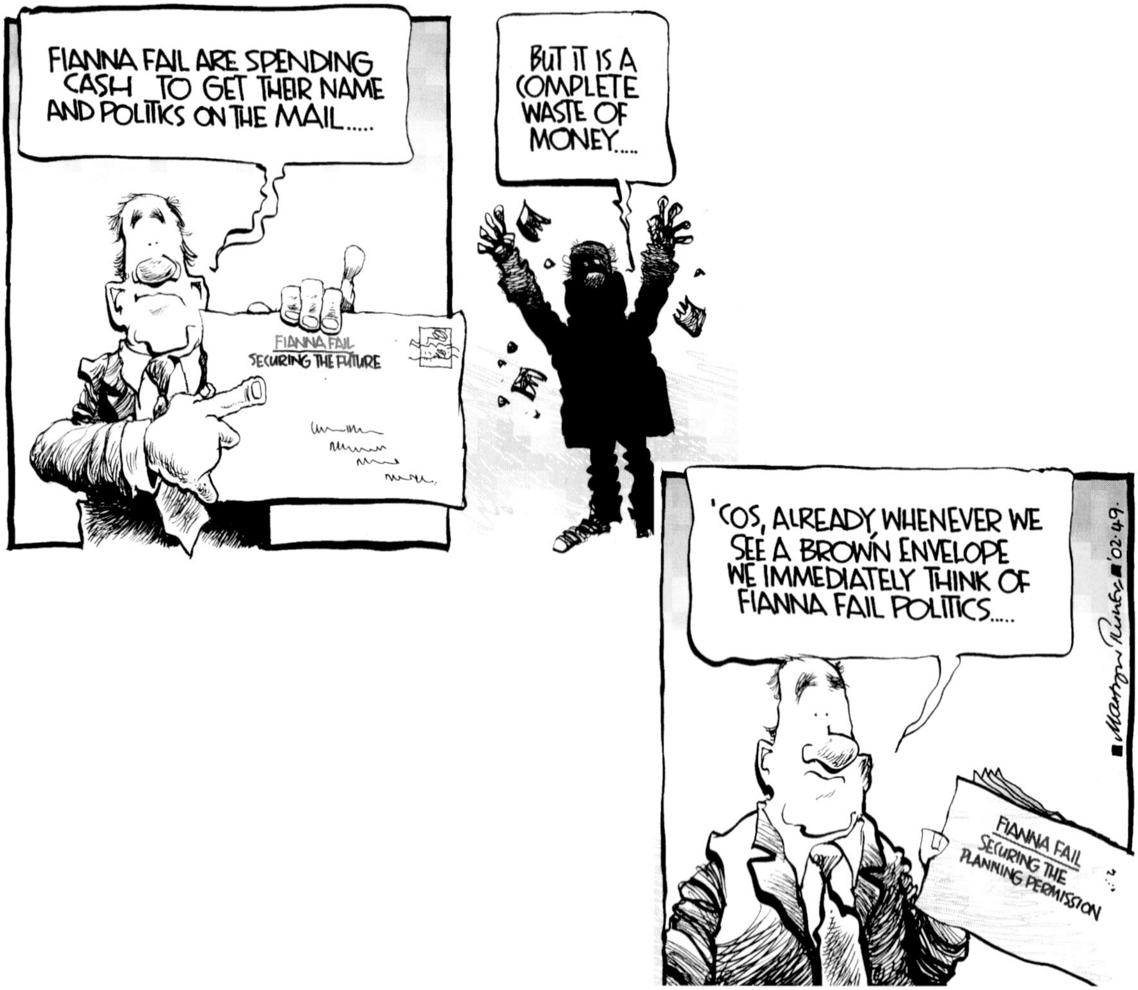
FIANNA FAIL ARE SPENDING CASH TO GET THEIR NAME AND POLITICS ON THE MAIL.....
FIANNA FAIL
SECURING THE FUTURE
BUT IT IS A COMPLETE WASTE OF MONEY....
'COS, ALREADY, WHENEVER WE SEE A BROWN ENVELOPE WE IMMEDIATELY THINK OF FIANNA FAIL POLITICS.....
FIANNA FAIL
SECURING THE PLANNING PERMISSION

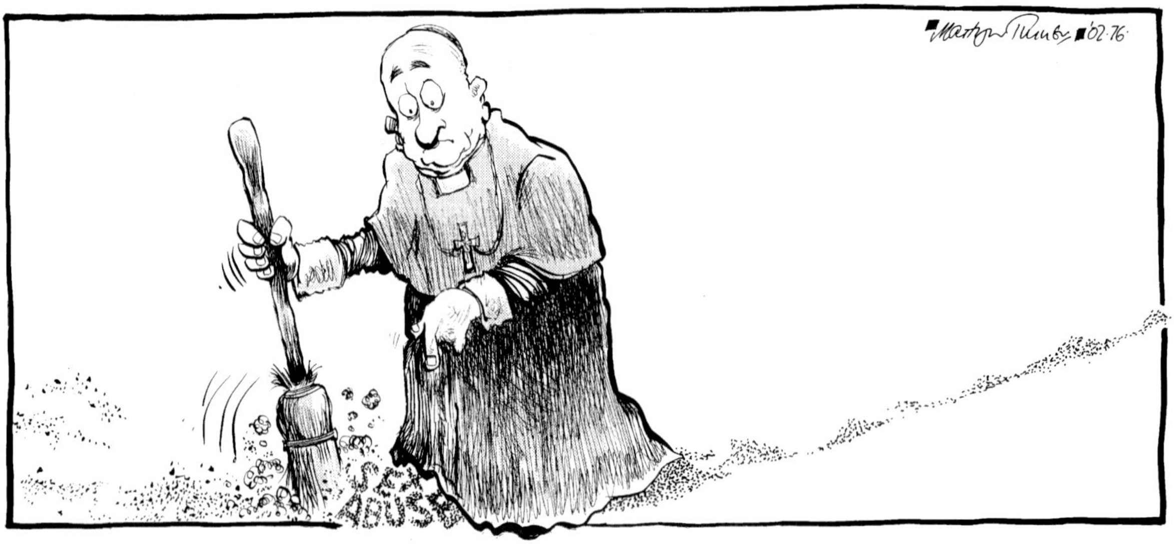
ABUSE

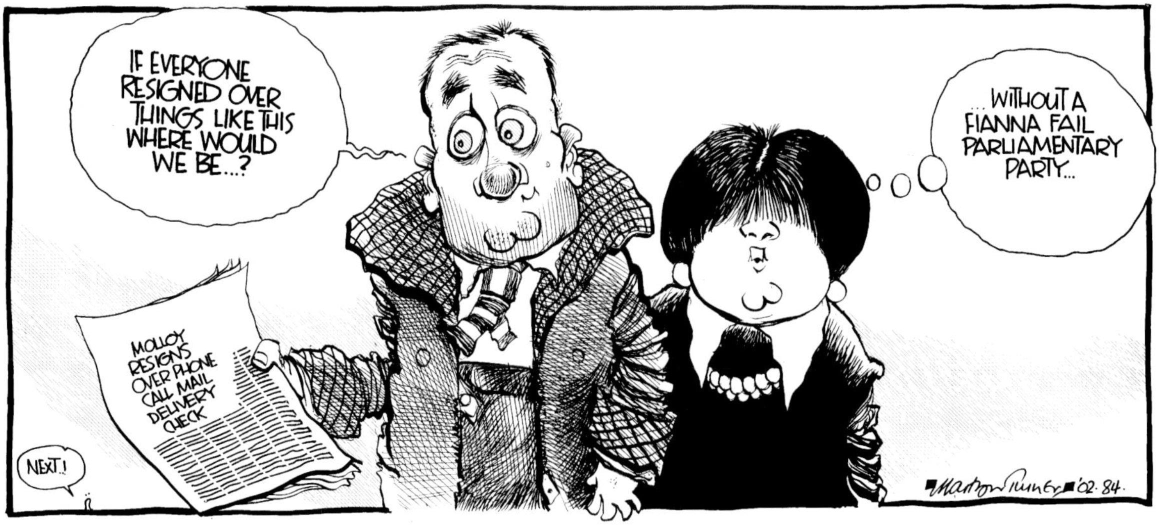
IF EVERYONE RESIGNED OVER THINGS LIKE THIS WHERE WOULD WE BE...?
...WITHOUT A FIANNA FAIL PARLIAMENTARY PARTY...
MOLLOY RESIGNS OVER PHONE CALL MAIL DELIVERY CHECK
NEXT!
Martyn Turner '02.84.

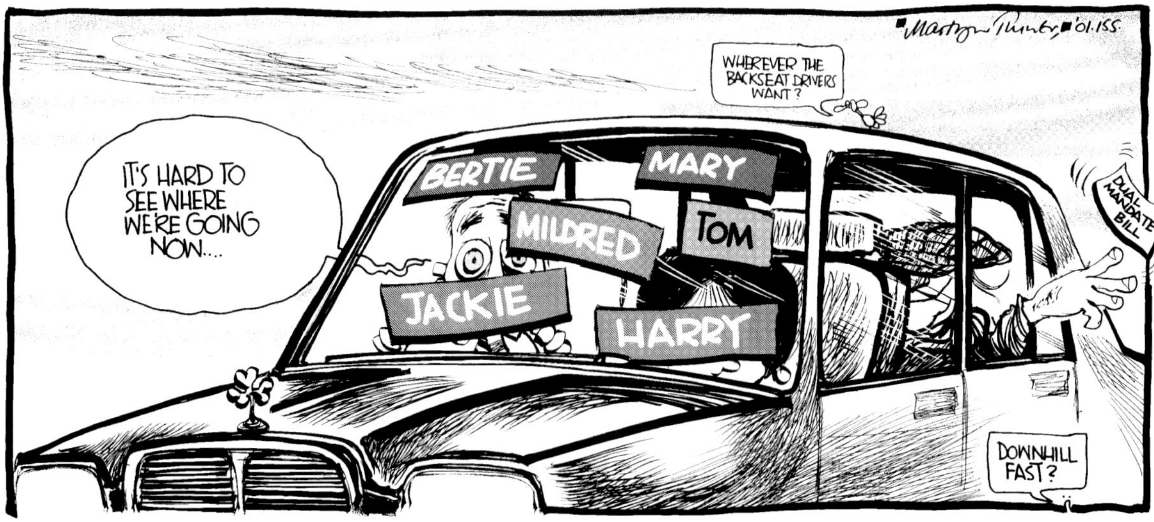
Martyn Turner '01.155.
WHEREVER THE BACKSEAT DRIVERS WANT?
IT'S HARD TO SEE WHERE WE'RE GOING NOW....
BERTIE
MARY
MILDRED
TOM
JACKIE
HARRY
DUAL MANDATE BILL
DOWNHILL FAST?

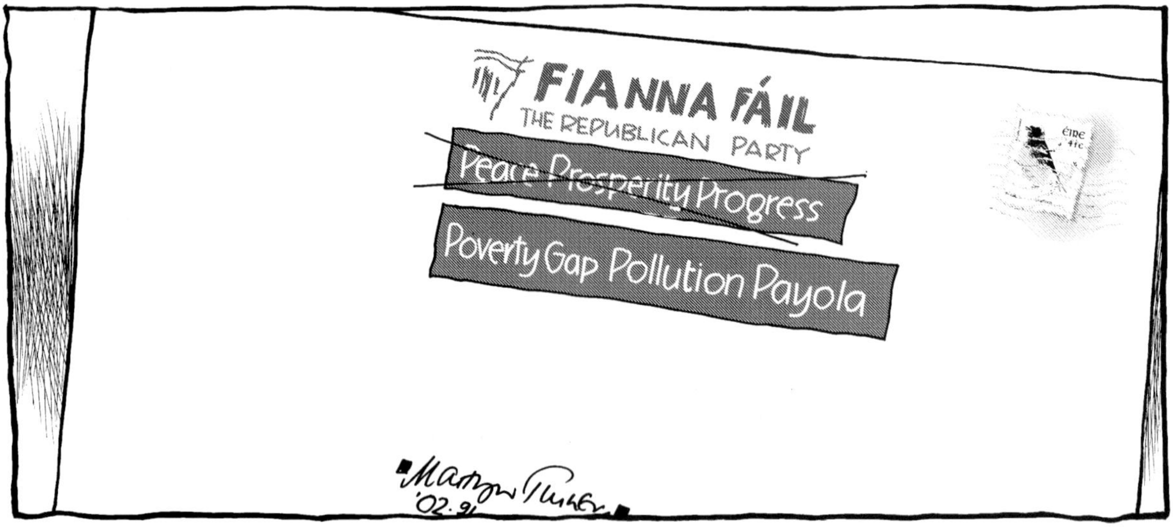
FIANNA FÁIL
THE REPUBLICAN PARTY
Peace Prosperity Progress
Poverty Gap Pollution Payola
éire
Martyn Turner
'02.91

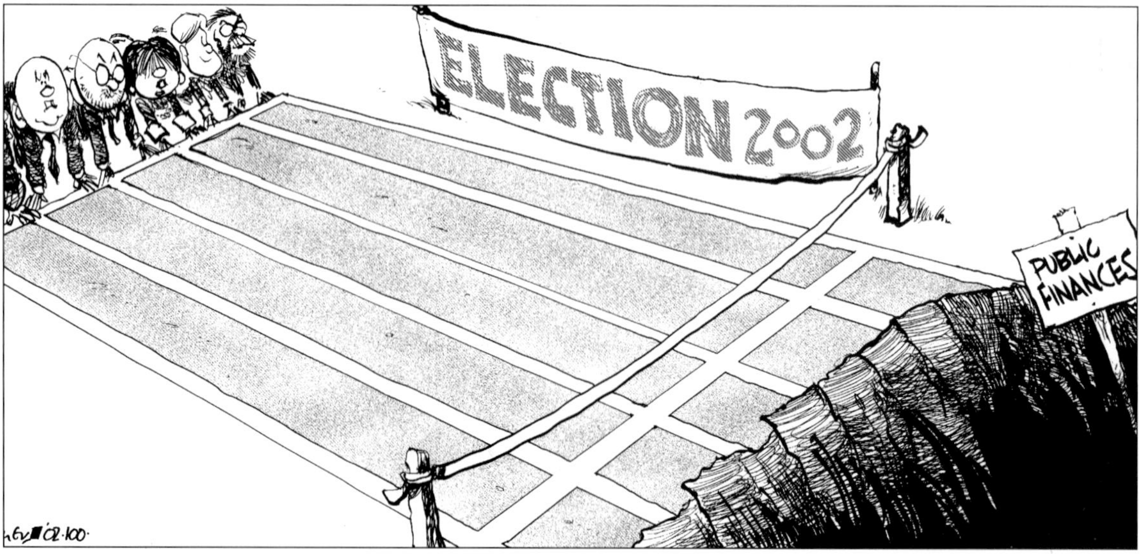
ELECTION 2002
PUBLIC FINANCES
'02.100

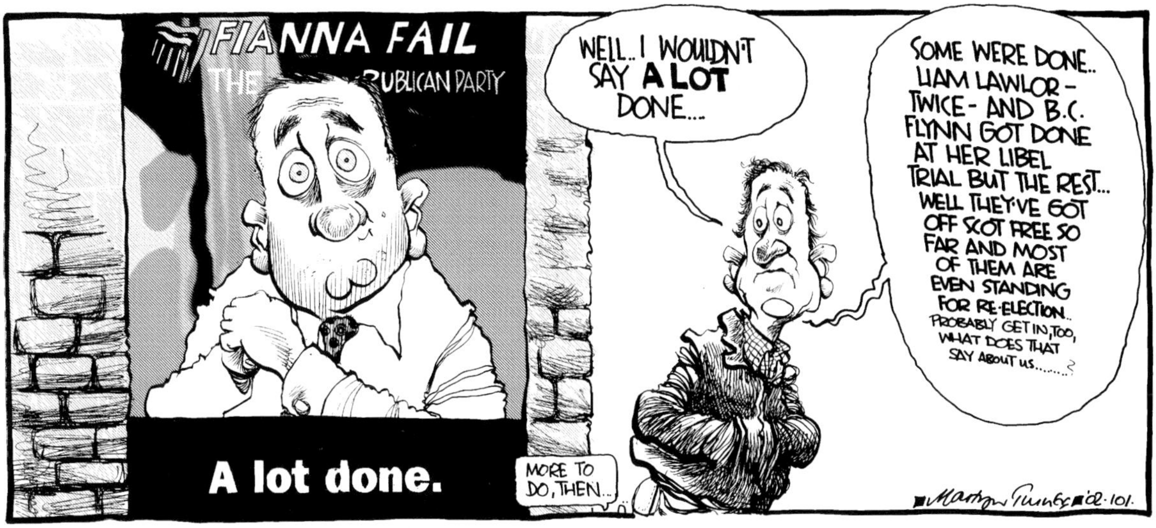
FIANNA FAIL
THE RUBLICAN PARTY
A lot done.
WELL.. I WOULDN'T SAY A LOT DONE....
SOME WERE DONE.. LIAM LAWLOR – TWICE – AND B.C. FLYNN GOT DONE AT HER LIBEL TRIAL BUT THE REST... WELL THEY'VE GOT OFF SCOT FREE SO FAR AND MOST OF THEM ARE EVEN STANDING FOR RE-ELECTION.. PROBABLY GET IN, TOO, WHAT DOES THAT SAY ABOUT US.......?
MORE TO DO, THEN...
Martyn Turner '02.101.

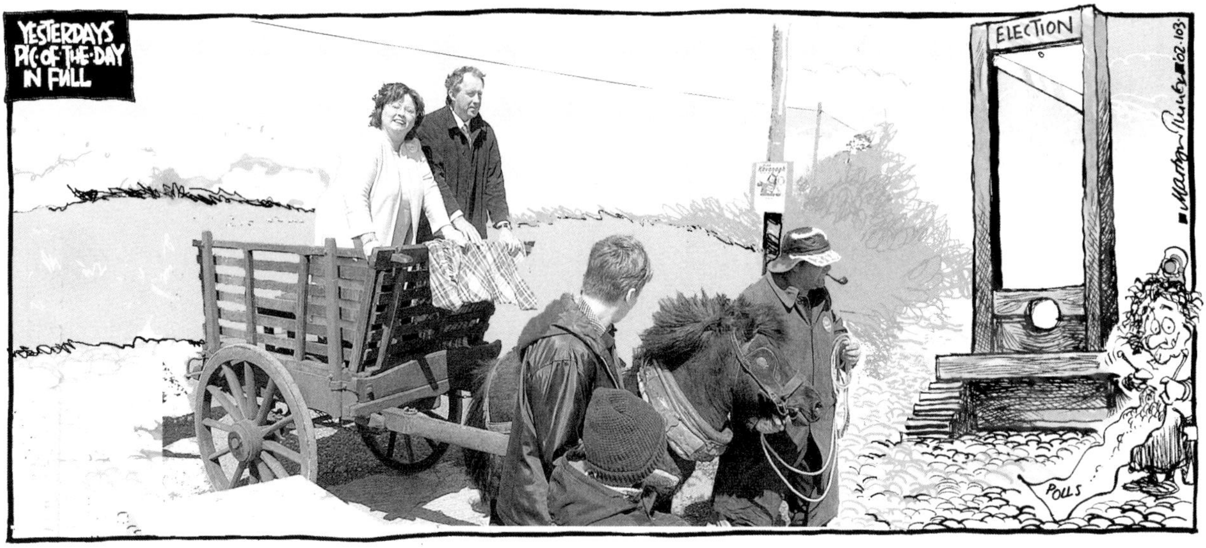
YESTERDAYS PIC-OF-THE-DAY IN FULL
ELECTION
POLLS
Martyn Turner '02.103.

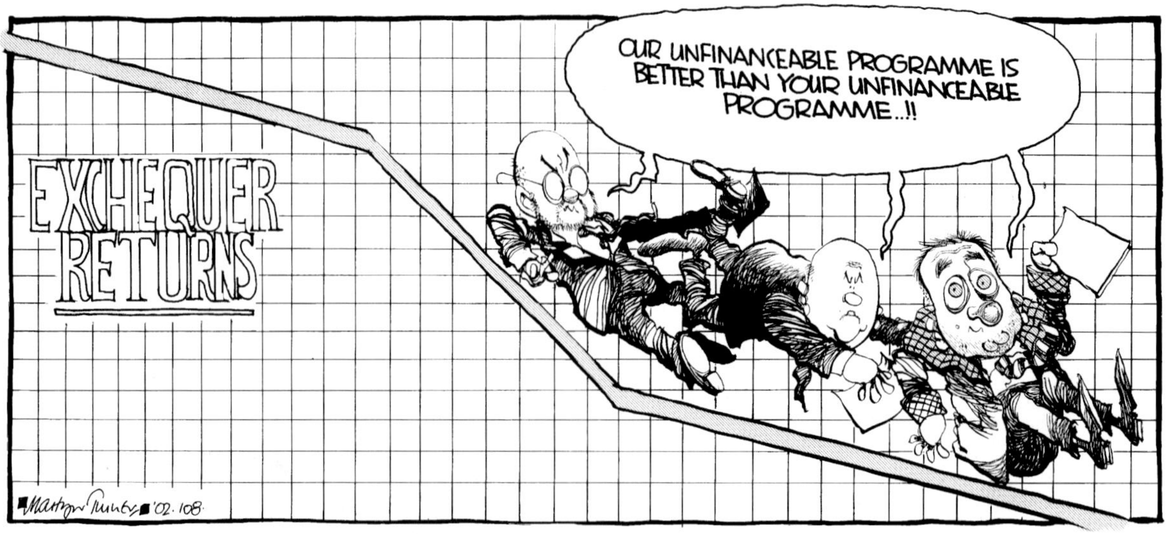
OUR UNFINANCEABLE PROGRAMME IS BETTER THAN YOUR UNFINANCEABLE PROGRAMME...!!
EXCHEQUER RETURNS
Martyn Turner '02.108

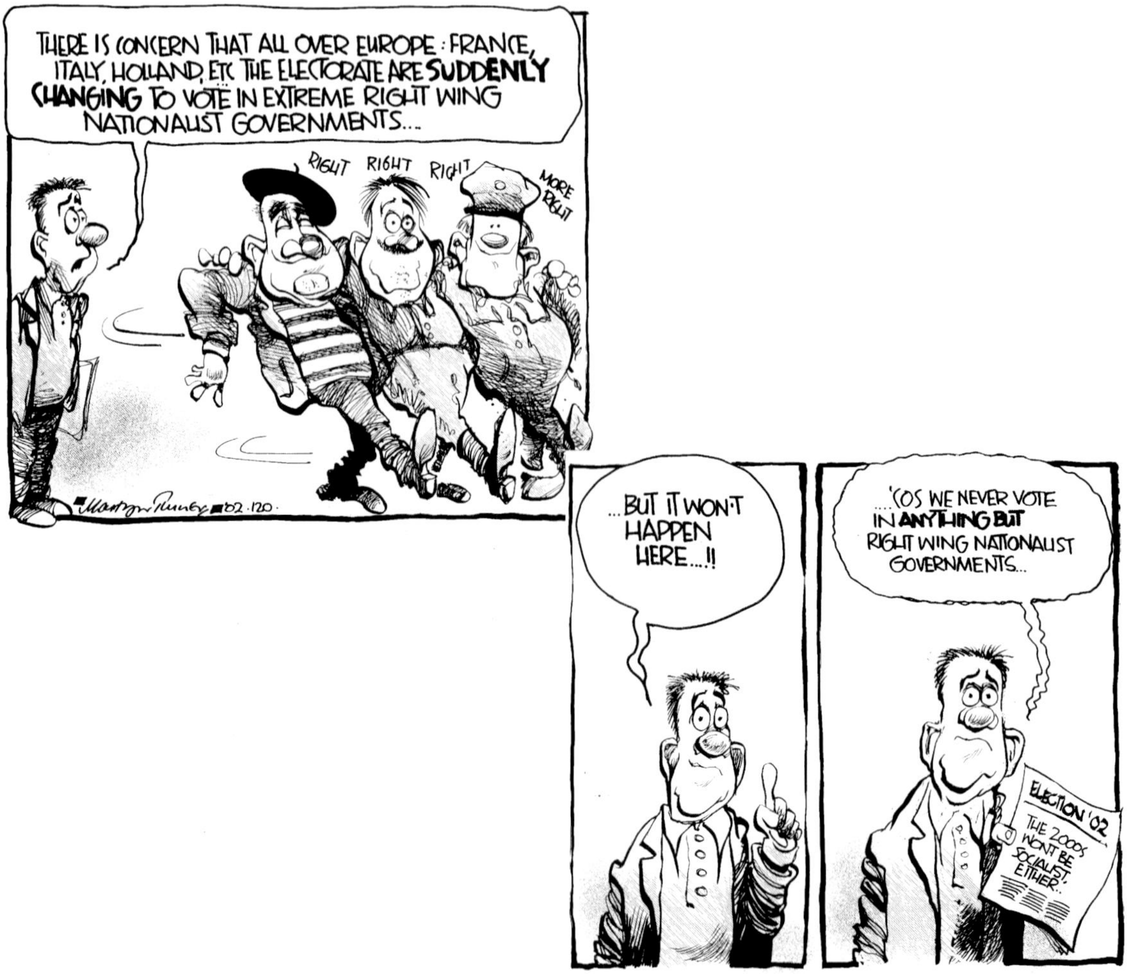
THERE IS CONCERN THAT ALL OVER EUROPE: FRANCE, ITALY, HOLLAND, ETC THE ELECTORATE ARE SUDDENLY CHANGING TO VOTE IN EXTREME RIGHT WING NATIONALIST GOVERNMENTS...
RIGHT
RIGHT
RIGHT
MORE RIGHT
Martyn Turner '02.120
...BUT IT WON'T HAPPEN HERE...!!
...'COS WE NEVER VOTE IN ANYTHING BUT RIGHT WING NATIONALIST GOVERNMENTS...
ELECTION '02
THE 2000s WONT BE SOCIALIST EITHER..

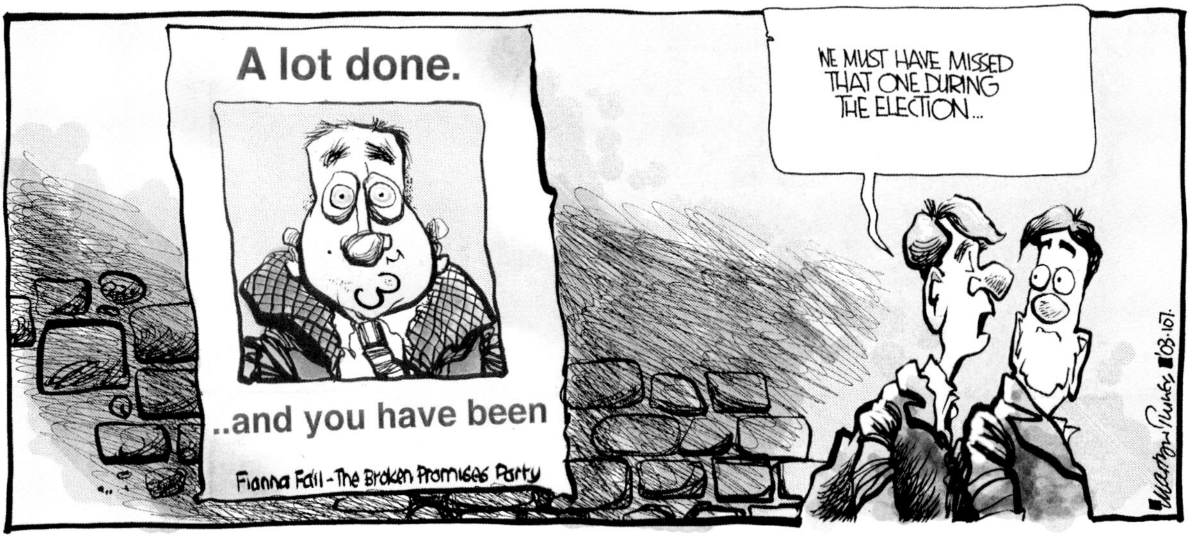
A lot done.
..and you have been
Fianna Fáil - The Broken Promises Party
WE MUST HAVE MISSED THAT ONE DURING THE ELECTION...
'03.10?

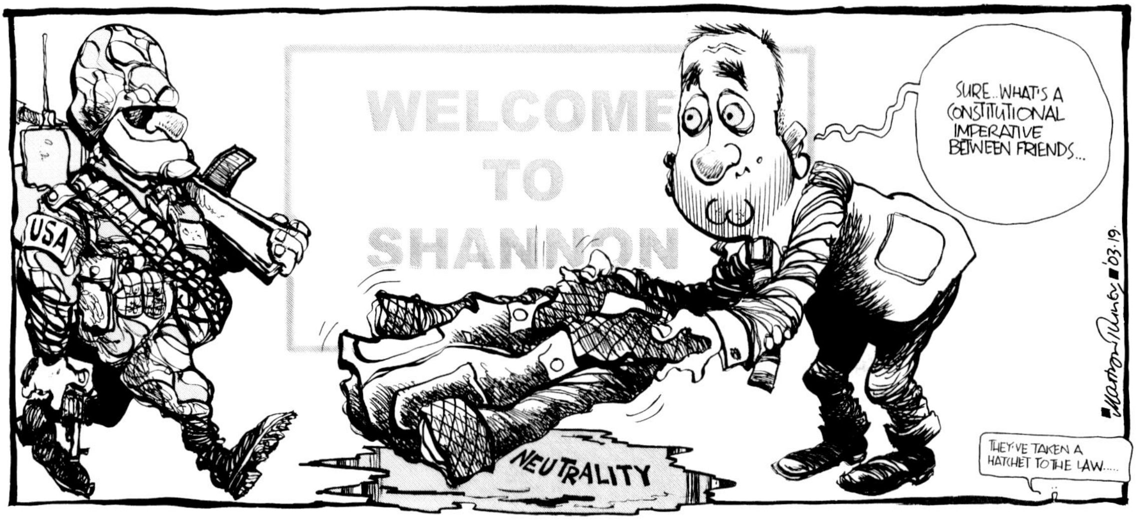
WELCOME TO SHANNON
USA
SURE..WHAT'S A CONSTITUTIONAL IMPERATIVE BETWEEN FRIENDS...
NEUTRALITY
THEY'VE TAKEN A HATCHET TO THE LAW.....
'03.19

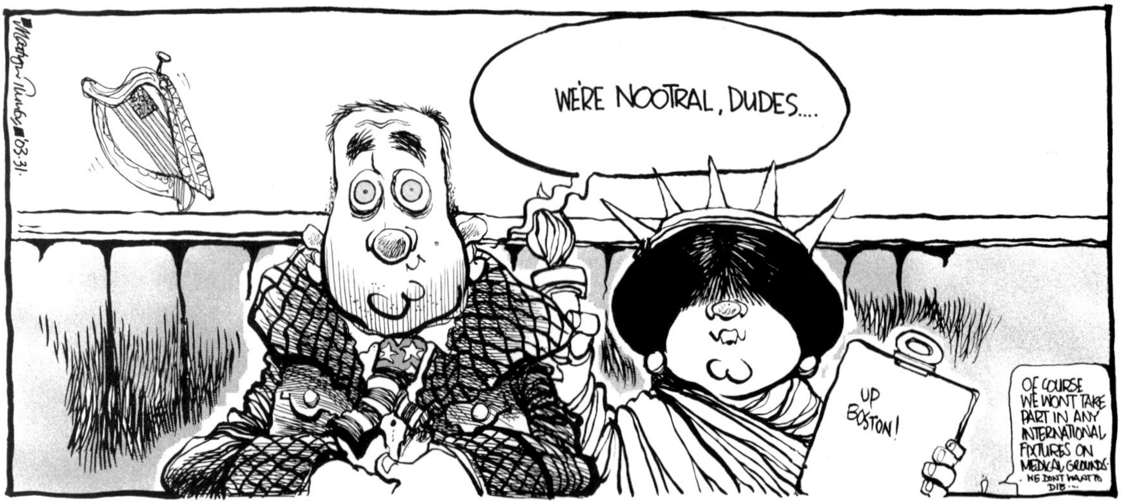
WE'RE NOOTRAL, DUDES....
UP BOSTON!
OF COURSE WE WONT TAKE PART IN ANY INTERNATIONAL FIXTURES ON MEDICAL GROUNDS. WE DONT WANT TO DIE...

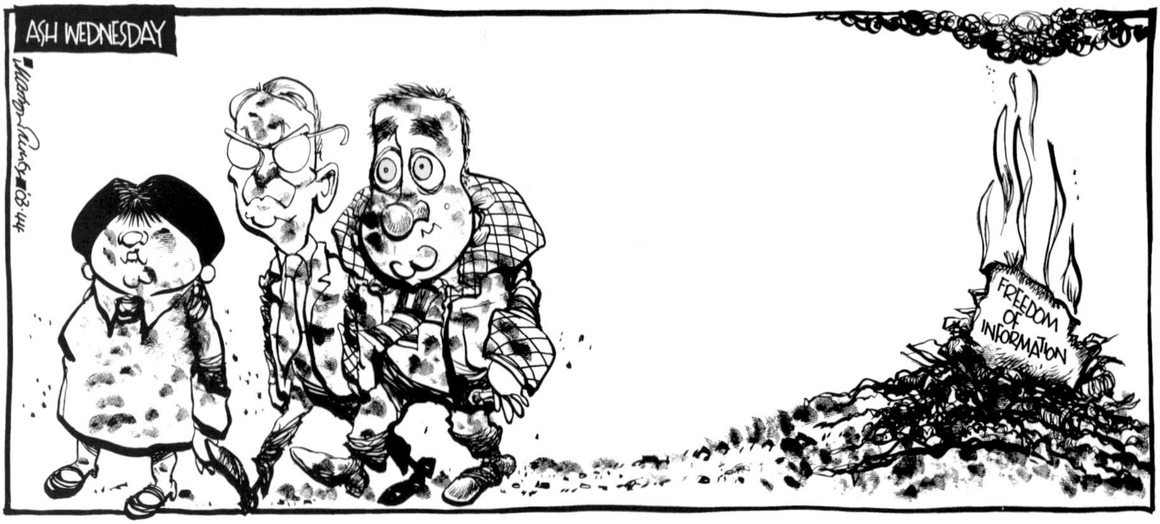
ASH WEDNESDAY
FREEDOM OF INFORMATION

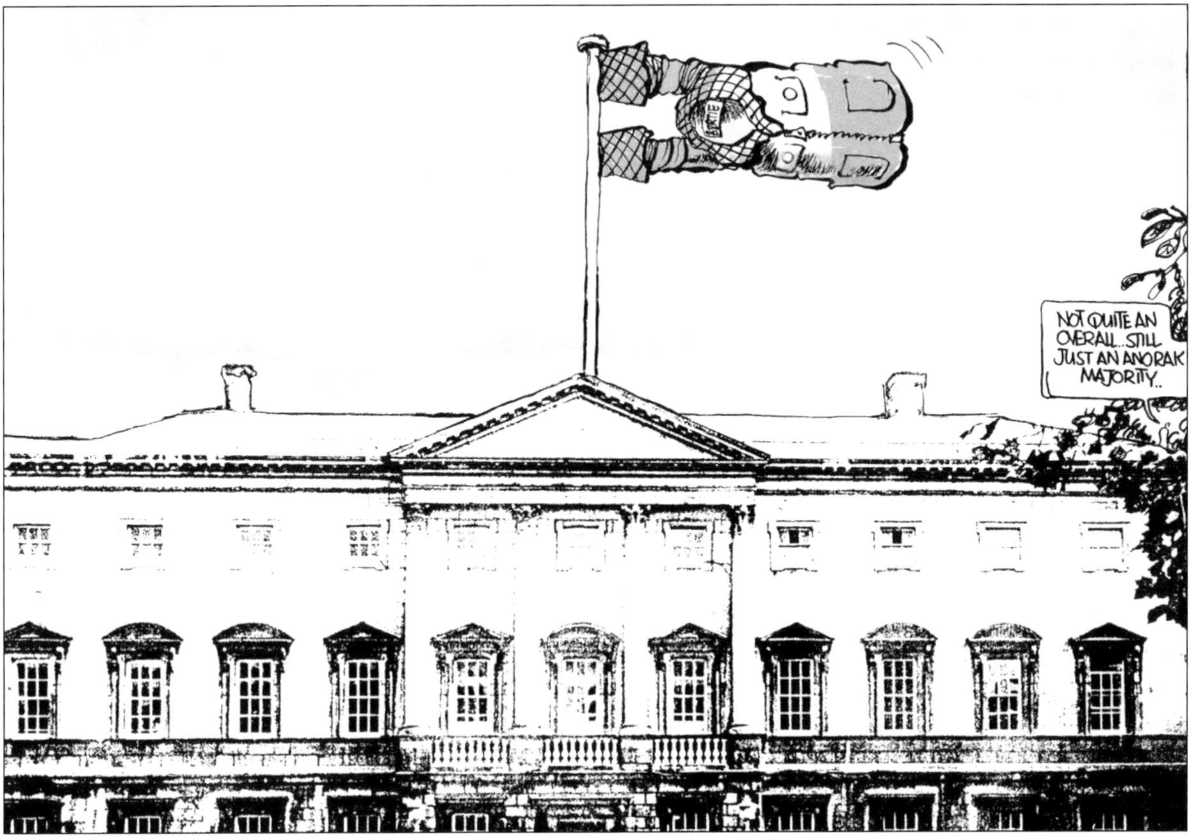
NOT QUITE AN OVERALL.. STILL JUST AN ANORAK MAJORITY..

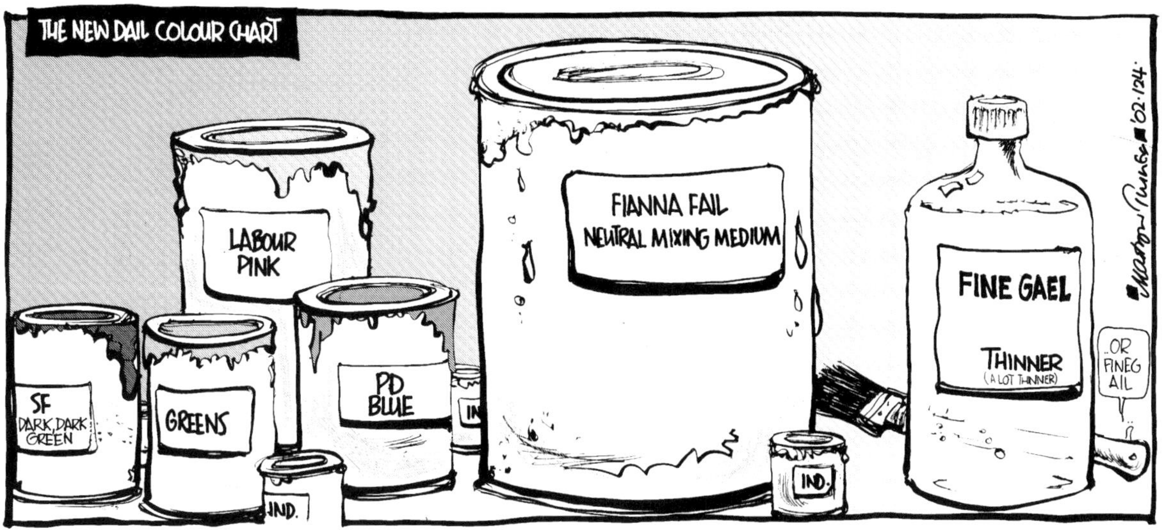
THE NEW DAIL COLOUR CHART
LABOUR PINK
FIANNA FAIL NEUTRAL MIXING MEDIUM
FINE GAEL
THINNER
(A LOT THINNER)
..OR FINEG AIL
SF DARK, DARK GREEN
GREENS
PD BLUE
IND.
IND.

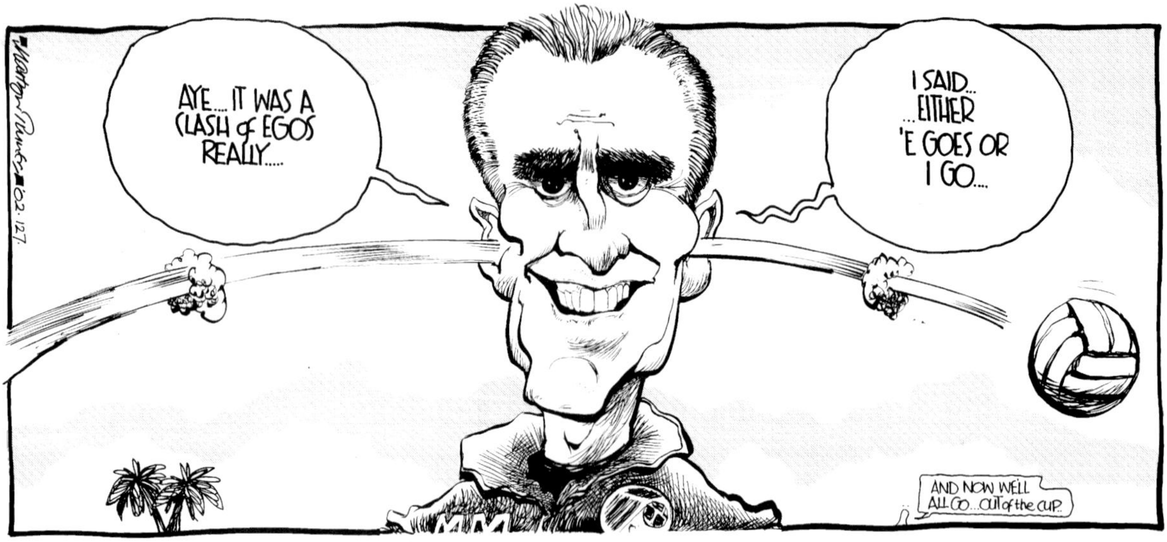
AYE.... IT WAS A CLASH of EGOS REALLY.....
I SAID... ...EITHER 'E GOES OR I GO...
AND NOW WE'LL ALL GO... OUT of the CUP..

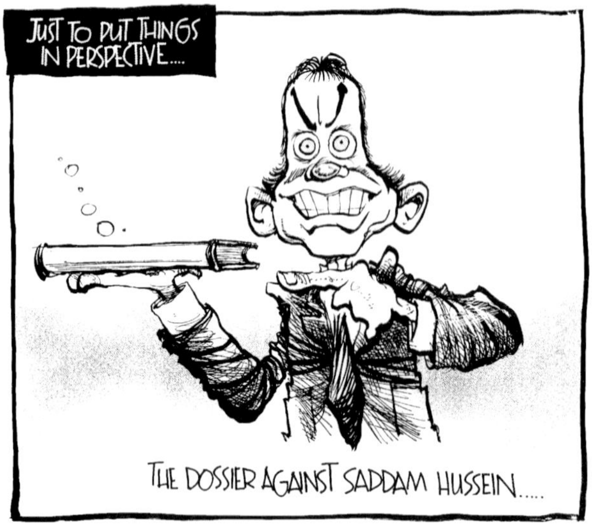
JUST TO PUT THINGS IN PERSPECTIVE....
THE DOSSIER AGAINST SADDAM HUSSEIN.....

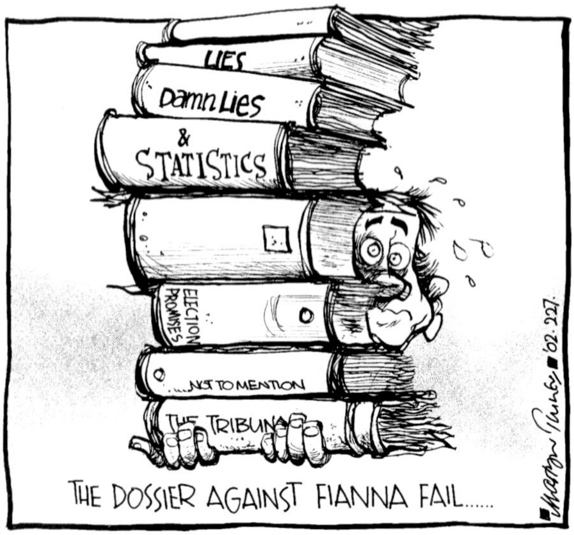
LIES
Damn Lies
&
STATISTICS
ELECTION PROMISES
...NOT TO MENTION
THE TRIBUNA
THE DOSSIER AGAINST FIANNA FAIL......

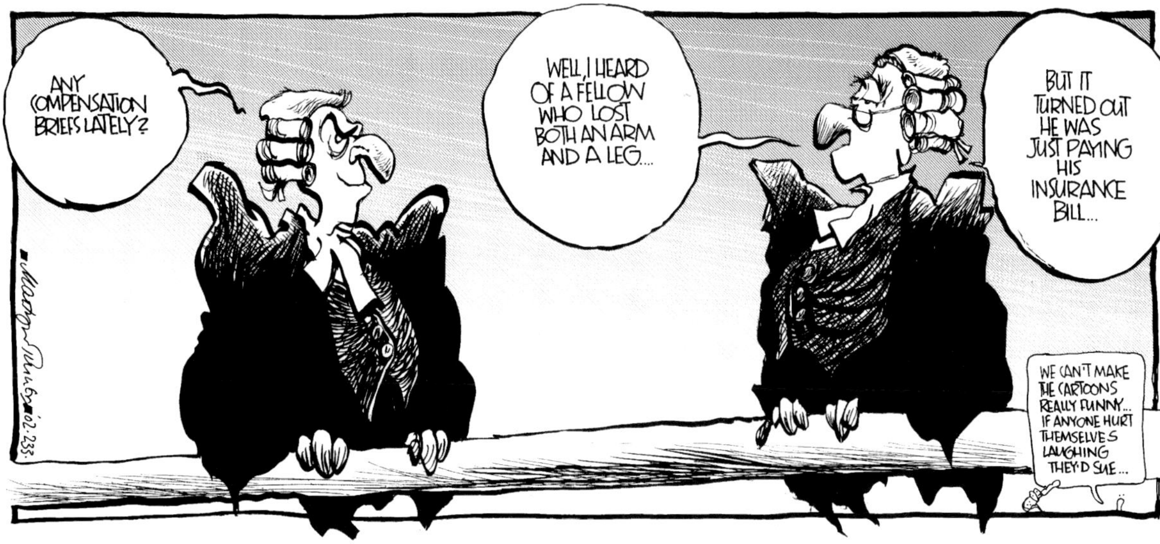
ANY COMPENSATION BRIEFS LATELY?
WELL, I HEARD OF A FELLOW WHO LOST BOTH AN ARM AND A LEG....
BUT IT TURNED OUT HE WAS JUST PAYING HIS INSURANCE BILL...
WE CAN'T MAKE THE CARTOONS REALLY FUNNY... IF ANYONE HURT THEMSELVES LAUGHING THEY'D SUE...

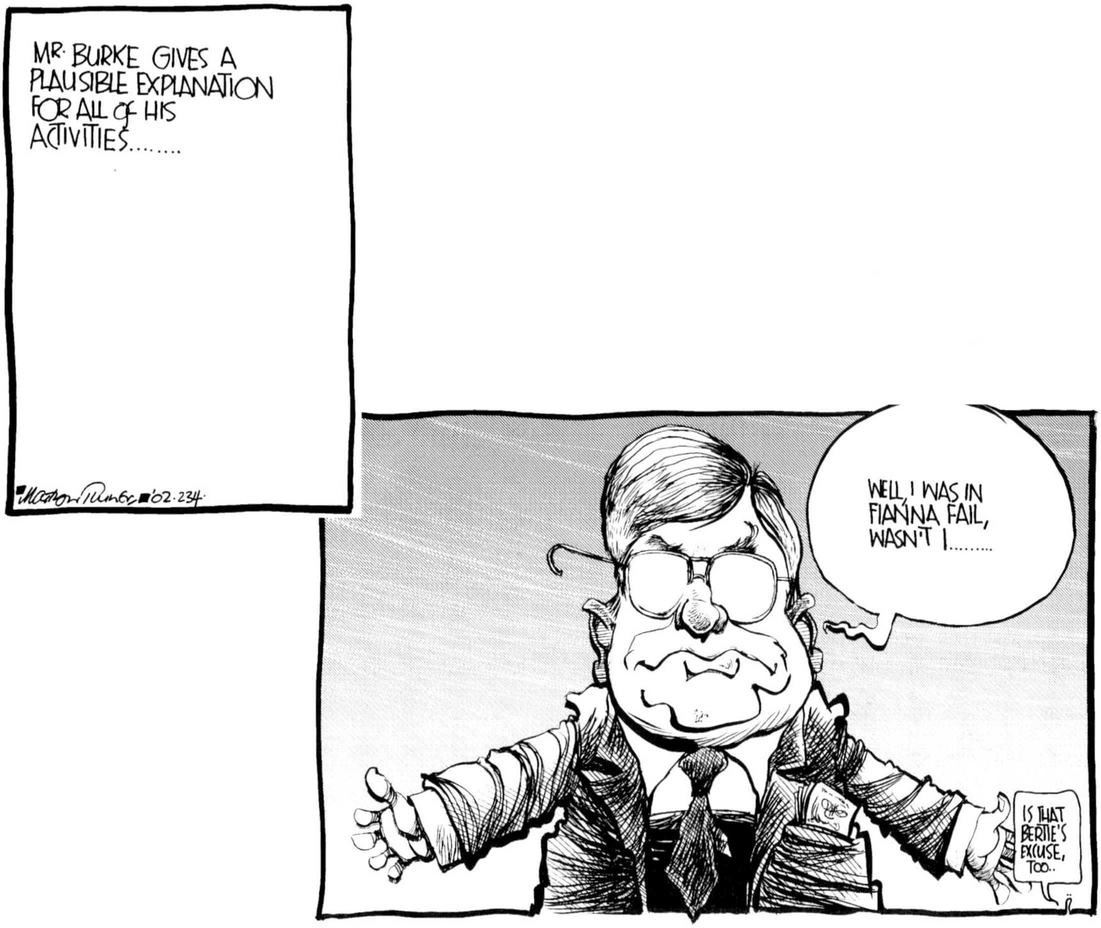
MR. BURKE GIVES A PLAUSIBLE EXPLANATION FOR ALL OF HIS ACTIVITIES........
WELL, I WAS IN FIANNA FAIL, WASN'T I........
IS THAT BERTIE'S EXCUSE, TOO..

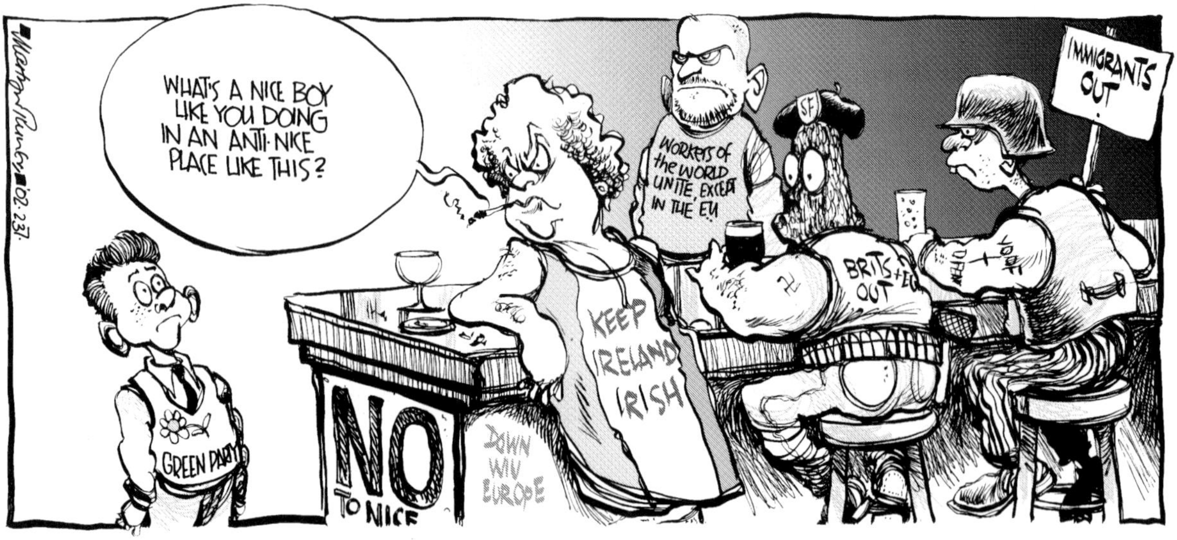
Martyn Turner 02·237
WHAT'S A NICE BOY LIKE YOU DOING IN AN ANTI·NICE PLACE LIKE THIS?
GREEN PARTY
NO TO NICE
DOWN WIV EUROPE
KEEP IRELAND IRISH
WORKERS OF THE WORLD UNITE, EXCEPT IN THE EU
SF
BRITS + EU OUT
IMMIGRANTS OUT

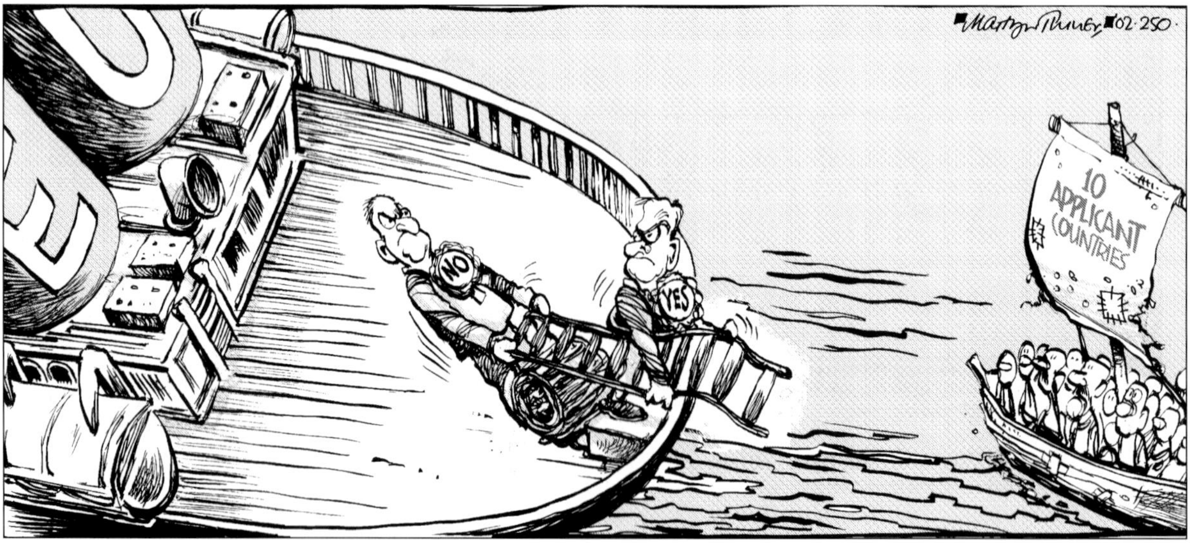
Martyn Turner 02·250
NO
YES
10 APPLICANT COUNTRIES

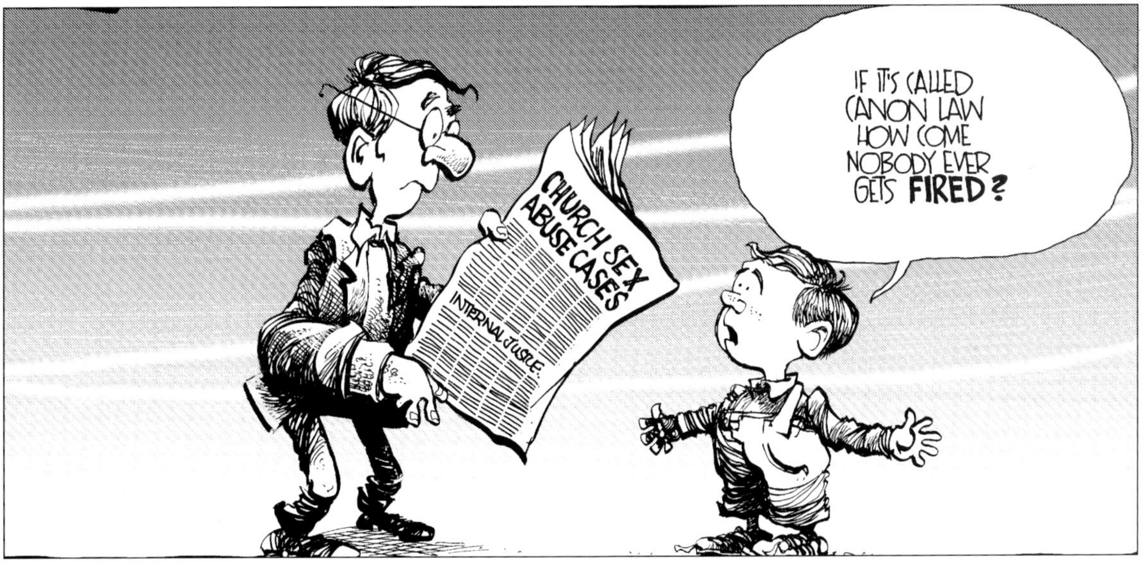
CHURCH SEX ABUSE CASES
INTERNAL JUSTICE
IF IT'S CALLED CANON LAW HOW COME NOBODY EVER GETS FIRED?

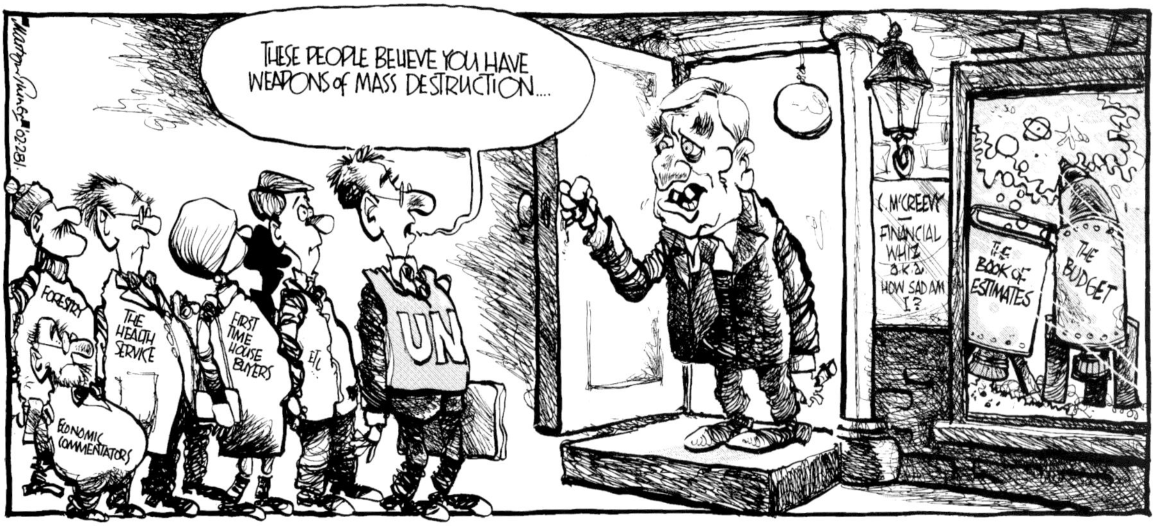
THESE PEOPLE BELIEVE YOU HAVE WEAPONS of MASS DESTRUCTION....
FORESTRY
THE HEALTH SERVICE
FIRST TIME HOUSE BUYERS
ETC
UN
ECONOMIC COMMENTATORS
C. M^cCREEVY — FINANCIAL WHIZ a.k.a. HOW SAD AM I?
THE BOOK OF ESTIMATES
THE BUDGET

MORIARTY
ESAT MODULE
Martyn Turner 02.2.95

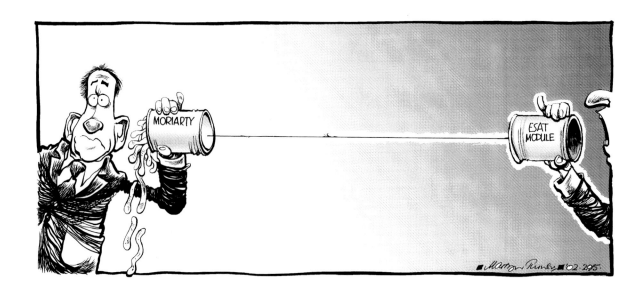

The Environment

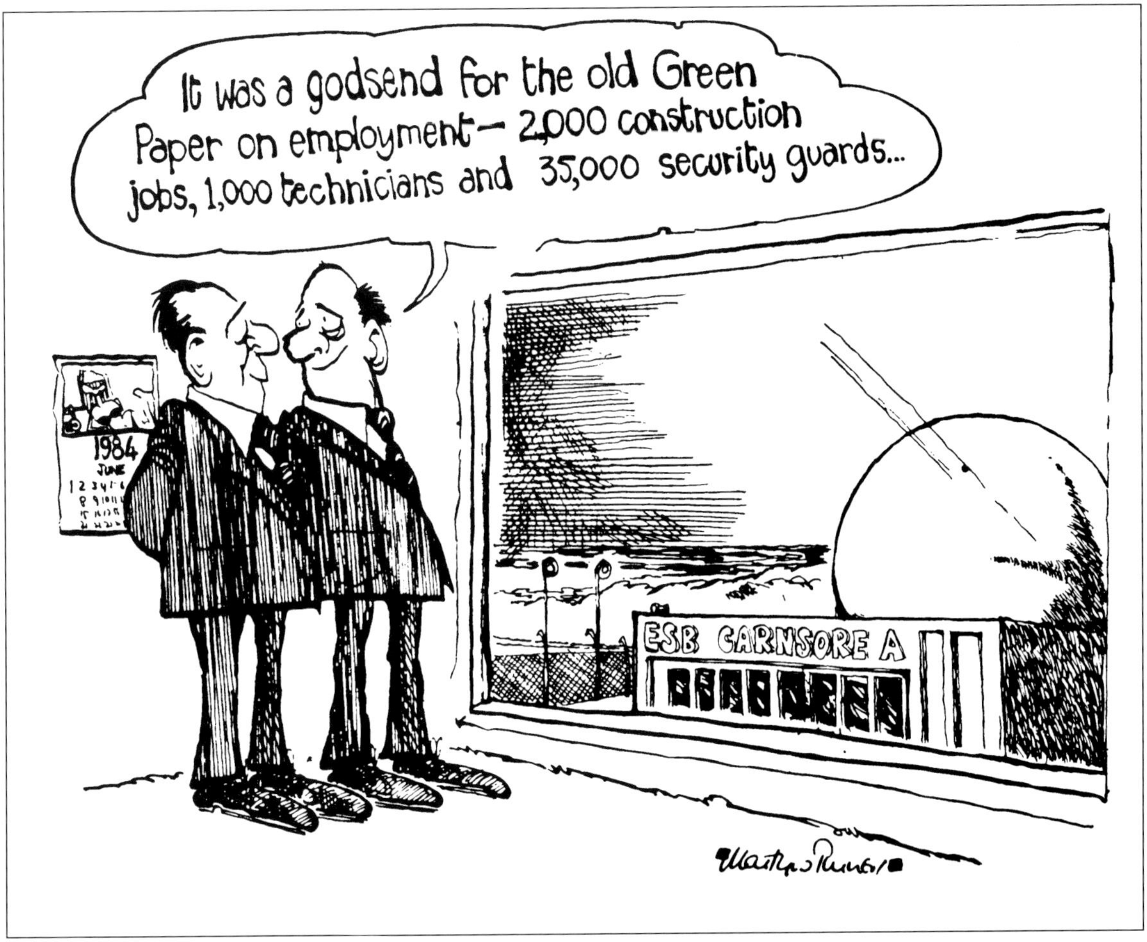
It was a godsend for the old Green Paper on employment — 2,000 construction jobs, 1,000 technicians and 35,000 security guards...
1984
JUNE
ESB CARNSORE A

Here are a few cartoons that loosely come under the heading 'environmental'. They are mostly self-explanatory except, perhaps, for younger readers, those concerning Carnsore Point. It may be hard to believe that the political parties who so actively object to Sellafield these days actively intended Ireland to have its very own nuclear power plant back in the early 70s. Carnsore Point. Those of us who objected at the time were given the usual abuse. The Chernobyl and Three Mile Island disasters changed minds that our arguments had not.

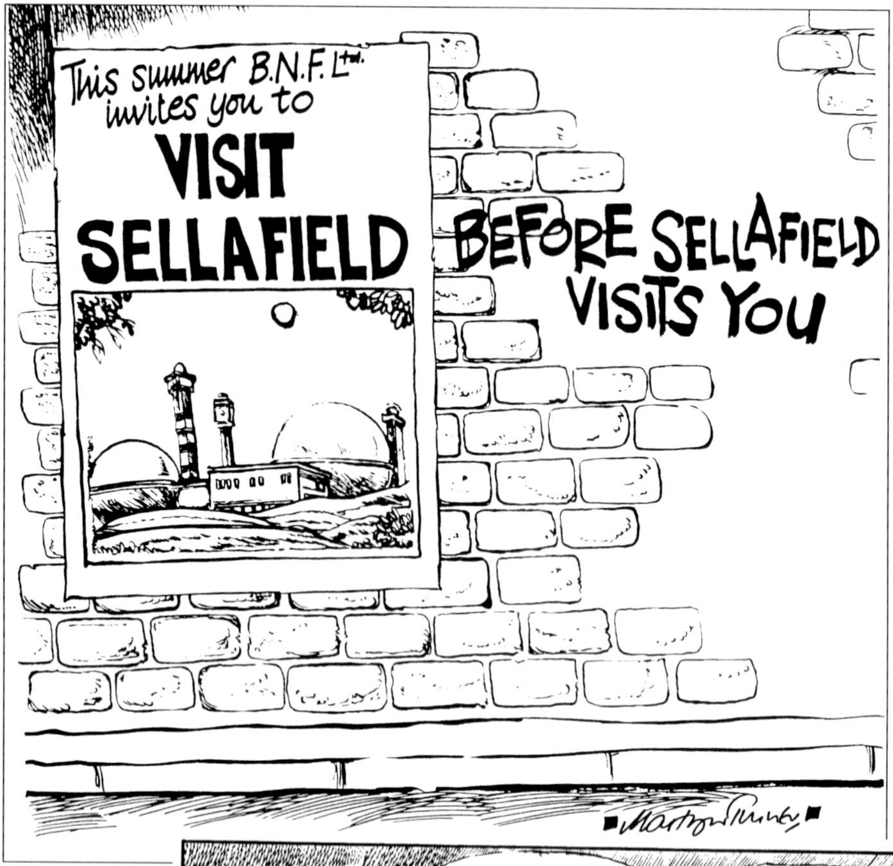
This summer B.N.F. Ltd. invites you to
VISIT SELLAFIELD
BEFORE SELLAFIELD VISITS YOU
Martyn Turner

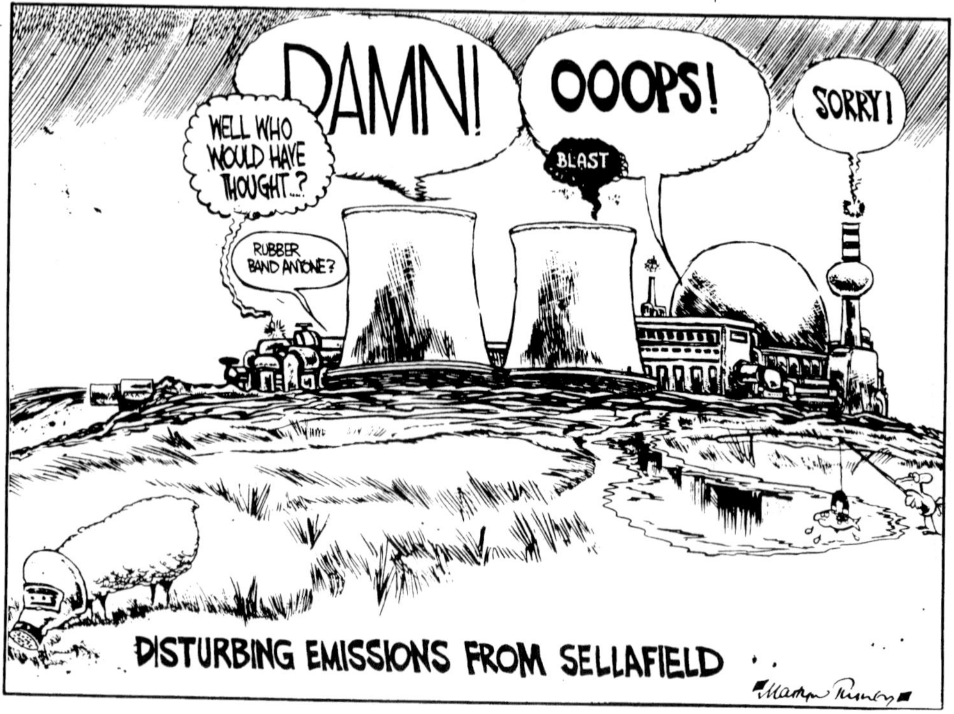
DAMN!
OOOPS!
SORRY!
WELL WHO WOULD HAVE THOUGHT..?
BLAST
RUBBER BAND ANYONE?
DISTURBING EMISSIONS FROM SELLAFIELD
Martyn Turner

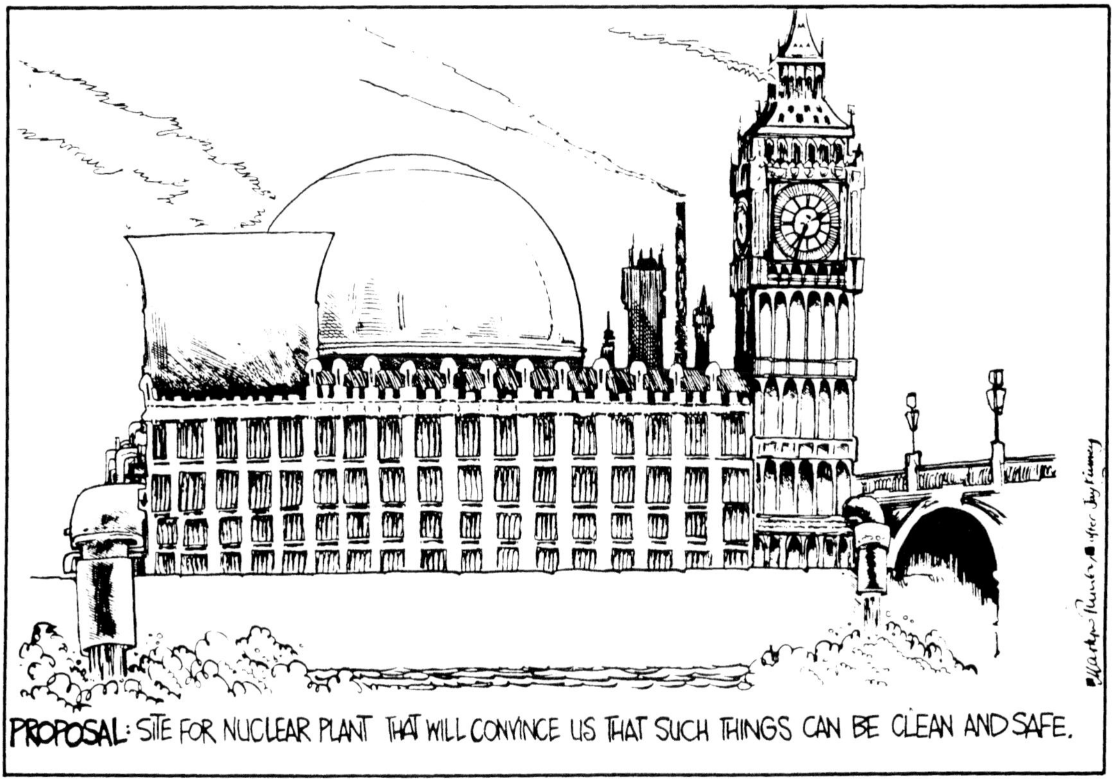
PROPOSAL: SITE FOR NUCLEAR PLANT THAT WILL CONVINCE US THAT SUCH THINGS CAN BE CLEAN AND SAFE.

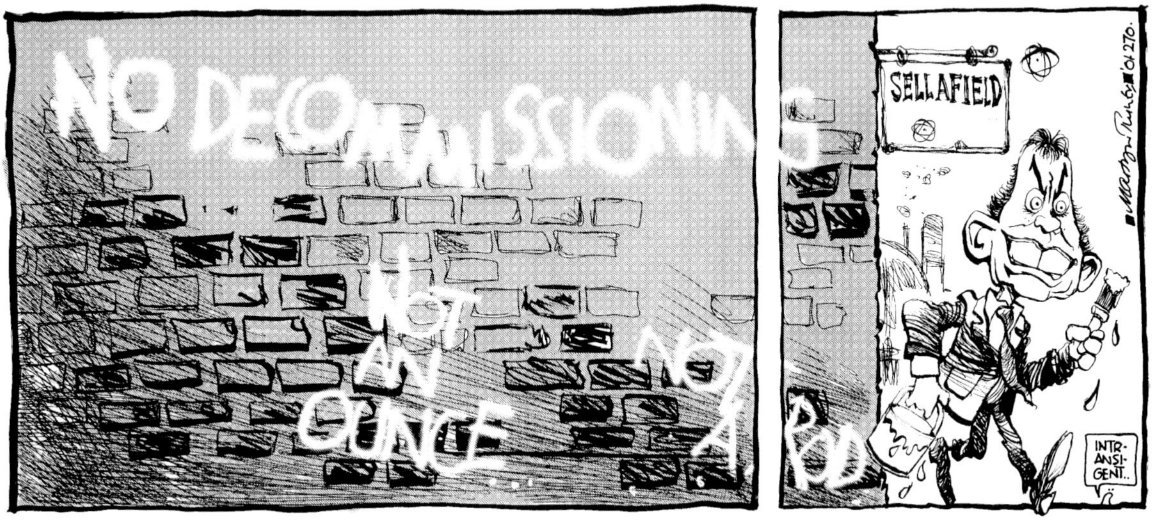
NO DECOMMISSIONING
NOT AN OUNCE
NOT A ROD
SELLAFIELD
INTRANSIGENT..

WE'RE NOT IRRESPONSIBLE.. IN THE CURRENT CIRCUMSTANCES WE WILL RING THE SITE WITH SECURITY
SELLAFIELD
MOX
VOX
TOXIC
OOOOPS!
AERIAL VIEW
TAKE AIM...

SELLAFIELD IS COMPLAINING BECAUSE THEY ARE DIRECTLY DOWNWIND FROM OUR TOXIC ILLEGAL DUMPS.....
HOSPITAL WASTE

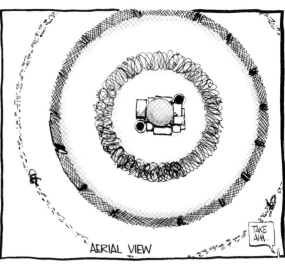

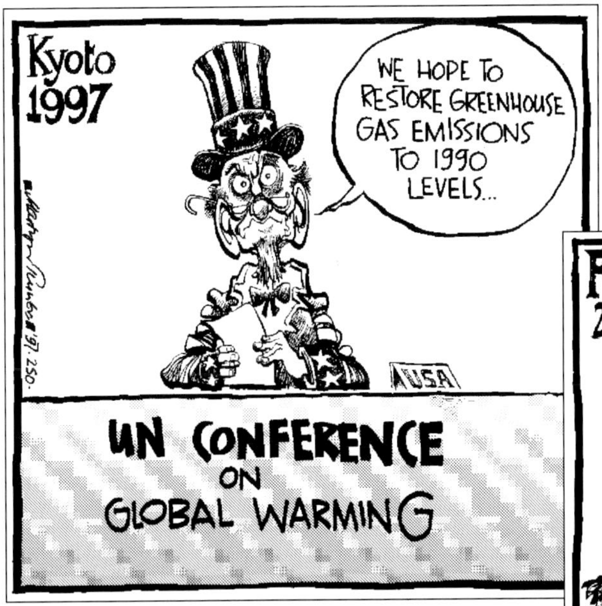
Kyoto
1997
WE HOPE TO RESTORE GREENHOUSE GAS EMISSIONS TO 1990 LEVELS...
USA
UN CONFERENCE ON GLOBAL WARMING

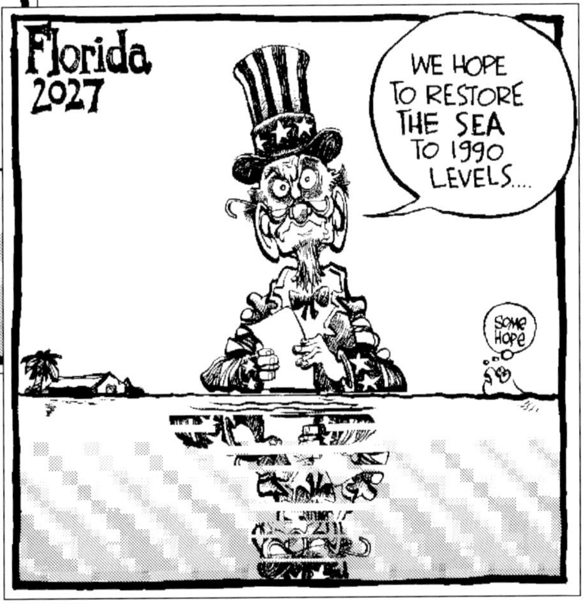
Florida
2027
WE HOPE TO RESTORE THE SEA TO 1990 LEVELS....
SOME HOPE

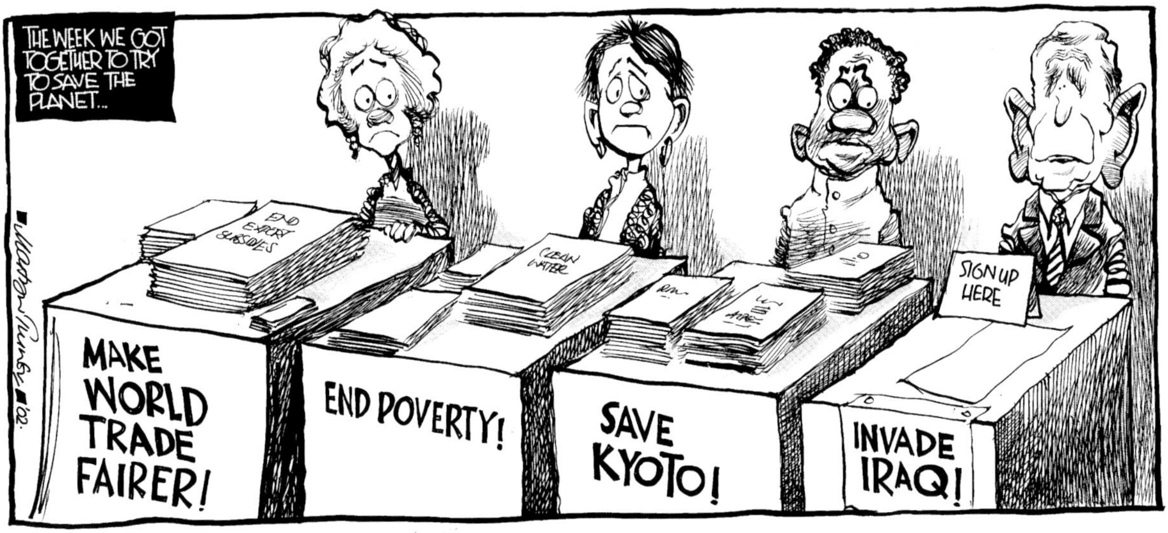
THE WEEK WE GOT TOGETHER TO TRY TO SAVE THE PLANET...
END EXPORT SUBSIDIES
SIGN UP HERE
MAKE WORLD TRADE FAIRER!
END POVERTY!
SAVE KYOTO!
INVADE IRAQ!

Proposed tree design for next time someone decides to create a rain forest...
THIS WAY UP
Martyn Turner

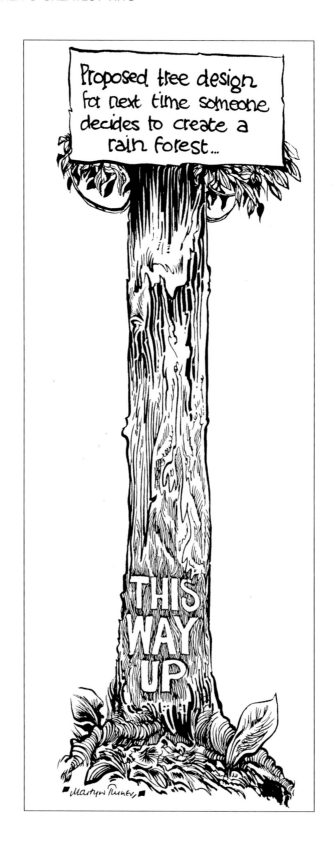

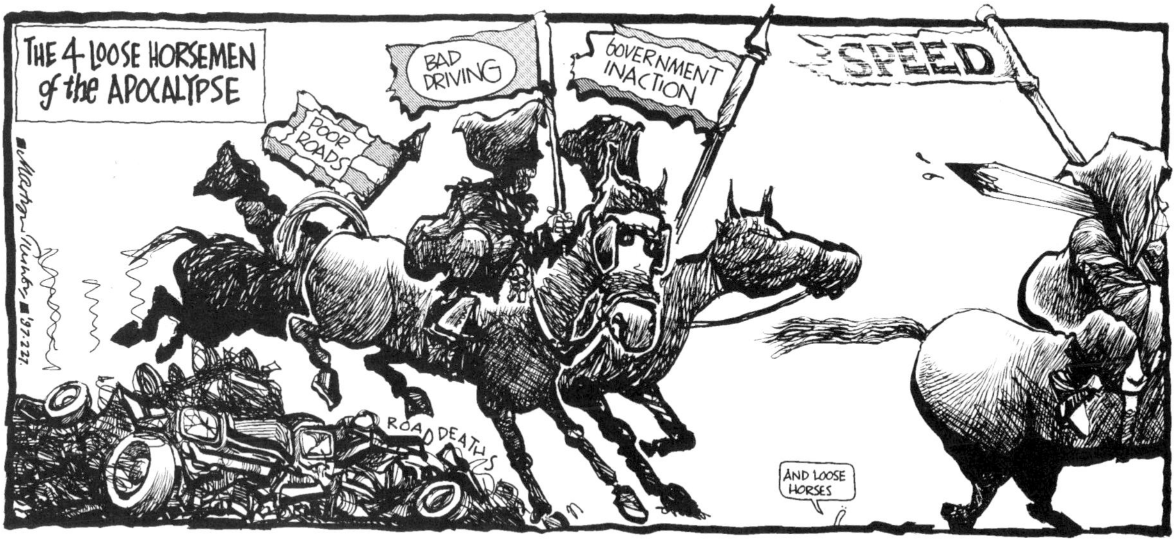
THE 4 LOOSE HORSEMEN of the APOCALYPSE
POOR ROADS
BAD DRIVING
GOVERNMENT INACTION
SPEED
ROAD DEATHS
AND LOOSE HORSES

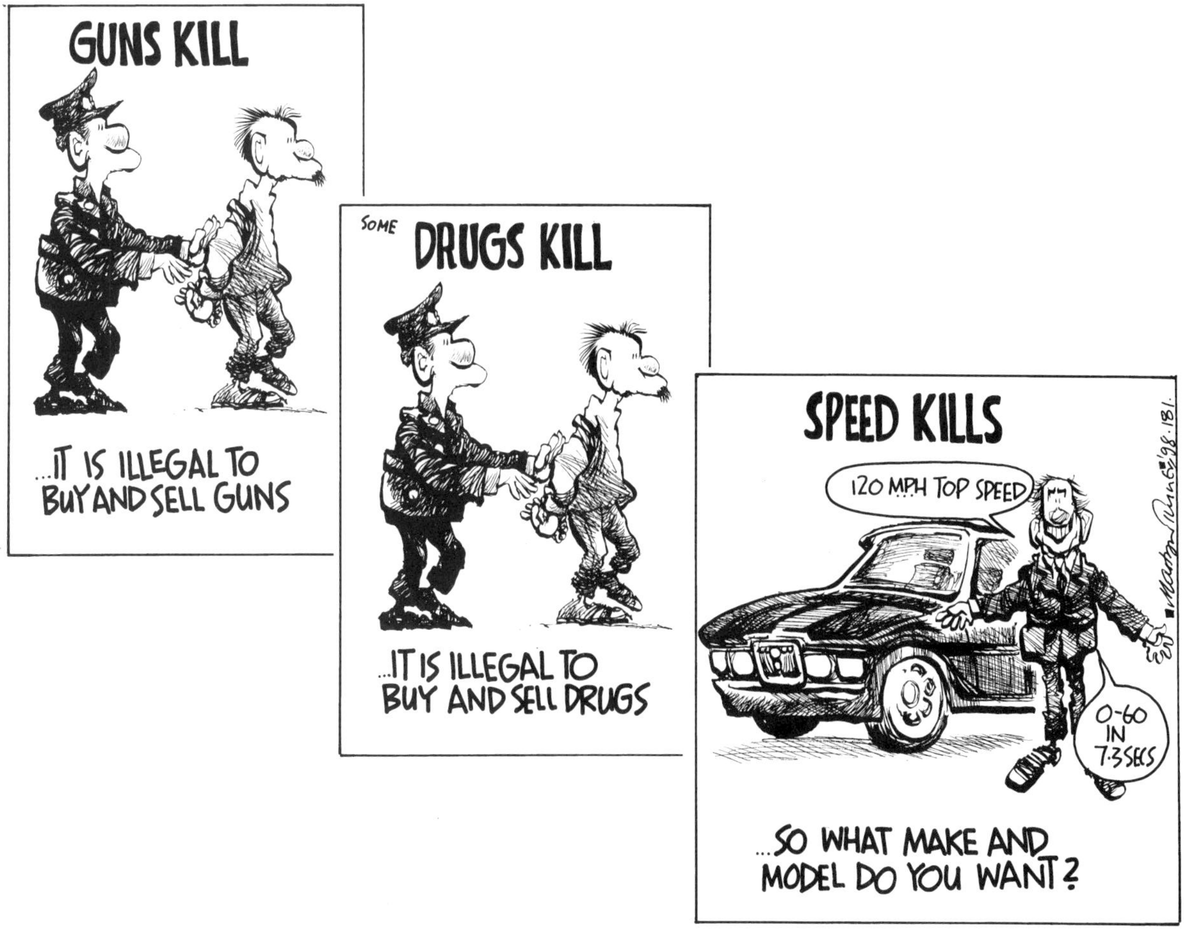
GUNS KILL
...IT IS ILLEGAL TO BUY AND SELL GUNS
SOME DRUGS KILL
...IT IS ILLEGAL TO BUY AND SELL DRUGS
SPEED KILLS
120 MPH TOP SPEED
0-60 IN 7.3 SECS
...SO WHAT MAKE AND MODEL DO YOU WANT?

IRELAND
UNACCOMPANIED LEARNERS, DRUNKS, THE YOUNG AND THE TOO QUICK.....
Martyn Turner '00.162.

YOU WERE DOING A HUNDRED MILES AN HOUR !!! EXPLAIN YOURSELF..
I WAS TRYING TO CATCH UP WITH THE MINISTER'S CAR TO DISCUSS ROAD SAFETY WITH HIM.....
Martyn Turner '00.141.

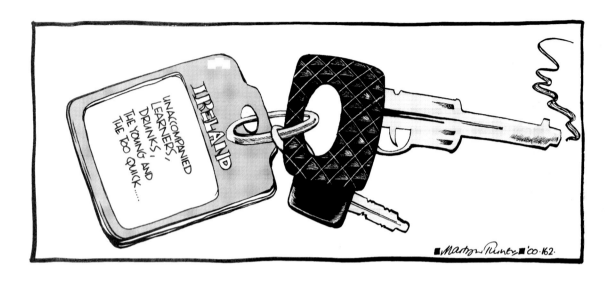

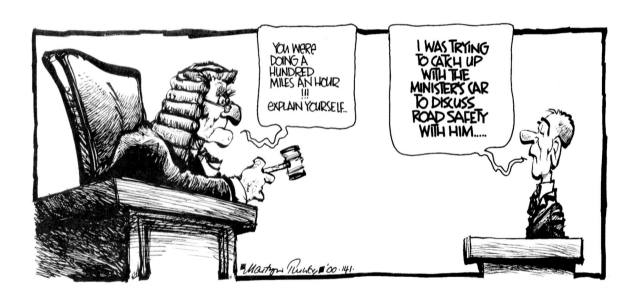

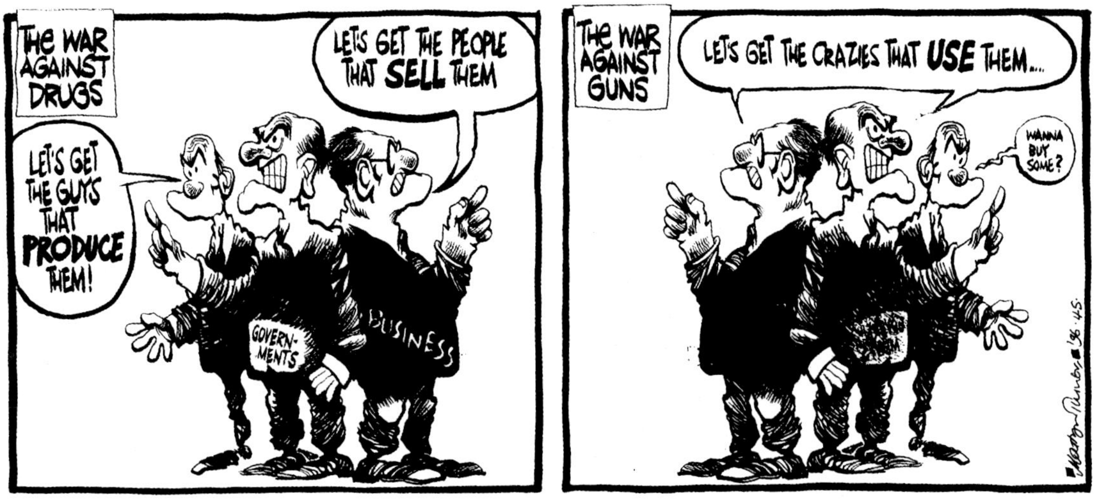
THE WAR AGAINST DRUGS
LET'S GET THE GUYS THAT PRODUCE THEM!
LET'S GET THE PEOPLE THAT SELL THEM
GOVERN-MENTS
BUSINESS
THE WAR AGAINST GUNS
LET'S GET THE CRAZIES THAT USE THEM...
WANNA BUY SOME?

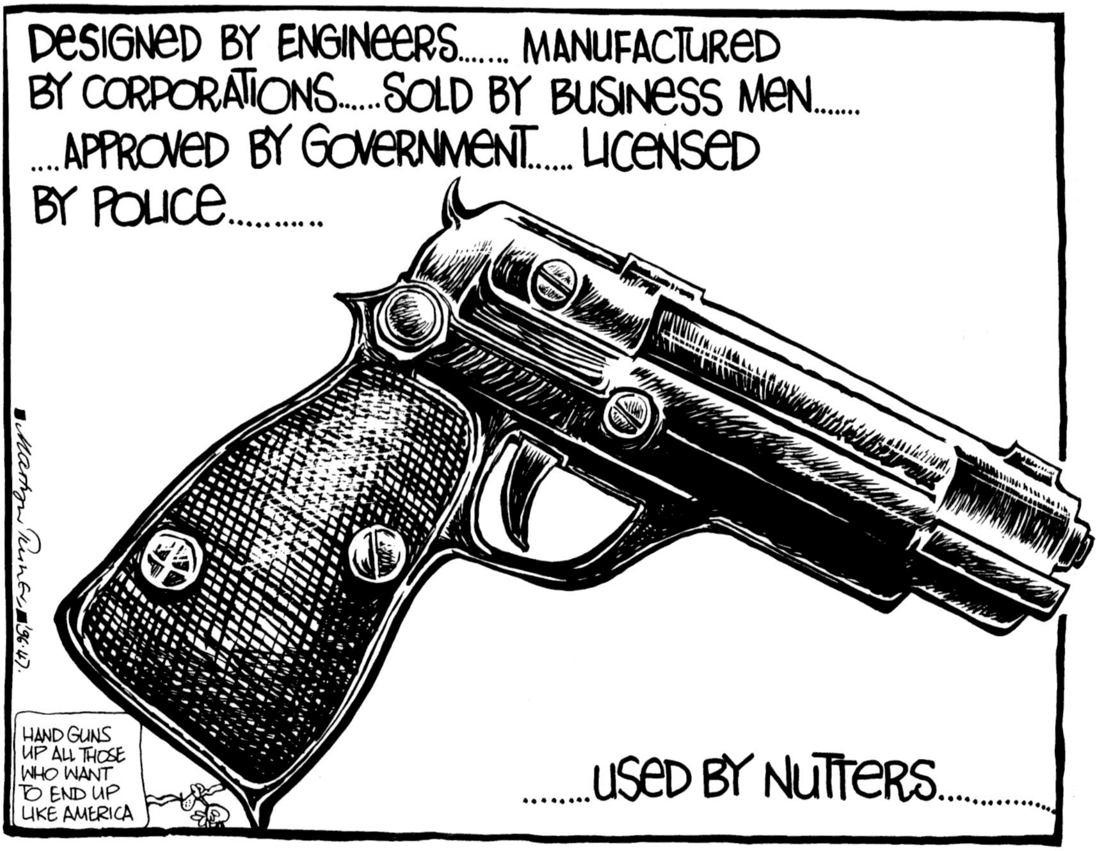
DESIGNED BY ENGINEERS....... MANUFACTURED BY CORPORATIONS......SOLD BY BUSINESS MEN.......
.....APPROVED BY GOVERNMENT...... LICENSED BY POLICE..........
........USED BY NUTTERS................
HAND GUNS UP ALL THOSE WHO WANT TO END UP LIKE AMERICA

The North

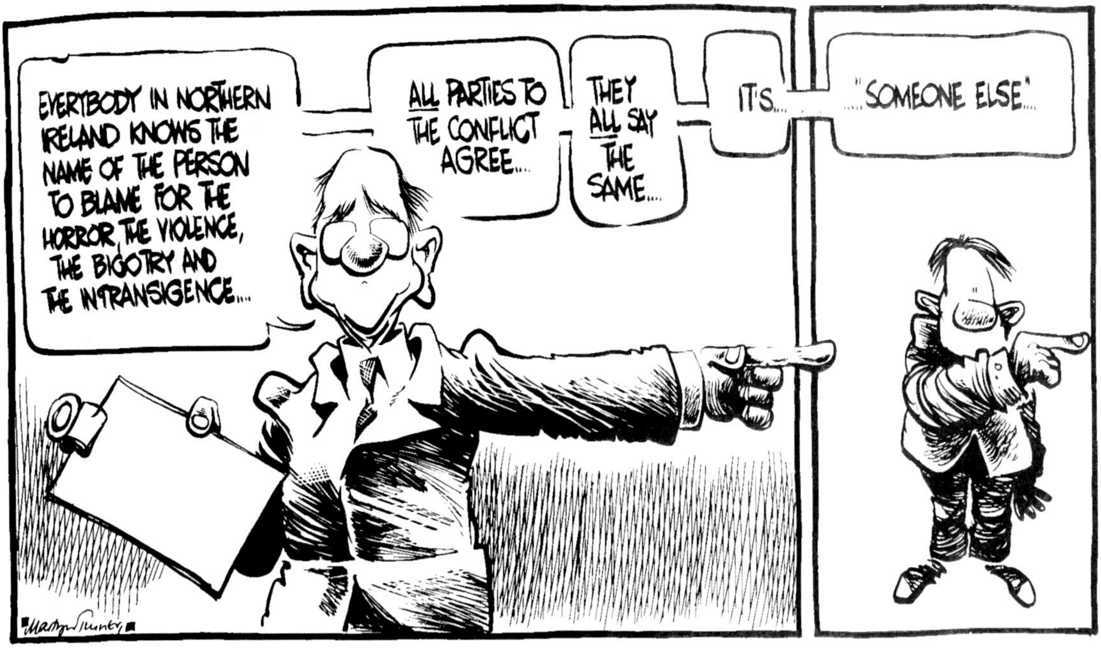
EVERYBODY IN NORTHERN IRELAND KNOWS THE NAME OF THE PERSON TO BLAME FOR THE HORROR, THE VIOLENCE, THE BIGOTRY AND THE INTRANSIGENCE...
ALL PARTIES TO THE CONFLICT AGREE...
THEY ALL SAY THE SAME...
IT'S...
..."SOMEONE ELSE"...
Martyn Turner

This is one section that needs no explanatory text since the same things happen over and over again, ad nauseam, in the North. Even the main actors don't seem to change too much. These are probably all the same cartoon. As I write this in April, whilst George W. Bush is in Hillsborough, we are told this is the most momentous week in the North's politics since the last momentous week. Hopefully, as this book is produced these cartoons can be consigned to history, and the peace process can become just…peace.

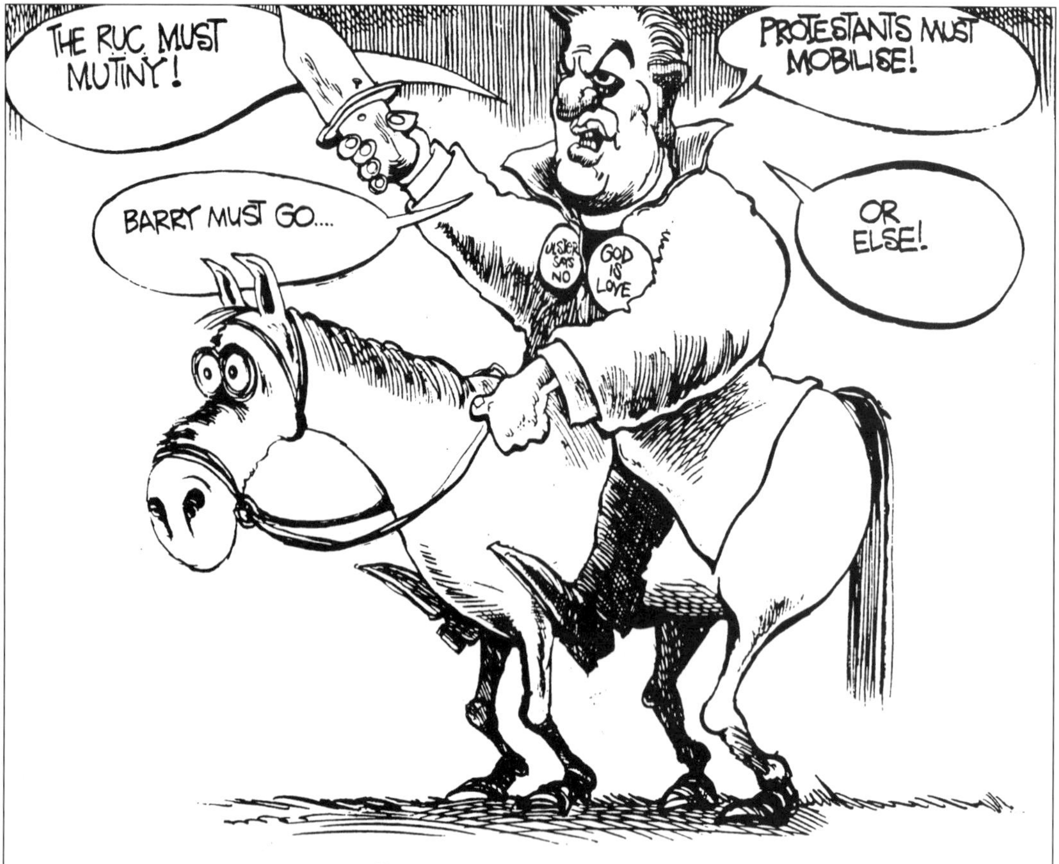
THE RUC MUST MUTINY!
PROTESTANTS MUST MOBILISE!
BARRY MUST GO....
OR ELSE!
ULSTER SAYS NO
GOD IS LOVE

KING BULLY

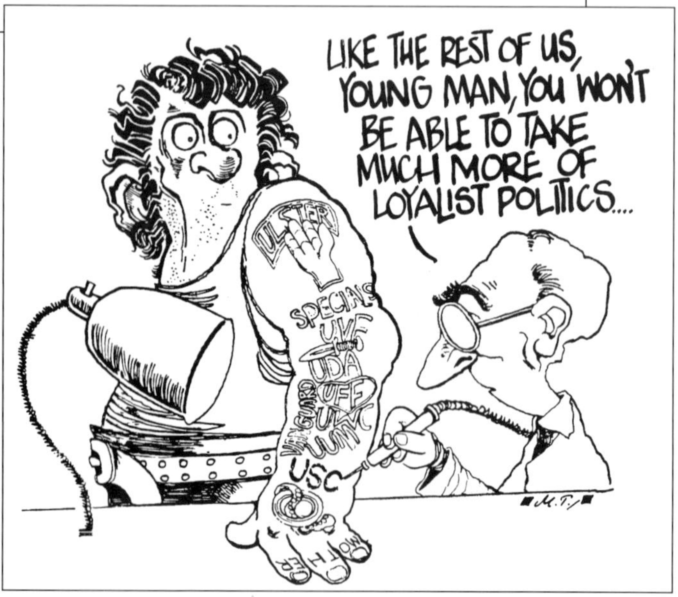
LIKE THE REST OF US, YOUNG MAN, YOU WON'T BE ABLE TO TAKE MUCH MORE OF LOYALIST POLITICS....
ULSTER
SPECIALS
UVF
UDA
UFF
VANGUARD
USC
MOTHER

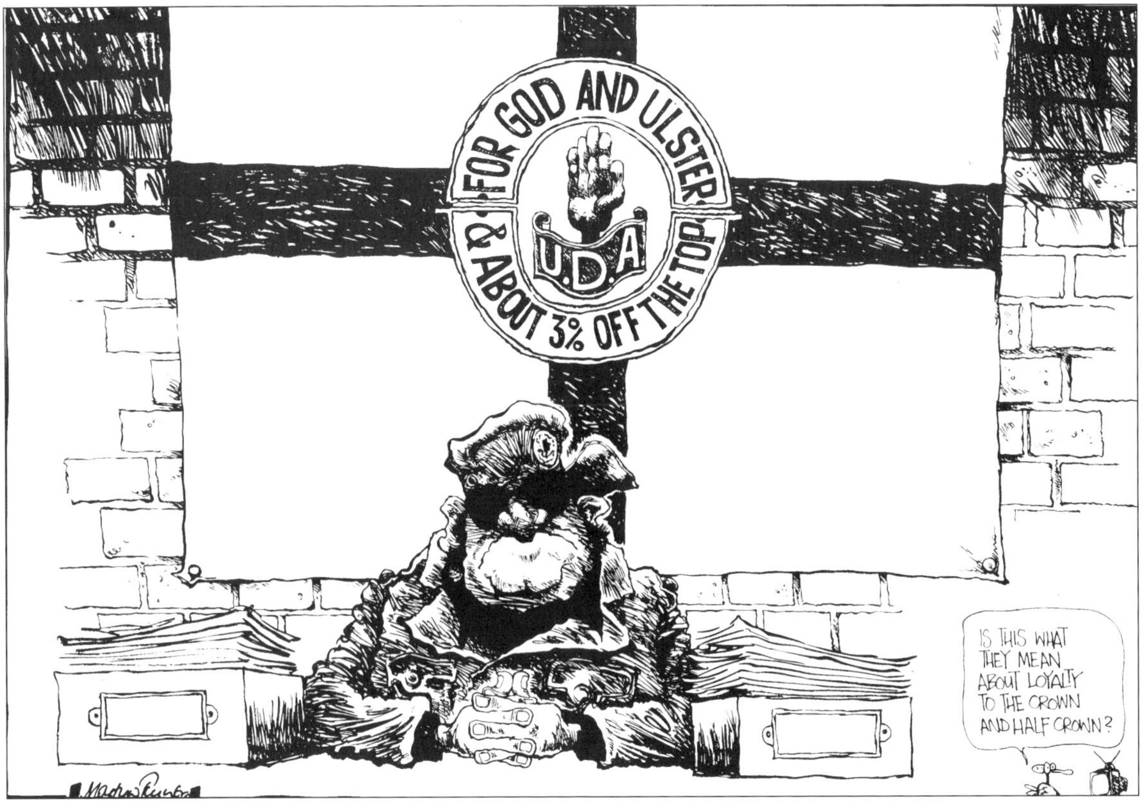
FOR GOD AND ULSTER & ABOUT 3% OFF THE TOP
U.D.A
IS THIS WHAT THEY MEAN ABOUT LOYALTY TO THE CROWN AND HALF CROWN?

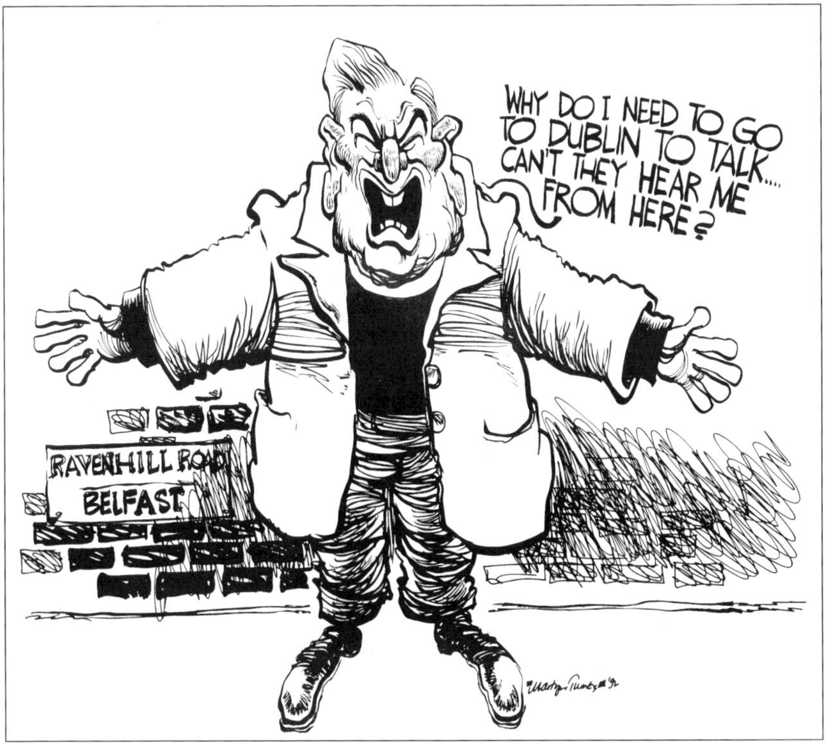
WHY DO I NEED TO GO TO DUBLIN TO TALK.... CAN'T THEY HEAR ME FROM HERE?
RAVENHILL ROAD
BELFAST

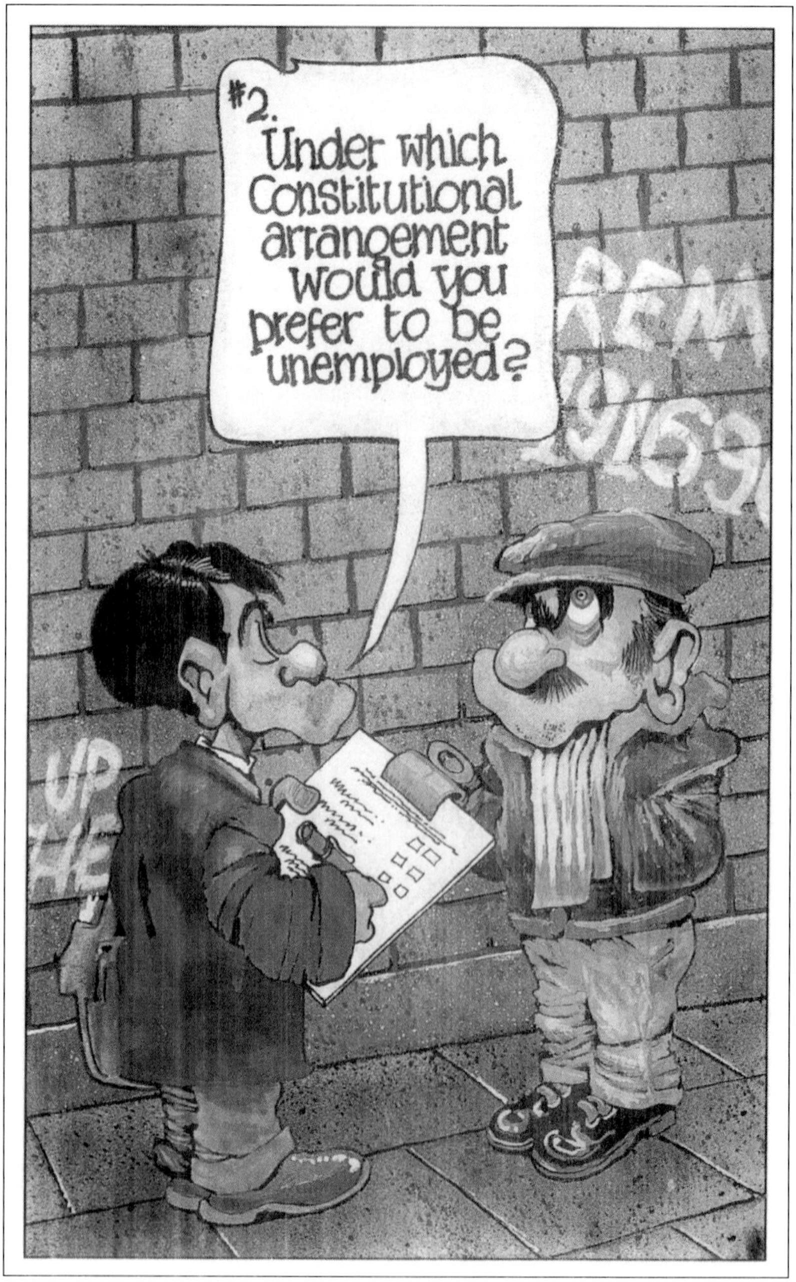
#2. Under which Constitutional arrangement would you prefer to be unemployed?
UP

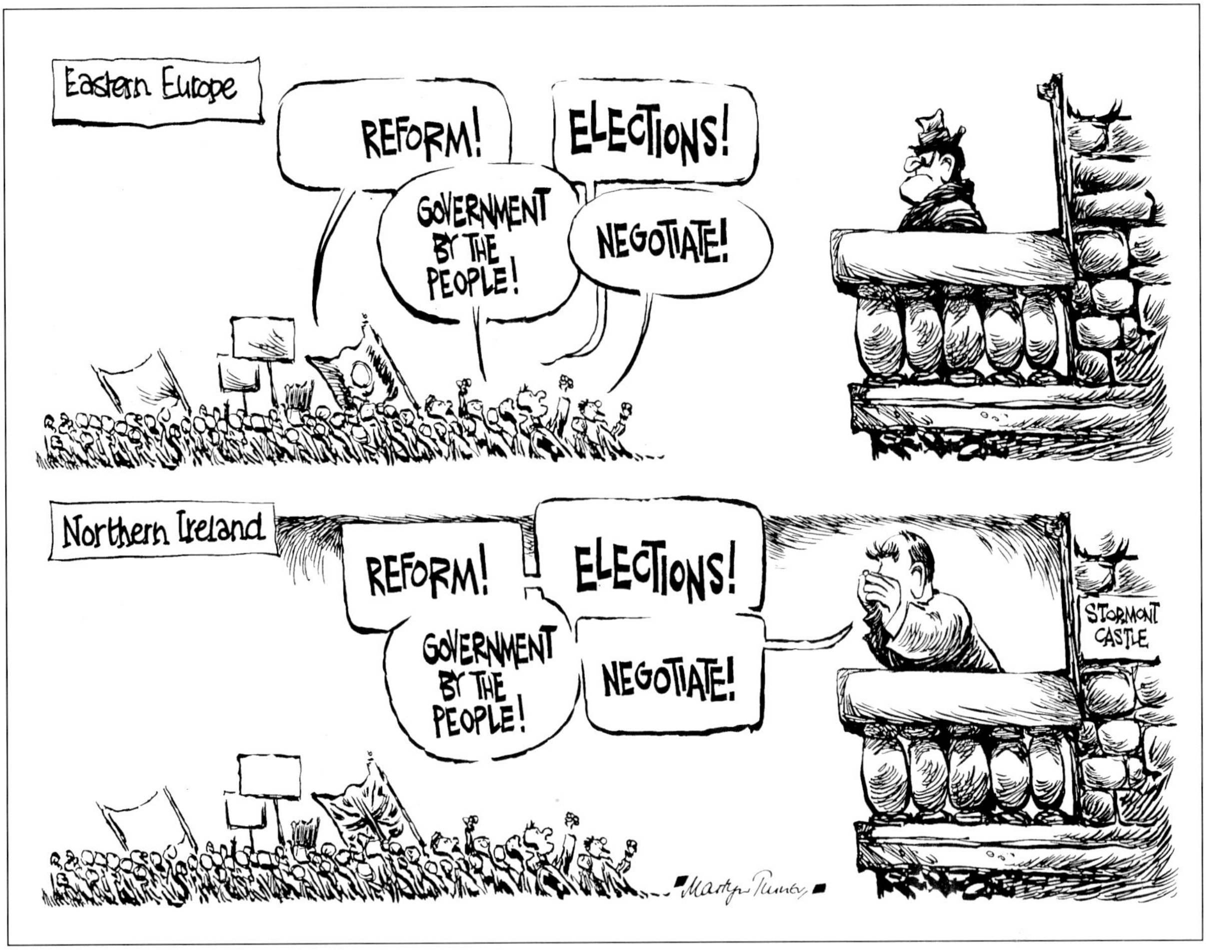
Eastern Europe
REFORM!
ELECTIONS!
GOVERNMENT BY THE PEOPLE!
NEGOTIATE!
Northern Ireland
REFORM!
ELECTIONS!
GOVERNMENT BY THE PEOPLE!
NEGOTIATE!
STORMONT CASTLE

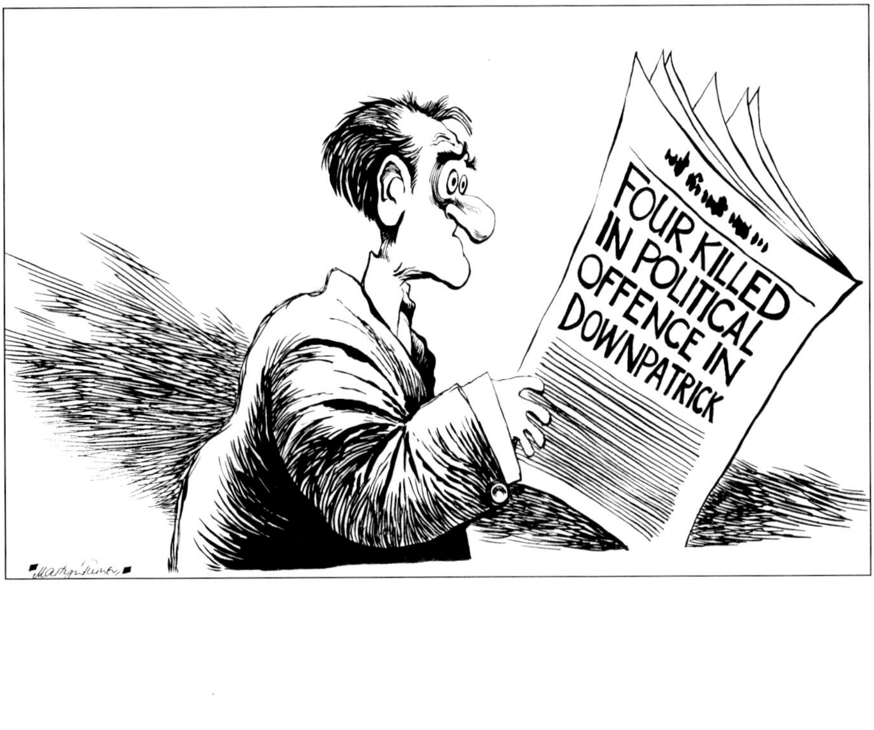
FOUR KILLED IN POLITICAL OFFENCE IN DOWNPATRICK

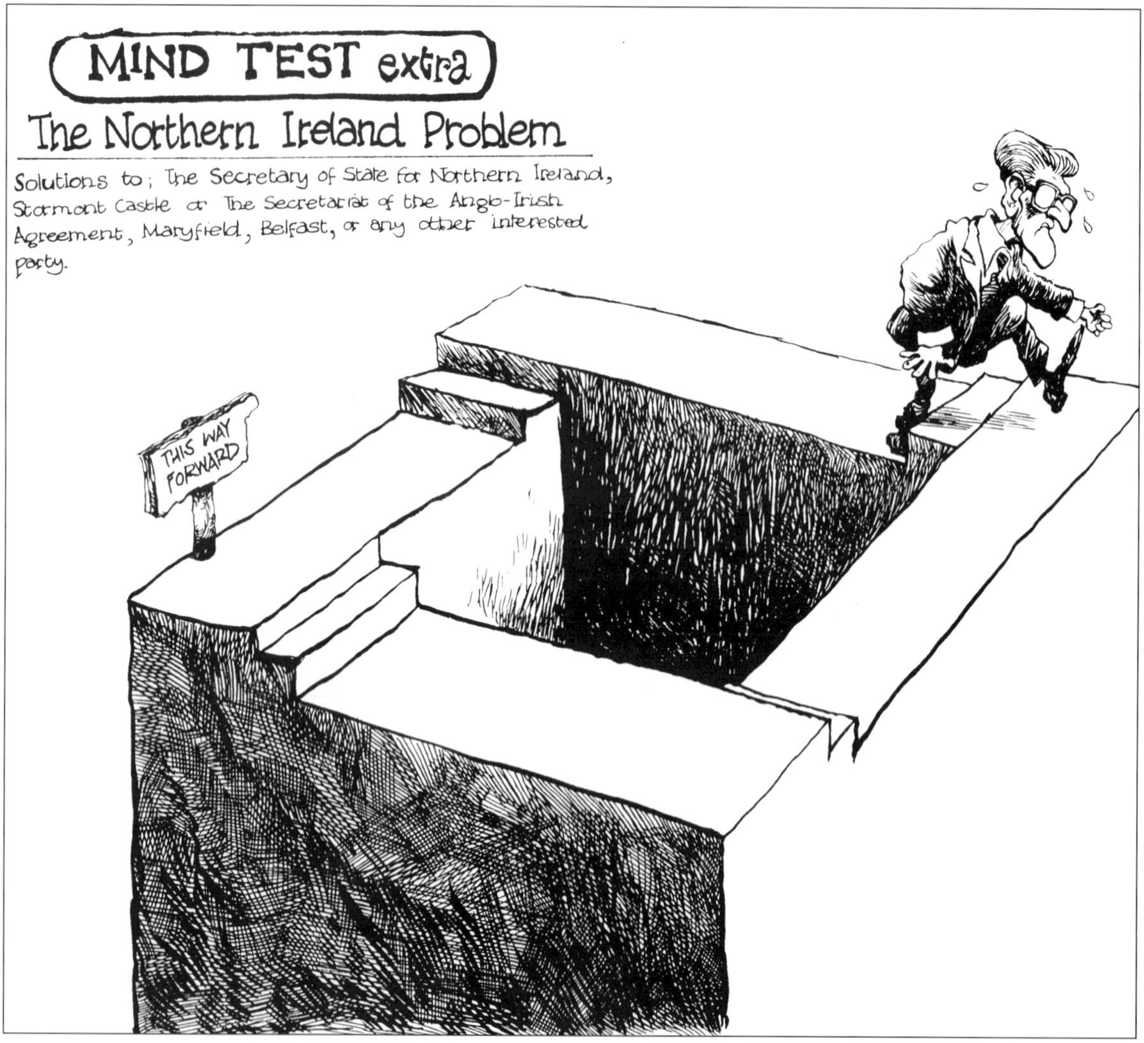
MIND TEST extra
The Northern Ireland Problem
Solutions to; The Secretary of State for Northern Ireland, Stormont Castle or The Secretariat of the Anglo-Irish Agreement, Maryfield, Belfast, or any other interested party.
THIS WAY FORWARD

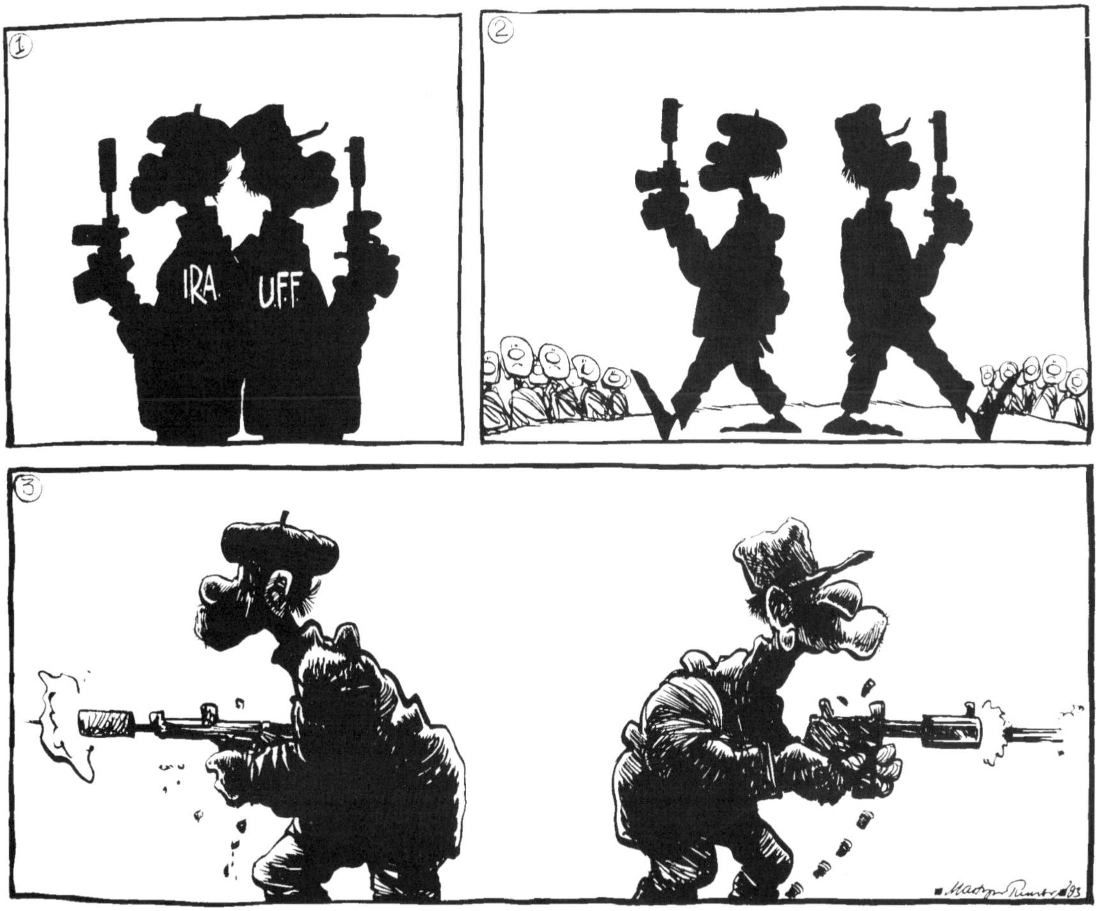
1
IRA.
U.F.F.
2
3

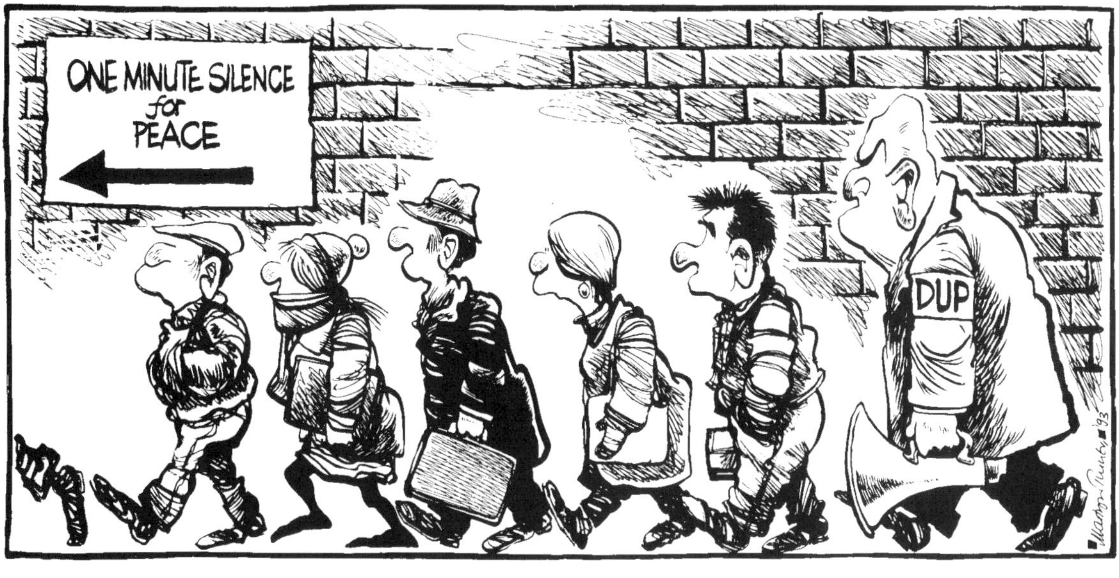
ONE MINUTE SILENCE for PEACE
DUP

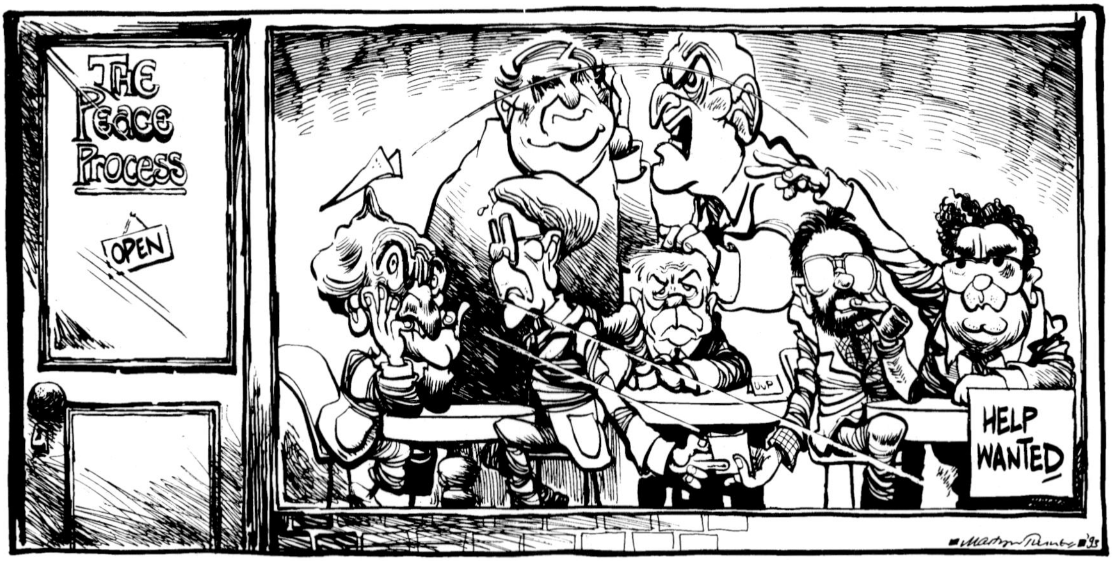
THE Peace Process
OPEN
DUP
HELP WANTED

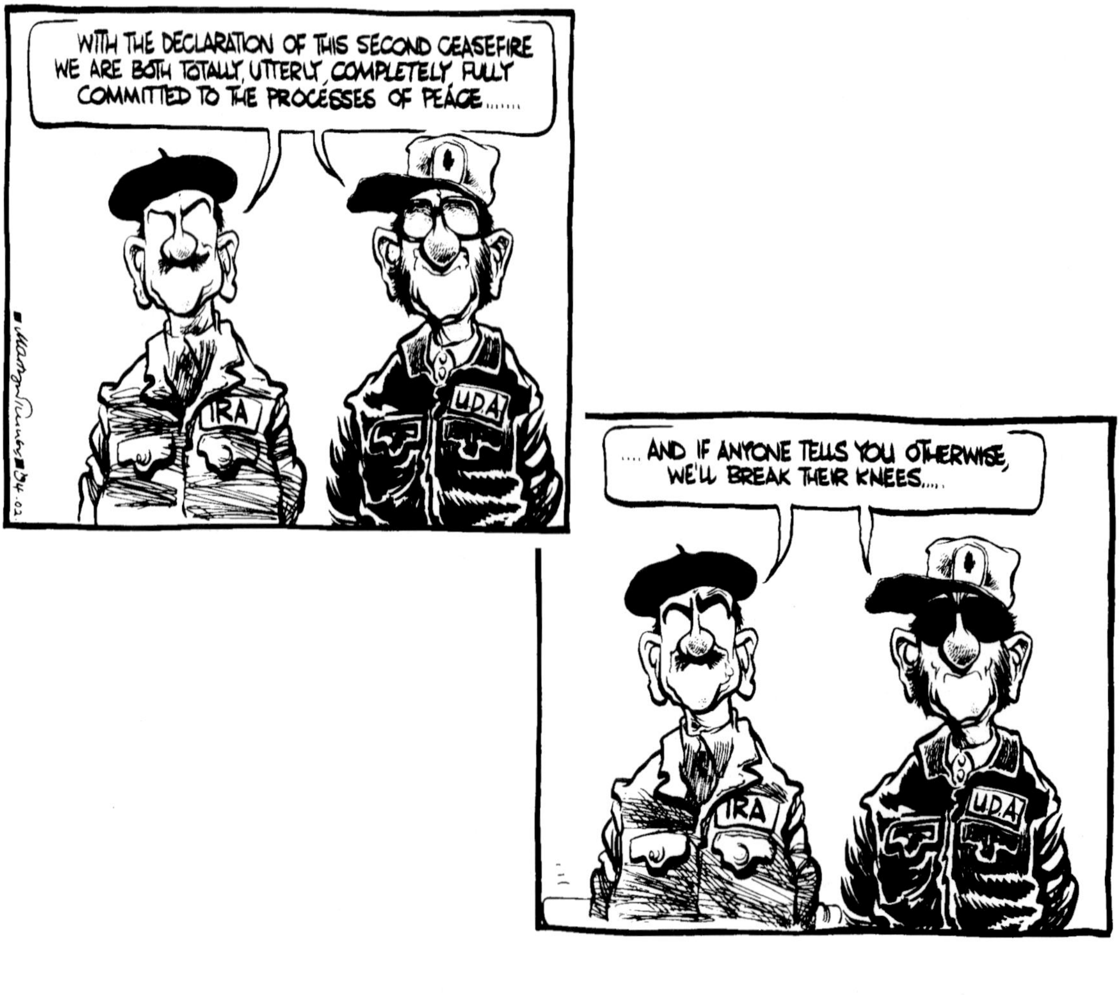
WITH THE DECLARATION OF THIS SECOND CEASEFIRE WE ARE BOTH TOTALLY, UTTERLY, COMPLETELY, FULLY COMMITTED TO THE PROCESSES OF PEACE.......
IRA
UDA
.... AND IF ANYONE TELLS YOU OTHERWISE, WE'LL BREAK THEIR KNEES.....
IRA
UDA

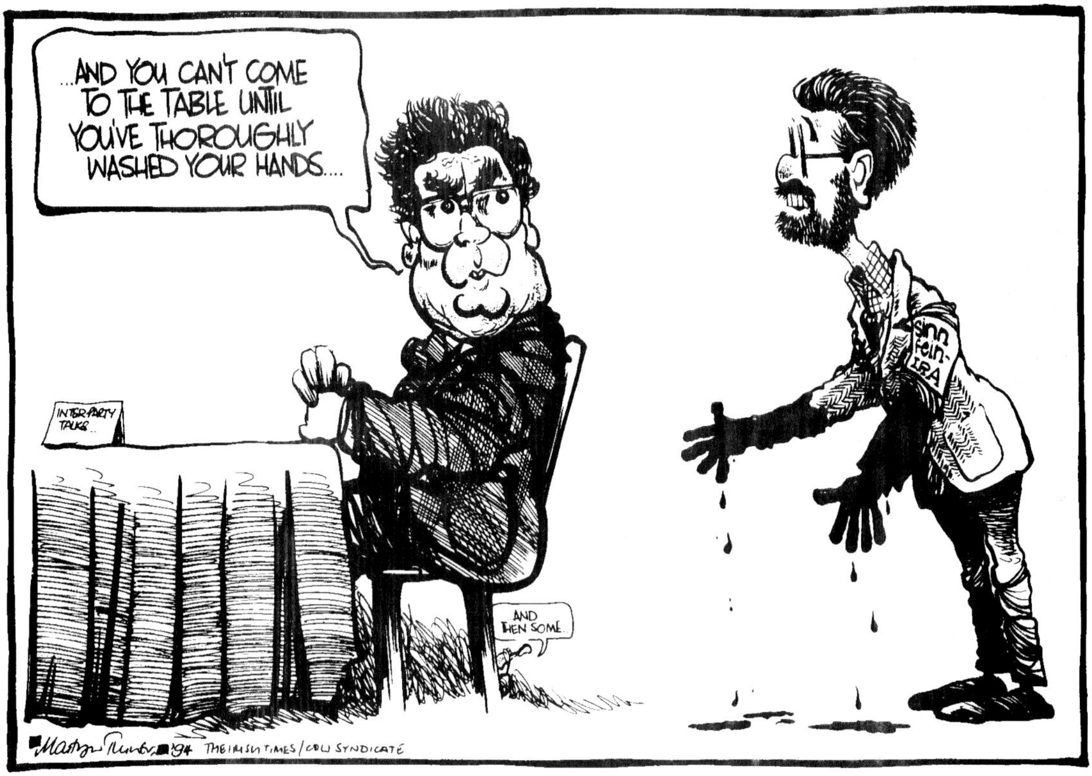
...AND YOU CAN'T COME TO THE TABLE UNTIL YOU'VE THOROUGHLY WASHED YOUR HANDS....
INTER-PARTY TALKS...
Sinn Fein-IRA
AND THEN SOME.
Martyn Turner '94
THE IRISH TIMES/CWS SYNDICATE

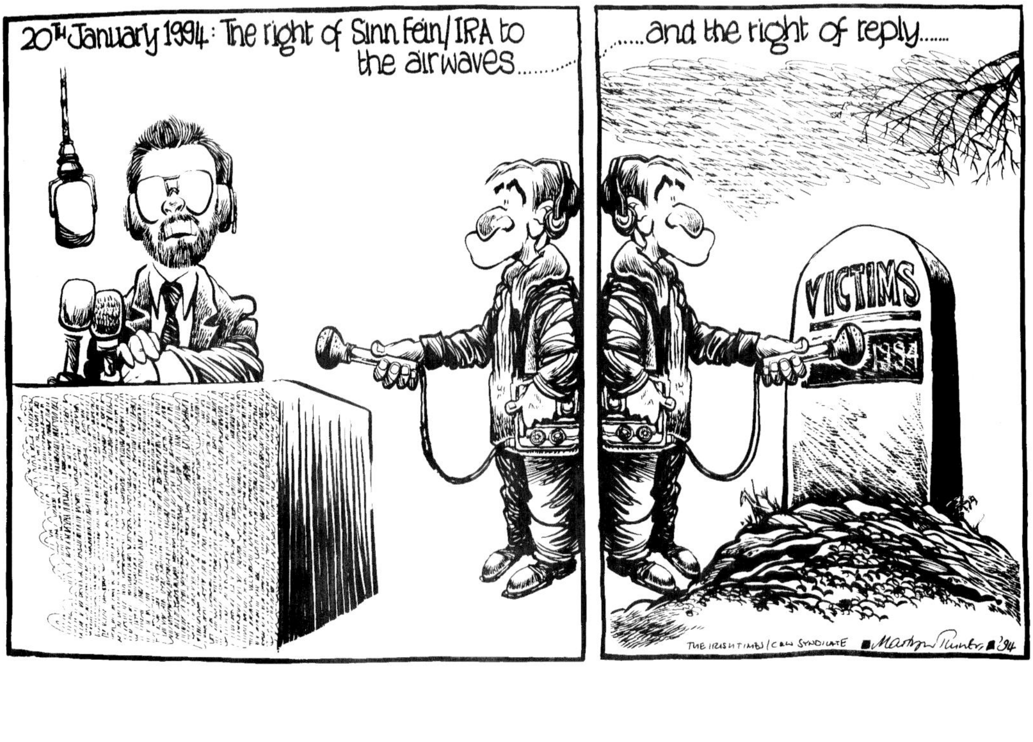
20TH January 1994: The right of Sinn Fein/IRA to the airwaves........
......and the right of reply.......
VICTIMS
1994
THE IRISH TIMES/CWS SYNDICATE
Martyn Turner '94

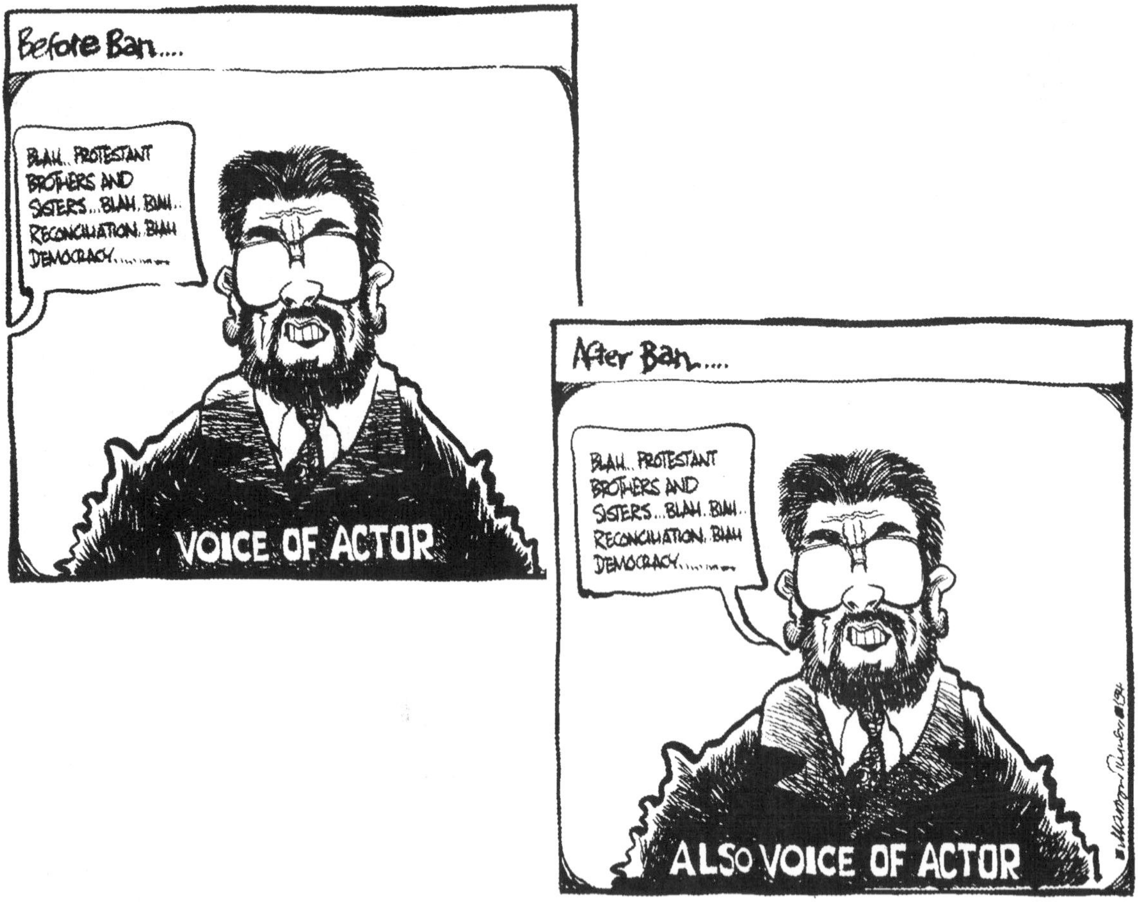
Before Ban....
BLAH... PROTESTANT BROTHERS AND SISTERS... BLAH, BLAH... RECONCILIATION, BLAH DEMOCRACY......
VOICE OF ACTOR
After Ban....
BLAH... PROTESTANT BROTHERS AND SISTERS... BLAH, BLAH... RECONCILIATION, BLAH DEMOCRACY......
ALSO VOICE OF ACTOR

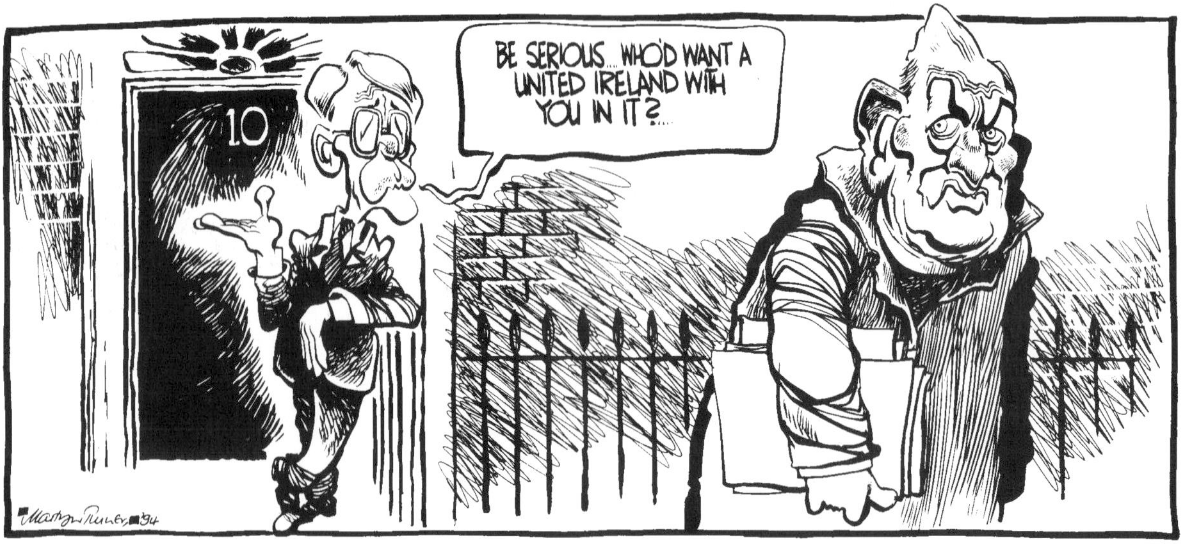
10
BE SERIOUS... WHO'D WANT A UNITED IRELAND WITH YOU IN IT?...

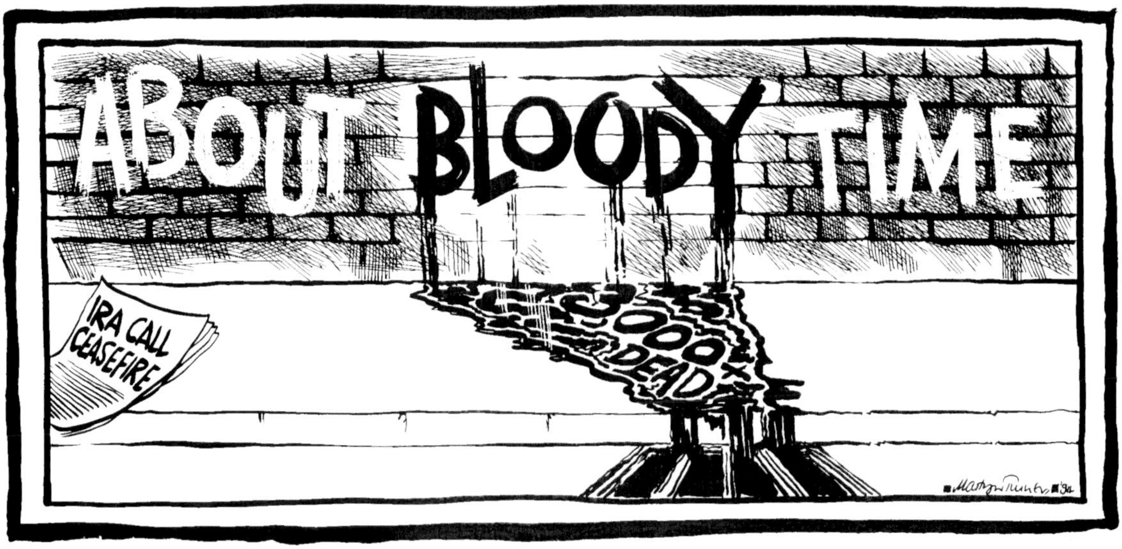
ABOUT BLOODY TIME
IRA CALL CEASEFIRE
3000+ DEAD

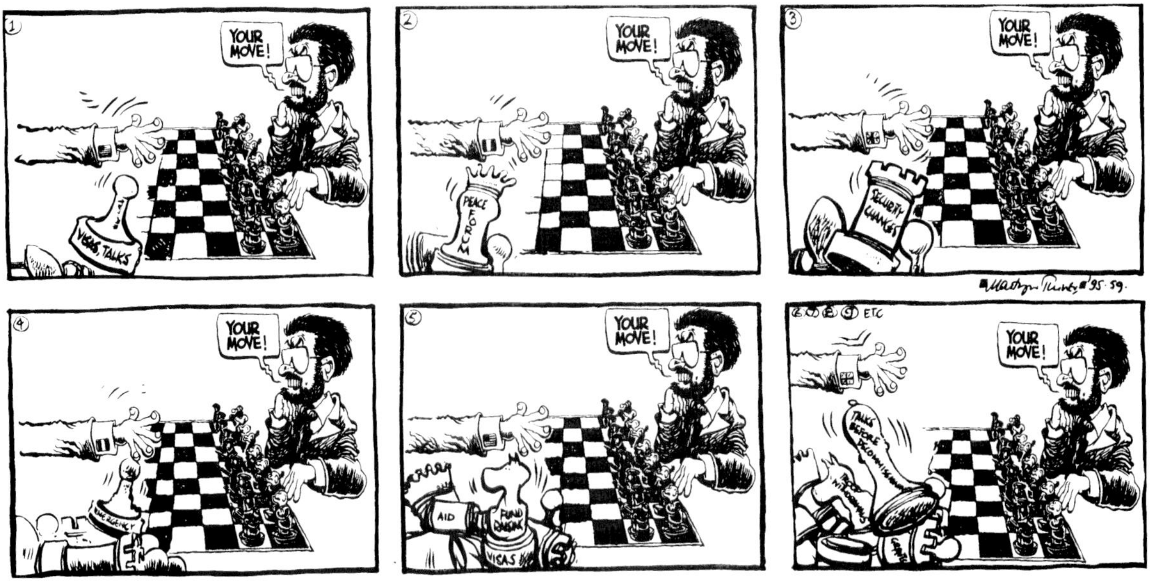
1
YOUR MOVE!
VISAS, TALKS
2
YOUR MOVE!
PEACE FORUM
3
YOUR MOVE!
SECURITY CHANGES
4
YOUR MOVE!
EMERGENCY
5
YOUR MOVE!
AID
FUND RAISING
VISAS
ETC
YOUR MOVE!
TALKS BEFORE DECOMMISSIONING

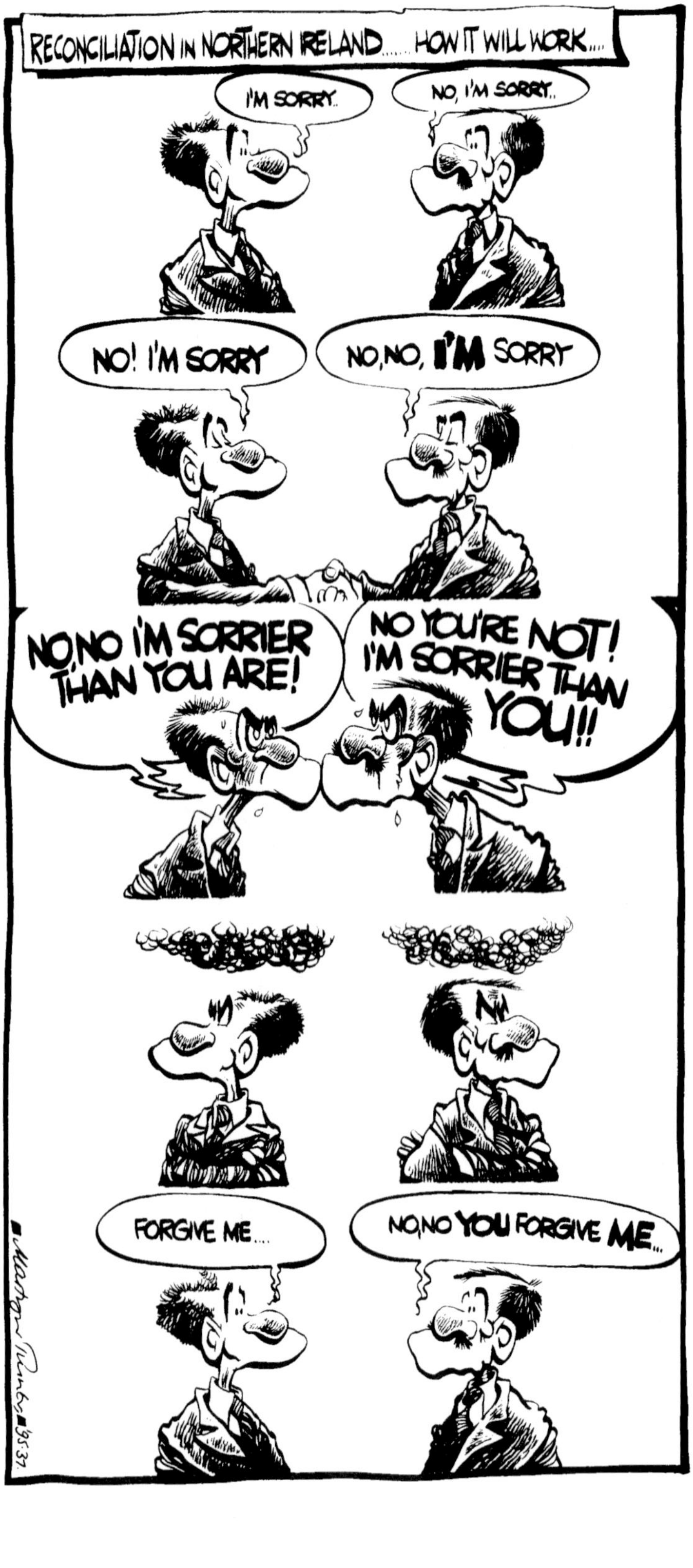
RECONCILIATION IN NORTHERN IRELAND...... HOW IT WILL WORK....
I'M SORRY..
NO, I'M SORRY..
NO! I'M SORRY
NO,NO, I'M SORRY
NO,NO I'M SORRIER THAN YOU ARE!
NO YOU'RE NOT! I'M SORRIER THAN YOU!!
FORGIVE ME....
NO,NO YOU FORGIVE ME...

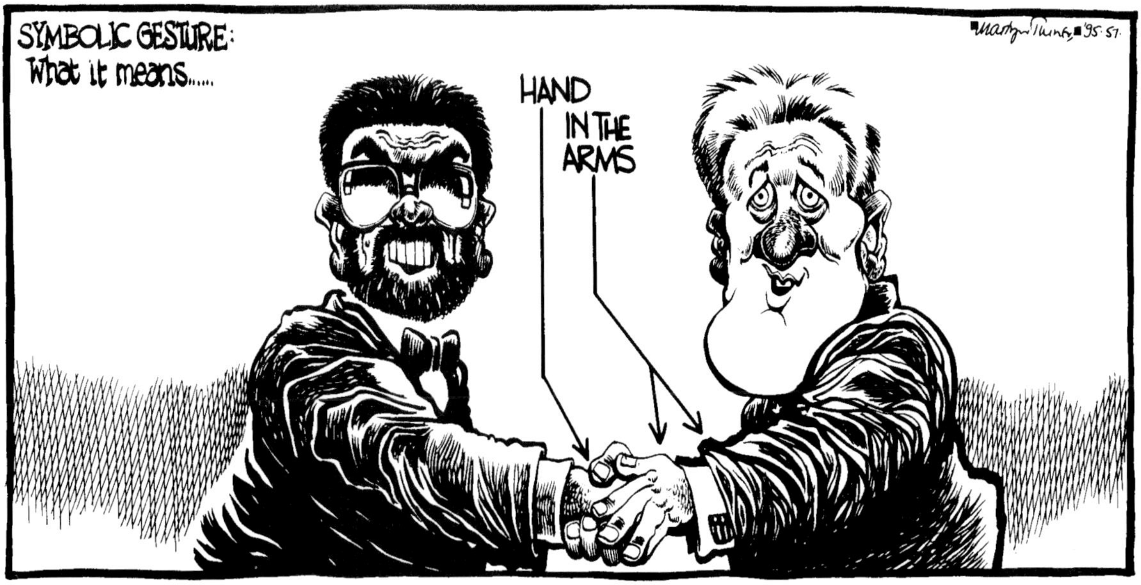
SYMBOLIC GESTURE:
What it means.....
HAND
IN THE
ARMS

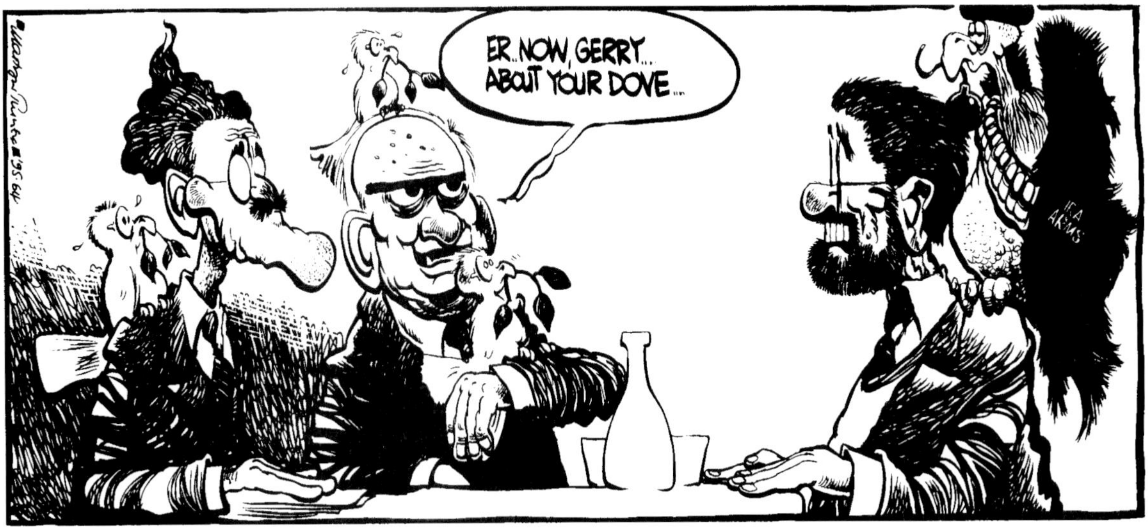
ER..NOW, GERRY...
ABOUT YOUR DOVE...
IRA
ARMS

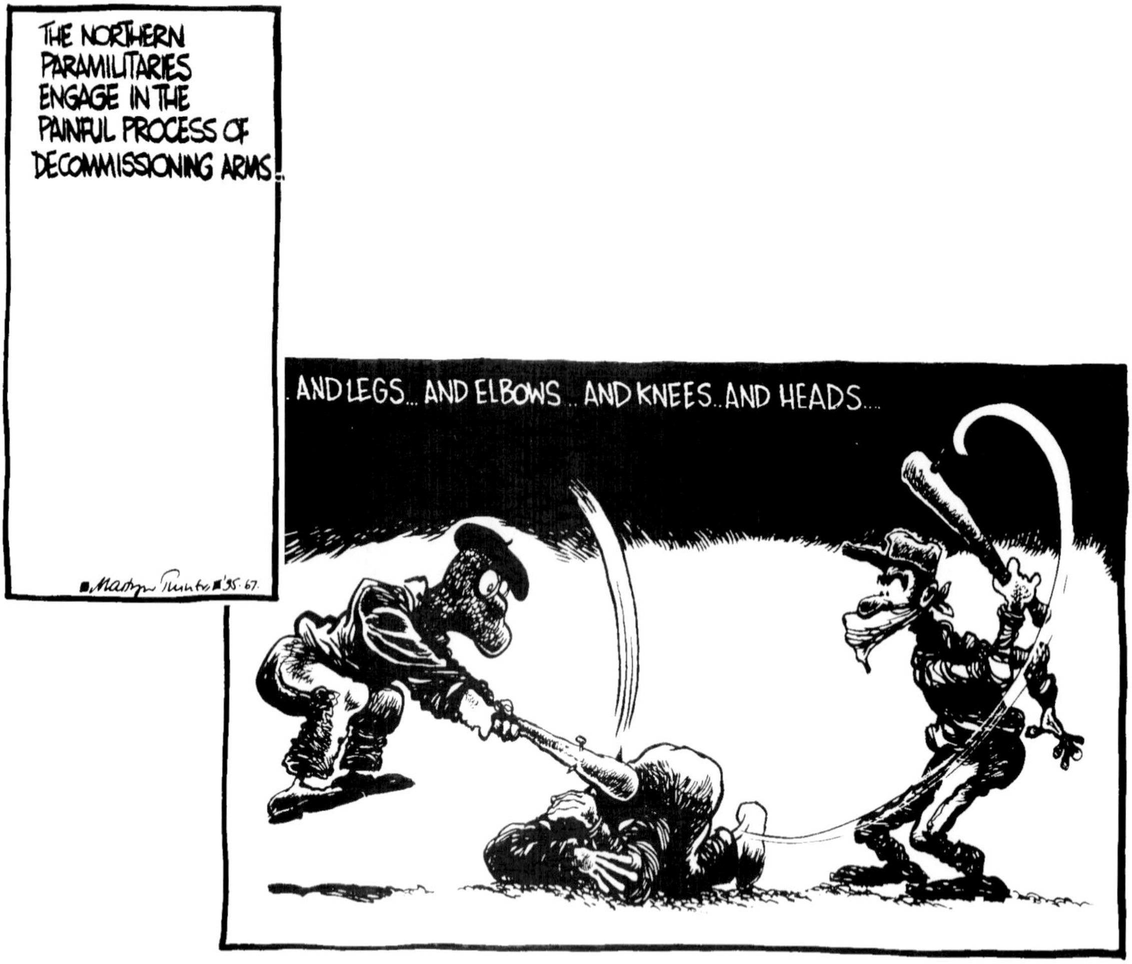
THE NORTHERN PARAMILITARIES ENGAGE IN THE PAINFUL PROCESS OF DECOMMISSIONING ARMS..
..AND LEGS... AND ELBOWS... AND KNEES..AND HEADS....

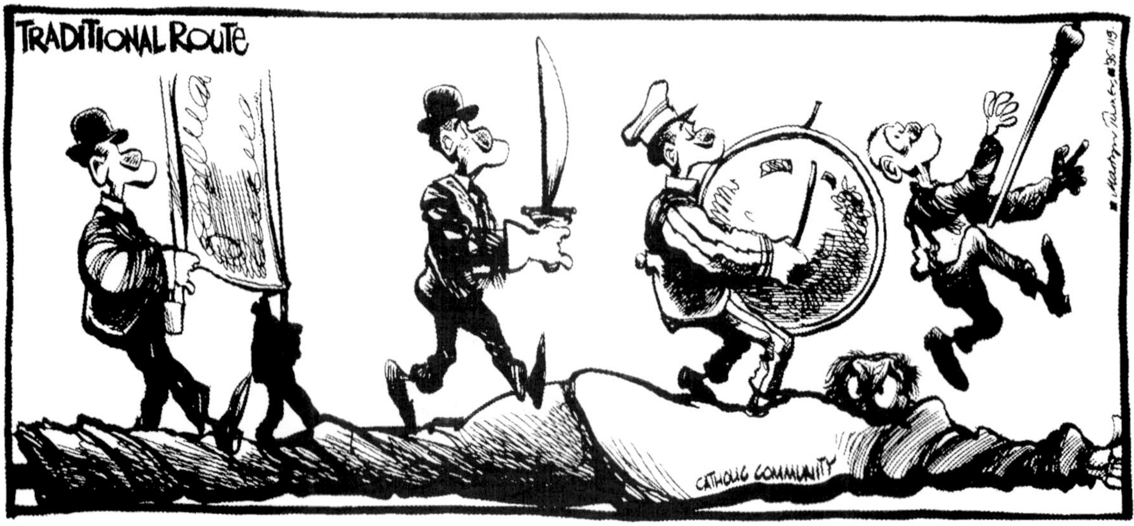
TRADITIONAL ROUTE
CATHOLIC COMMUNITY

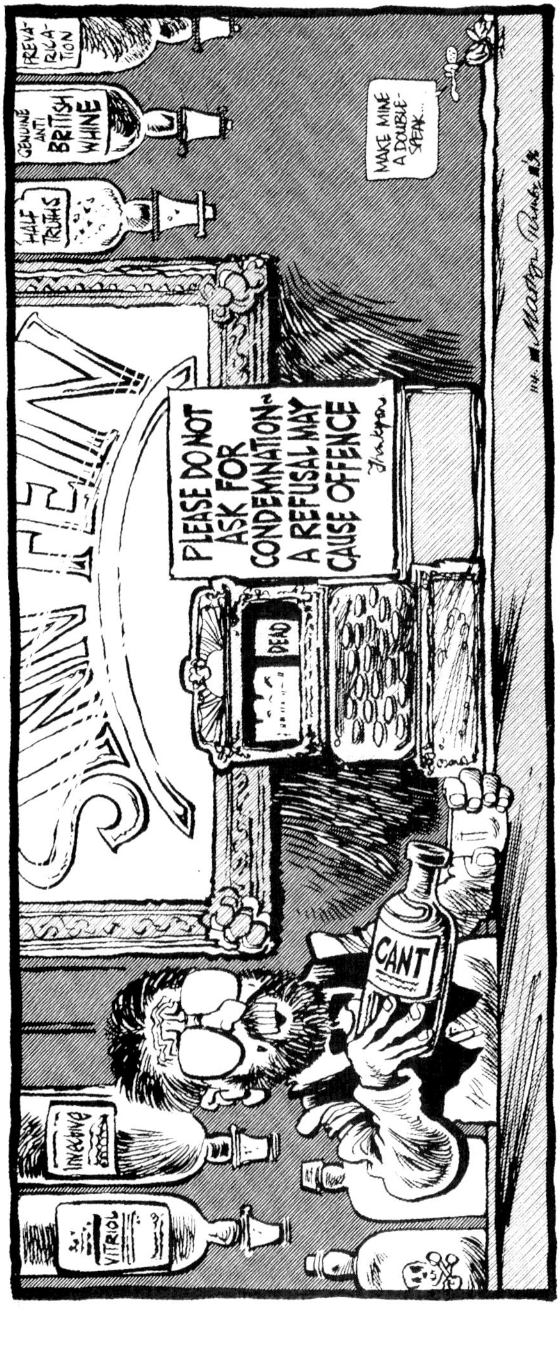
PREVA-RICA-TION
GENUINE ANTI BRITISH WHINE
HALF TRUTHS
SINN FEIN
PLEASE DO NOT ASK FOR CONDEMNATION. A REFUSAL MAY CAUSE OFFENCE
DEAD
CANT
INVECTIVE
VITRIOL
MAKE MINE A DOUBLE-SPEAK...

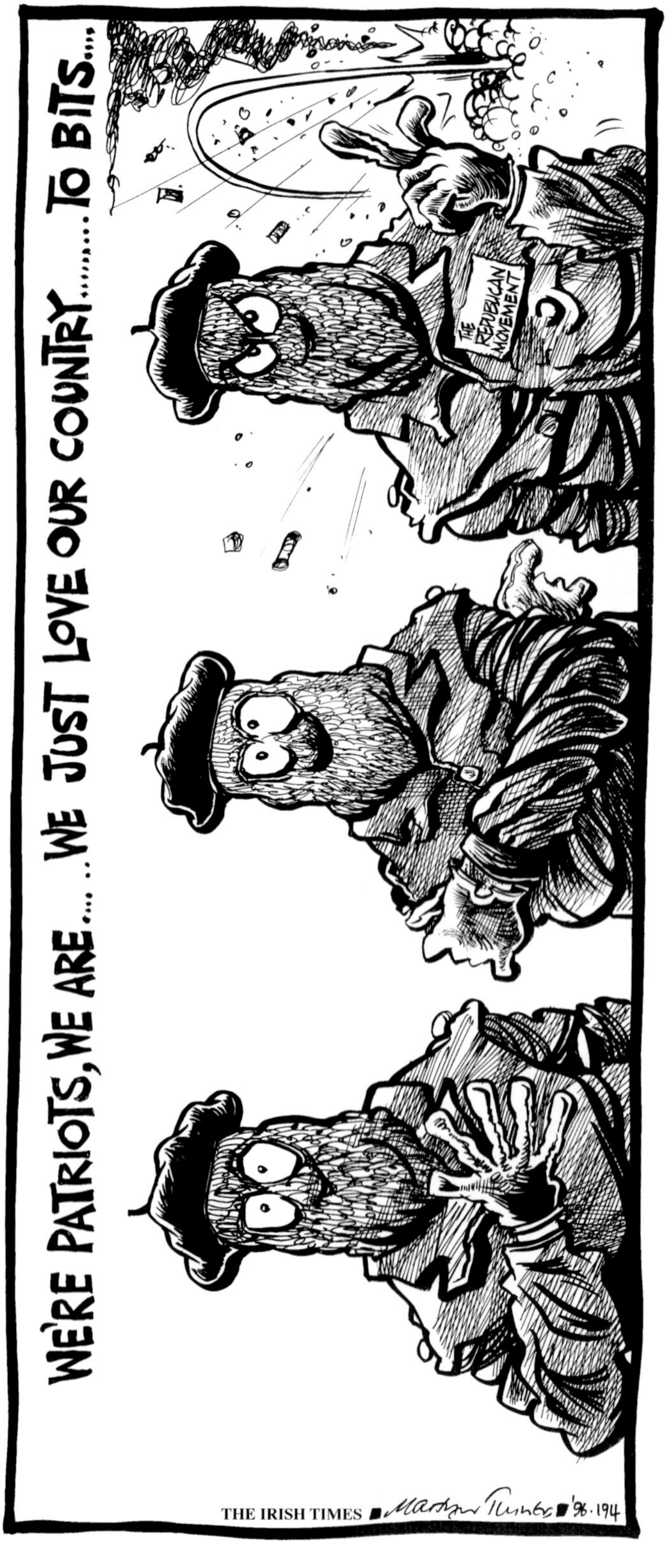
WE'RE PATRIOTS, WE ARE.... ...WE JUST LOVE OUR COUNTRY........TO BITS....
THE REPUBLICAN MOVEMENT
THE IRISH TIMES Martyn Turner '96.194

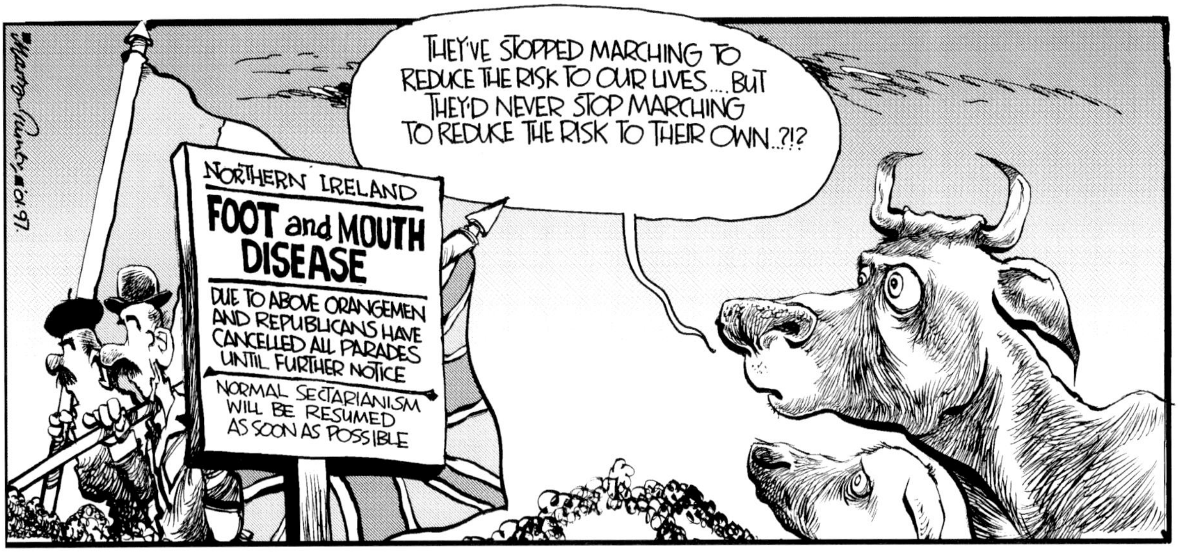
THEY'VE STOPPED MARCHING TO REDUCE THE RISK TO OUR LIVES.... BUT THEY'D NEVER STOP MARCHING TO REDUCE THE RISK TO THEIR OWN..?!?
NORTHERN IRELAND
FOOT and MOUTH DISEASE
DUE TO ABOVE ORANGEMEN AND REPUBLICANS HAVE CANCELLED ALL PARADES UNTIL FURTHER NOTICE
NORMAL SECTARIANISM WILL BE RESUMED AS SOON AS POSSIBLE

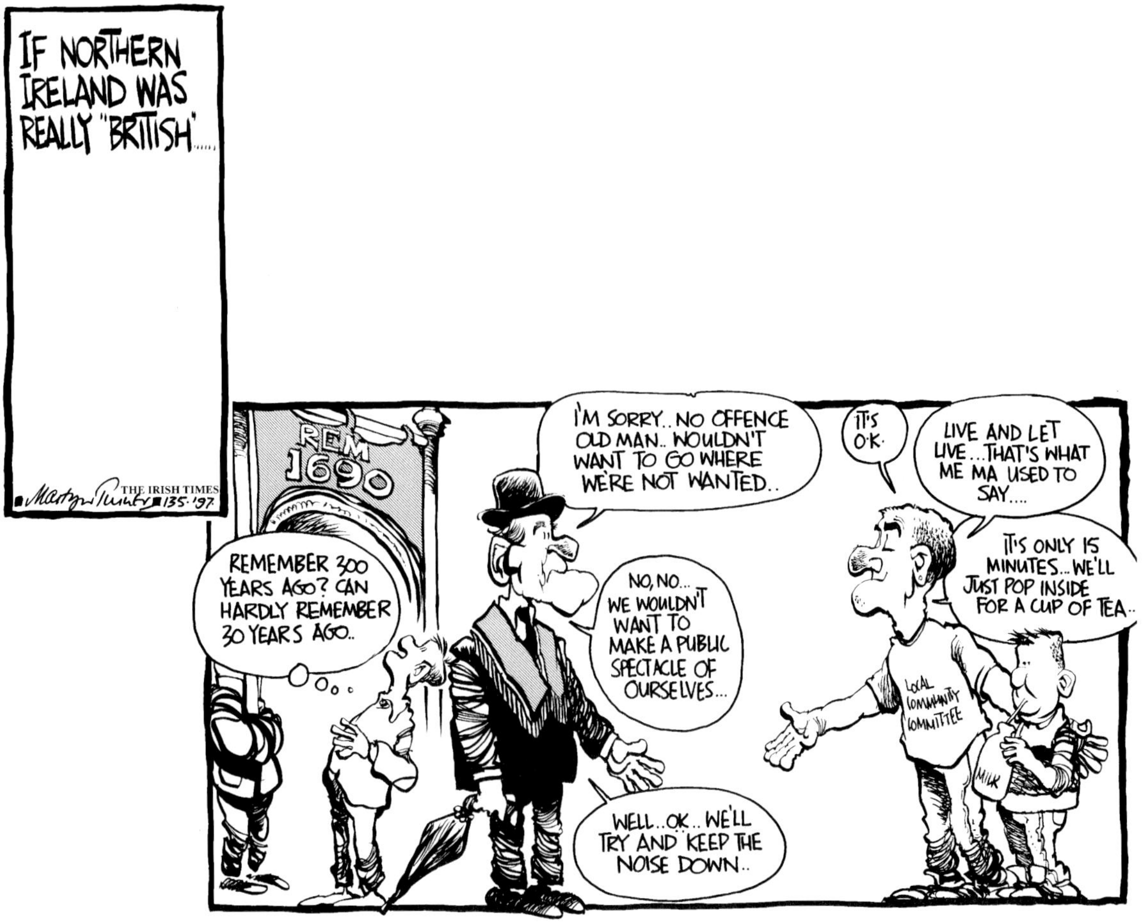
IF NORTHERN IRELAND WAS REALLY "BRITISH".....
THE IRISH TIMES 135·'97.
REM 1690
I'M SORRY.. NO OFFENCE OLD MAN.. WOULDN'T WANT TO GO WHERE WE'RE NOT WANTED..
IT'S O.K.
LIVE AND LET LIVE... THAT'S WHAT ME MA USED TO SAY....
REMEMBER 300 YEARS AGO? CAN HARDLY REMEMBER 30 YEARS AGO..
NO, NO... WE WOULDN'T WANT TO MAKE A PUBLIC SPECTACLE OF OURSELVES...
IT'S ONLY 15 MINUTES... WE'LL JUST POP INSIDE FOR A CUP OF TEA..
LOCAL COMMUNITY COMMITTEE
MILK
WELL.. OK.. WE'LL TRY AND KEEP THE NOISE DOWN..

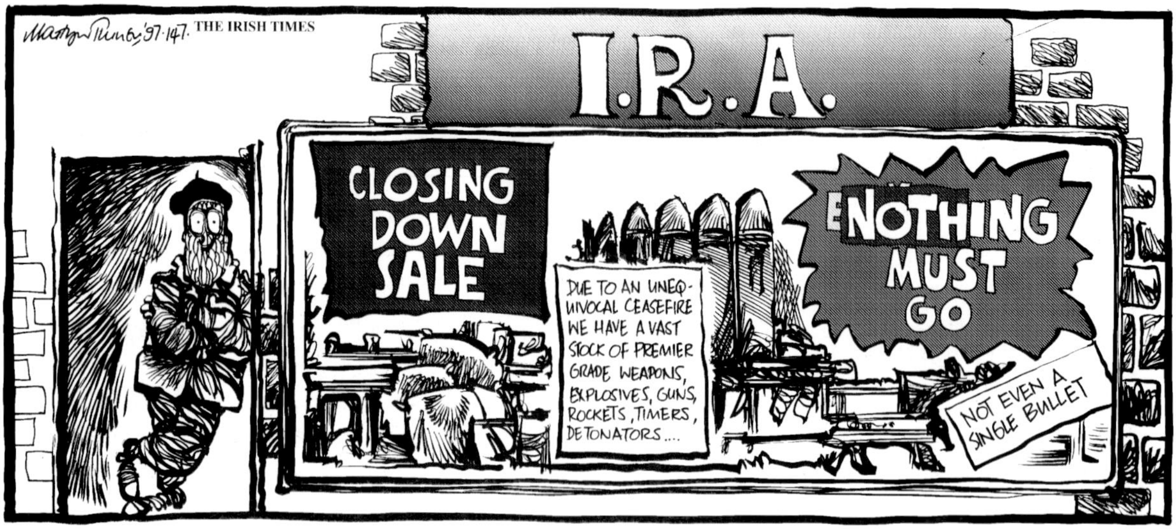
Martyn Turner '97.147. THE IRISH TIMES
I.R.A.
CLOSING DOWN SALE
DUE TO AN UNEQUIVOCAL CEASEFIRE WE HAVE A VAST STOCK OF PREMIER GRADE WEAPONS, EXPLOSIVES, GUNS, ROCKETS, TIMERS, DETONATORS....
ENOTHING MUST GO
NOT EVEN A SINGLE BULLET

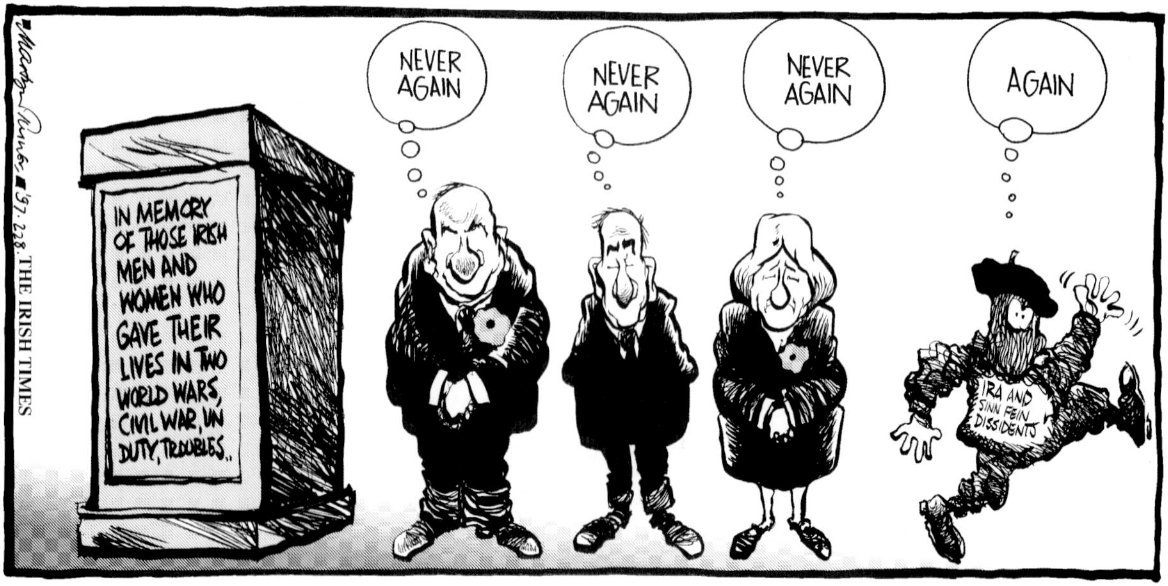
Martyn Turner '97.228. THE IRISH TIMES
IN MEMORY OF THOSE IRISH MEN AND WOMEN WHO GAVE THEIR LIVES IN TWO WORLD WARS, CIVIL WAR, UN DUTY, TROUBLES..
NEVER AGAIN
NEVER AGAIN
NEVER AGAIN
AGAIN
IRA AND SINN FEIN DISSIDENTS

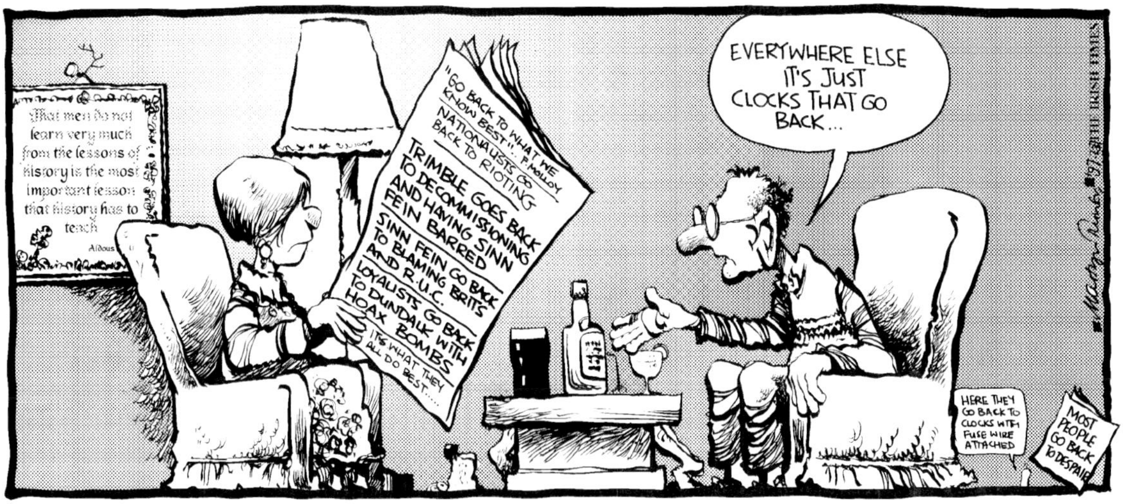
That men do not learn very much from the lessons of history is the most important lesson that history has to teach
Aldous
"GO BACK TO WHAT WE KNOW BEST!".. P. MOLLOY
NATIONALISTS GO BACK TO RIOTING
TRIMBLE GOES BACK TO DECOMMISSIONING AND HAVING SINN FEIN BARRED
SINN FEIN GO BACK TO BLAMING BRITS AND R.U.C.
LOYALISTS GO BACK TO DUNDALK WITH HOAX BOMBS
IT'S WHAT THEY ALL DO BEST....
EVERYWHERE ELSE IT'S JUST CLOCKS THAT GO BACK...
HERE THEY GO BACK TO CLOCKS WITH FUSE WIRE ATTACHED
MOST PEOPLE GO BACK TO DESPAIR
Martyn Turner '97 THE IRISH TIMES

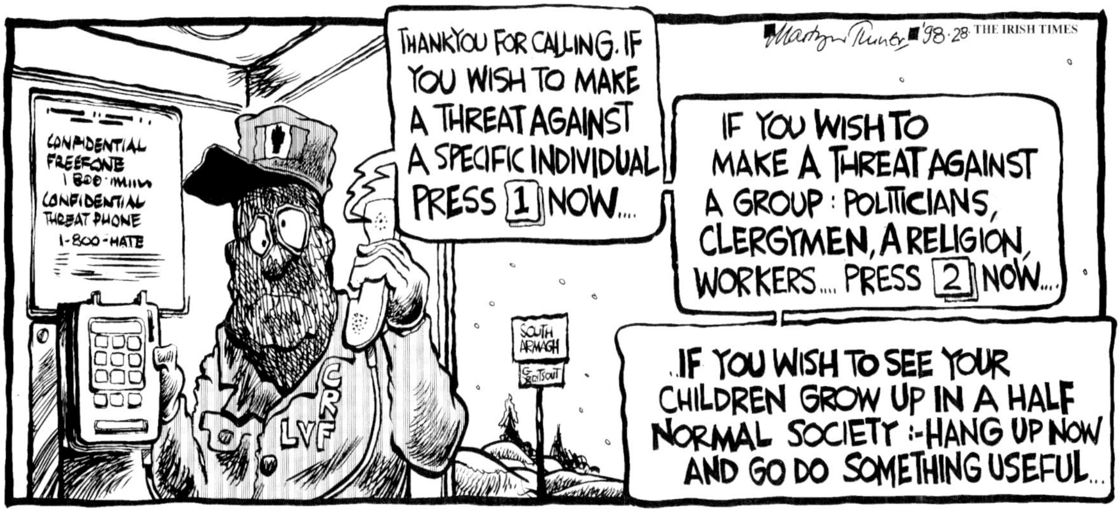
Martyn Turner '98·28 THE IRISH TIMES
CONFIDENTIAL FREEFONE 1 800 ·
CONFIDENTIAL THREAT PHONE 1-800-HATE
SOUTH ARMAGH
LVF
CRF
THANKYOU FOR CALLING. IF YOU WISH TO MAKE A THREAT AGAINST A SPECIFIC INDIVIDUAL PRESS 1 NOW....
IF YOU WISH TO MAKE A THREAT AGAINST A GROUP: POLITICIANS, CLERGYMEN, A RELIGION, WORKERS.... PRESS 2 NOW...
..IF YOU WISH TO SEE YOUR CHILDREN GROW UP IN A HALF NORMAL SOCIETY :- HANG UP NOW AND GO DO SOMETHING USEFUL...

'98·34· THE IRISH TIMES
TO: N.I.
LOVE
MURDERS
PUNISHMENT BEATINGS
TALKS ROWS
SCHOOL ATTACK
LOVE

THE IRISH TIMES
The HAND of HISTORY

UKUP
LVF
SPIRIT of DRUMCREE
DUP
CIRA
INLA
32 COUNTY SOV
RSF
The CLAWS of HISTORY

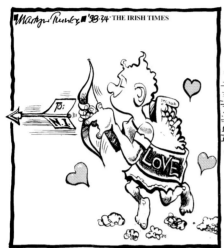

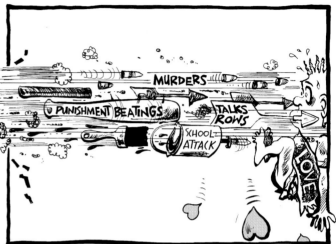

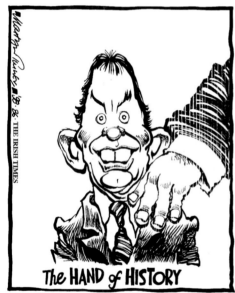

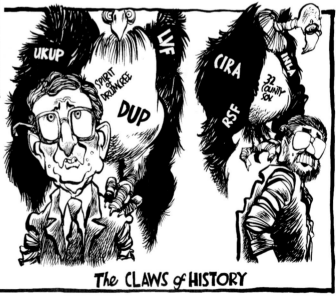

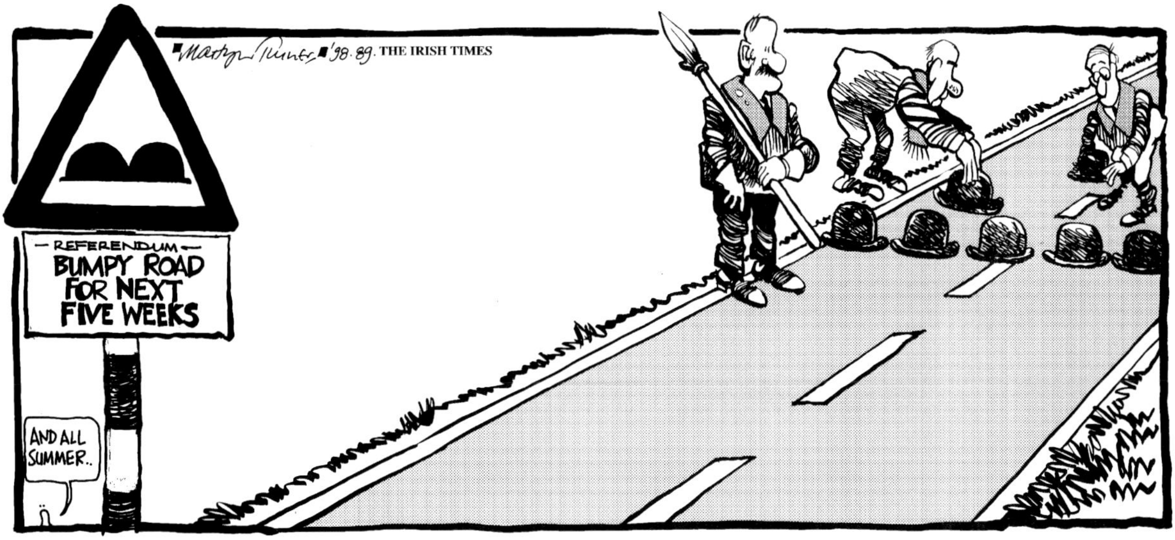

Martyn Turner '98.89. THE IRISH TIMES
— REFERENDUM —
BUMPY ROAD FOR NEXT FIVE WEEKS
AND ALL SUMMER..

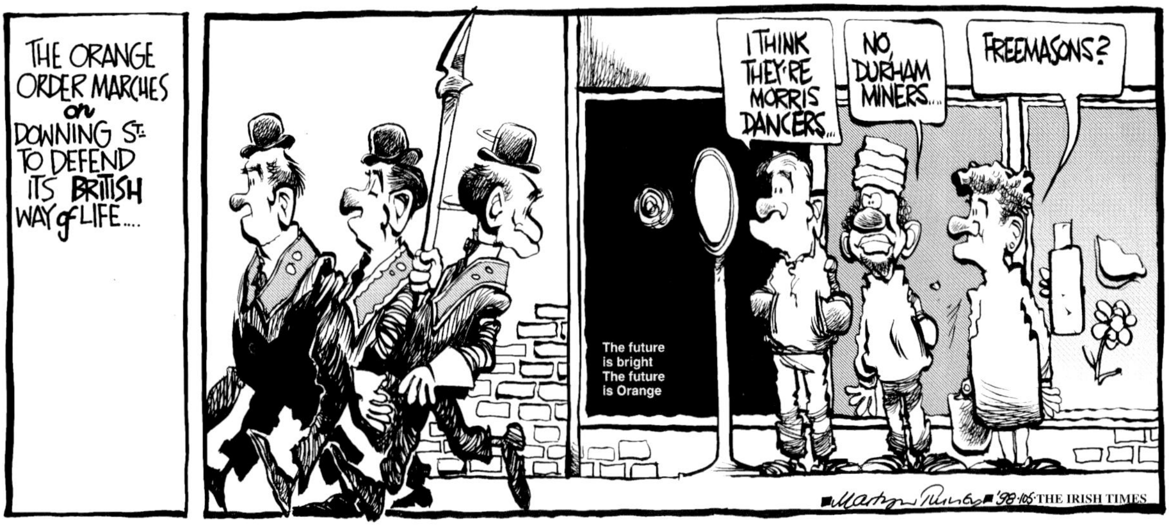

THE ORANGE ORDER MARCHES on DOWNING ST. TO DEFEND ITS BRITISH WAY of LIFE....
I THINK THEY'RE MORRIS DANCERS...
NO, DURHAM MINERS...
FREEMASONS?
The future is bright The future is Orange
Martyn Turner '98.105 THE IRISH TIMES

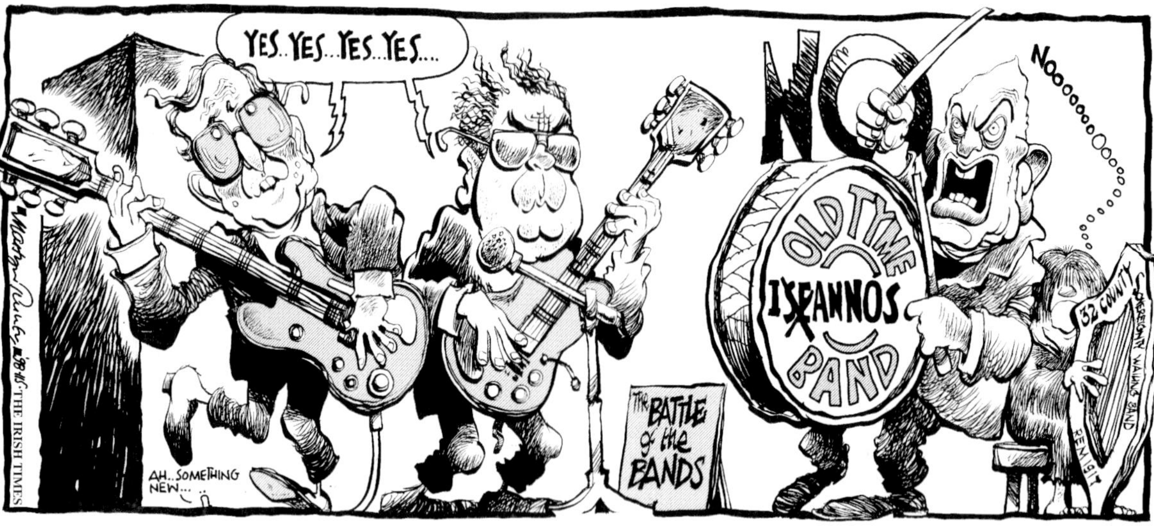
YES..YES...YES..YES....
NO
Noooooooooo
OLD TYME
ISPANNOS
BAND
THE BATTLE of the BANDS
32 COUNTY SOVEREIGNTY WAILING BAND
REM 1917
AH..SOMETHING NEW...
THE IRISH TIMES

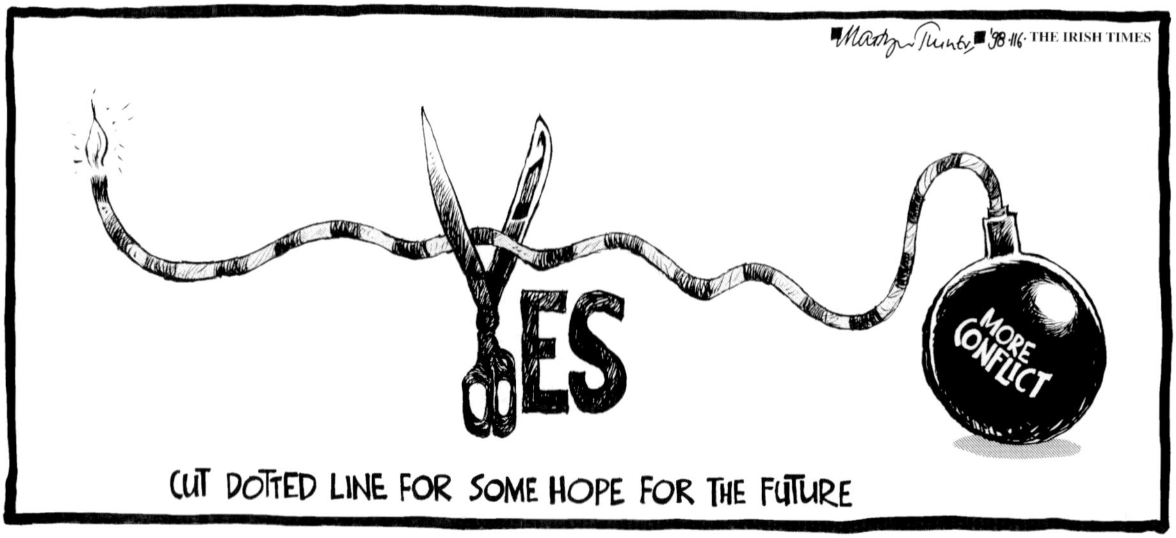
'98 ·116· THE IRISH TIMES
YES
MORE CONFLICT
CUT DOTTED LINE FOR SOME HOPE FOR THE FUTURE

101 USES for a PORTADOWN SASH
AS A BLINDFOLD YOUR SASH WILL HELP YOU IGNORE THE GUNMEN PETROL BOMBERS AND THUGS IN YOUR MIDST...
YOU'LL NEVER HEAR THOSE CALLS TO GIVE UP WITH A SASH BETWEEN YOUR EARS...
GO HOME!
HAVING WASHED YOUR HANDS OF RESPONSIBILITY FOR BALLYMONEY...USE IT TO DRY THEM...
'98·142·THE IRISH TIMES

SAYS NO
REM 1690
NOT AN INCH
REM 1916
BRITS OUT
JERICHO ST.
YES!
REM 1998
'98·119·THE IRISH TIMES

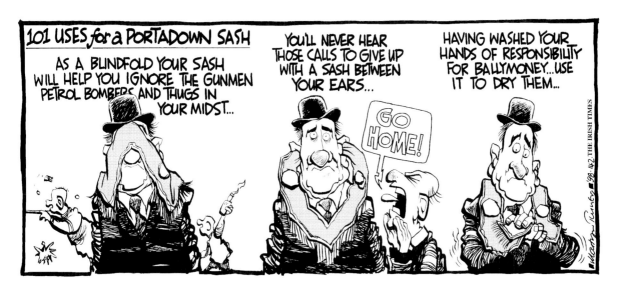

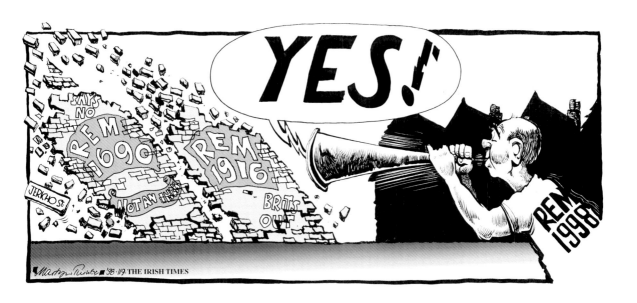

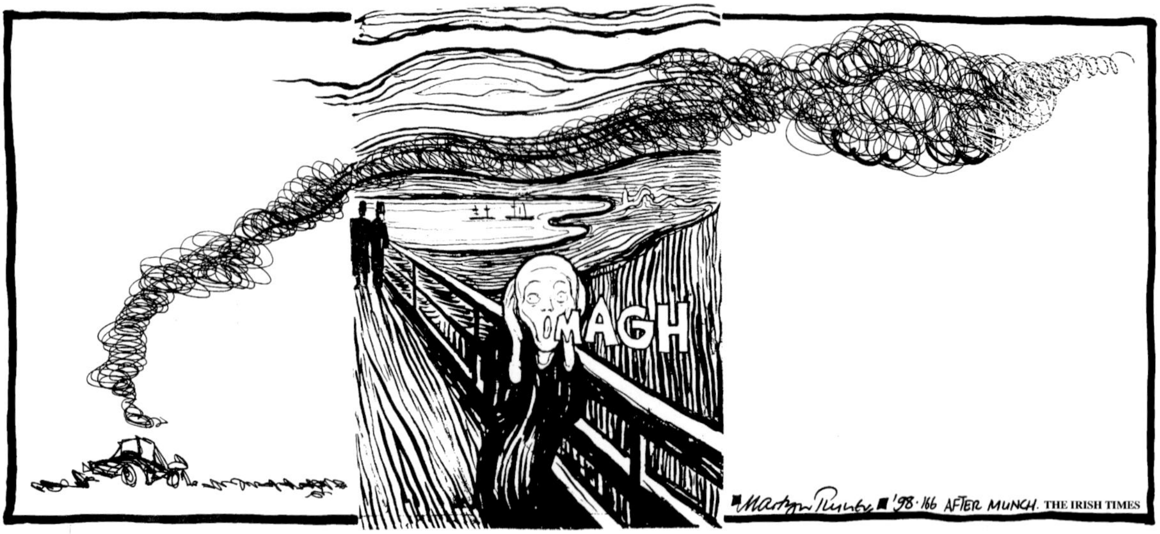
OMAGH
Martyn Turner '98·166 AFTER MUNCH. THE IRISH TIMES

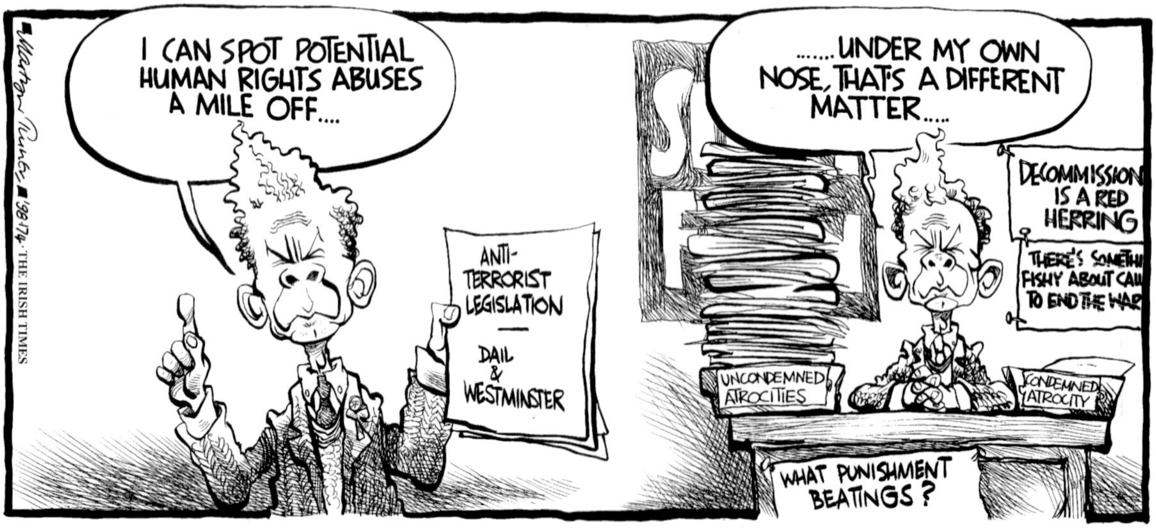
I CAN SPOT POTENTIAL HUMAN RIGHTS ABUSES A MILE OFF....
ANTI-TERRORIST LEGISLATION — DAIL & WESTMINSTER
.......UNDER MY OWN NOSE, THAT'S A DIFFERENT MATTER.....
DECOMMISSION IS A RED HERRING
THERE'S SOMETHI FISHY ABOUT CAL TO END THE WAR
UNCONDEMNED ATROCITIES
CONDEMNED ATROCITY
WHAT PUNISHMENT BEATINGS ?
Martyn Turner '98·174 THE IRISH TIMES

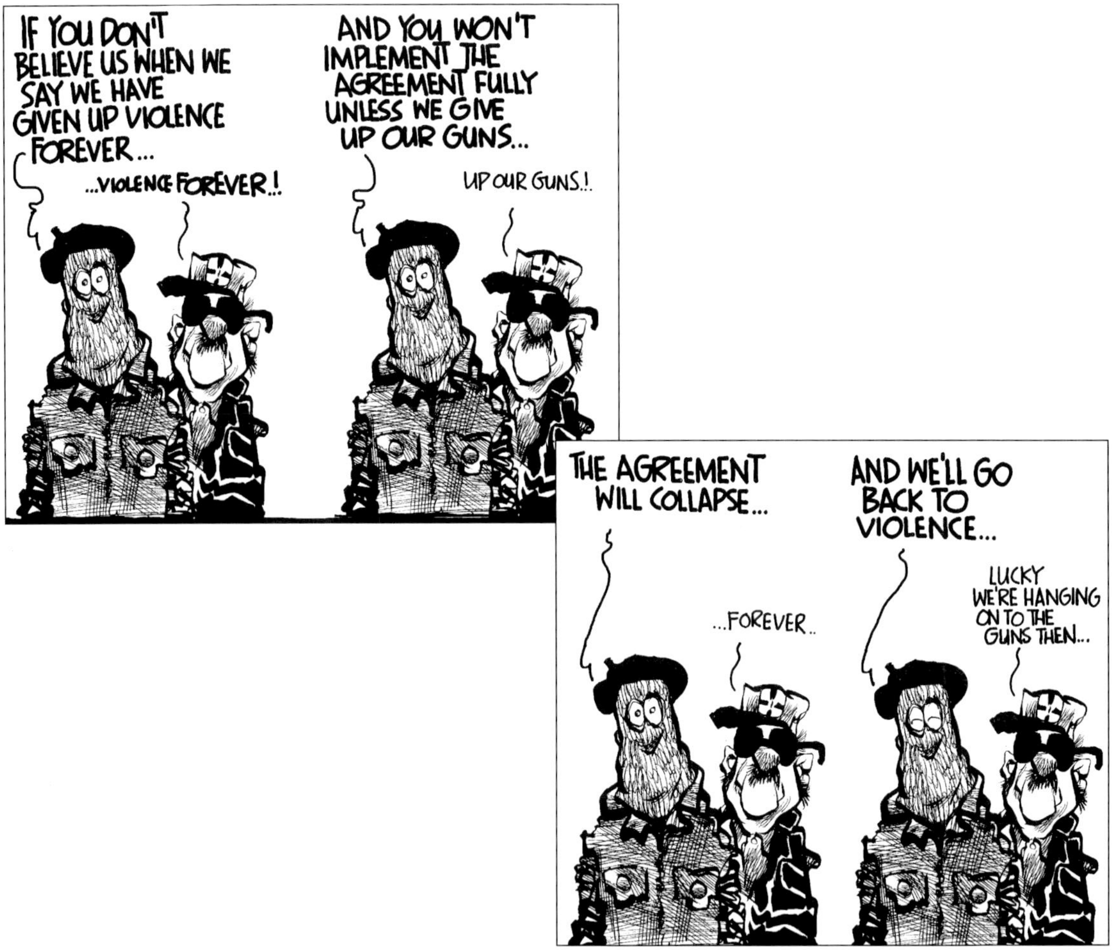
IF YOU DON'T BELIEVE US WHEN WE SAY WE HAVE GIVEN UP VIOLENCE FOREVER...
...VIOLENCE FOREVER.!
AND YOU WON'T IMPLEMENT THE AGREEMENT FULLY UNLESS WE GIVE UP OUR GUNS...
UP OUR GUNS.!
THE AGREEMENT WILL COLLAPSE...
...FOREVER..
AND WE'LL GO BACK TO VIOLENCE...
LUCKY WE'RE HANGING ON TO THE GUNS THEN...

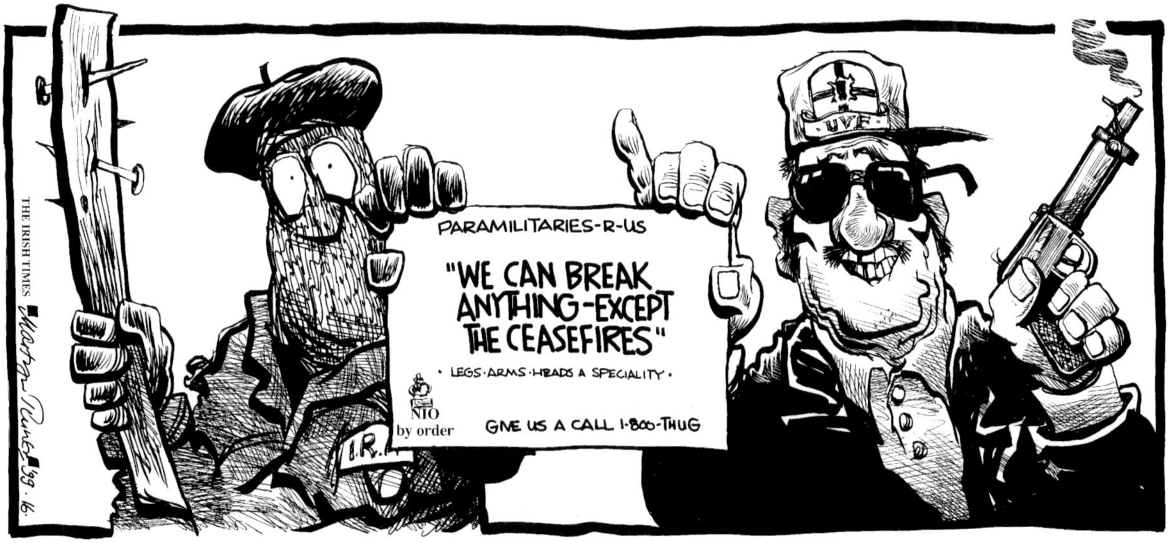
PARAMILITARIES-R-US
"WE CAN BREAK ANYTHING-EXCEPT THE CEASEFIRES"
• LEGS·ARMS·HEADS A SPECIALITY •
NIO by order
GIVE US A CALL 1-800-THUG
UVF
I.R.
THE IRISH TIMES

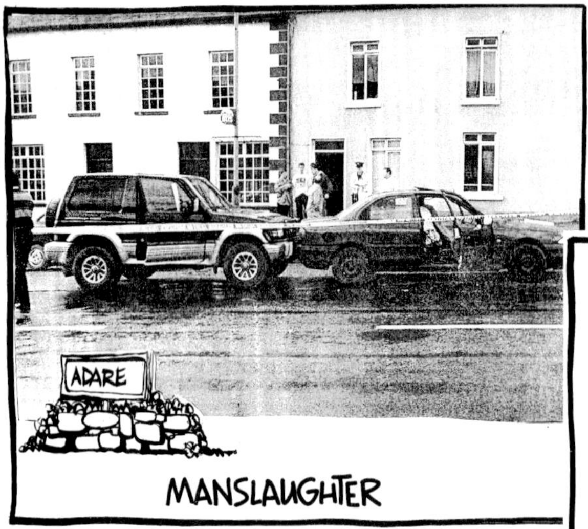
ADARE
MANSLAUGHTER

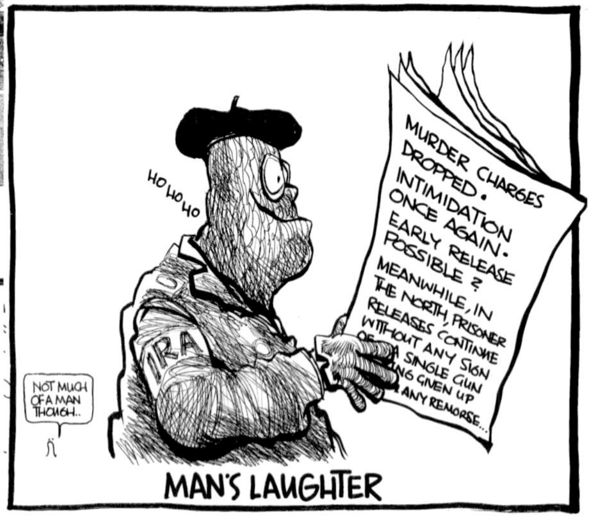
HO HO HO
MURDER CHARGES DROPPED.
INTIMIDATION ONCE AGAIN.
EARLY RELEASE POSSIBLE?
MEANWHILE, IN THE NORTH, PRISONER RELEASES CONTINUE WITHOUT ANY SIGN
A SINGLE GUN
NG GIVEN UP
ANY REMORSE..
IRA
NOT MUCH OF A MAN THOUGH..
MAN'S LAUGHTER

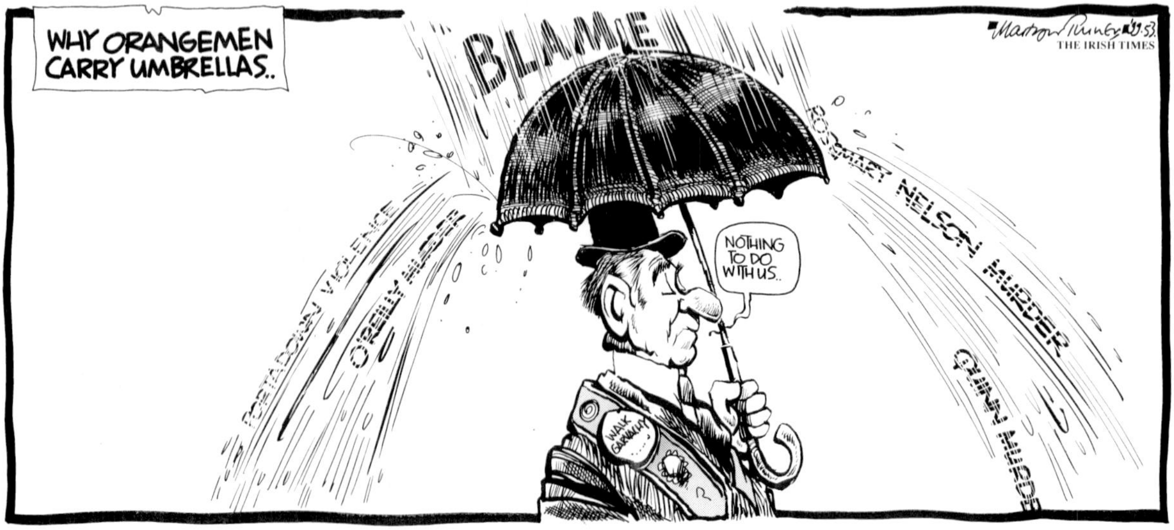
WHY ORANGEMEN CARRY UMBRELLAS..
BLAME
PORTADOWN VIOLENCE
O'REILLY MURDER
ROSEMARY NELSON MURDER
QUINN MURDER
NOTHING TO DO WITH US..
WALK GARVAGHY
THE IRISH TIMES

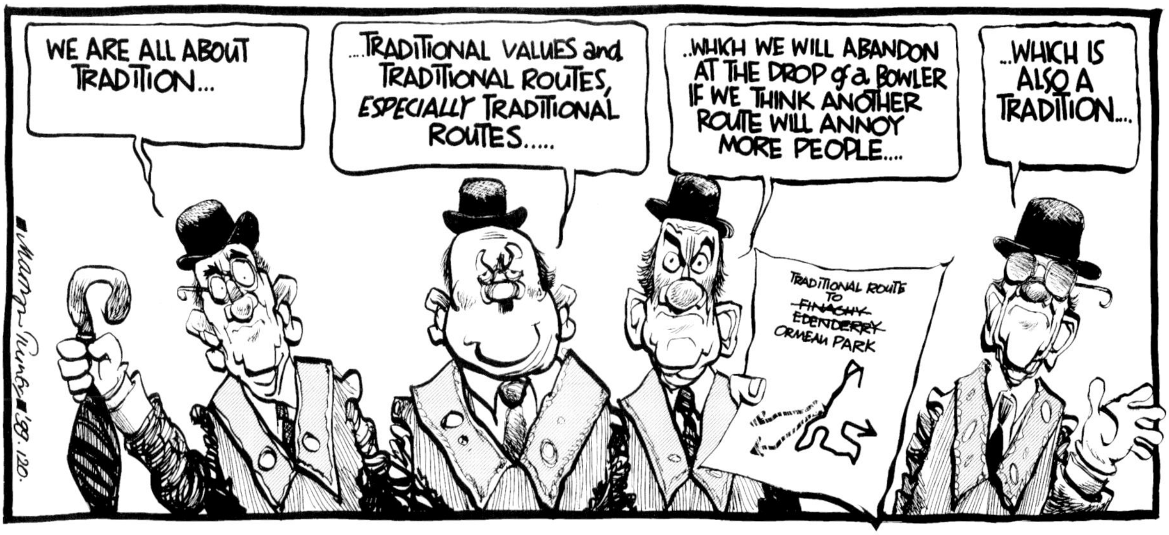
WE ARE ALL ABOUT TRADITION...
...TRADITIONAL VALUES and TRADITIONAL ROUTES, ESPECIALLY TRADITIONAL ROUTES.....
..WHICH WE WILL ABANDON AT THE DROP of a BOWLER IF WE THINK ANOTHER ROUTE WILL ANNOY MORE PEOPLE....
...WHICH IS ALSO A TRADITION....
TRADITIONAL ROUTE TO ~~FINAGHY~~ ~~EDENDERRY~~ ORMEAU PARK
Martyn Turner '98.120.

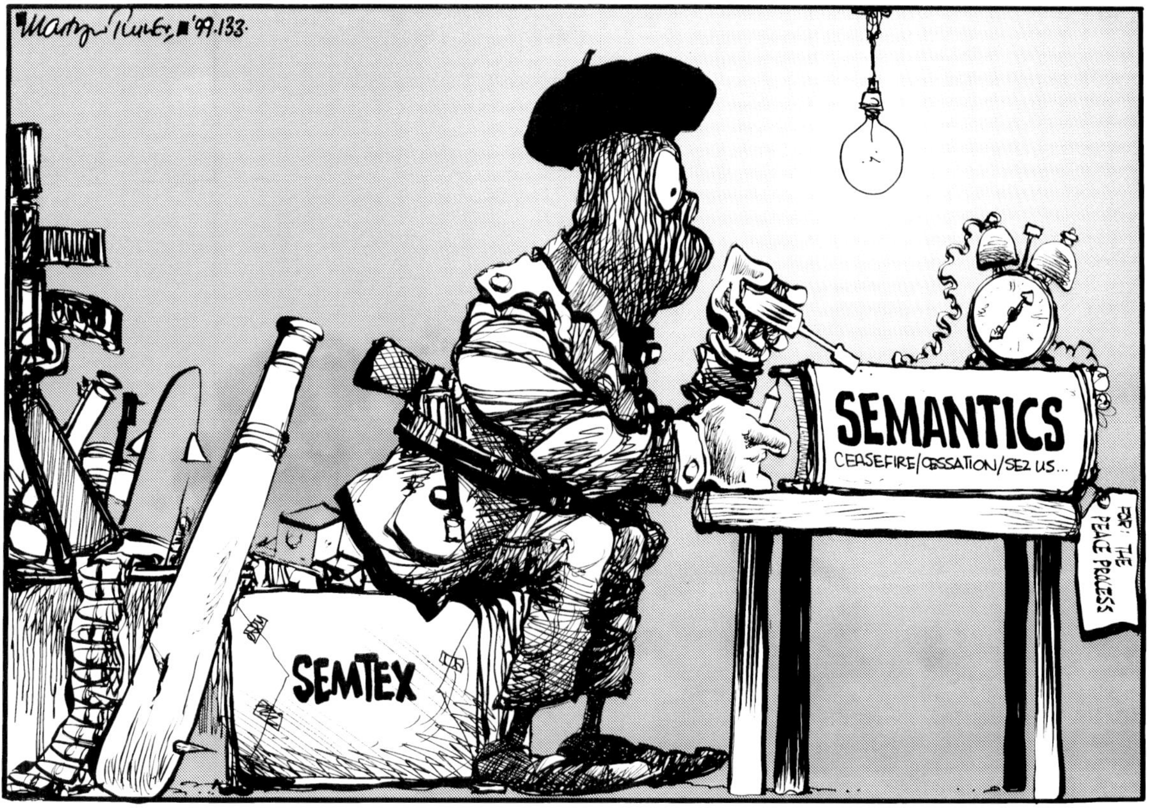
Martyn Turner '99.133.
SEMANTICS
CEASEFIRE/CESSATION/SEZ US...
FOR: THE PEACE PROCESS
SEMTEX

THE BOX SAYS "1-2 YEARS"....
AND I'VE ONLY TAKEN 21 MONTHS SO FAR....
THE N.I. JIGSAW
4 PIECES
GOVERNMENT
DEVOLUTION
REFORM
DECOMMISSIONING
THE OLD JOKES ARE BEST!
IF ONLY IT WAS A JOKE..
THE IRISH TIMES

AUSTRIA
WIEN
FREEDOM.. PARTY (FPÖ)
HOW DO WE HELP TO KEEP THE **EXTREME RIGHT** OUT OF GOVERNMENT ?
EU
USA
NORTHERN IRELAND
D.U.P.
S.F.
Bits of the OUP
HOW DO WE HELP TO KEEP THE **EXTREME RIGHT** IN GOVERNMENT ?
EU
USA

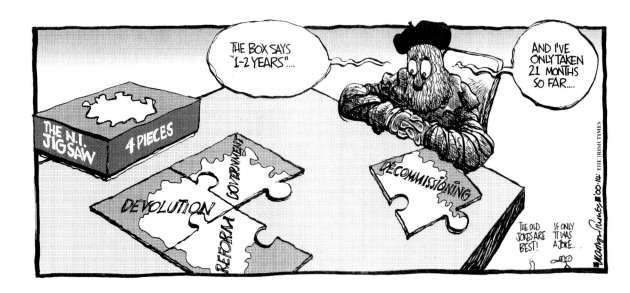

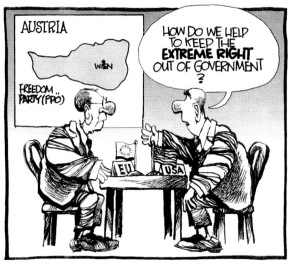

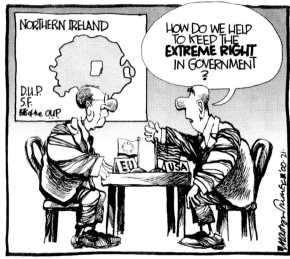

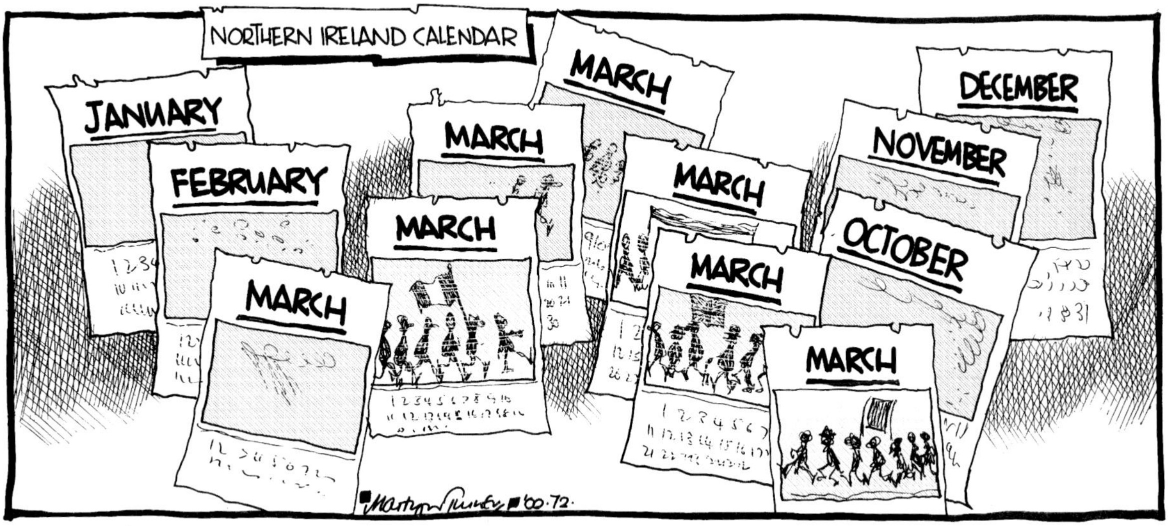
NORTHERN IRELAND CALENDAR
JANUARY
FEBRUARY
MARCH
MARCH
MARCH
MARCH
MARCH
MARCH
MARCH
DECEMBER
NOVEMBER
OCTOBER
Martyn Turner '00.72.

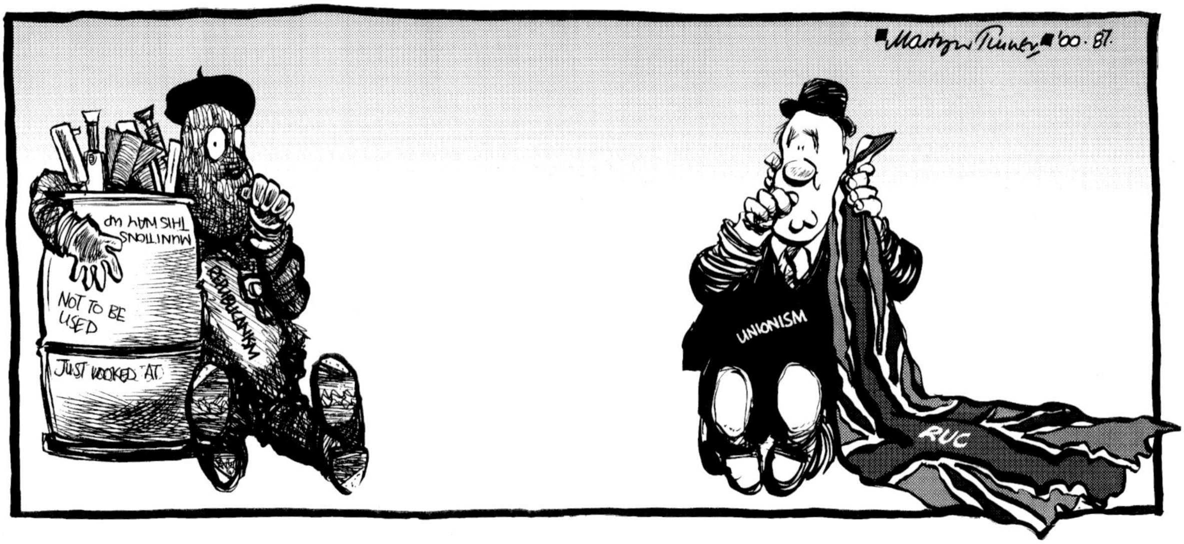
Martyn Turner '00.87.
MUNITIONS THIS WAY UP
NOT TO BE USED
JUST LOOKED AT
REPUBLICANISM
UNIONISM
RUC

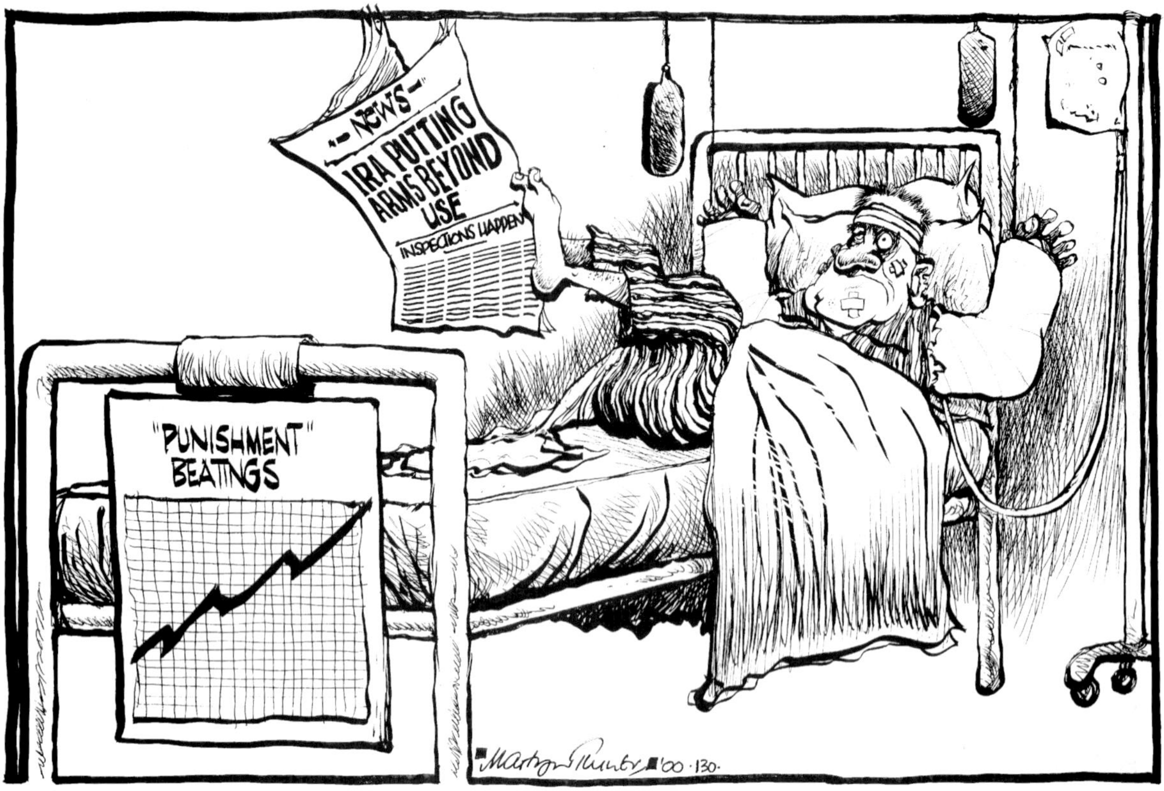

NEWS
IRA PUTTING ARMS BEYOND USE
INSPECTIONS HAPPEN
"PUNISHMENT" BEATINGS

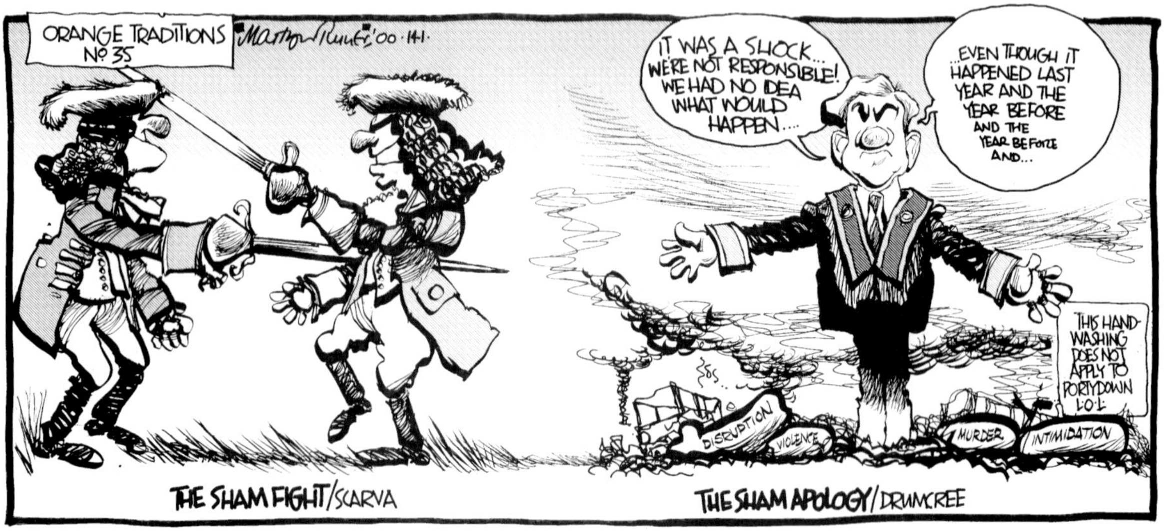

ORANGE TRADITIONS No 35
IT WAS A SHOCK... WE'RE NOT RESPONSIBLE! WE HAD NO IDEA WHAT WOULD HAPPEN....
...EVEN THOUGH IT HAPPENED LAST YEAR AND THE YEAR BEFORE AND THE YEAR BEFORE AND...
THIS HAND-WASHING DOES NOT APPLY TO PORTADOWN L.O.L.
DISRUPTION
VIOLENCE
MURDER
INTIMIDATION
THE SHAM FIGHT/SCARVA
THE SHAM APOLOGY/DRUMCREE

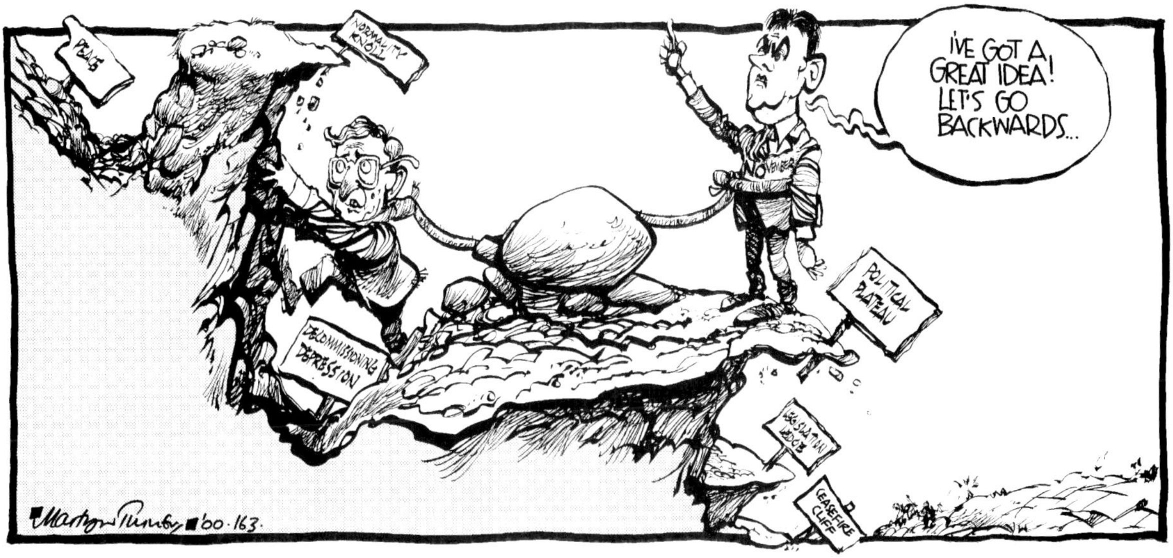
PEACE
NORMALITY KNOLL
I'VE GOT A GREAT IDEA! LET'S GO BACKWARDS...
NOVEMBER
POLITICAL PLATEAU
DECOMMISSIONING DEPRESSION
LEGISLATION LEDGE
CEASEFIRE CLIFF
Martyn Turner '00·163.

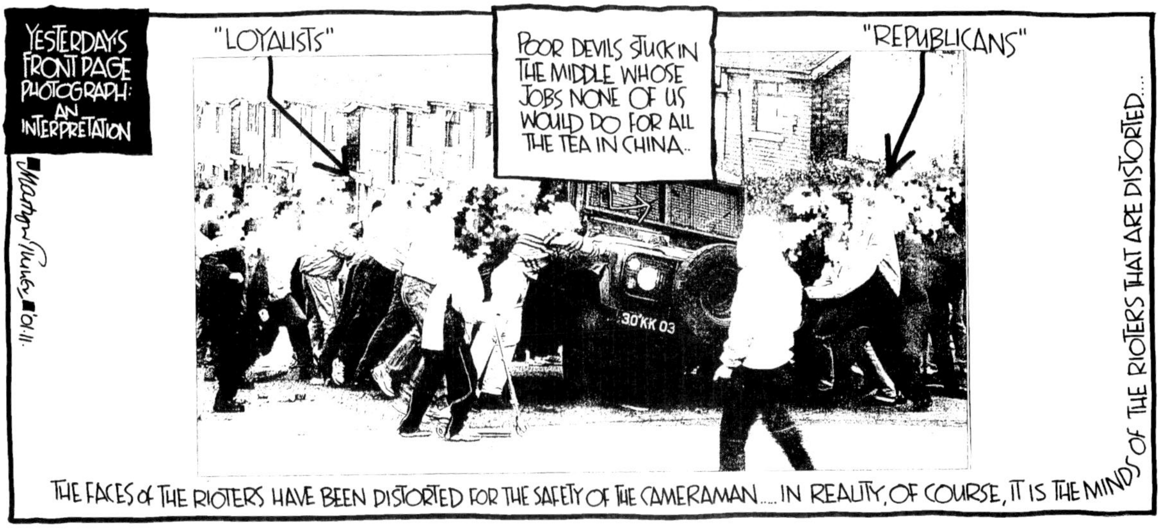
YESTERDAY'S FRONT PAGE PHOTOGRAPH: AN INTERPRETATION
"LOYALISTS"
POOR DEVILS STUCK IN THE MIDDLE WHOSE JOBS NONE OF US WOULD DO FOR ALL THE TEA IN CHINA..
"REPUBLICANS"
30 KK 03
Martyn Turner '01.11.
THE FACES OF THE RIOTERS HAVE BEEN DISTORTED FOR THE SAFETY OF THE CAMERAMAN..... IN REALITY, OF COURSE, IT IS THE MINDS OF THE RIOTERS THAT ARE DISTORTED....

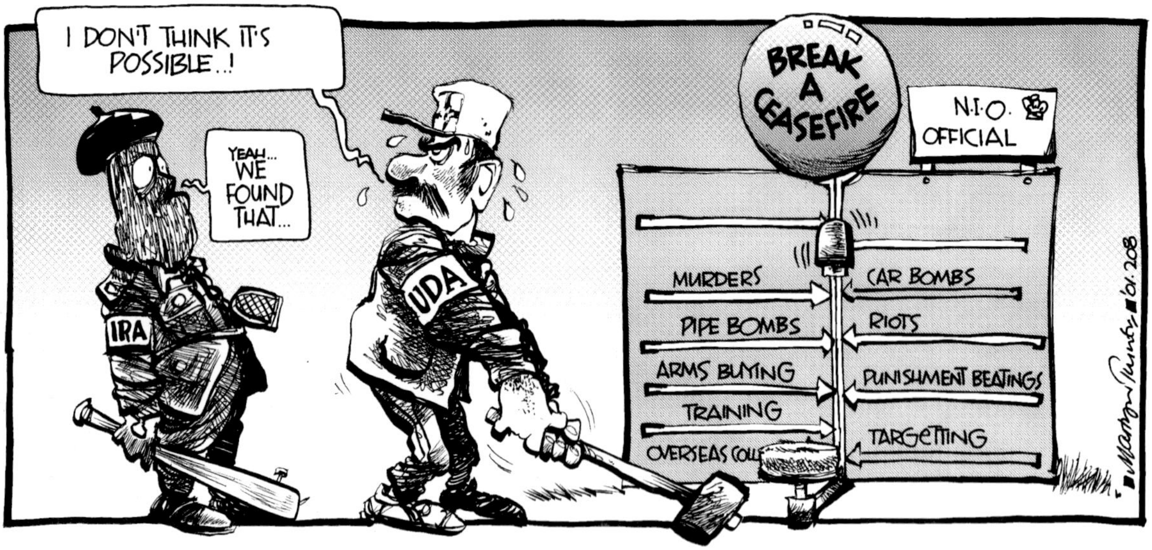
I DON'T THINK IT'S POSSIBLE..!
YEAH... WE FOUND THAT...
IRA
UDA
BREAK A CEASEFIRE
N.I.O. OFFICIAL
MURDERS
CAR BOMBS
PIPE BOMBS
RIOTS
ARMS BUYING
PUNISHMENT BEATINGS
TRAINING
TARGETTING
OVERSEAS

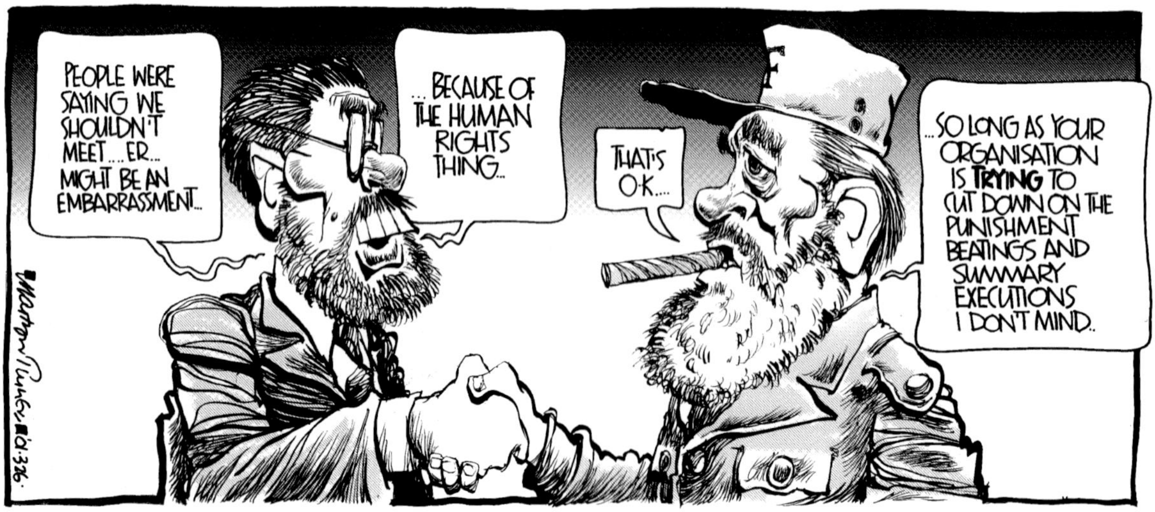
PEOPLE WERE SAYING WE SHOULDN'T MEET.... ER... MIGHT BE AN EMBARRASSMENT...
... BECAUSE OF THE HUMAN RIGHTS THING...
THAT'S O.K....
...SO LONG AS YOUR ORGANISATION IS TRYING TO CUT DOWN ON THE PUNISHMENT BEATINGS AND SUMMARY EXECUTIONS I DON'T MIND..

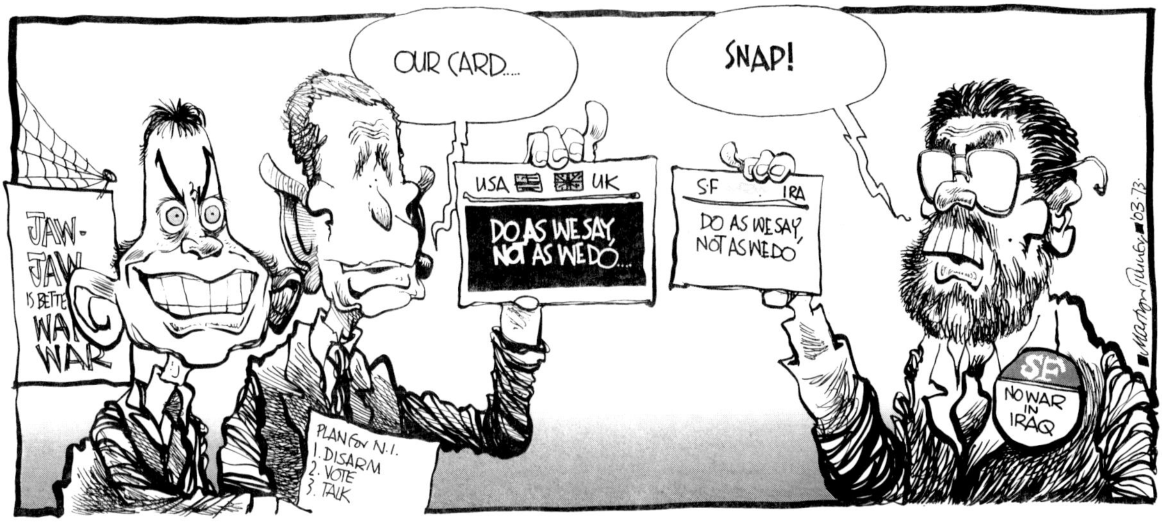
JAW-
JAW
IS BETTE
WA
WAR
OUR CARD....
USA UK
DO AS WE SAY, NOT AS WE DO...
PLAN for N.I.
1. DISARM
2. VOTE
3. TALK
SNAP!
S·F IRA
DO AS WE SAY, NOT AS WE DO
SF
NO WAR IN IRAQ

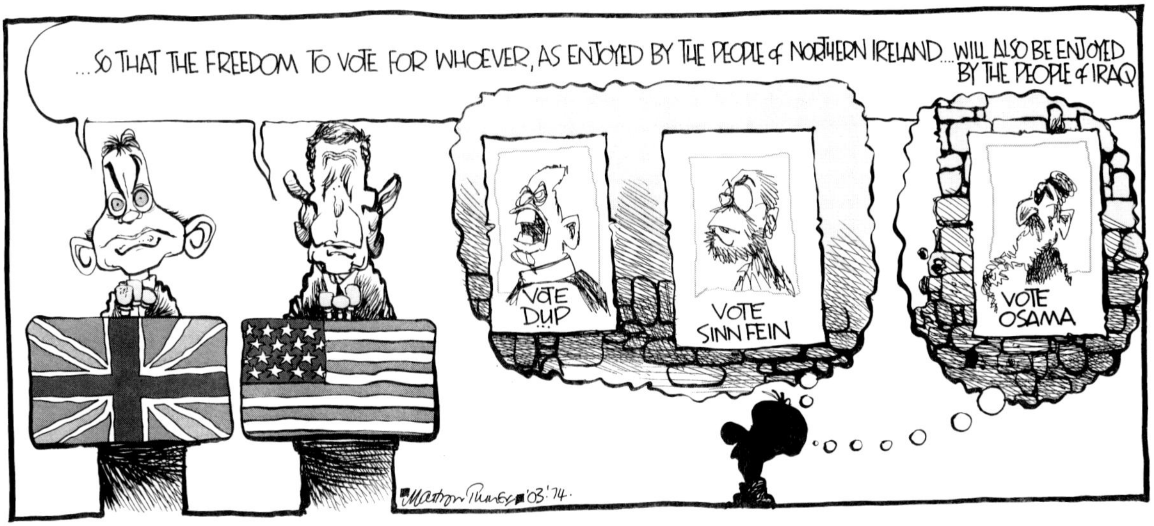
...SO THAT THE FREEDOM TO VOTE FOR WHOEVER, AS ENJOYED BY THE PEOPLE of NORTHERN IRELAND.... WILL ALSO BE ENJOYED BY THE PEOPLE of IRAQ
VOTE DUP...
VOTE SINN FEIN
VOTE OSAMA

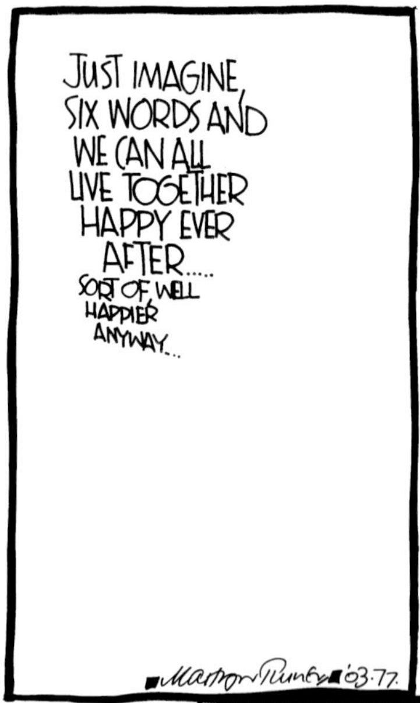
JUST IMAGINE, SIX WORDS AND WE CAN ALL LIVE TOGETHER HAPPY EVER AFTER.....
SORT OF, WELL HAPPIER ANYWAY...
'03.77.

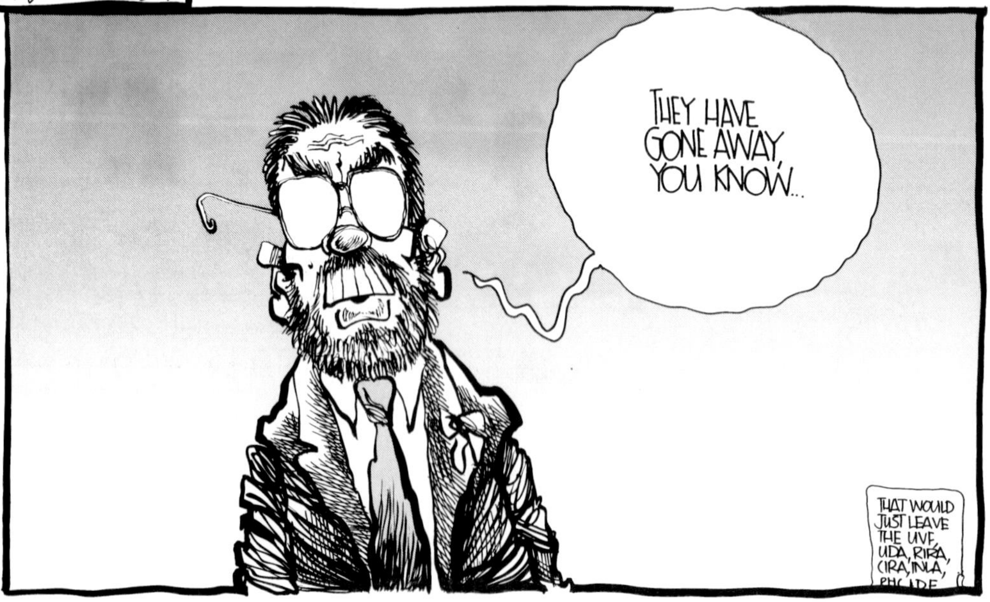
THEY HAVE GONE AWAY, YOU KNOW...
THAT WOULD JUST LEAVE THE UVF, UDA, RIRA, CIRA, INLA,

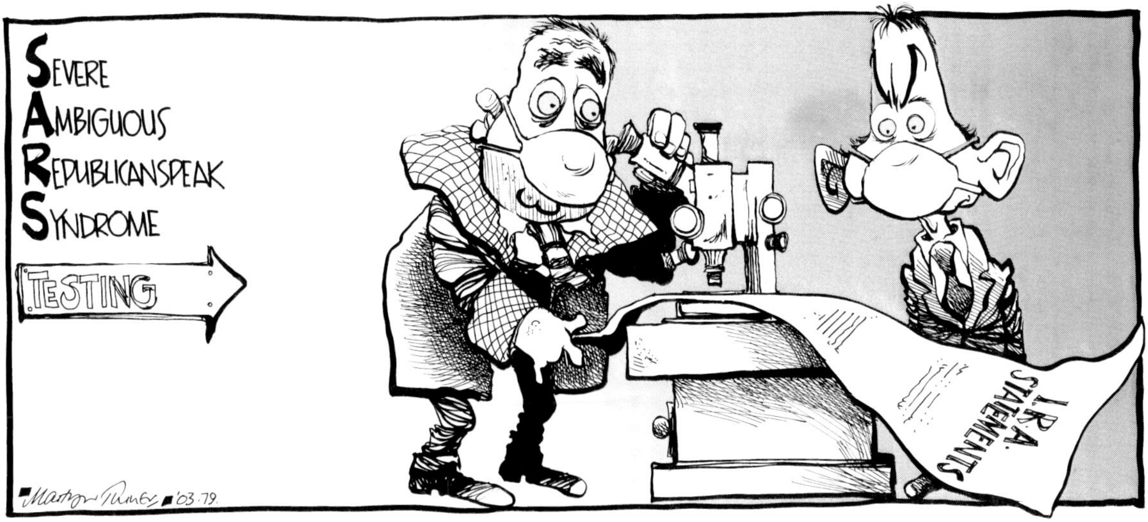
SEVERE
AMBIGUOUS
REPUBLICANSPEAK
SYNDROME
TESTING
I.R.A. STATEMENTS
Martyn Turner '03

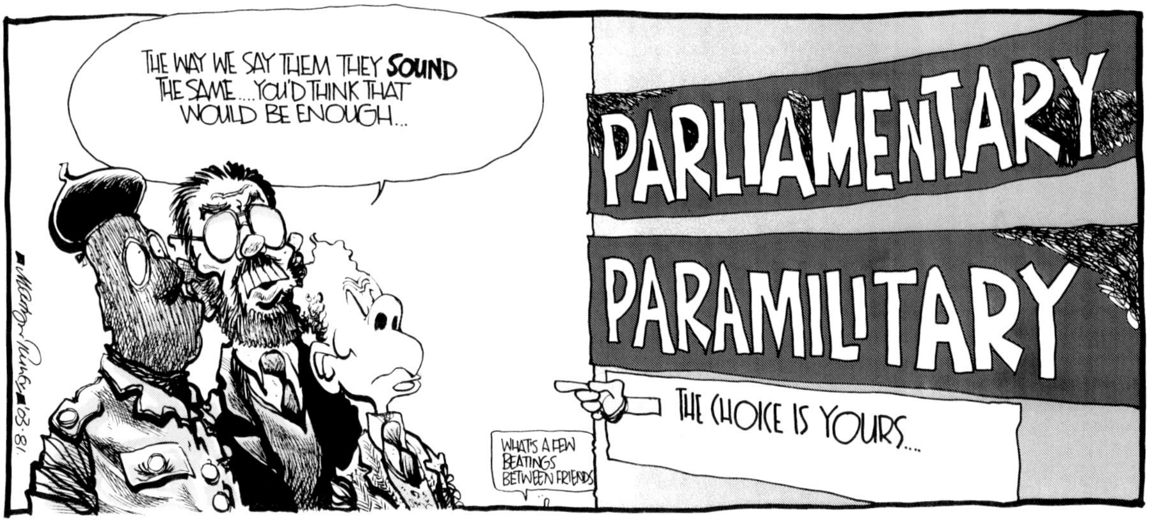
THE WAY WE SAY THEM THEY SOUND THE SAME.... YOU'D THINK THAT WOULD BE ENOUGH...
PARLIAMENTARY
PARAMILITARY
THE CHOICE IS YOURS....
WHAT'S A FEW BEATINGS BETWEEN FRIENDS
Martyn Turner '03

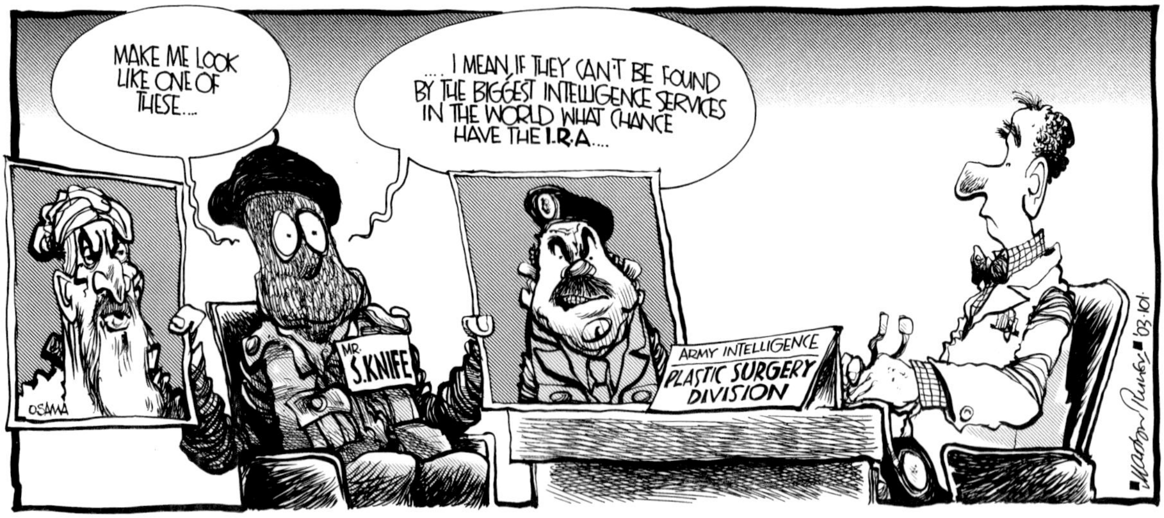
MAKE ME LOOK LIKE ONE OF THESE....
....I MEAN, IF THEY CAN'T BE FOUND BY THE BIGGEST INTELLIGENCE SERVICES IN THE WORLD WHAT CHANCE HAVE THE I.R.A....
OSAMA
MR. S.KNIFE
ARMY INTELLIGENCE
PLASTIC SURGERY DIVISION

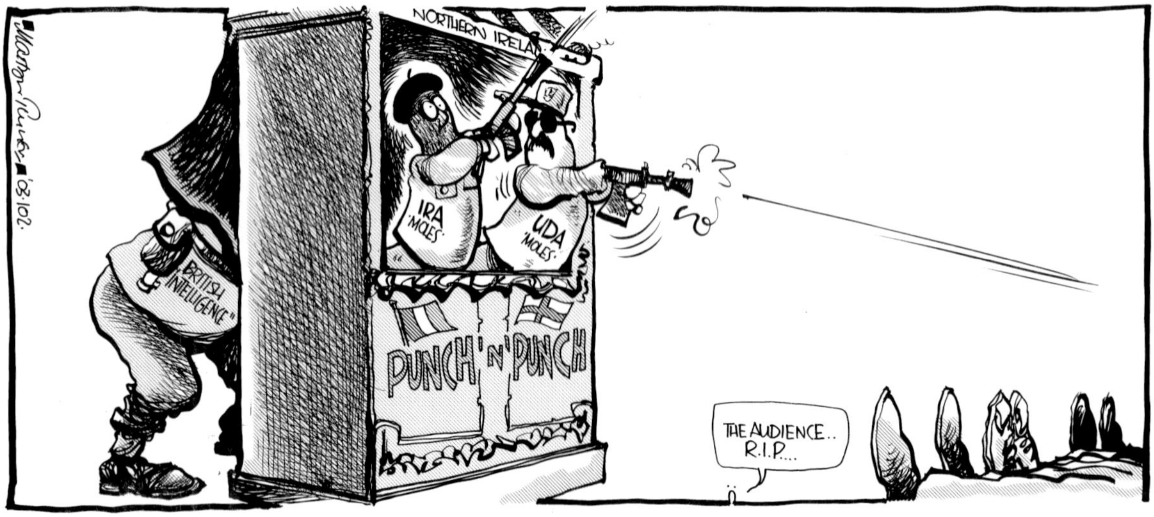
NORTHERN IRELA
IRA 'MOLES'
UDA 'MOLES'
"BRITISH INTELLIGENCE"
PUNCH 'N' PUNCH
THE AUDIENCE.. R.I.P....

New World Order in slightly random order

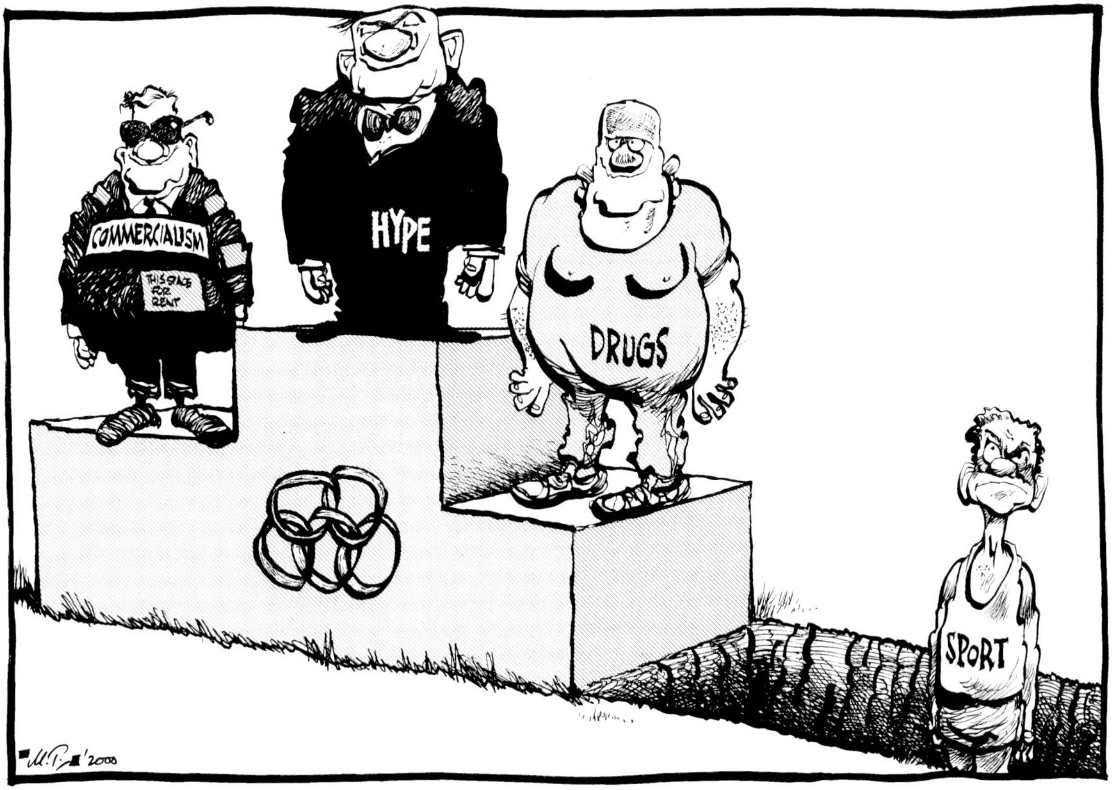
COMMERCIALISM
THIS SPACE FOR RENT
HYPE
DRUGS
SPORT

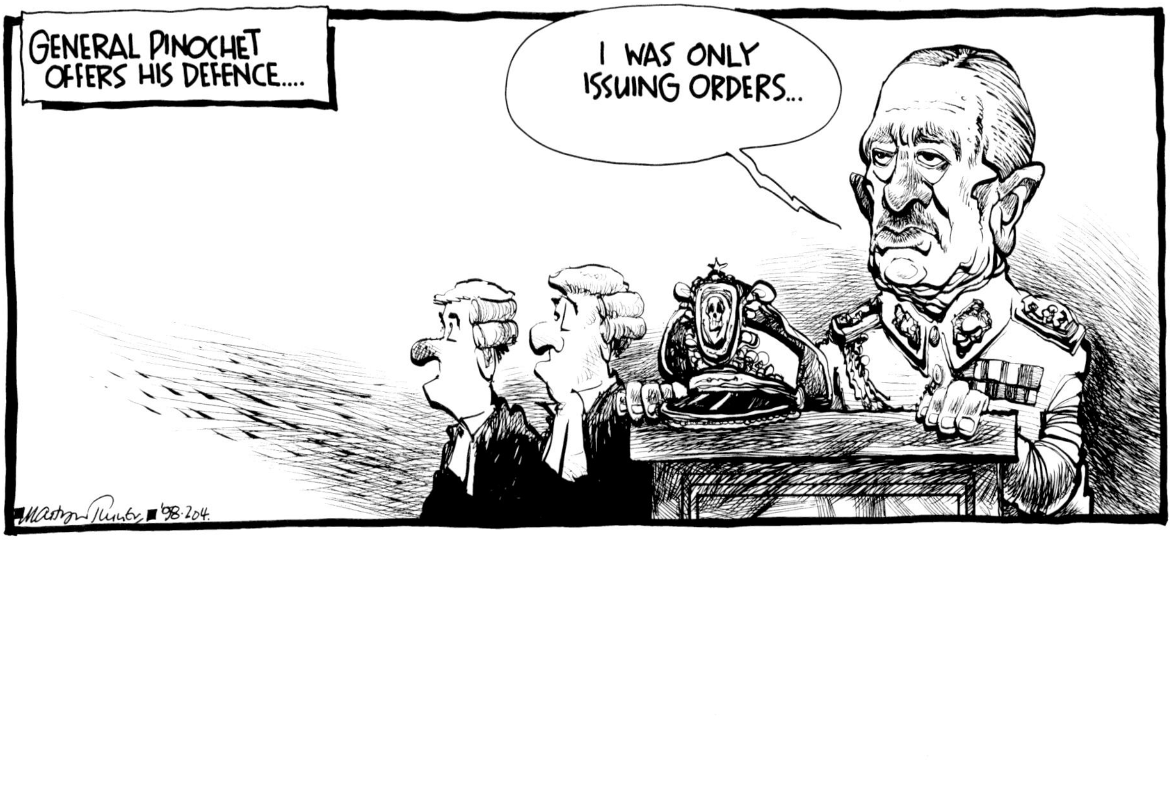
GENERAL PINOCHET OFFERS HIS DEFENCE....
I WAS ONLY ISSUING ORDERS...

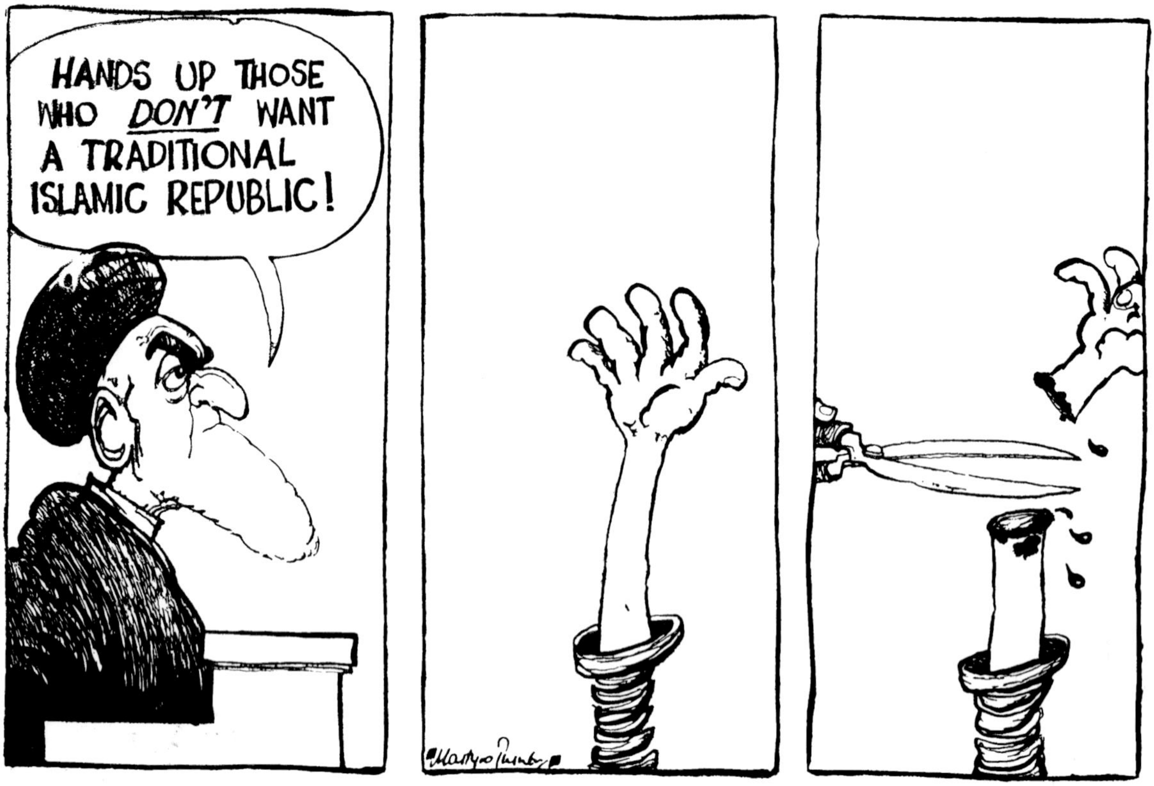
HANDS UP THOSE WHO DON'T WANT A TRADITIONAL ISLAMIC REPUBLIC!

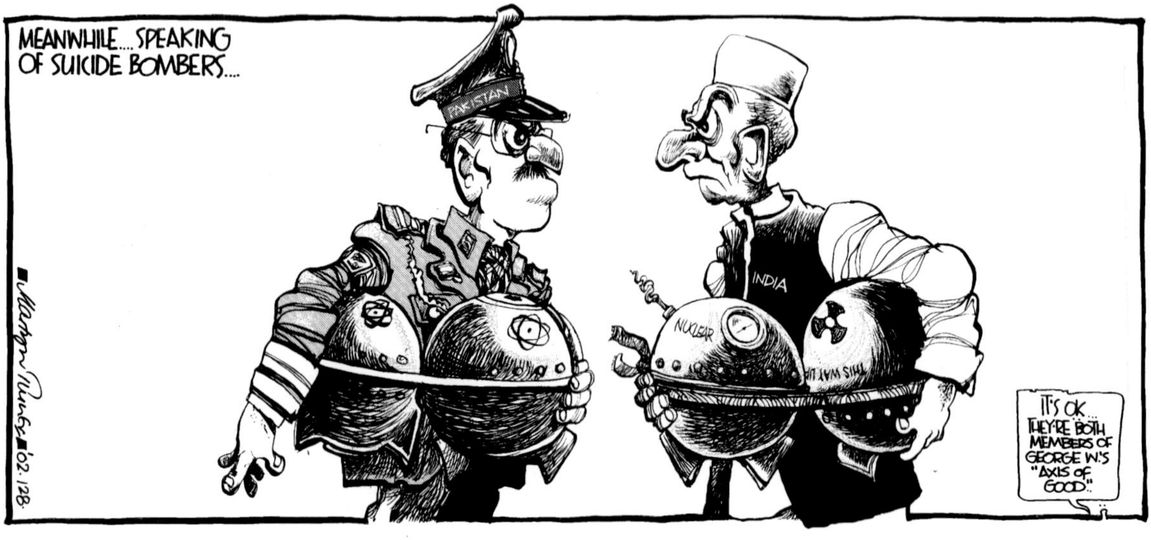
MEANWHILE.... SPEAKING OF SUICIDE BOMBERS....
PAKISTAN
INDIA
NUCLEAR
IT'S OK... THEY'RE BOTH MEMBERS OF GEORGE W.'S "AXIS OF GOOD".

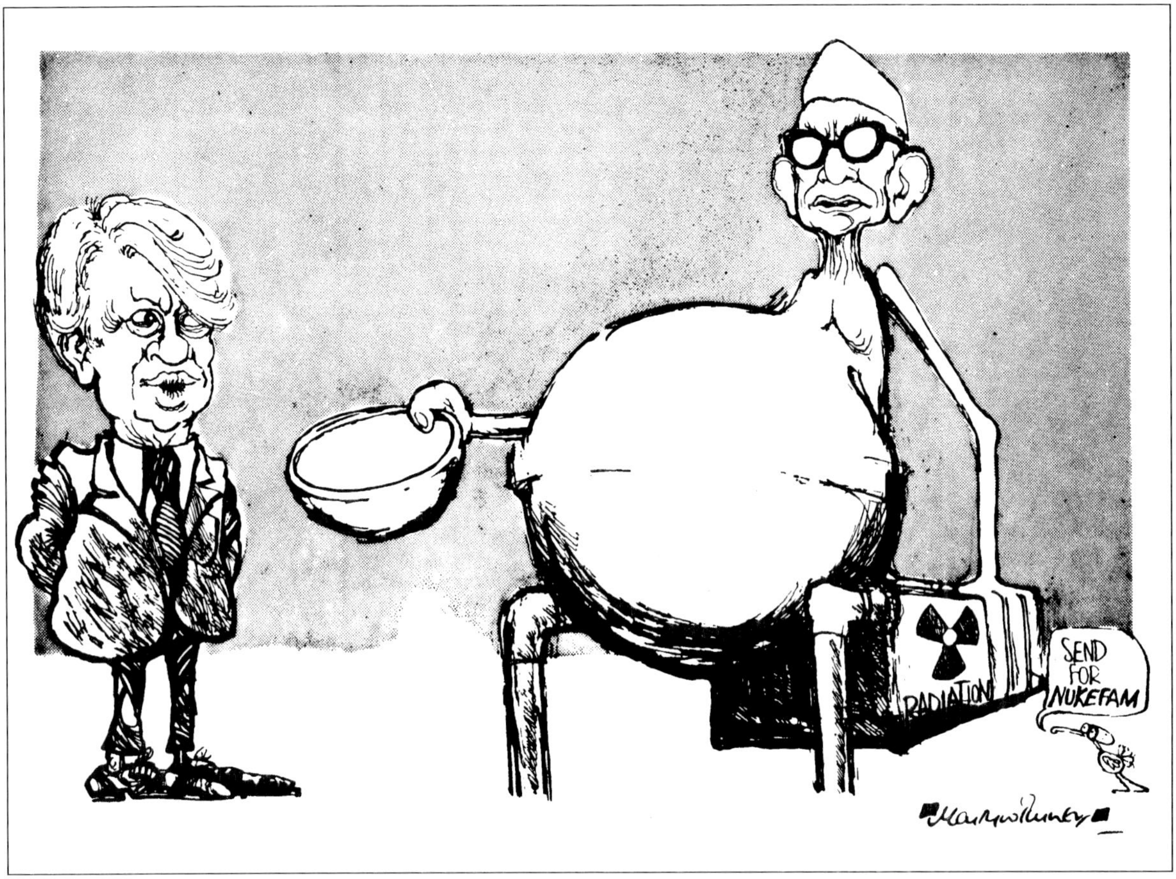
RADIATION
SEND FOR NUKEFAM

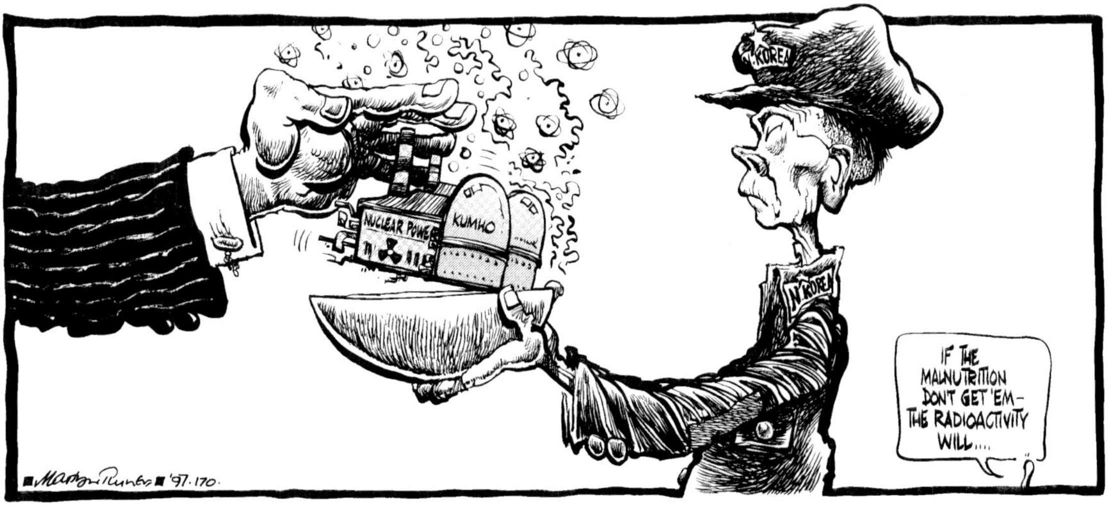
KOREA
NUCLEAR POWE
KUMHO
N'KOREA
IF THE MALNUTRITION DON'T GET 'EM - THE RADIOACTIVITY WILL....
'97.170.

Hands up those who would believe a report that says there is little evidence that Chernobyl has damaged health...

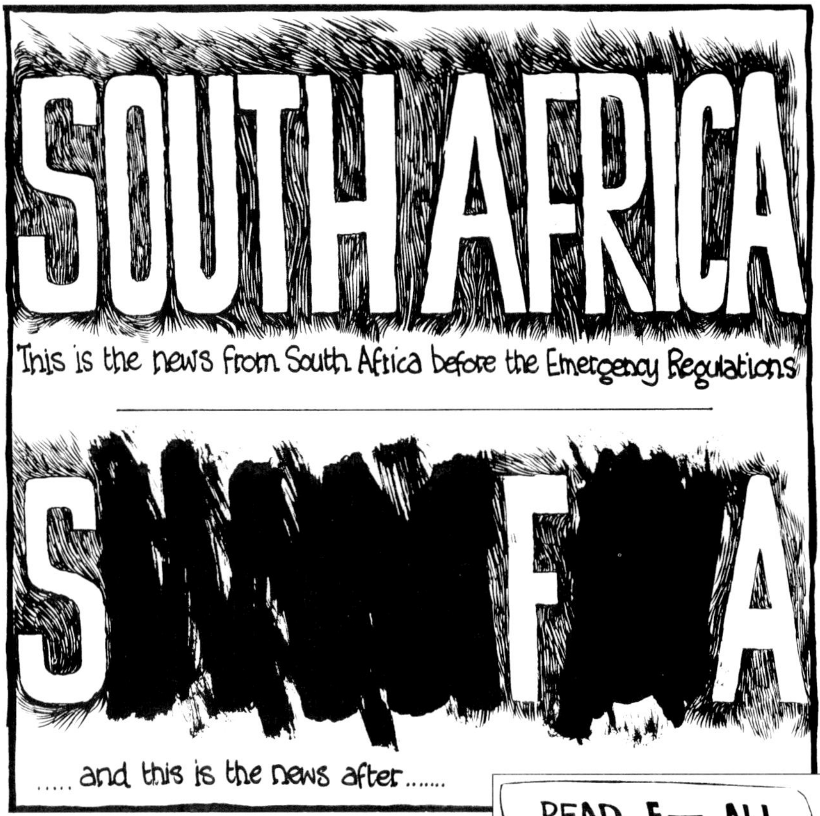
SOUTH AFRICA
This is the news from South Africa before the Emergency Regulations
S F A
..... and this is the news after.......

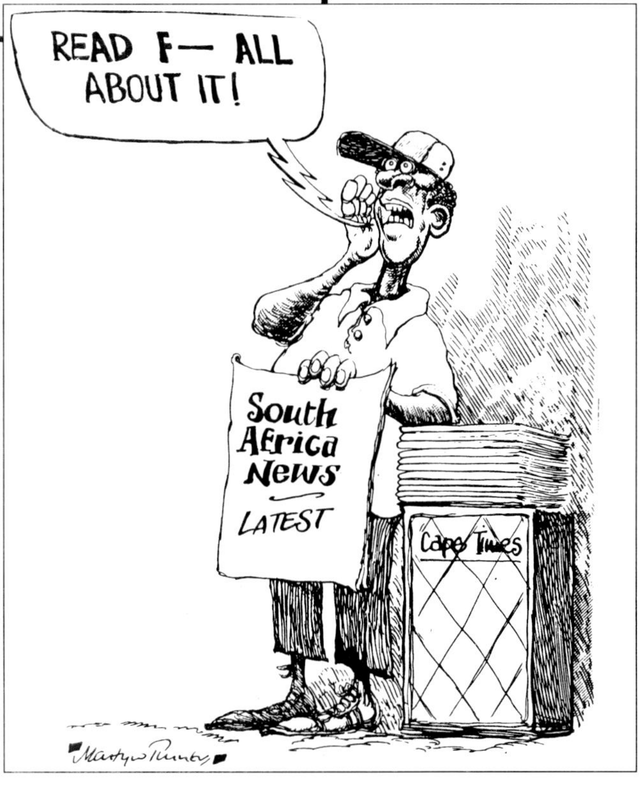
READ F— ALL ABOUT IT!
South Africa News
LATEST
Cape Times

APART HEID
ECONOMICS

IN EVENT OF EMERGENCY
BREAK GLASS
CENSORSHIP
Indemnity Law
WAR WAR IS BETTER THAN JAW JAW
P.W. BOTHA
QUITE SIMILAR TO NORMALITY REALLY

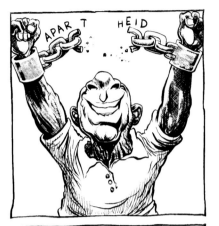

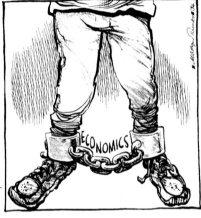

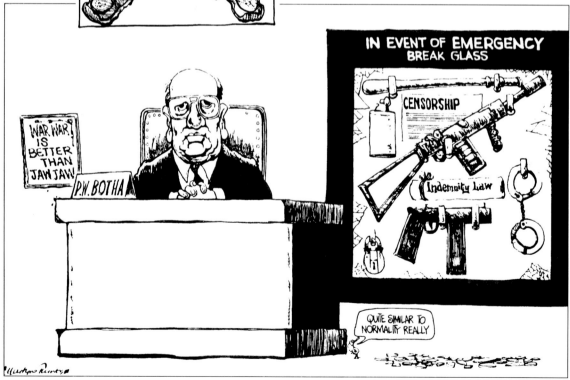

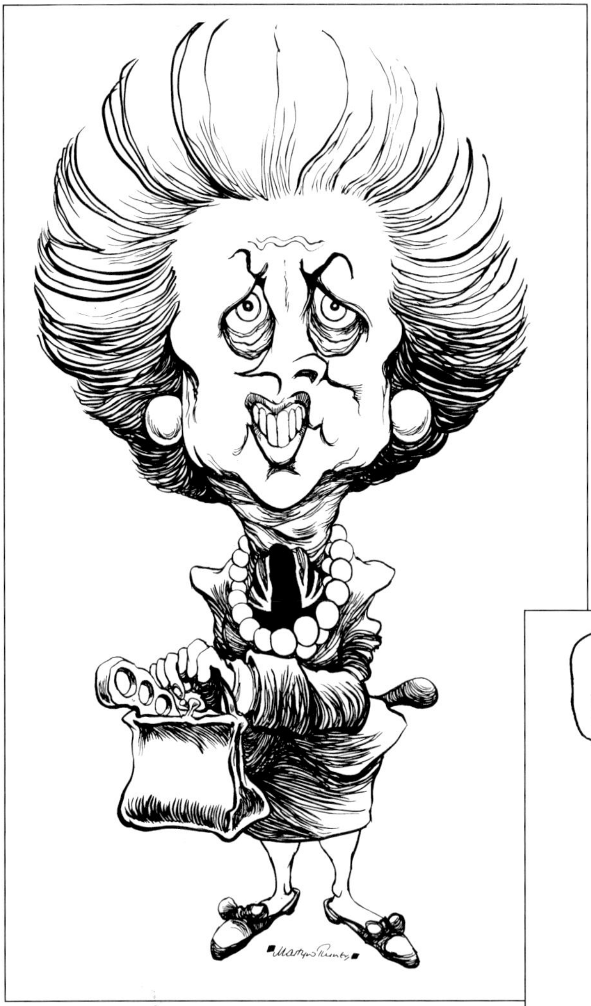

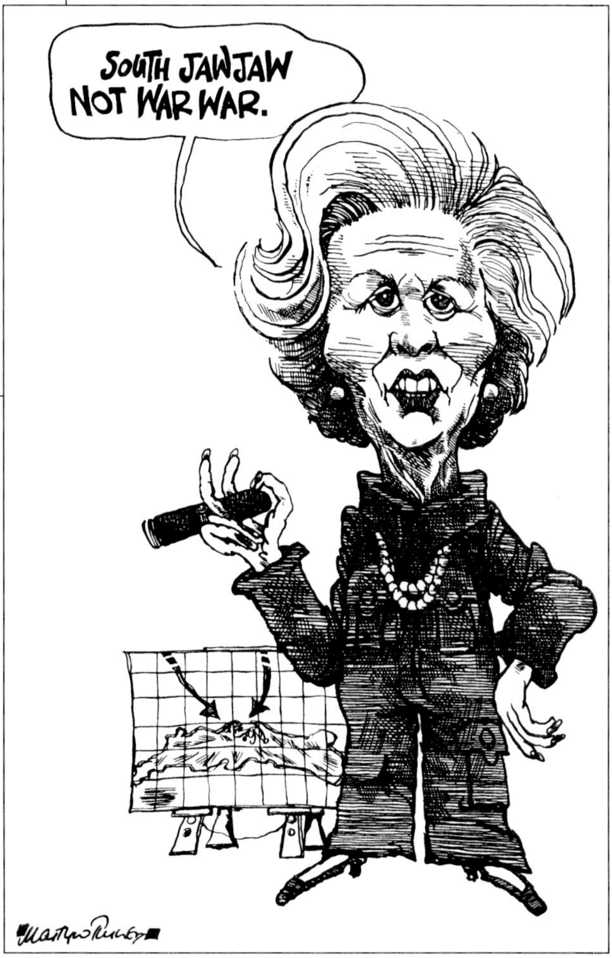
SOUTH JAWJAW
NOT WAR WAR.

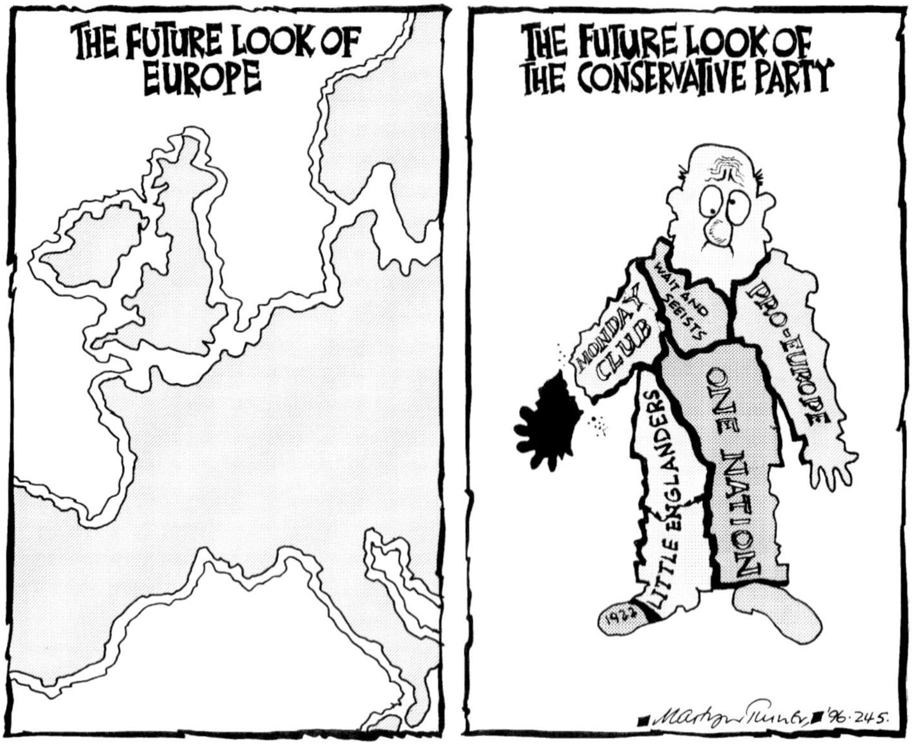
THE FUTURE LOOK OF EUROPE
THE FUTURE LOOK OF THE CONSERVATIVE PARTY
WAIT AND SEEISTS
MONDAY CLUB
PRO-EUROPE
ONE NATION
LITTLE ENGLANDERS
1922
Martyn Turner '96·245.

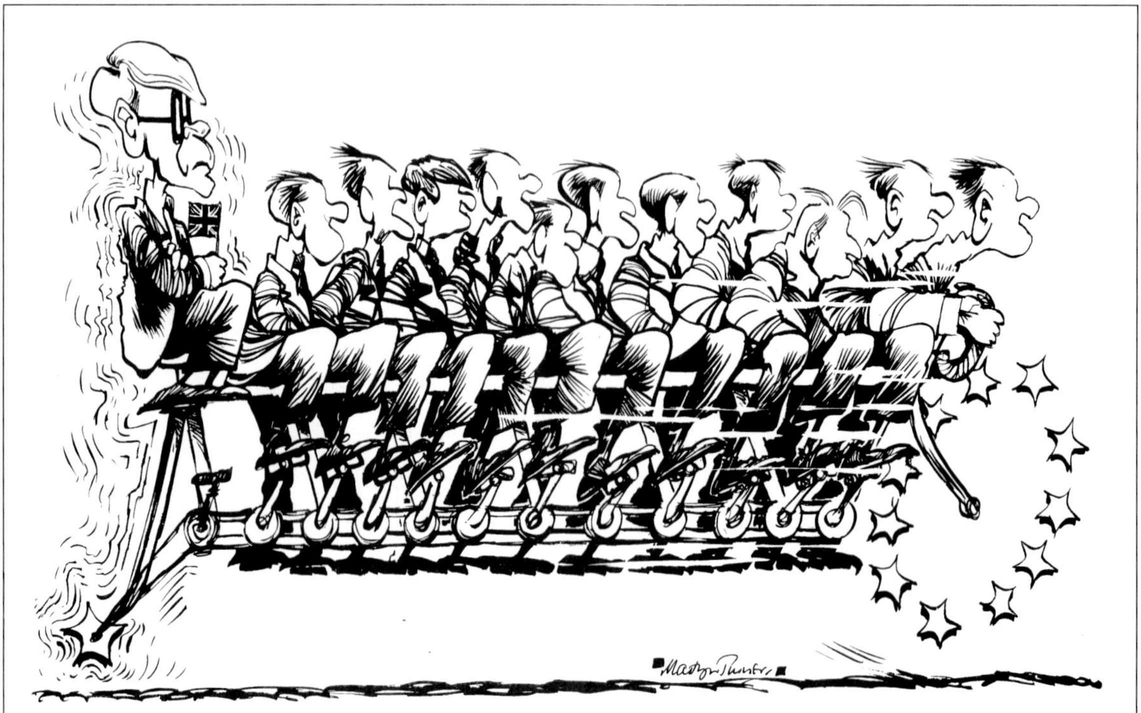
Martyn Turner

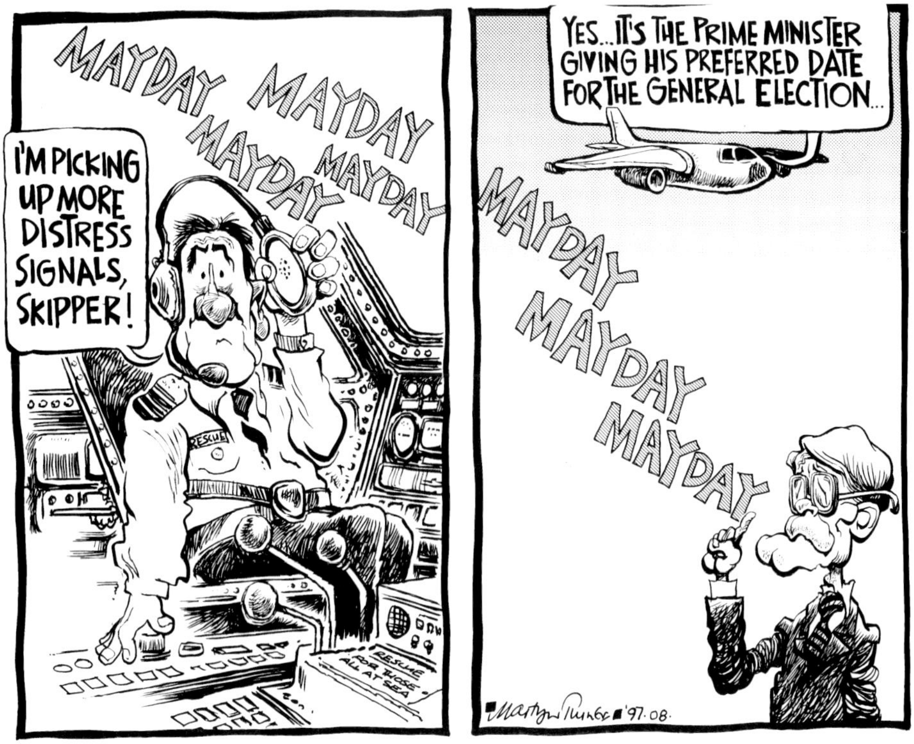
MAYDAY MAYDAY MAYDAY MAYDAY MAYDAY
I'M PICKING UP MORE DISTRESS SIGNALS, SKIPPER!
RESCUE
RESCUE FOR THOSE ALL AT SEA
YES...IT'S THE PRIME MINISTER GIVING HIS PREFERRED DATE FOR THE GENERAL ELECTION...
MAYDAY MAYDAY MAYDAY
Martyn Turner '97.08.

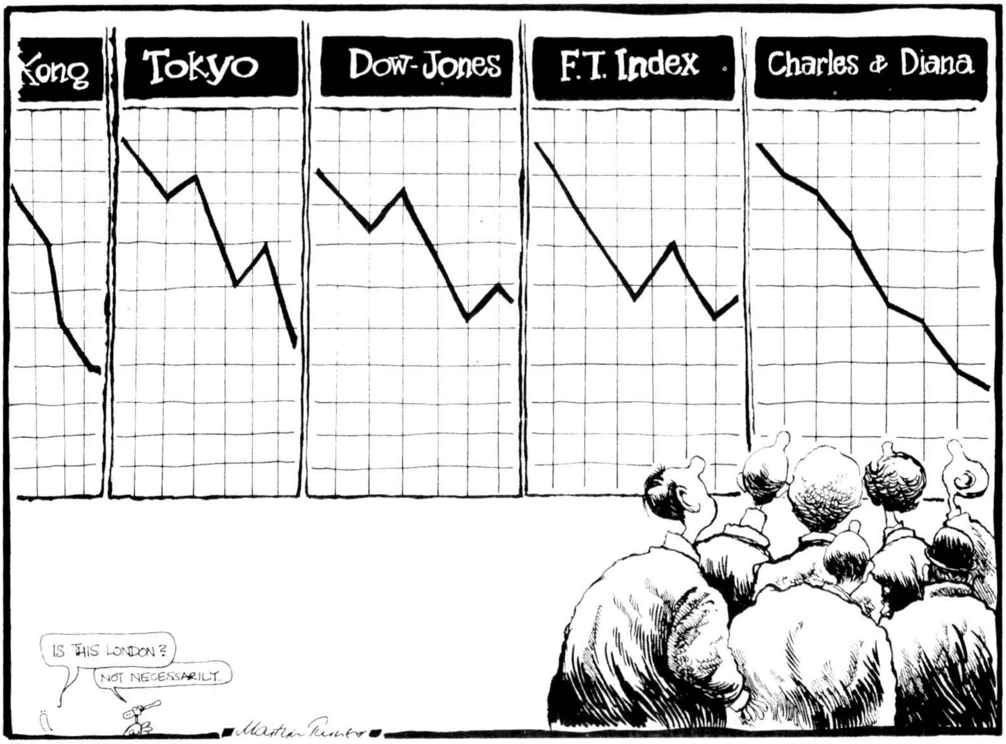
Kong
Tokyo
Dow-Jones
F.T. Index
Charles & Diana
IS THIS LONDON?
NOT NECESSARILY
Martyn Turner

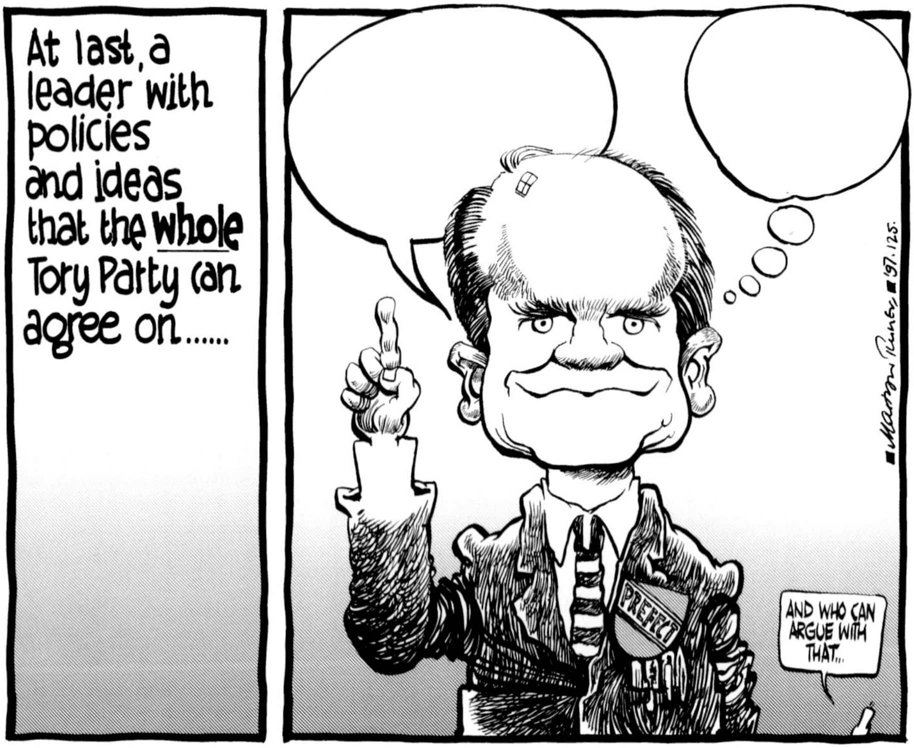

At last, a leader with policies and ideas that the whole Tory Party can agree on......
PREFECT
AND WHO CAN ARGUE WITH THAT...
Martyn Turner '97.125.

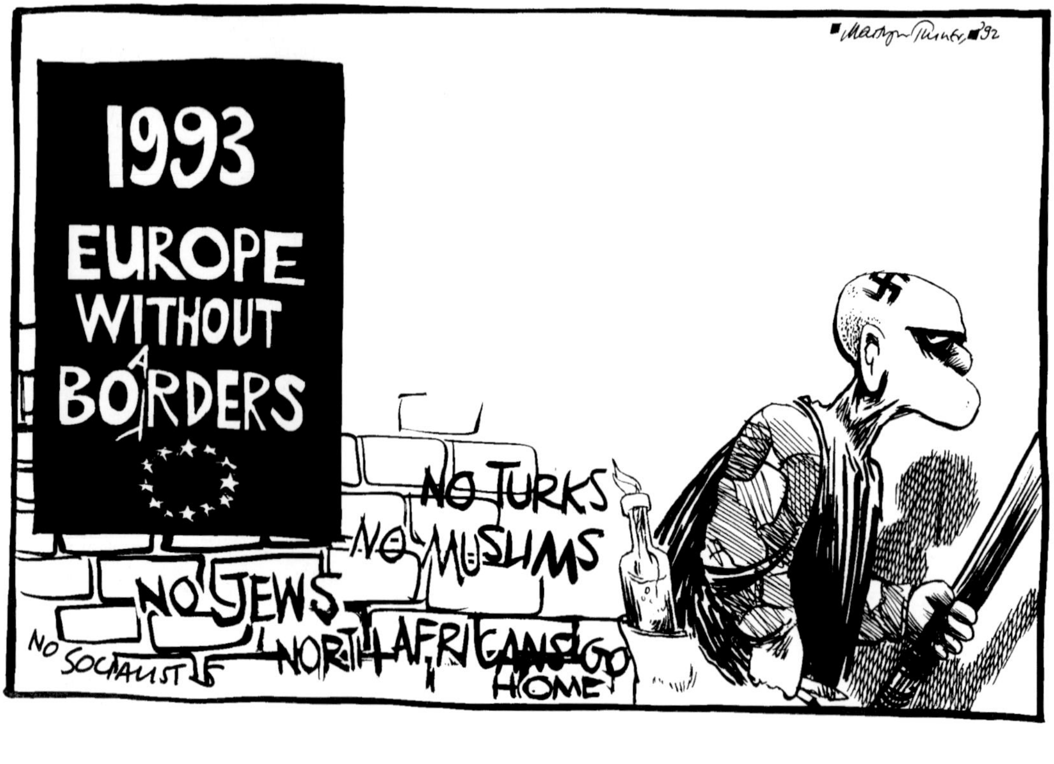

Martyn Turner '92
1993
EUROPE WITHOUT A BORDERS
NO TURKS
NO MUSLIMS
NO JEWS
NO SOCIALISTS
NORTH AFRICANS GO HOME

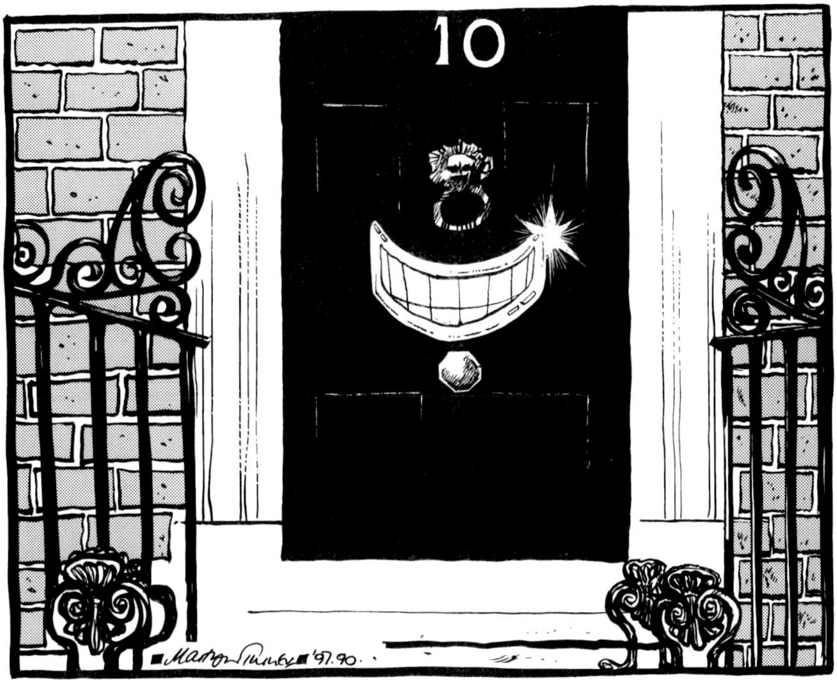
10

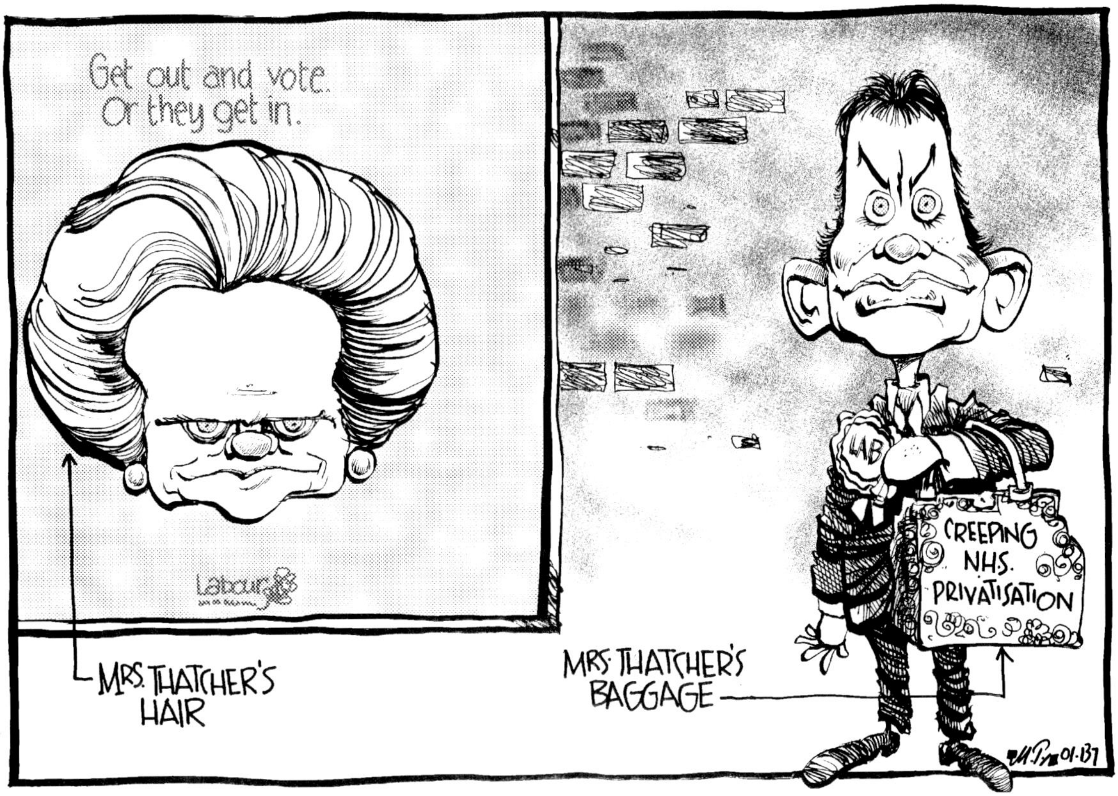
Get out and vote.
Or they get in.
Labour
MRS. THATCHER'S HAIR
LAB
CREEPING NHS. PRIVATISATION
MRS. THATCHER'S BAGGAGE

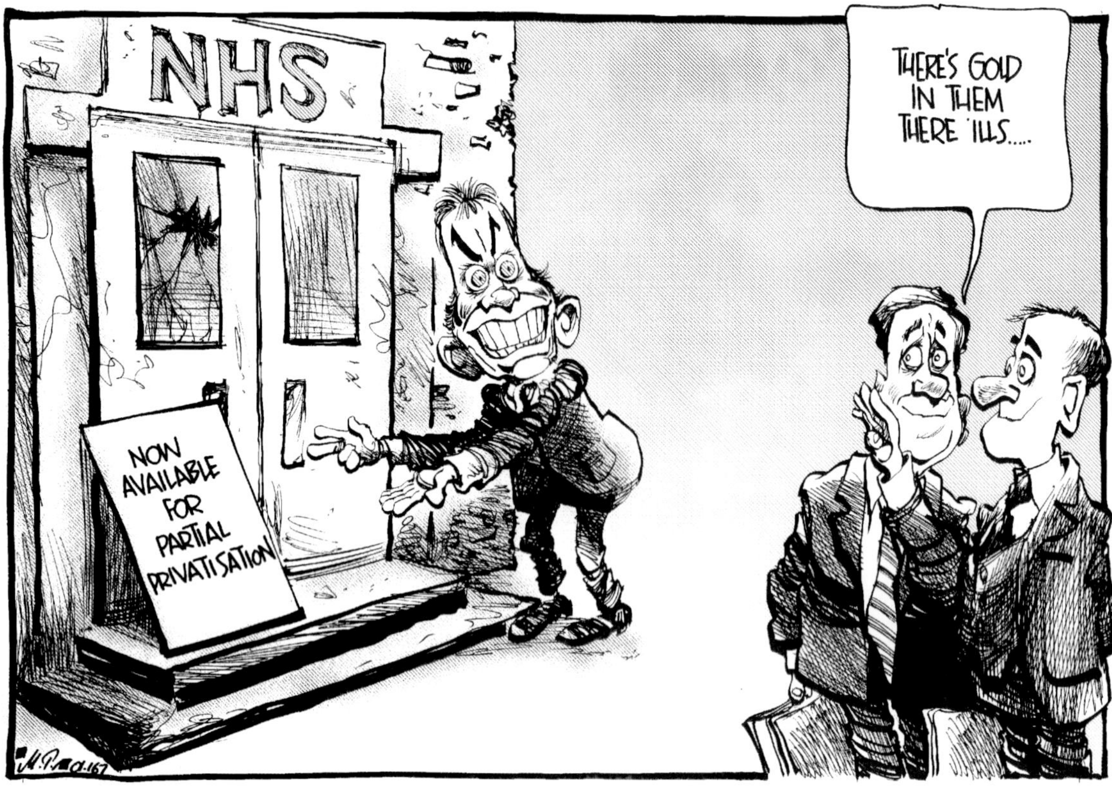
NHS
NOW AVAILABLE FOR PARTIAL PRIVATISATION
THERE'S GOLD IN THEM THERE 'ILLS.....

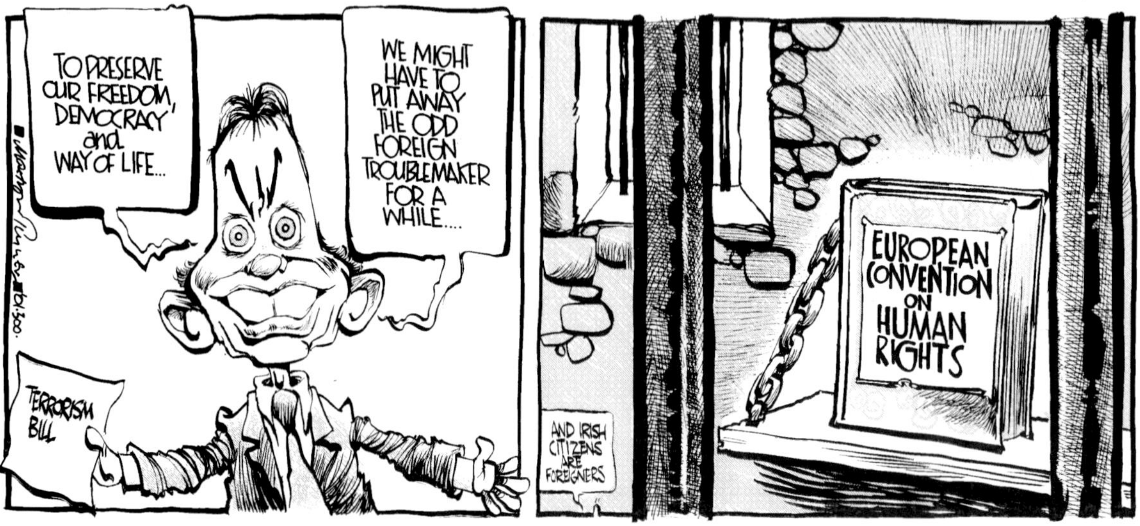
TO PRESERVE OUR FREEDOM, DEMOCRACY and WAY OF LIFE...
WE MIGHT HAVE TO PUT AWAY THE ODD FOREIGN TROUBLEMAKER FOR A WHILE....
TERRORISM BILL
AND IRISH CITIZENS ARE FOREIGNERS
EUROPEAN CONVENTION ON HUMAN RIGHTS

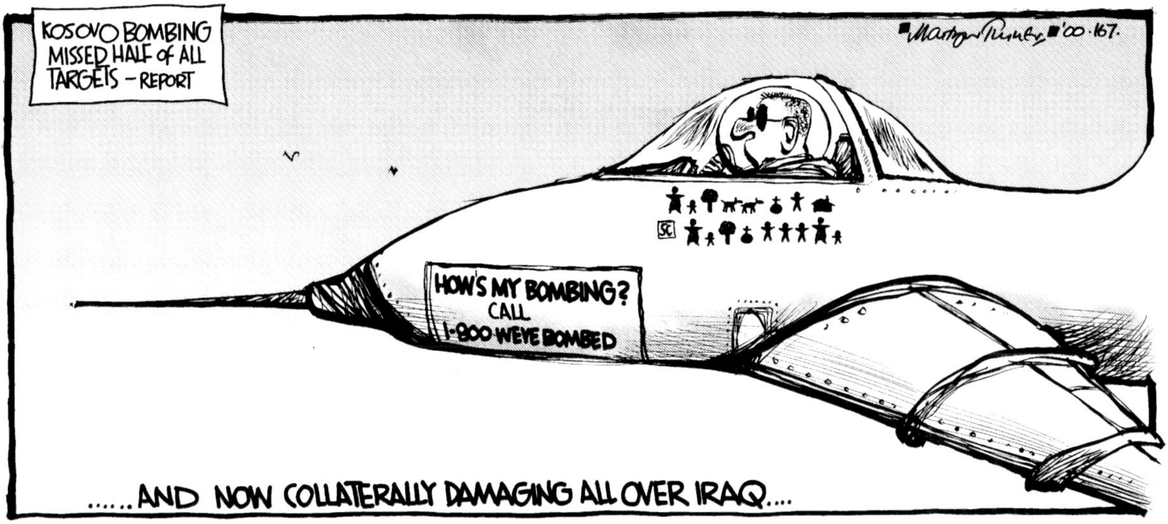
KOSOVO BOMBING MISSED HALF OF ALL TARGETS – REPORT
HOW'S MY BOMBING? CALL 1-800-WEVE BOMBED
......AND NOW COLLATERALLY DAMAGING ALL OVER IRAQ....

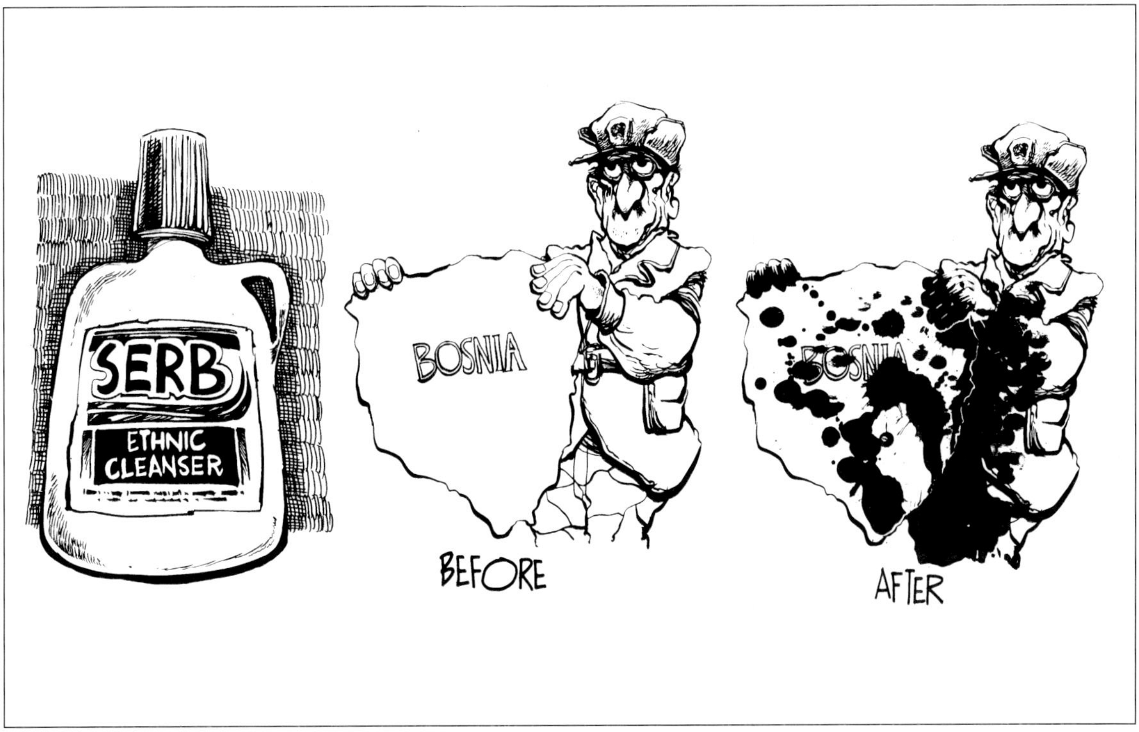
SERB
ETHNIC CLEANSER
BOSNIA
BEFORE
AFTER

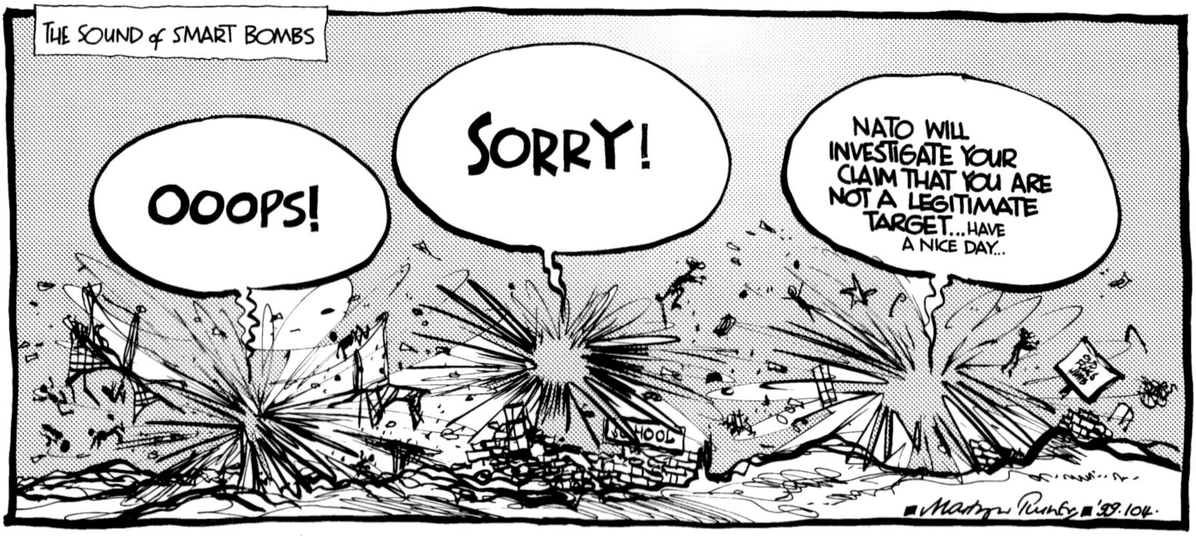
THE SOUND of SMART BOMBS
OOOPS!
SORRY!
NATO WILL INVESTIGATE YOUR CLAIM THAT YOU ARE NOT A LEGITIMATE TARGET... HAVE A NICE DAY...
SCHOOL

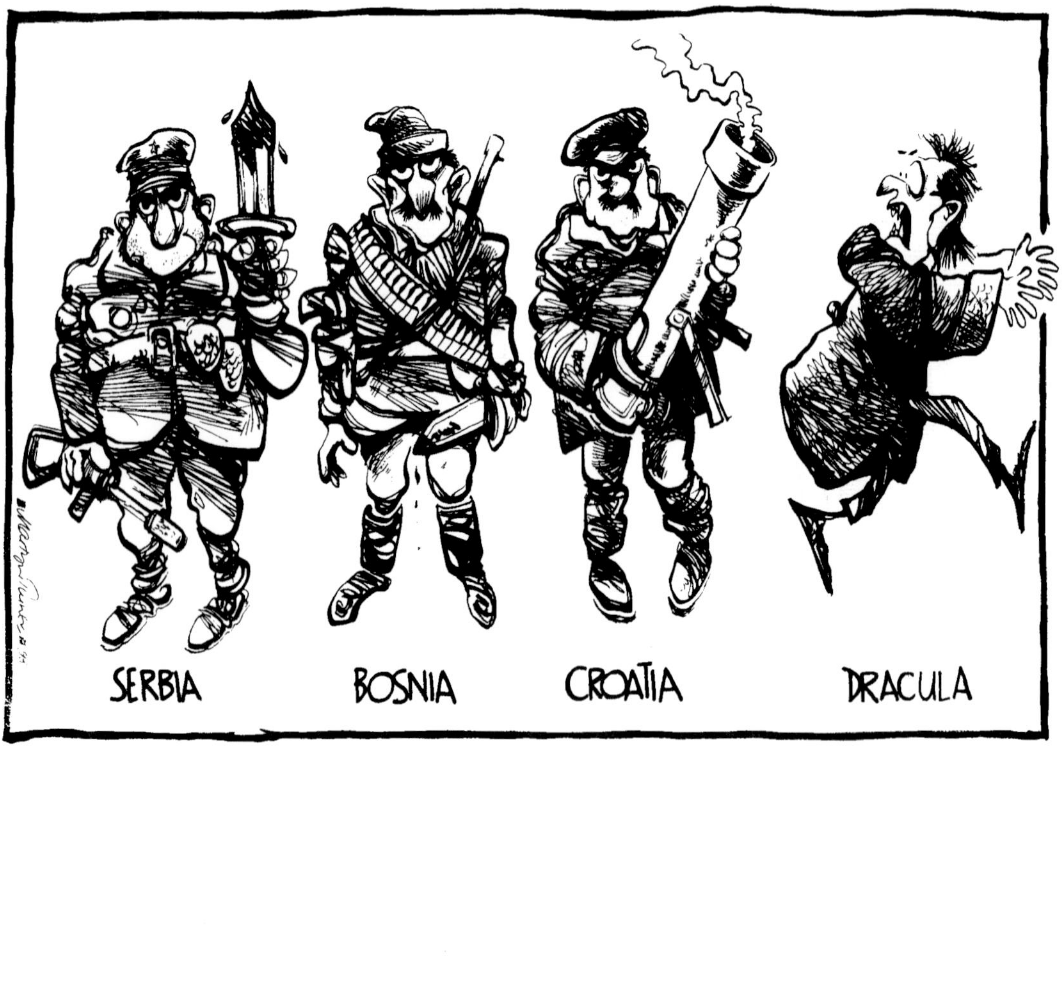
SERBIA
BOSNIA
CROATIA
DRACULA

Q. What has 500 black bras and 2,000 pairs of shoes?
A. An Imeldapede.

MARCOS
W
W
W
W

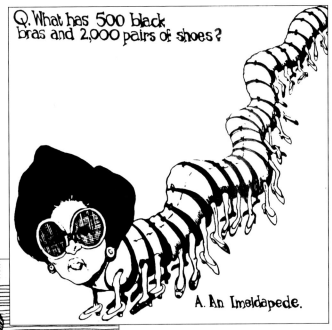

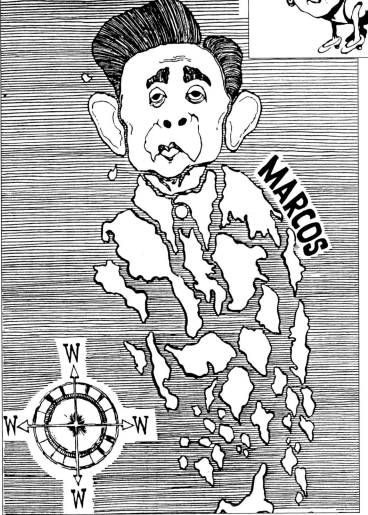

Imelda and Ferdinand Marcos

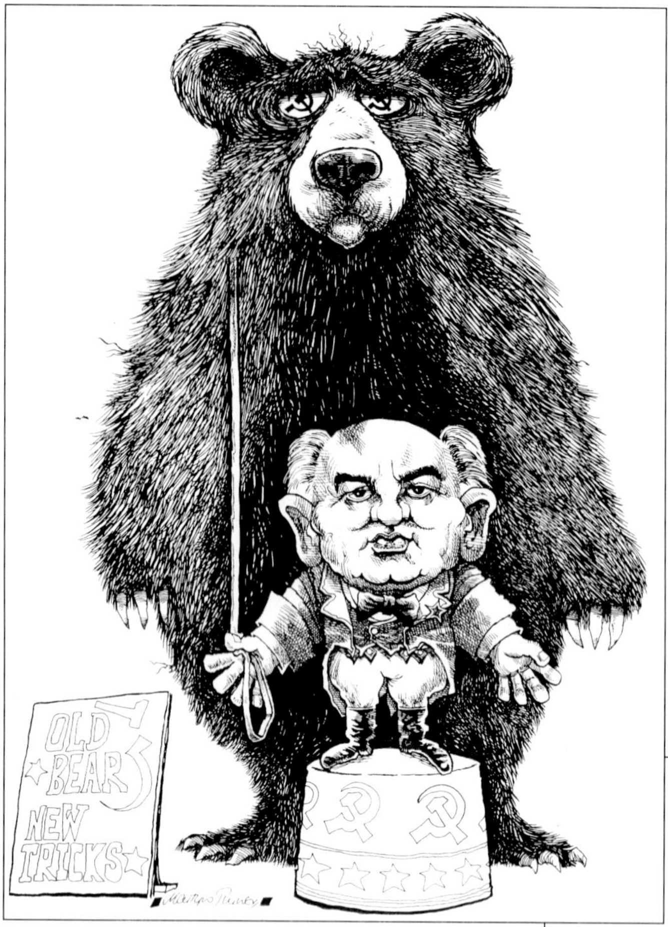
OLD
BEAR
NEW
TRICKS

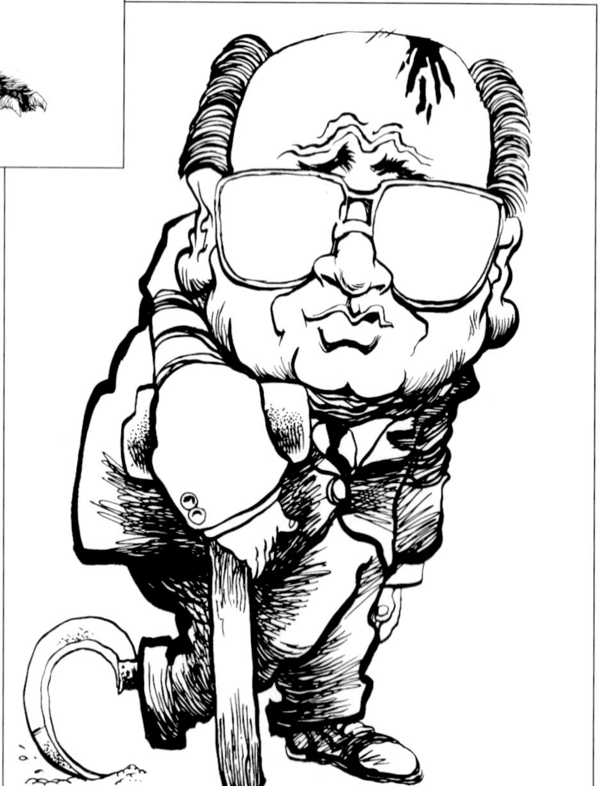

Gorbachev

Gaddafi

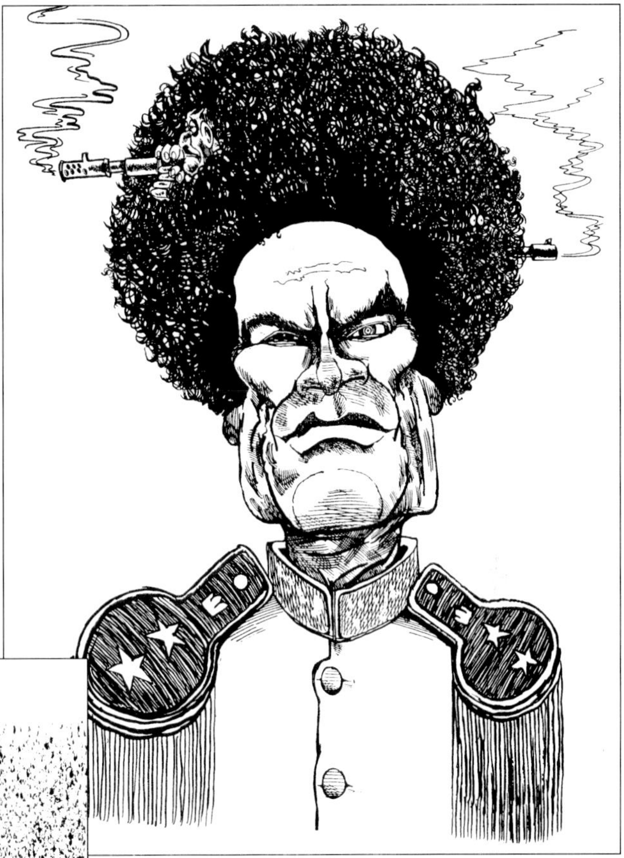

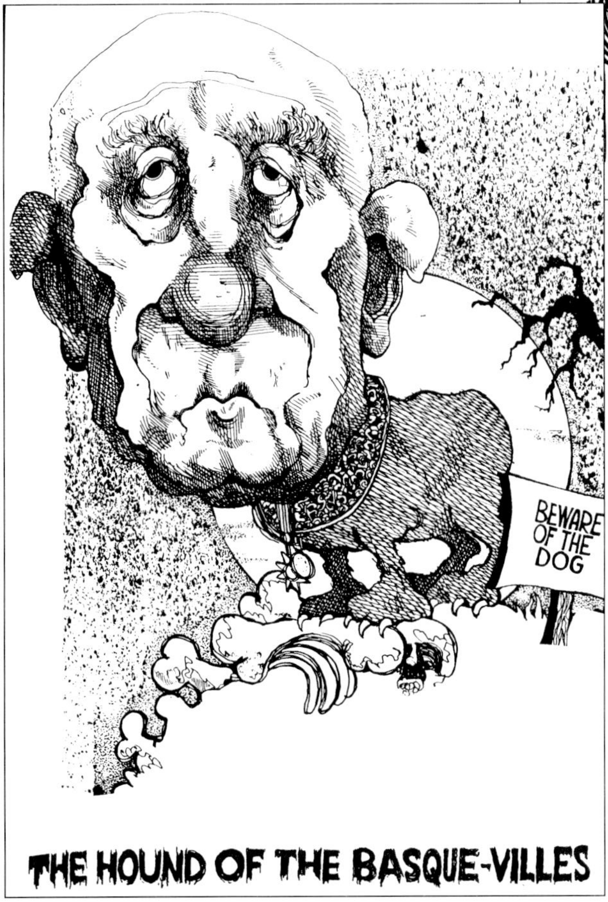
BEWARE OF THE DOG
THE HOUND OF THE BASQUE-VILLES

Franco

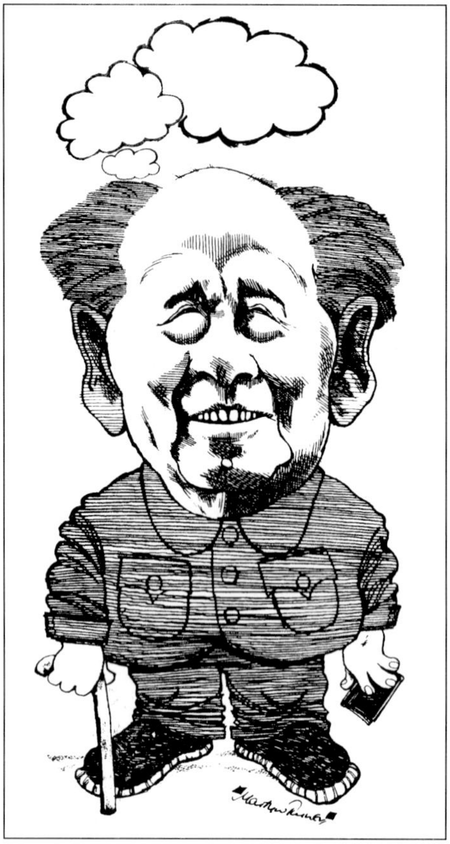

Mao

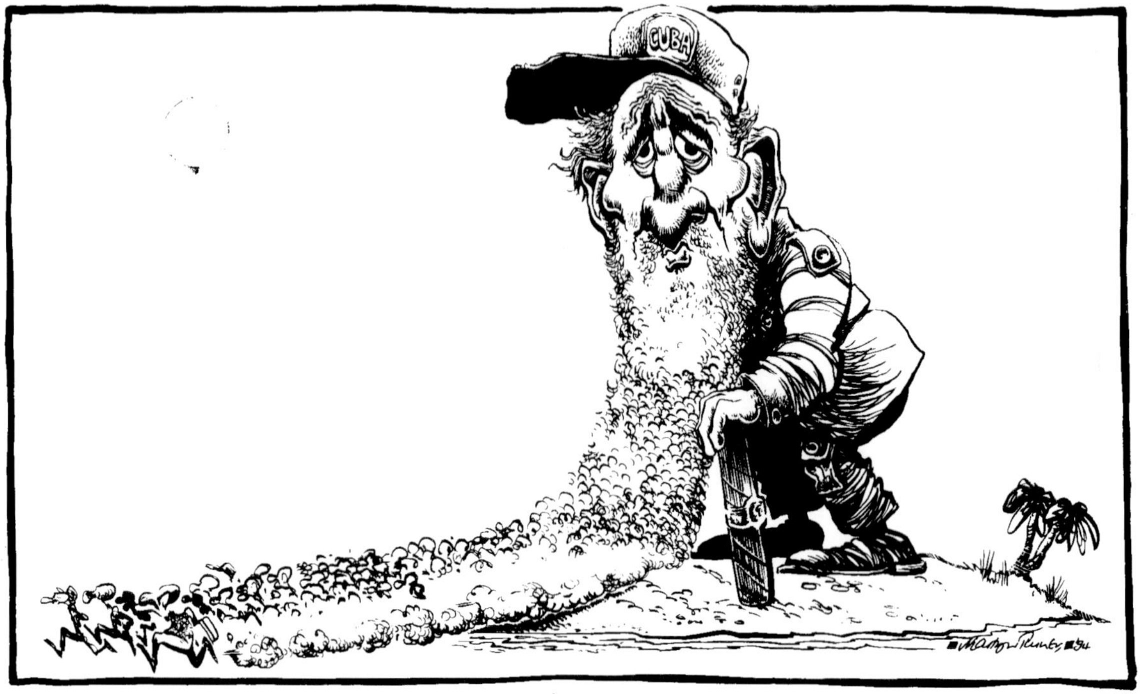
CUBA

Castro

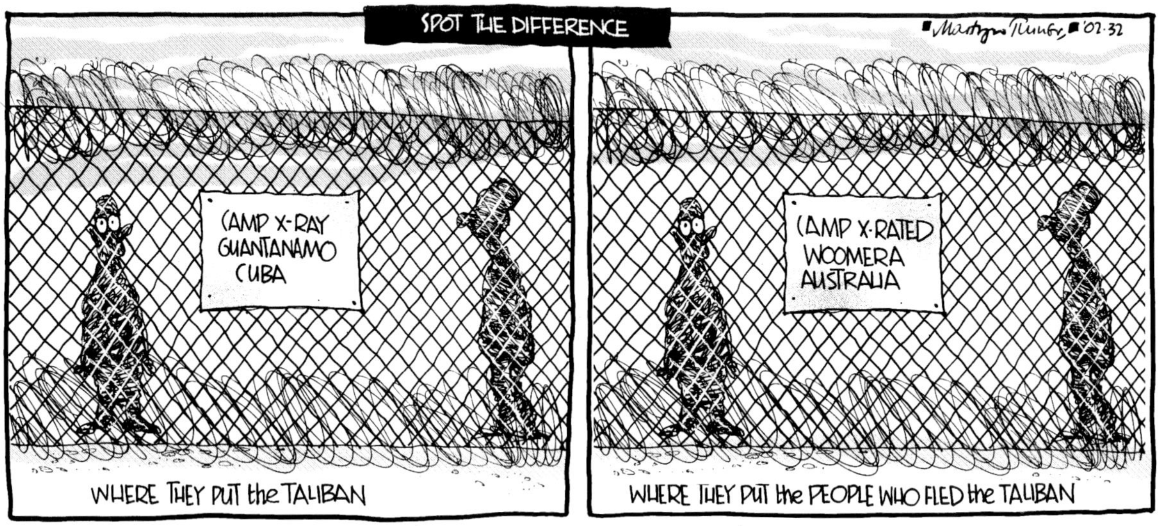
SPOT THE DIFFERENCE
Martyn Turner '02.32
CAMP X-RAY GUANTANAMO CUBA
WHERE THEY PUT the TALIBAN
CAMP X-RATED WOOMERA AUSTRALIA
WHERE THEY PUT the PEOPLE WHO FLED the TALIBAN

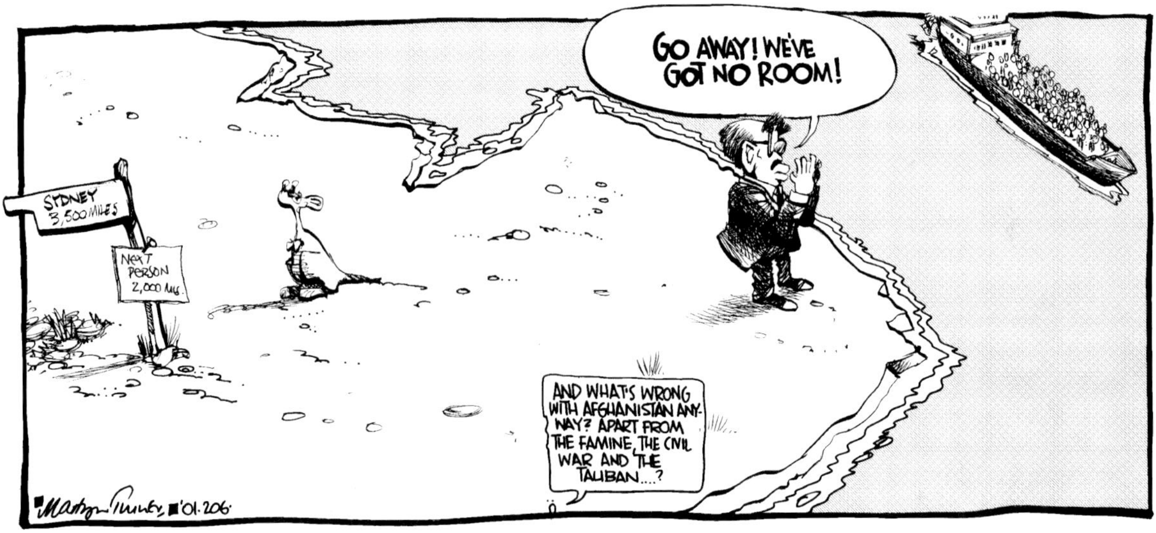
GO AWAY! WE'VE GOT NO ROOM!
SYDNEY 3,500 MILES
NEXT PERSON 2,000 MLS.
AND WHAT'S WRONG WITH AFGHANISTAN ANYWAY? APART FROM THE FAMINE, THE CIVIL WAR AND THE TALIBAN....?
Martyn Turner '01.206

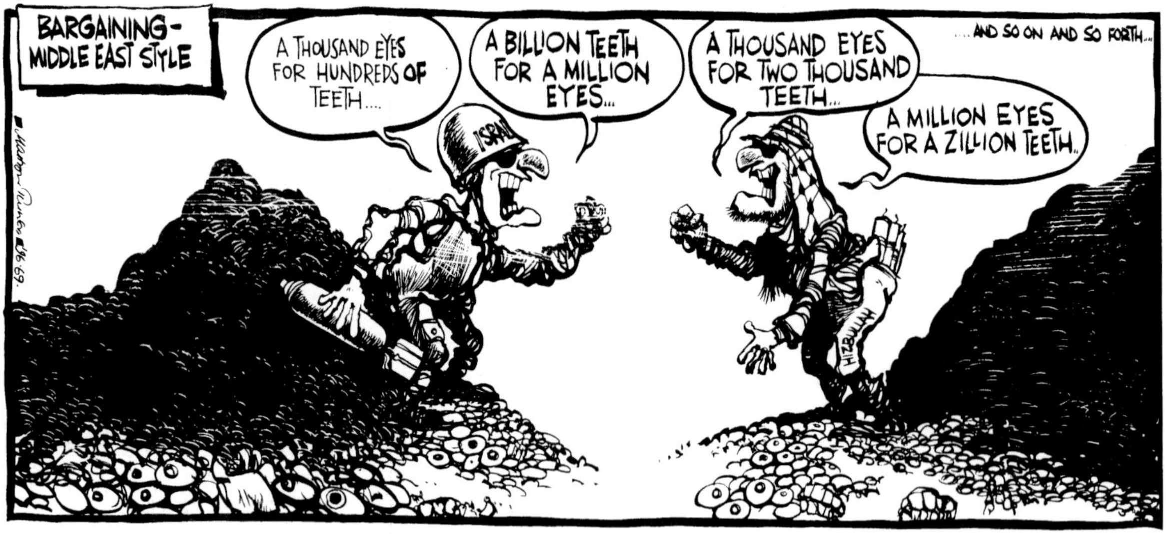
BARGAINING - MIDDLE EAST STYLE
A THOUSAND EYES FOR HUNDREDS OF TEETH....
A BILLION TEETH FOR A MILLION EYES...
A THOUSAND EYES FOR TWO THOUSAND TEETH...
A MILLION EYES FOR A ZILLION TEETH..
....AND SO ON AND SO FORTH...
ISRAEL
HIZBULLAH

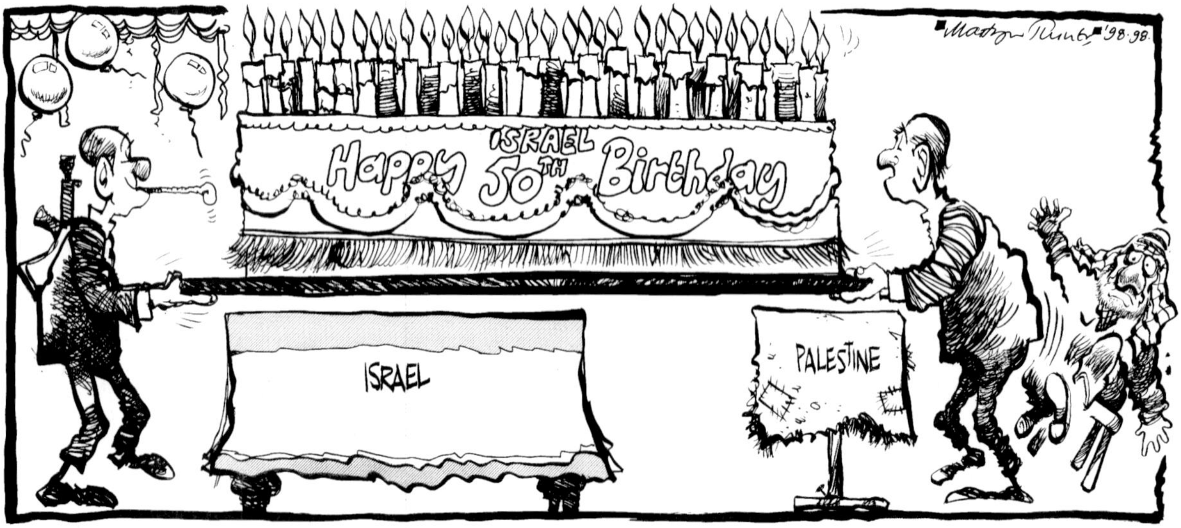
Happy ISRAEL 50TH Birthday
ISRAEL
PALESTINE

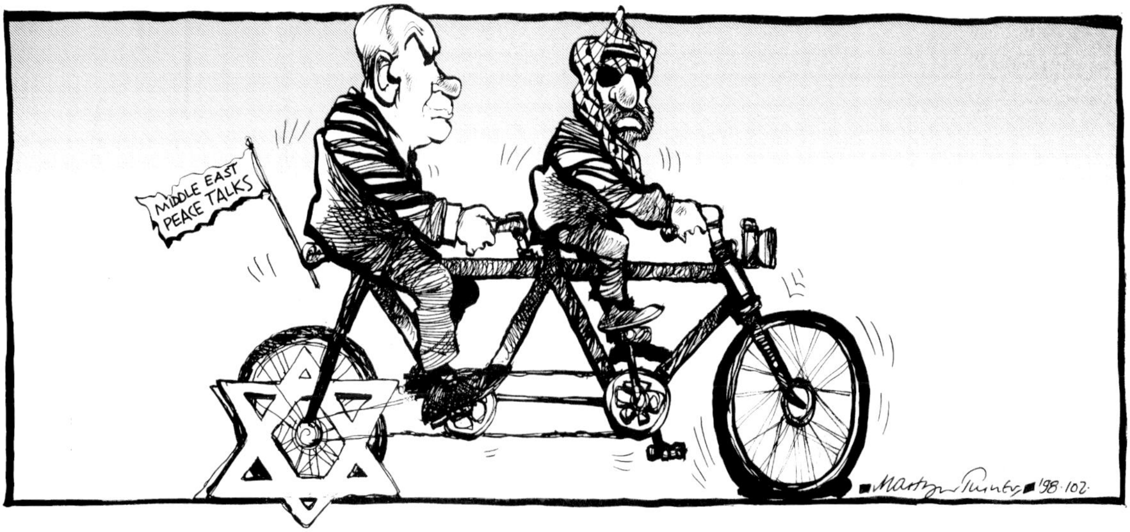
MIDDLE EAST PEACE TALKS
Martyn Turner '98·102·

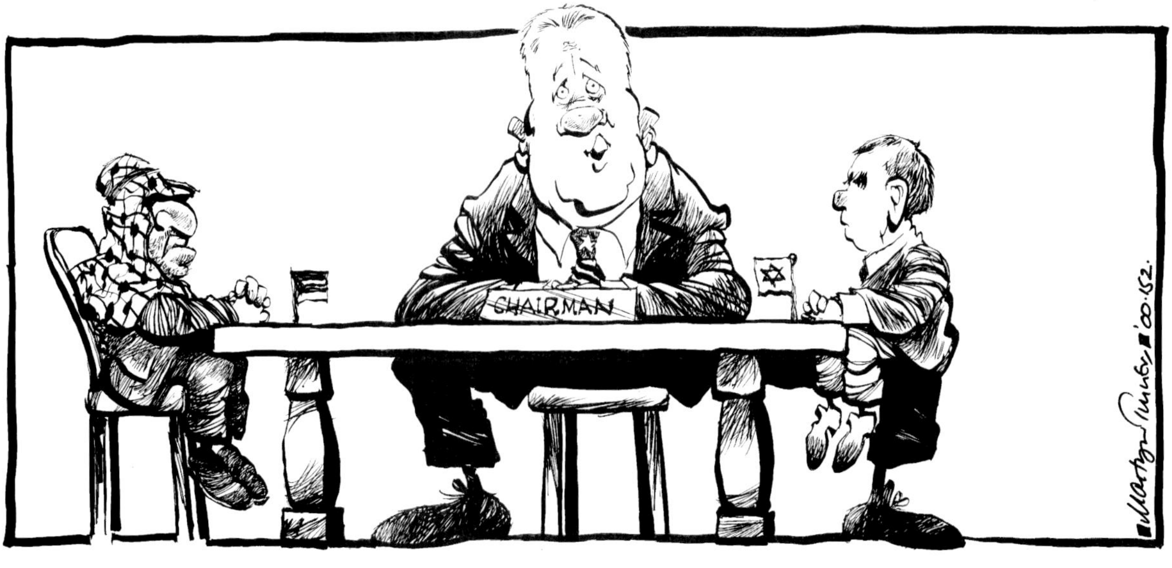
CHAIRMAN
Martyn Turner '00·152·

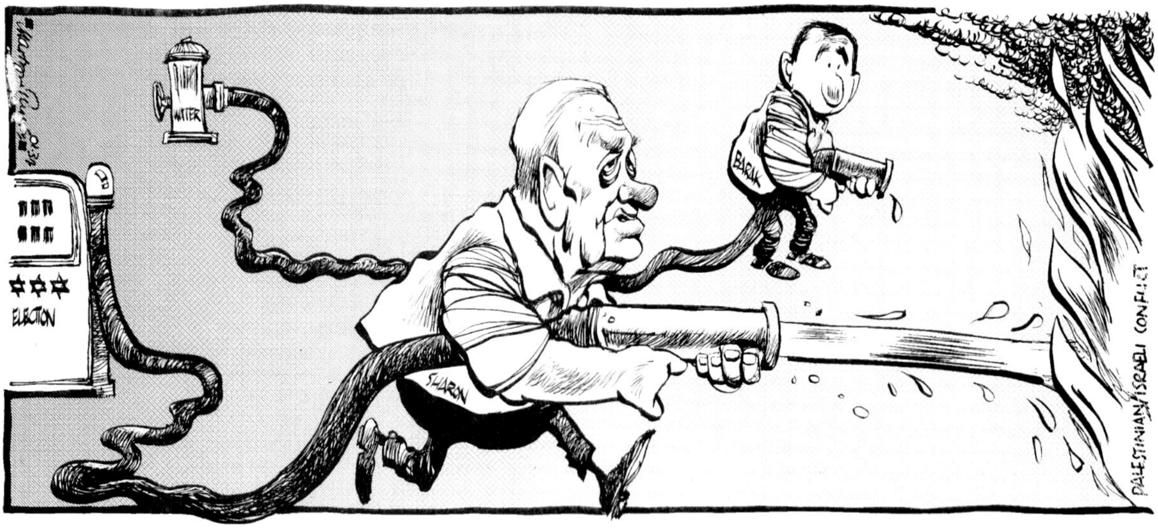
WATER
ELECTION
SHARON
BARAK
PALESTINIAN/ISRAELI CONFLICT

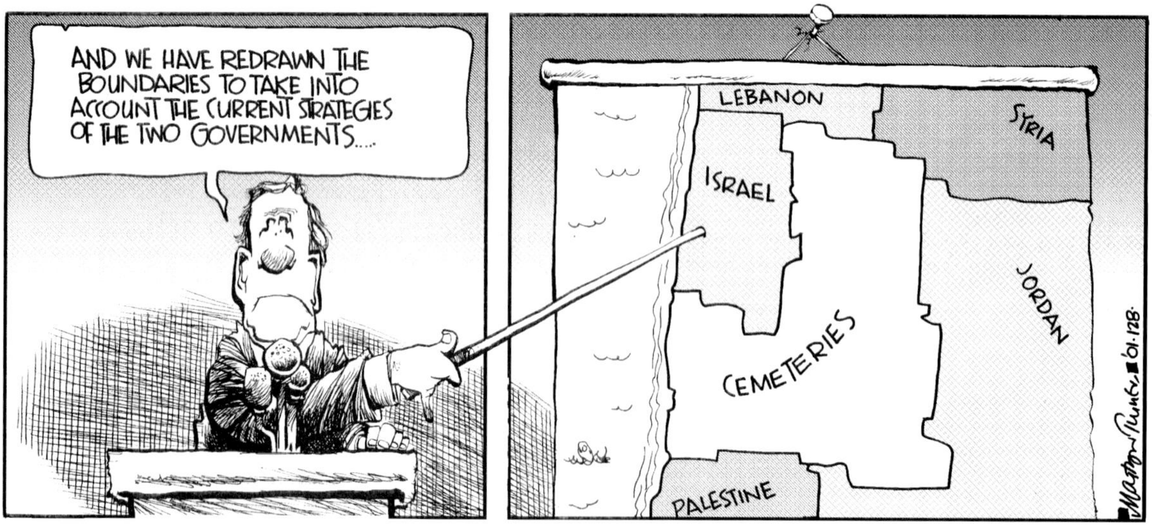
AND WE HAVE REDRAWN THE BOUNDARIES TO TAKE INTO ACCOUNT THE CURRENT STRATEGIES OF THE TWO GOVERNMENTS.....
LEBANON
SYRIA
ISRAEL
JORDAN
CEMETERIES
PALESTINE

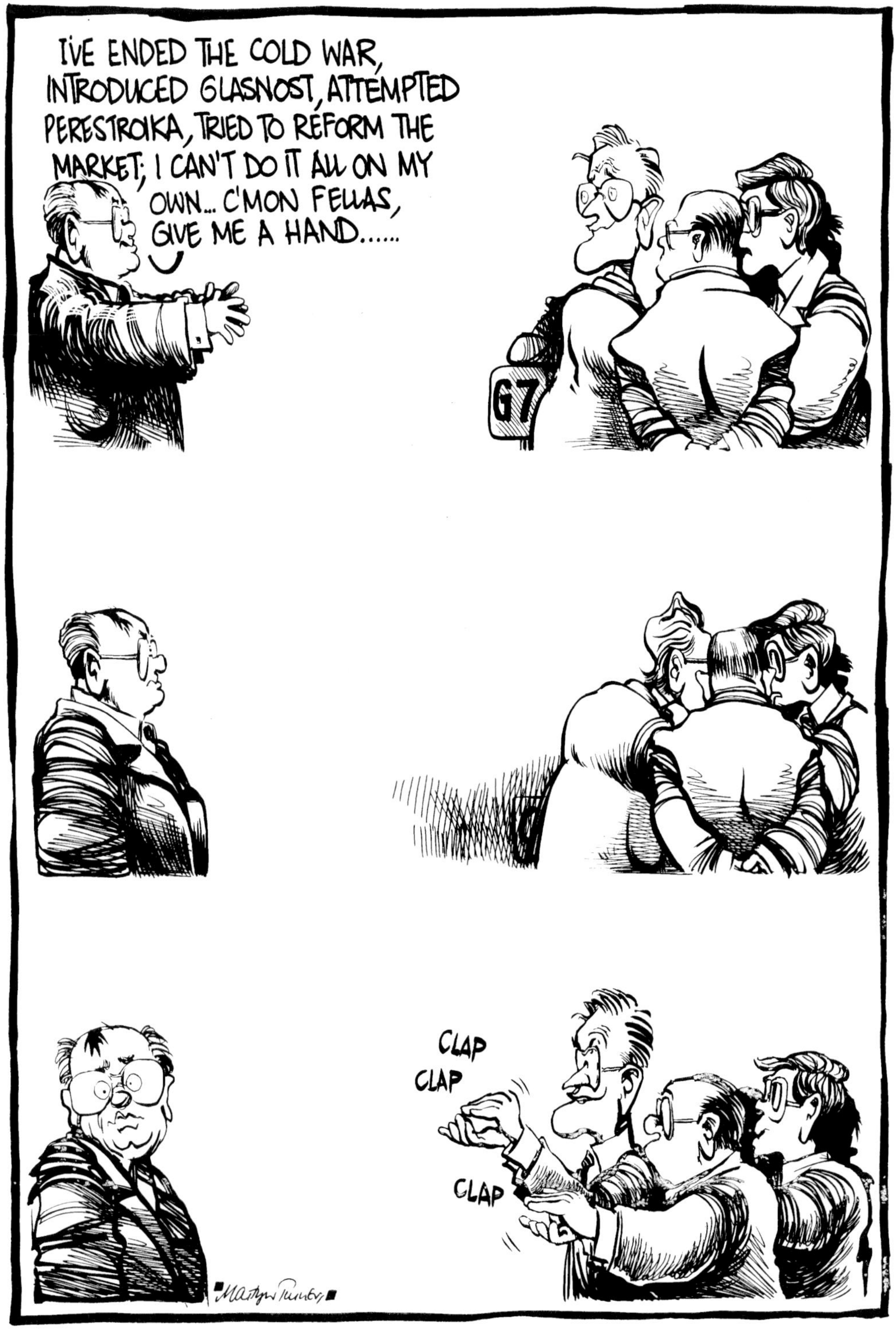
I'VE ENDED THE COLD WAR, INTRODUCED GLASNOST, ATTEMPTED PERESTROIKA, TRIED TO REFORM THE MARKET; I CAN'T DO IT ALL ON MY OWN... C'MON FELLAS, GIVE ME A HAND......
G7
CLAP
CLAP
CLAP
Martyn Turner

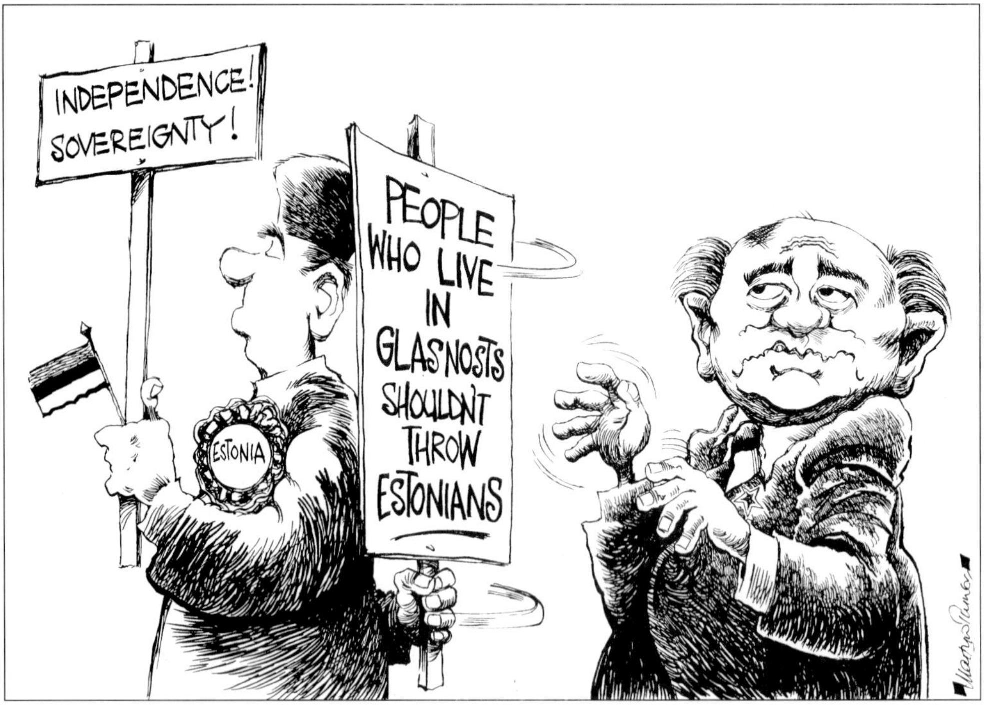
INDEPENDENCE!
SOVEREIGNTY!
ESTONIA
PEOPLE WHO LIVE IN GLASNOSTS SHOULDN'T THROW ESTONIANS
Martyn Turner

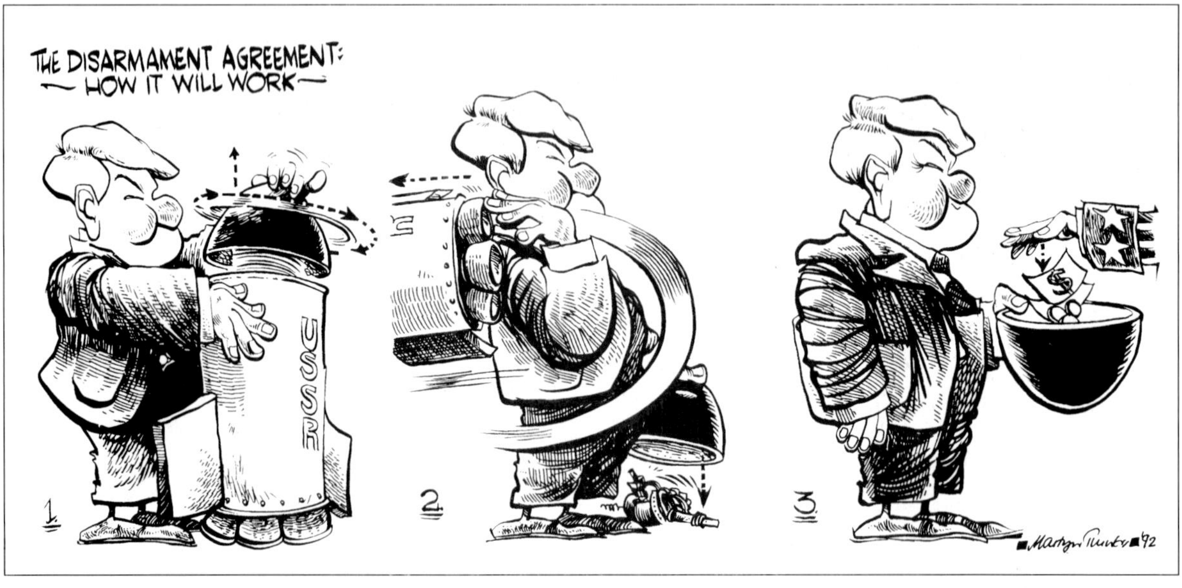
THE DISARMAMENT AGREEMENT:
HOW IT WILL WORK
USSR
1.
2.
3.
Martyn Turner '92

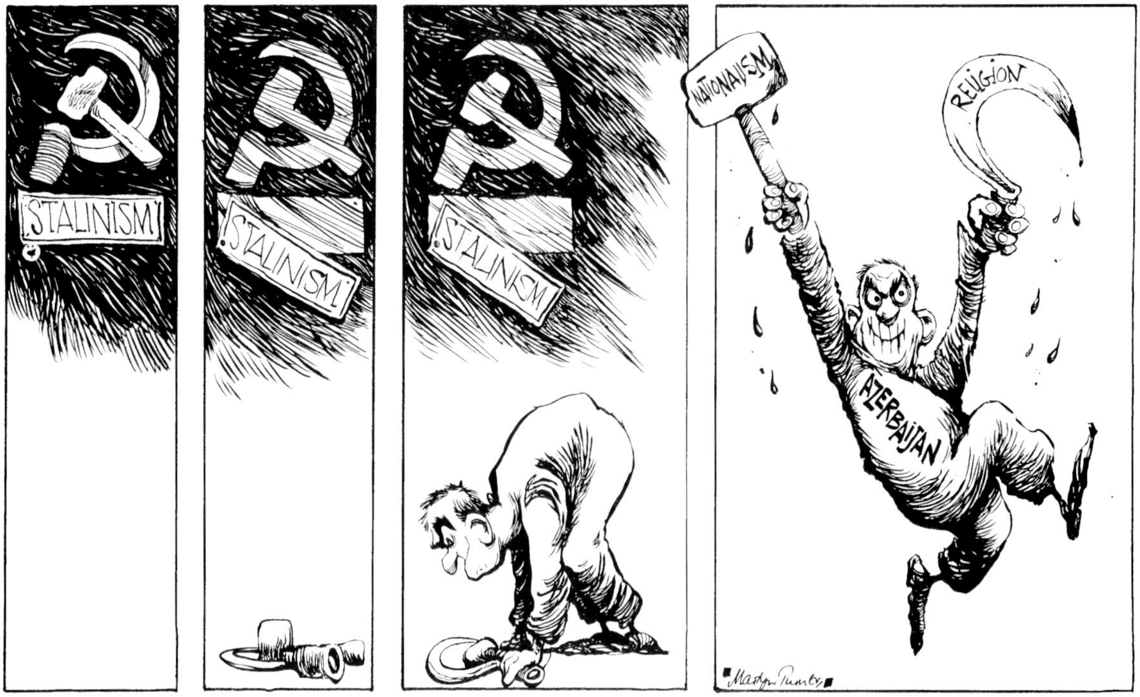
STALINISM
STALINISM
STALINISM
NATIONALISM
RELIGION
AZERBAIJAN

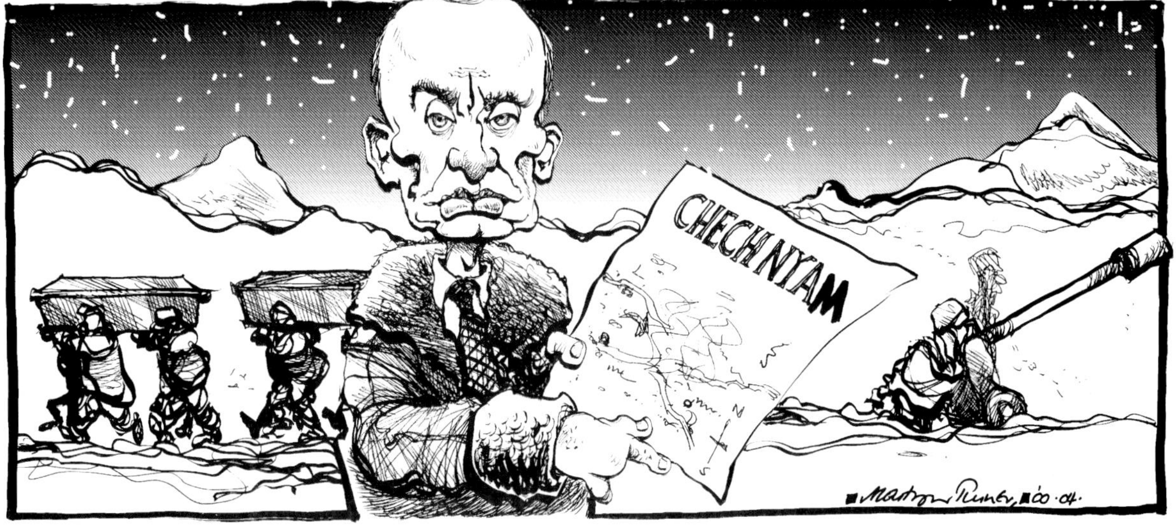
CHECHNYAM

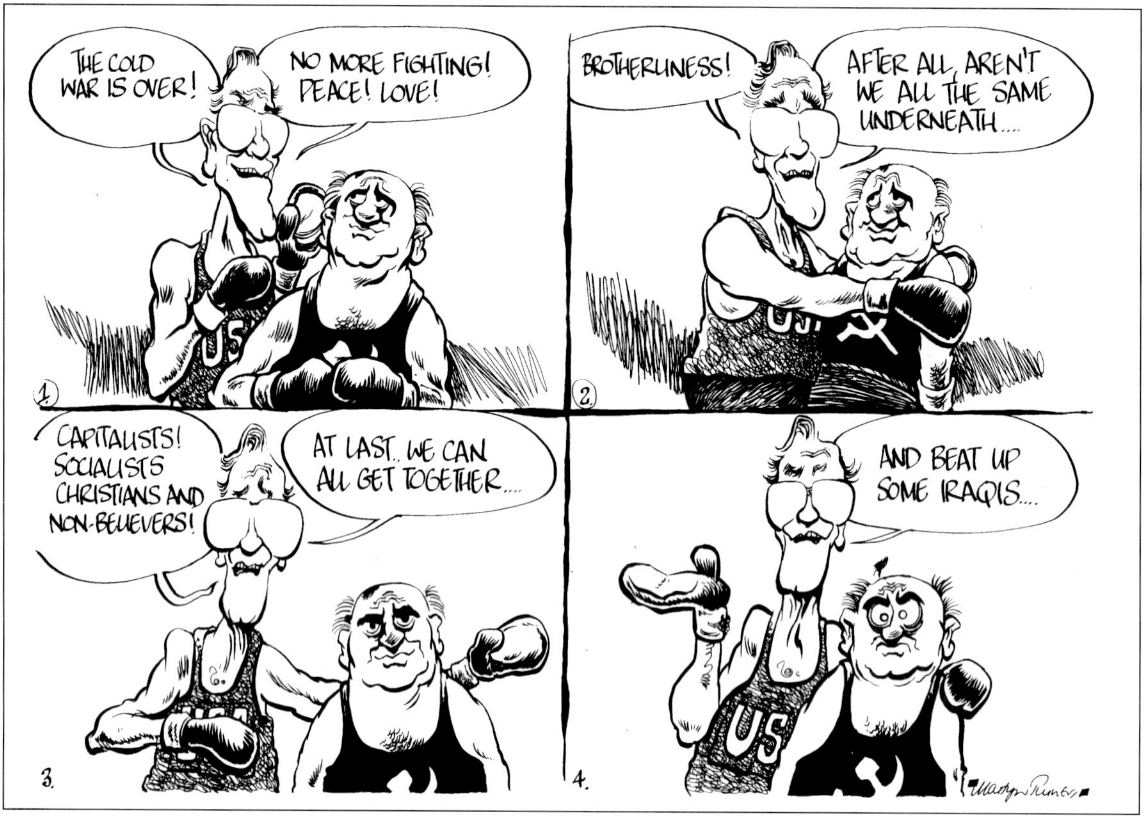
THE COLD WAR IS OVER!
NO MORE FIGHTING! PEACE! LOVE!
US
1.
BROTHERLINESS!
AFTER ALL, AREN'T WE ALL THE SAME UNDERNEATH....
2.
CAPITALISTS! SOCIALISTS CHRISTIANS AND NON-BELIEVERS!
AT LAST.. WE CAN ALL GET TOGETHER....
3.
AND BEAT UP SOME IRAQIS....
US
4.
Martyn Turner

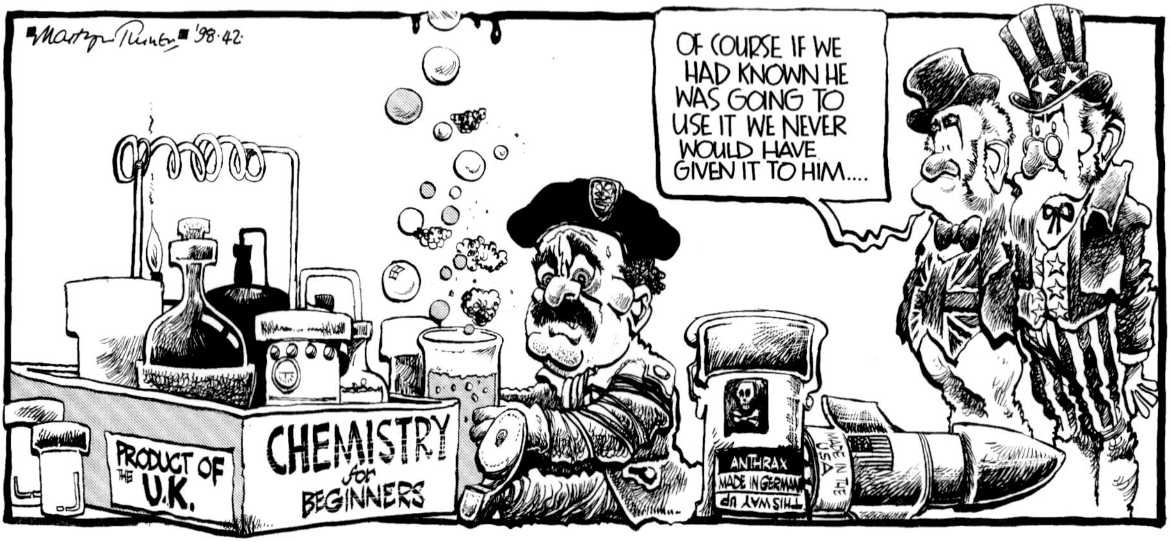
Martyn Turner '98.42.
OF COURSE IF WE HAD KNOWN HE WAS GOING TO USE IT WE NEVER WOULD HAVE GIVEN IT TO HIM....
PRODUCT OF THE U.K.
CHEMISTRY for BEGINNERS
ANTHRAX
MADE IN GERMANY
THIS WAY UP
MADE IN THE USA

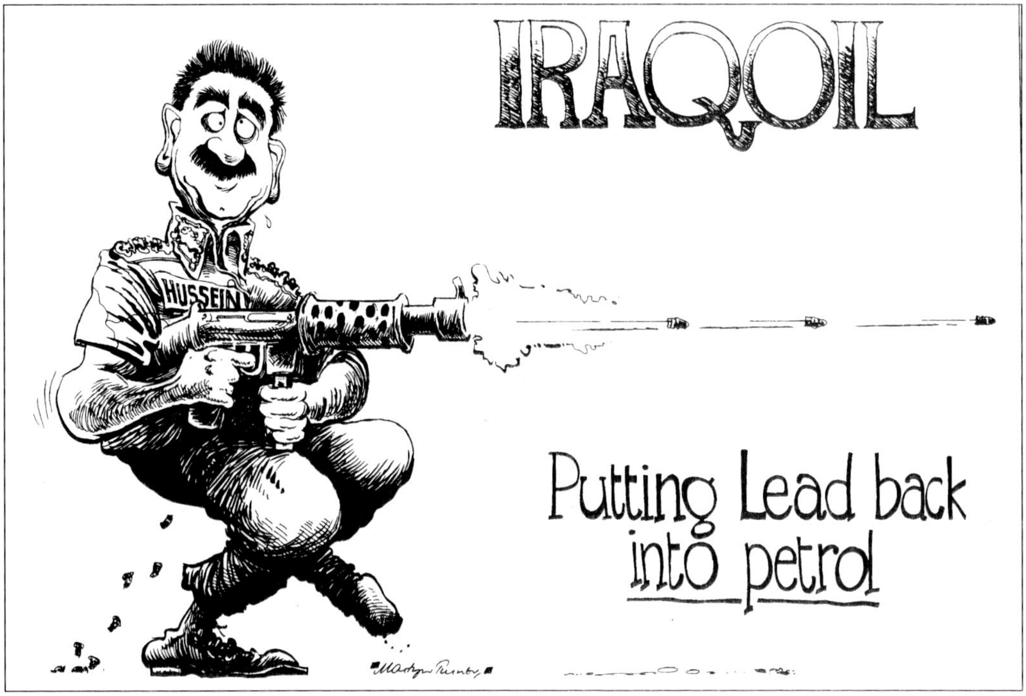
IRAQOIL
HUSSEIN
Putting Lead back into petrol

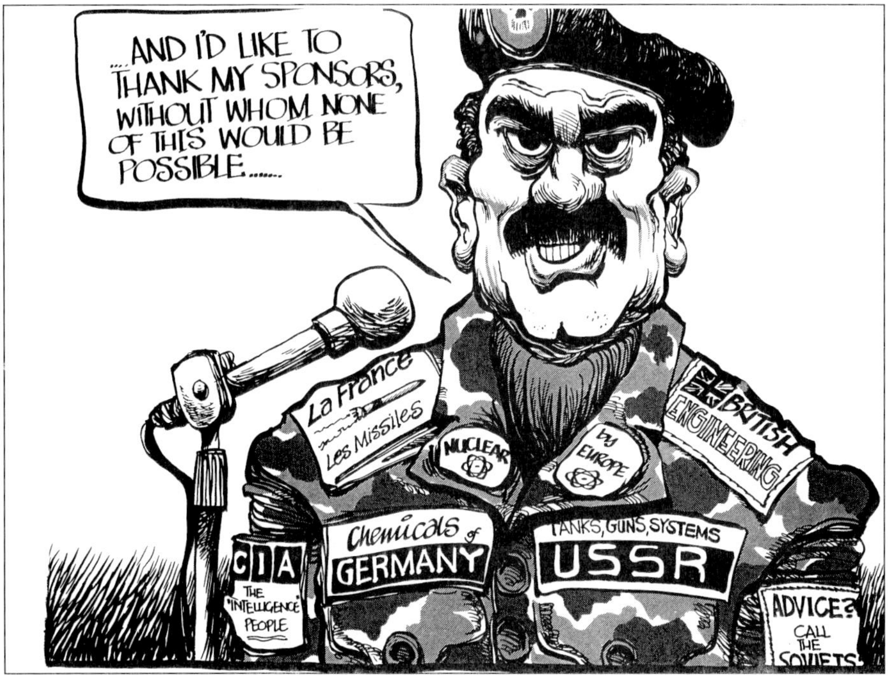
....AND I'D LIKE TO THANK MY SPONSORS, WITHOUT WHOM NONE OF THIS WOULD BE POSSIBLE.......
La France
Les Missiles
NUCLEAR
by EUROPE
BRITISH ENGINEERING
Chemicals of GERMANY
TANKS, GUNS, SYSTEMS
USSR
CIA
THE "INTELLIGENCE" PEOPLE
ADVICE?
CALL THE

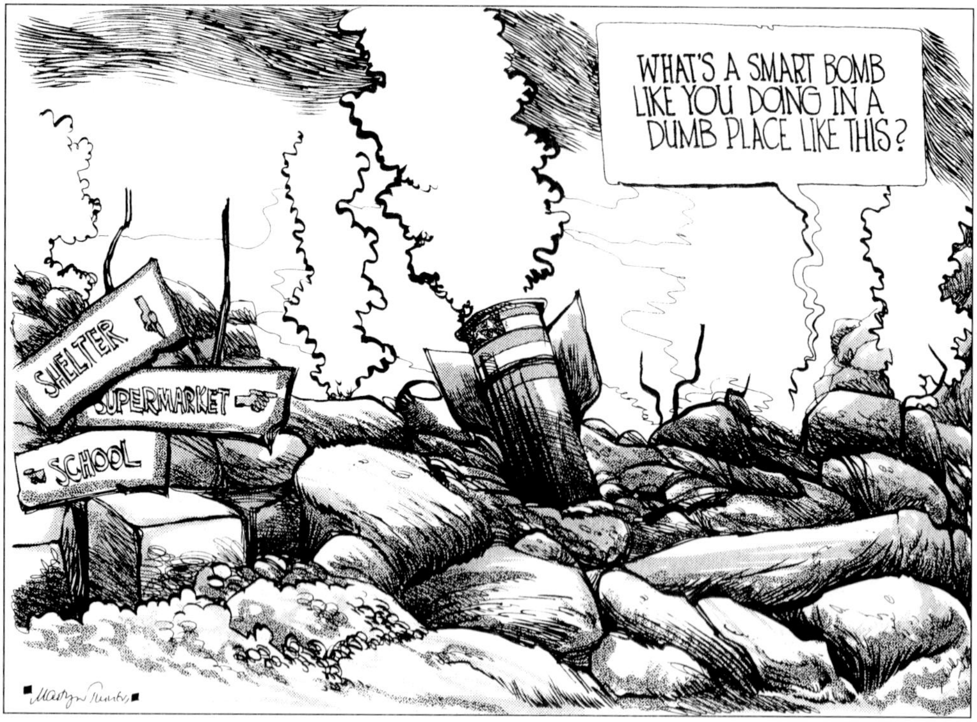
WHAT'S A SMART BOMB LIKE YOU DOING IN A DUMB PLACE LIKE THIS?
SHELTER
SUPERMARKET
SCHOOL
Martyn Turner

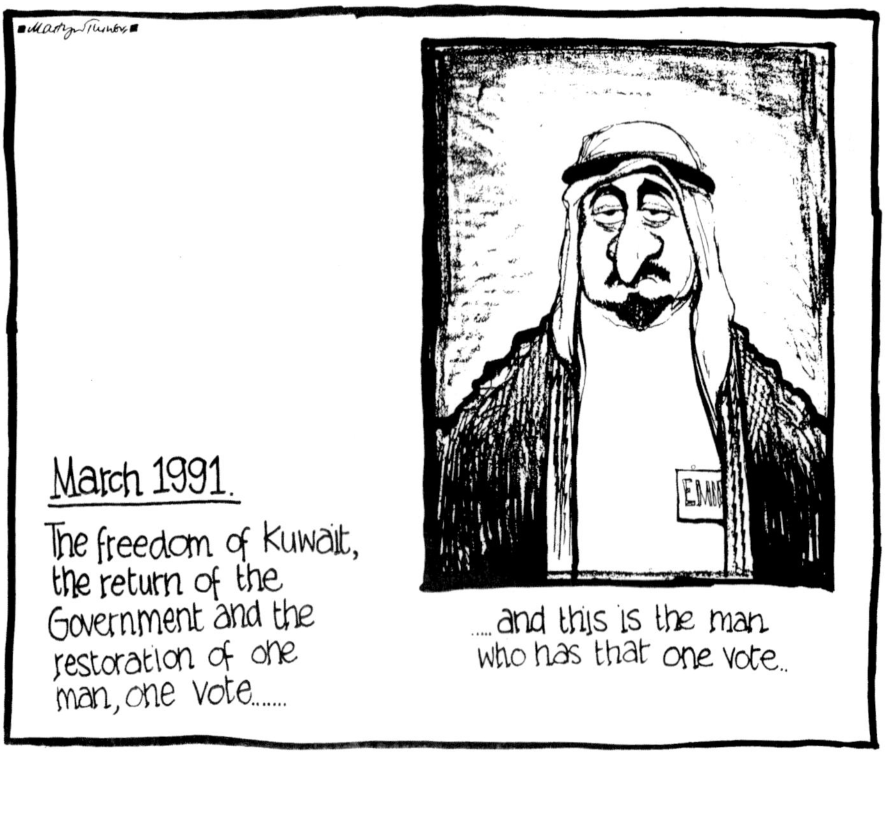
Martyn Turner
March 1991.
The freedom of Kuwait, the return of the Government and the restoration of one man, one vote.......
....and this is the man who has that one vote..

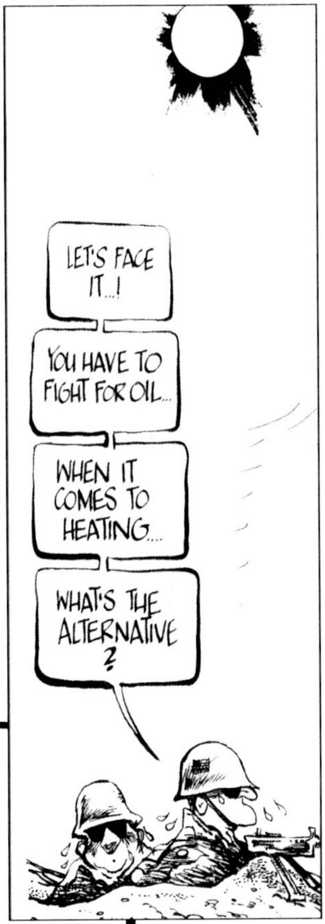
LET'S FACE IT...!
YOU HAVE TO FIGHT FOR OIL...
WHEN IT COMES TO HEATING....
WHAT'S THE ALTERNATIVE ?

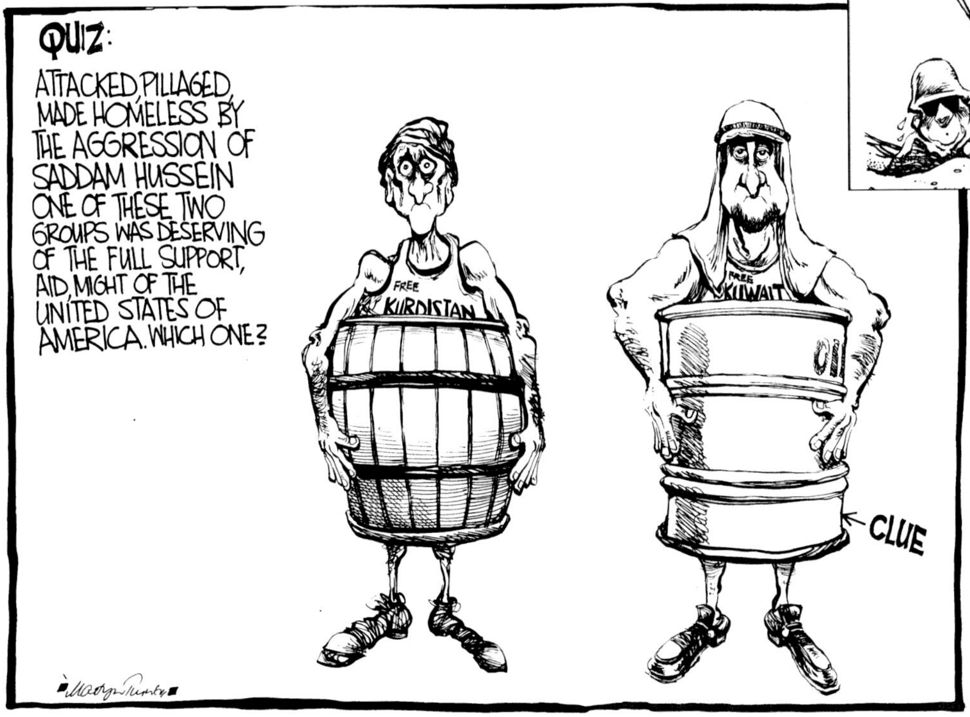
QUIZ:
ATTACKED, PILLAGED, MADE HOMELESS BY THE AGGRESSION OF SADDAM HUSSEIN ONE OF THESE TWO GROUPS WAS DESERVING OF THE FULL SUPPORT, AID, MIGHT OF THE UNITED STATES OF AMERICA. WHICH ONE?
FREE KURDISTAN
FREE KUWAIT
CLUE

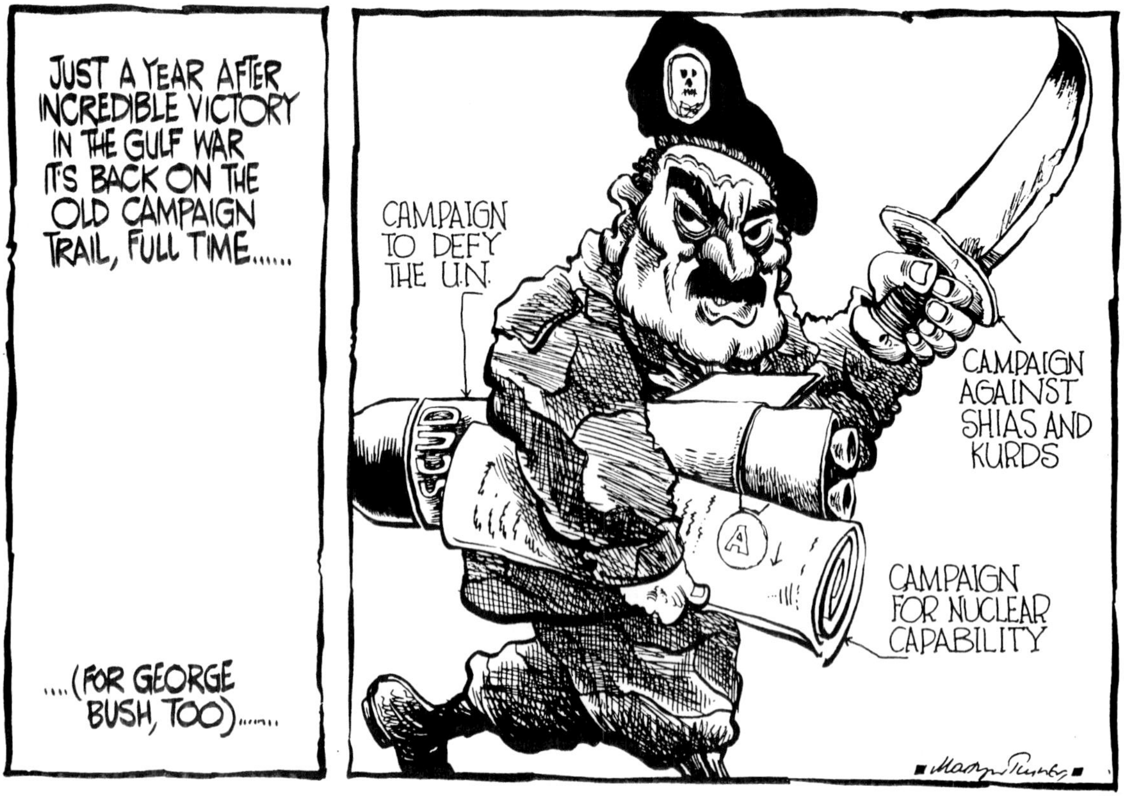
JUST A YEAR AFTER INCREDIBLE VICTORY IN THE GULF WAR IT'S BACK ON THE OLD CAMPAIGN TRAIL, FULL TIME......
....(FOR GEORGE BUSH, TOO).......
CAMPAIGN TO DEFY THE U.N.
SCUD
CAMPAIGN AGAINST SHIAS AND KURDS
A
CAMPAIGN FOR NUCLEAR CAPABILITY

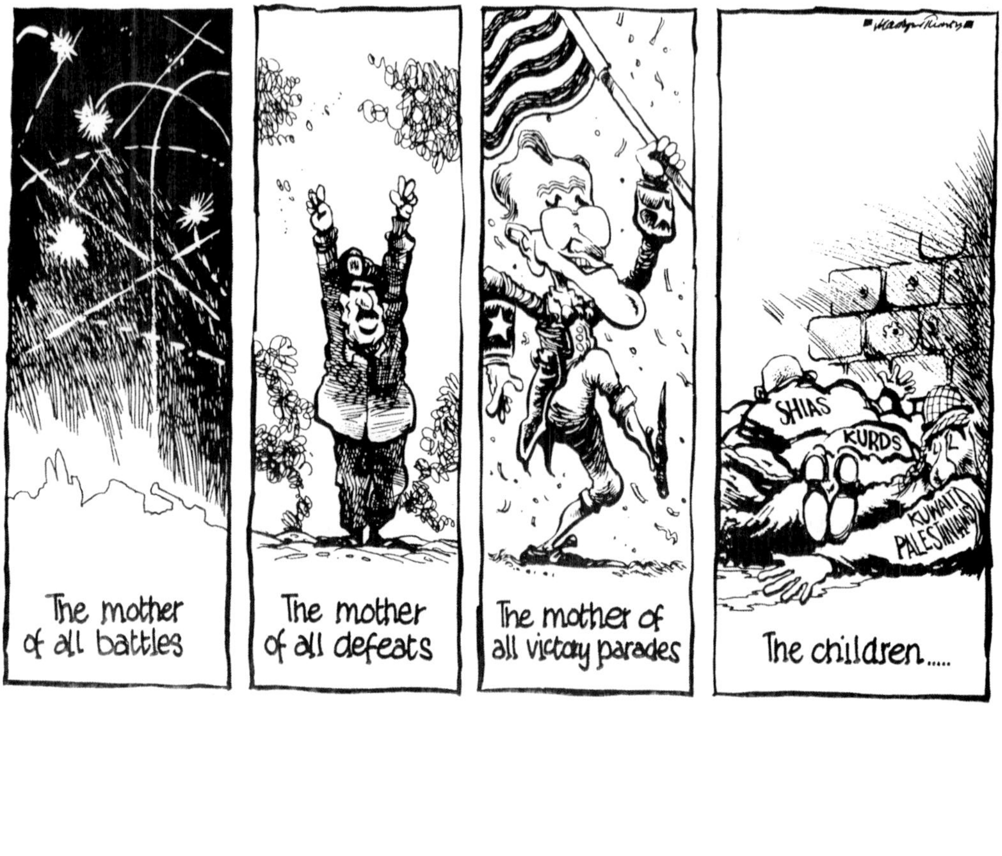
The mother of all battles
The mother of all defeats
The mother of all victory parades
SHIAS
KURDS
KUWAITI PALESTINIANS
The children.....

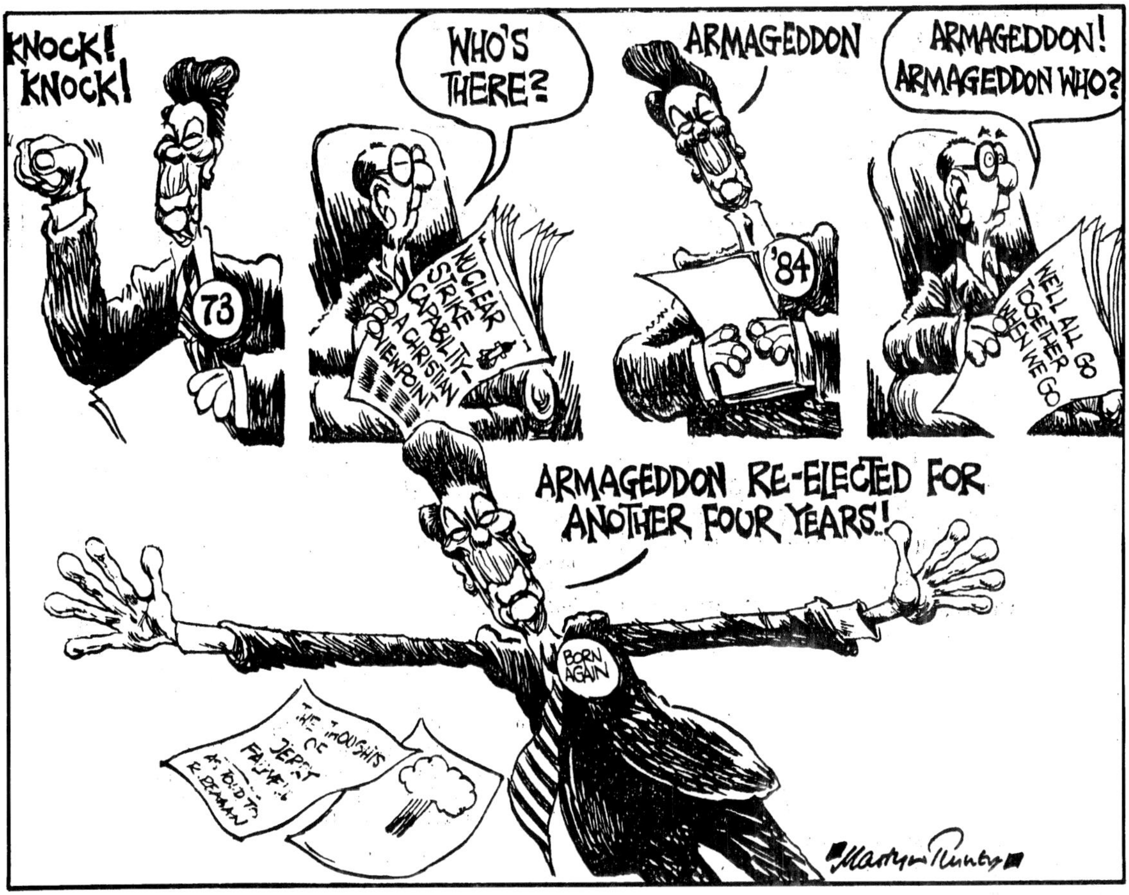
KNOCK! KNOCK!
73
WHO'S THERE?
NUCLEAR STRIKE CAPABILITY – A CHRISTIAN VIEWPOINT
ARMAGEDDON
'84
ARMAGEDDON! ARMAGEDDON WHO?
WE'LL ALL GO TOGETHER WHEN WE GO
ARMAGEDDON RE-ELECTED FOR ANOTHER FOUR YEARS!
BORN AGAIN
Martyn Turner

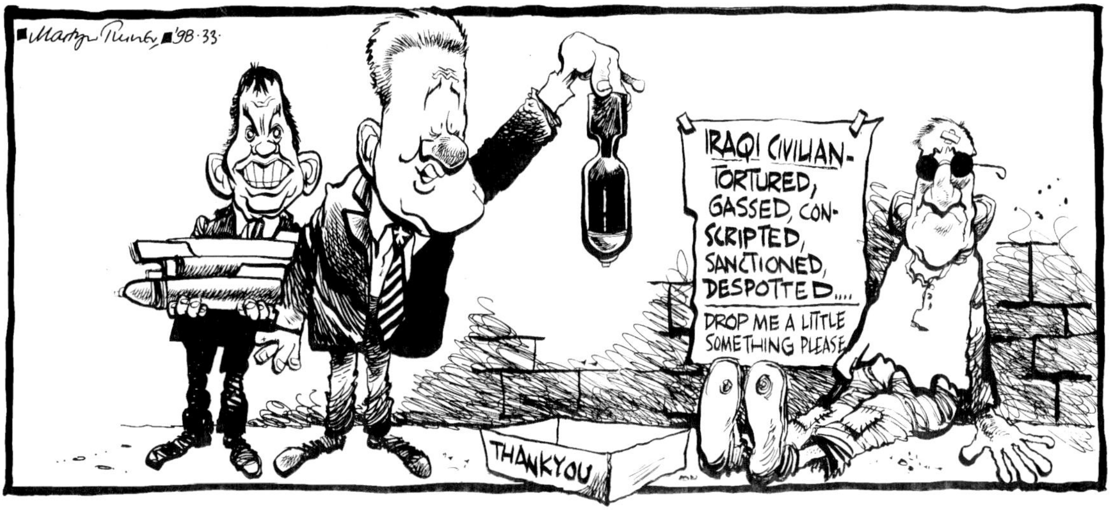
Martyn Turner '98·33·
IRAQI CIVILIAN – TORTURED, GASSED, CON-SCRIPTED, SANCTIONED, DESPOTTED....
DROP ME A LITTLE SOMETHING PLEASE
THANKYOU

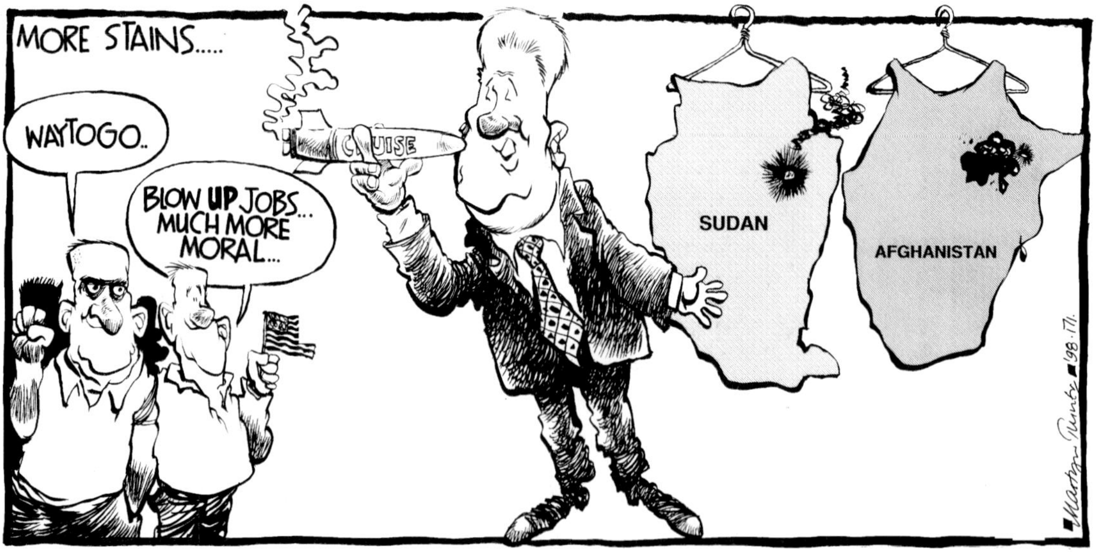
MORE STAINS.....
WAYTOGO..
BLOW UP JOBS... MUCH MORE MORAL...
CRUISE
SUDAN
AFGHANISTAN
Martyn Turner '98·171·

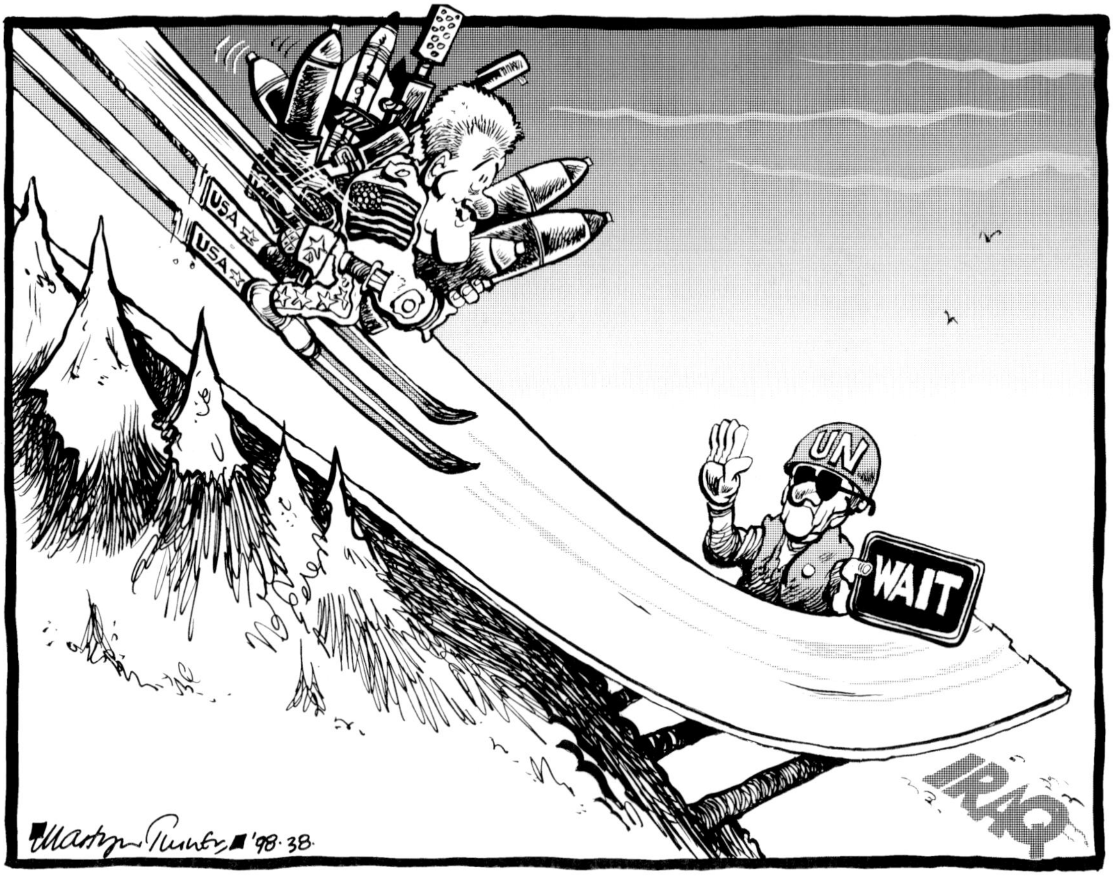
USA
USA
UN
WAIT
IRAQ
Martyn Turner '98·38·

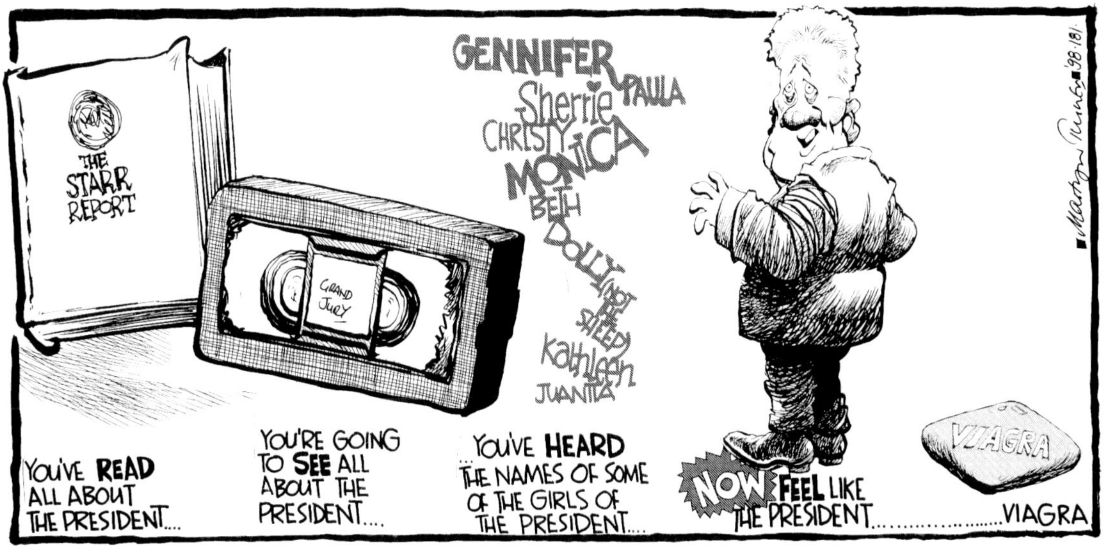
THE STARR REPORT
GRAND JURY
YOU'VE READ ALL ABOUT THE PRESIDENT....
YOU'RE GOING TO SEE ALL ABOUT THE PRESIDENT....
GENNIFER
PAULA
Sherrie
CHRISTY
MONICA
BETH
DOLLY (NOT THE SHEEP)
Kathleen
JUANITA
...YOU'VE HEARD THE NAMES OF SOME OF THE GIRLS OF THE PRESIDENT....
VIAGRA
NOW FEEL LIKE THE PRESIDENT.....................VIAGRA
'98·181

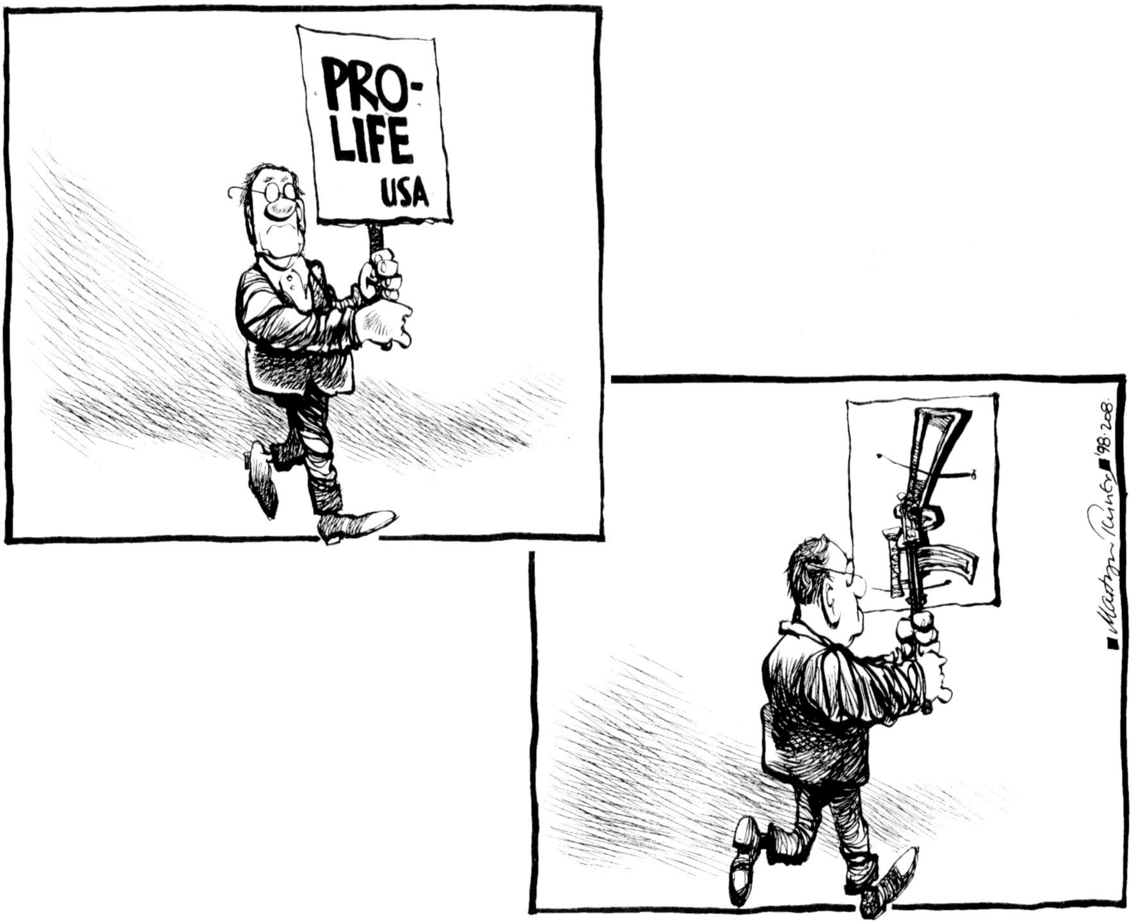
PRO-LIFE USA
'98·208

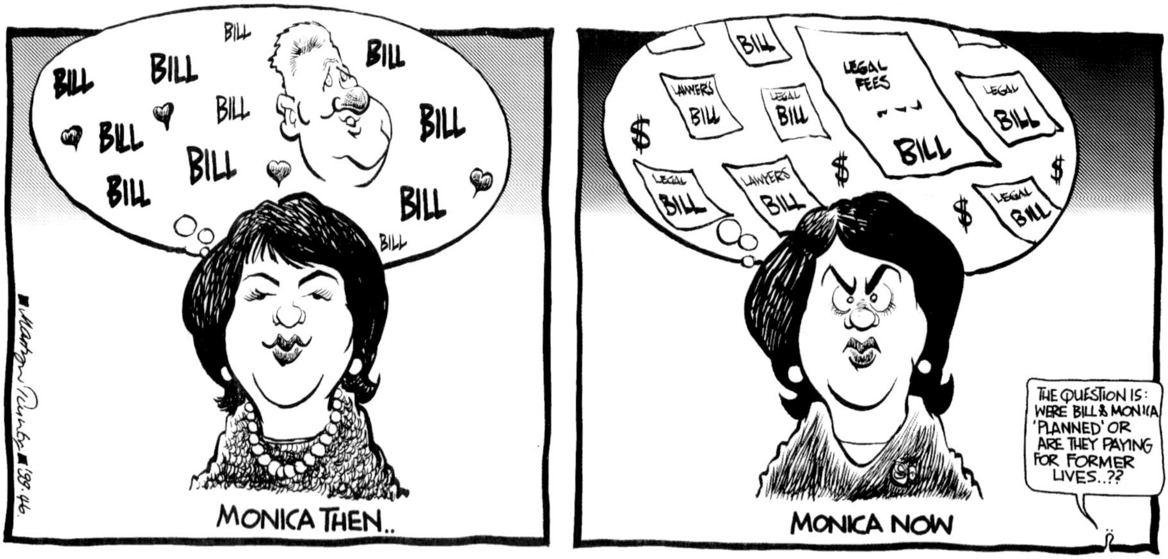
BILL
BILL
BILL
BILL
BILL
BILL
BILL
BILL
BILL
BILL
MONICA THEN..
BILL
LAWYERS BILL
LEGAL BILL
LEGAL FEES
BILL
LEGAL BILL
LEGAL BILL
LAWYERS BILL
LEGAL BILL
MONICA NOW
THE QUESTION IS: WERE BILL & MONICA 'PLANNED' OR ARE THEY PAYING FOR FORMER LIVES..??

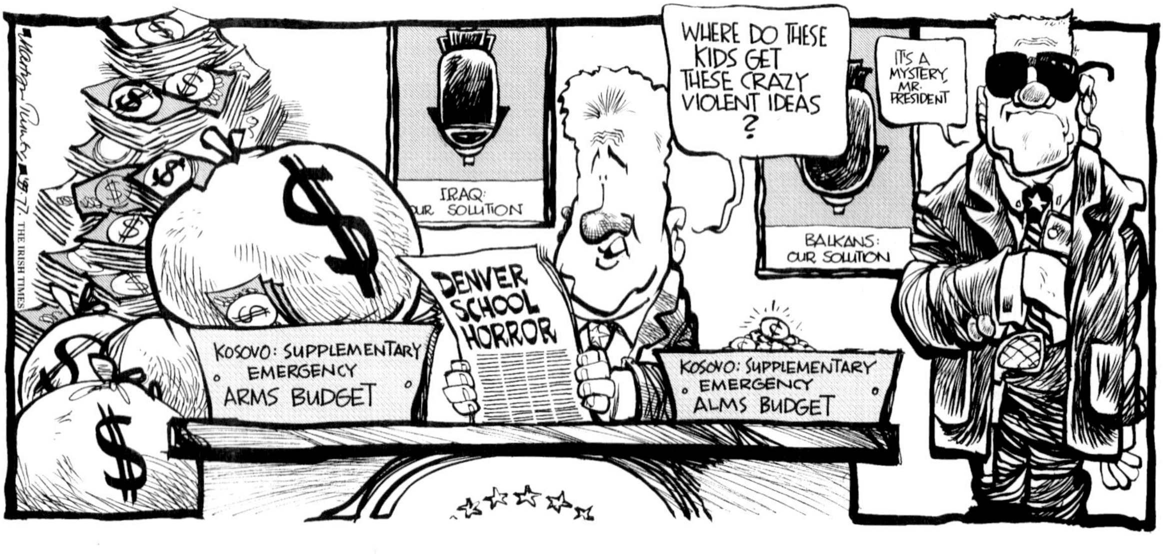
WHERE DO THESE KIDS GET THESE CRAZY VIOLENT IDEAS ?
IT'S A MYSTERY, MR. PRESIDENT
IRAQ: OUR SOLUTION
BALKANS: OUR SOLUTION
DENVER SCHOOL HORROR
KOSOVO: SUPPLEMENTARY EMERGENCY ARMS BUDGET
KOSOVO: SUPPLEMENTARY EMERGENCY ALMS BUDGET
THE IRISH TIMES

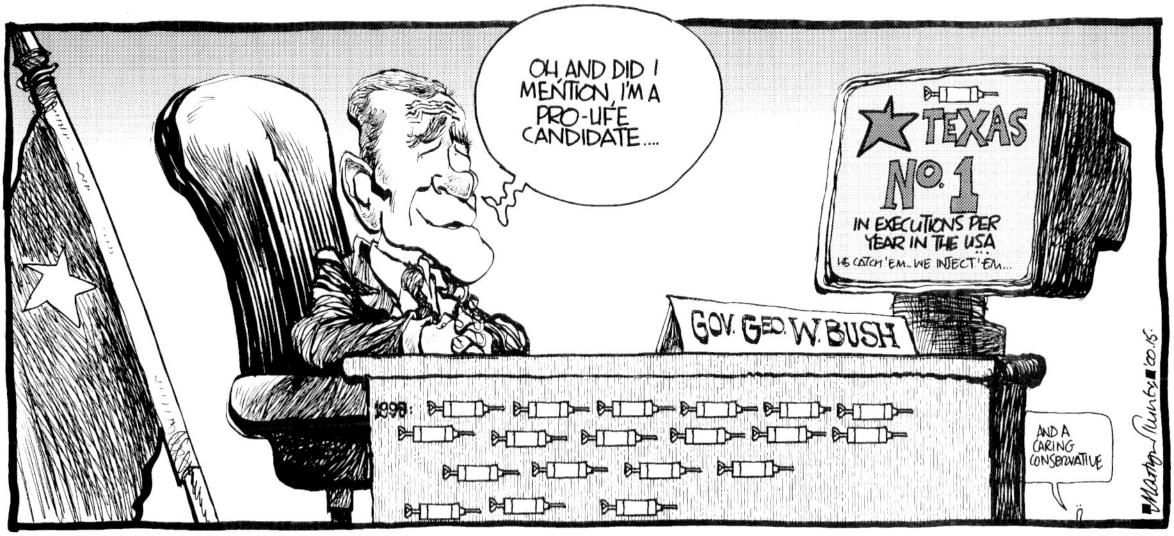
OH, AND DID I MENTION, I'M A PRO-LIFE CANDIDATE....
TEXAS
No. 1
IN EXECUTIONS PER YEAR IN THE USA
WE CATCH 'EM.. WE INJECT 'EM...
GOV. GEO. W. BUSH
1998:
AND A CARING CONSERVATIVE

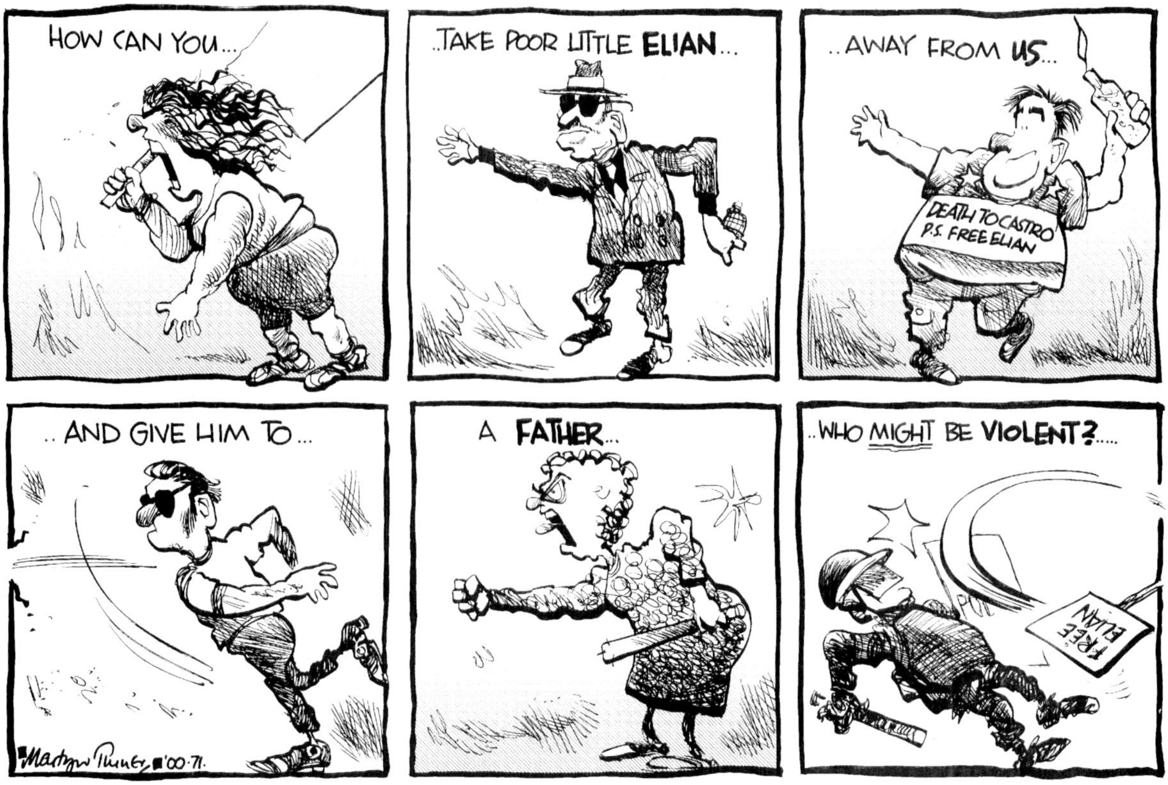
HOW CAN YOU...
..TAKE POOR LITTLE ELIAN...
..AWAY FROM US...
DEATH TO CASTRO
P.S. FREE ELIAN
..AND GIVE HIM TO...
A FATHER...
..WHO MIGHT BE VIOLENT?.....
FREE ELIAN

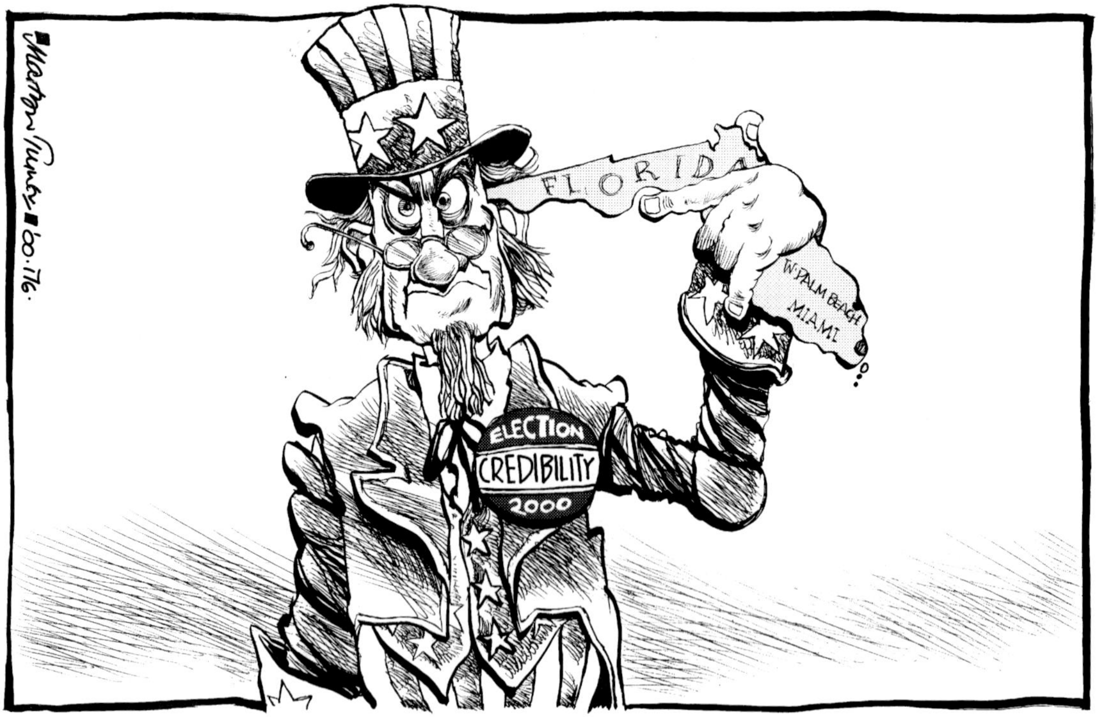
FLORIDA
W. PALM BEACH
MIAMI
ELECTION
CREDIBILITY
2000

And then there was the War . . .

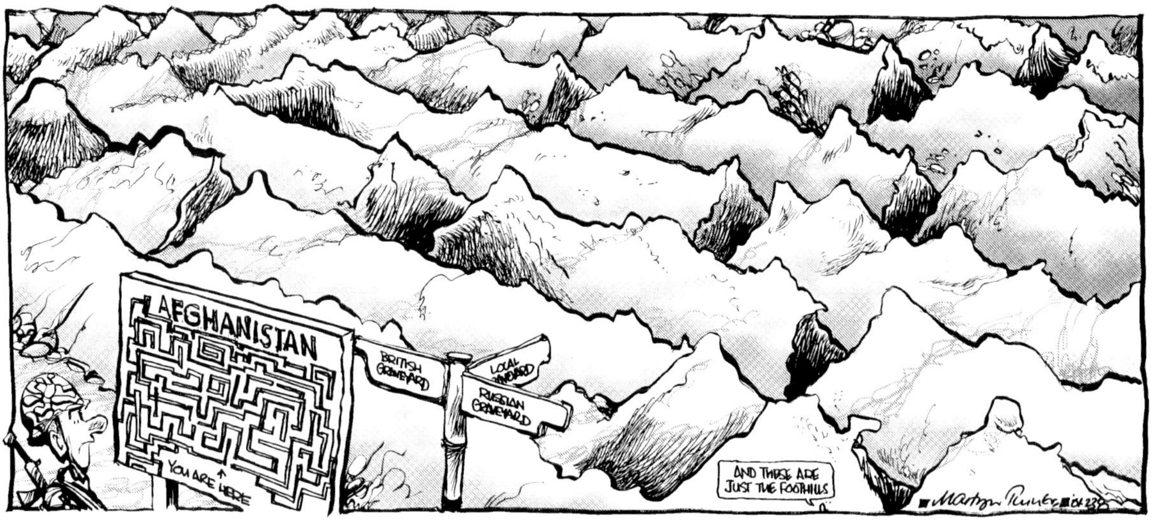
AFGHANISTAN
YOU ARE HERE
BRITISH GRAVEYARD
LOCAL GRAVEYARD
RUSSIAN GRAVEYARD
AND THESE ARE JUST THE FOOTHILLS
Martyn Turner

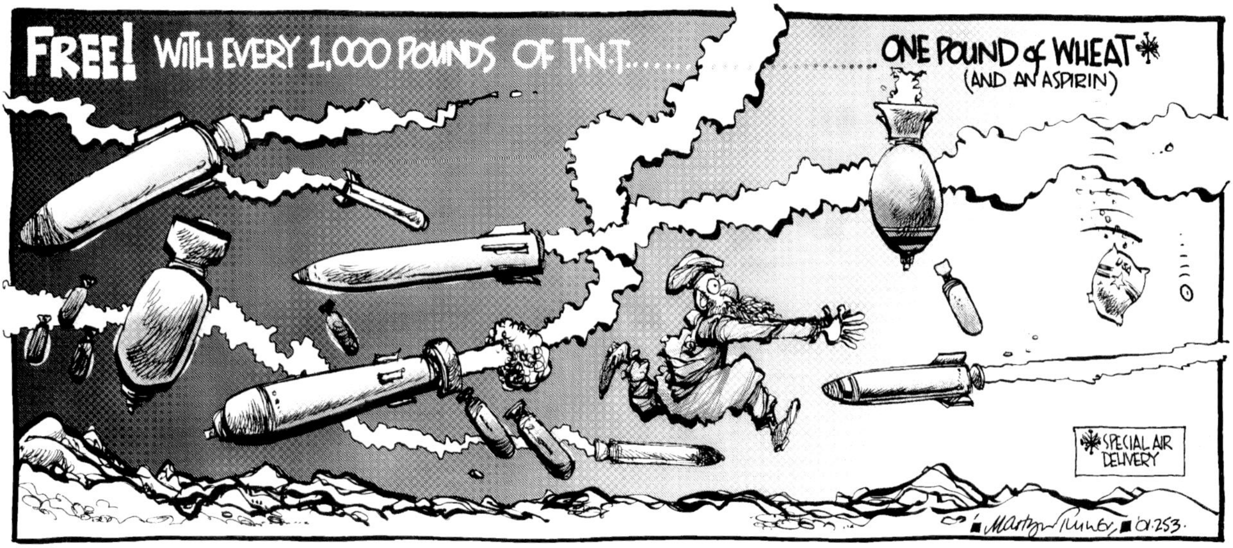
FREE! WITH EVERY 1,000 POUNDS OF T.N.T.......
ONE POUND of WHEAT*
(AND AN ASPIRIN)
USA
*SPECIAL AIR DELIVERY
Martyn Turner

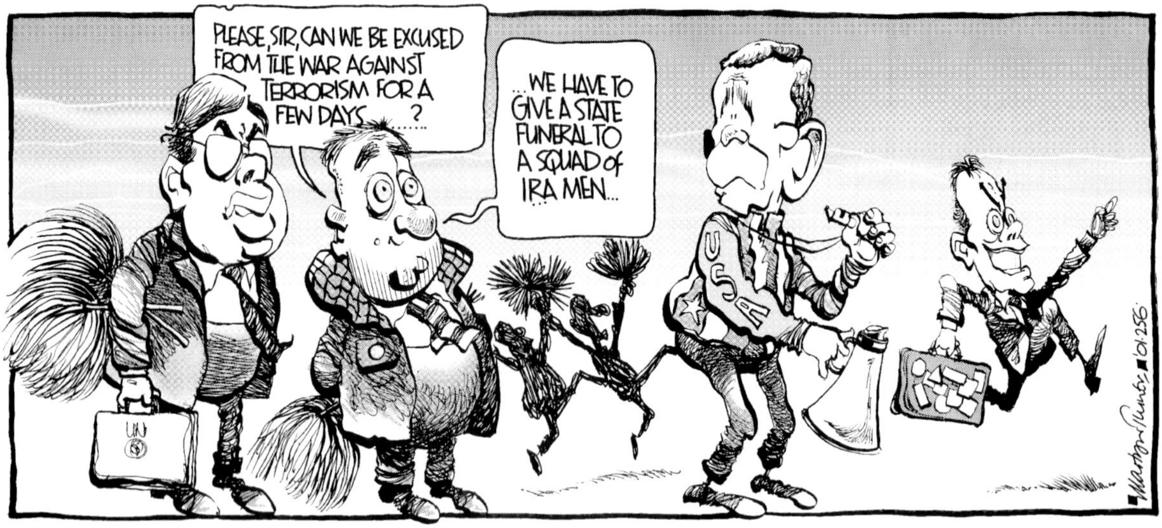
PLEASE, SIR, CAN WE BE EXCUSED FROM THE WAR AGAINST TERRORISM FOR A FEW DAYS.........?
...WE HAVE TO GIVE A STATE FUNERAL TO A SQUAD of IRA MEN...
UN
USA

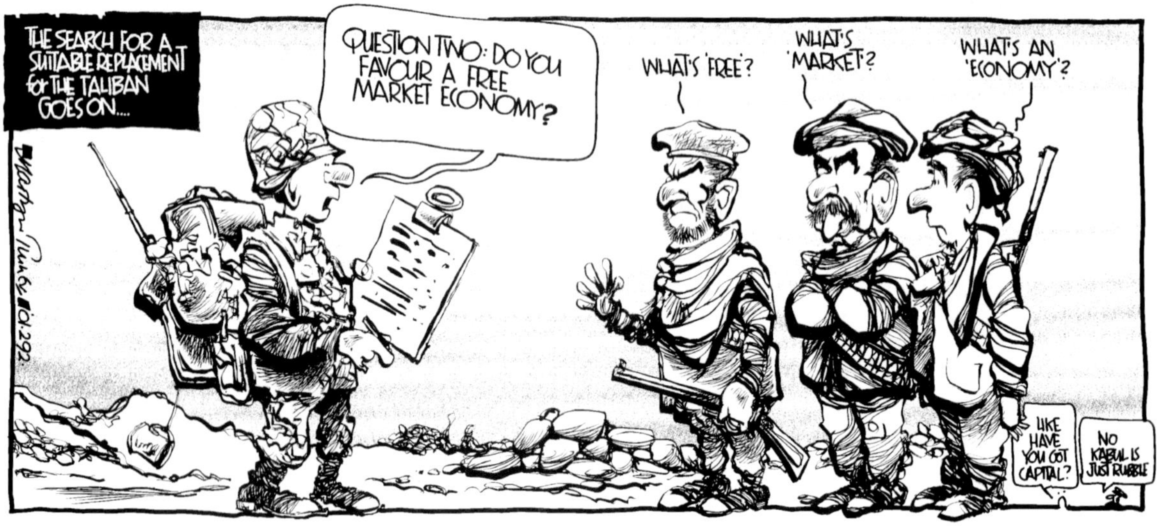
THE SEARCH FOR A SUITABLE REPLACEMENT for THE TALIBAN GOES ON....
QUESTION TWO: DO YOU FAVOUR A FREE MARKET ECONOMY?
WHAT'S 'FREE'?
WHAT'S 'MARKET'?
WHAT'S AN 'ECONOMY'?
LIKE HAVE YOU GOT CAPITAL?
NO KABUL IS JUST RUBBLE

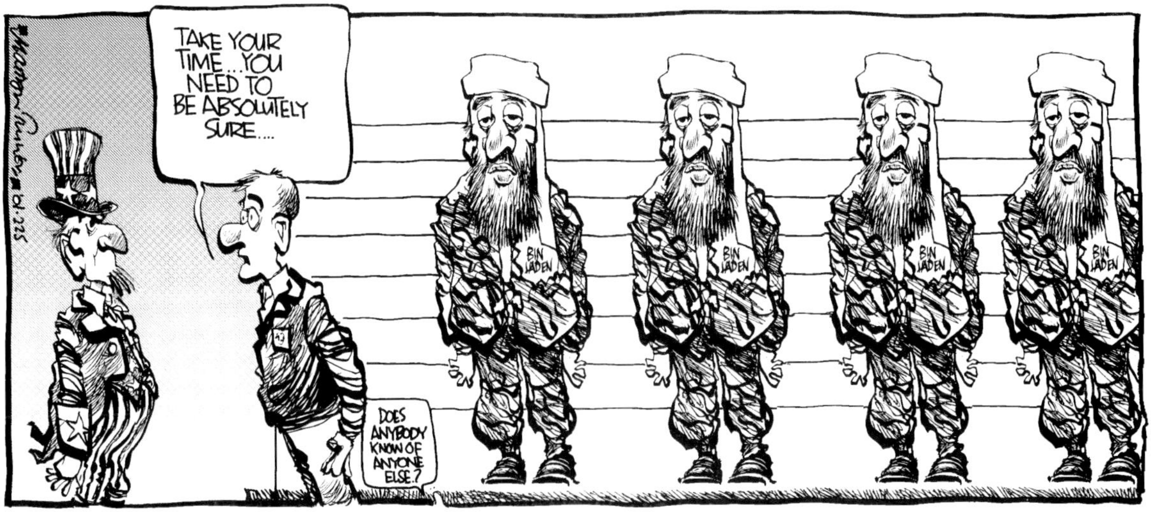
TAKE YOUR TIME... YOU NEED TO BE ABSOLUTELY SURE....
DOES ANYBODY KNOW OF ANYONE ELSE?
BIN LADEN
BIN LADEN
BIN LADEN
BIN LADEN
Martyn Turner 01.225

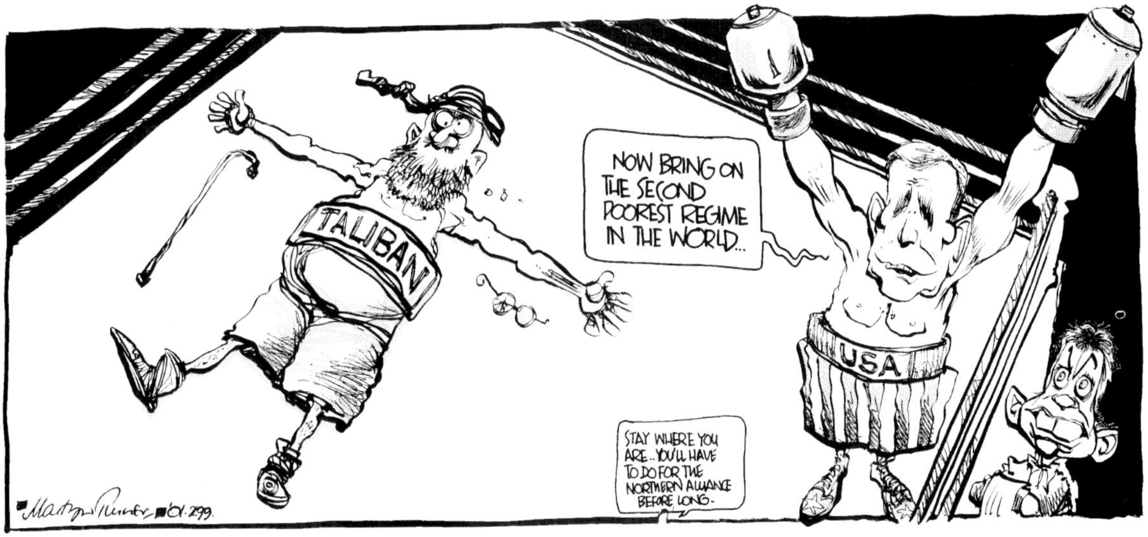
TALIBAN
NOW BRING ON THE SECOND POOREST REGIME IN THE WORLD...
USA
STAY WHERE YOU ARE... YOU'LL HAVE TO DO FOR THE NORTHERN ALLIANCE BEFORE LONG.
Martyn Turner 01.299.

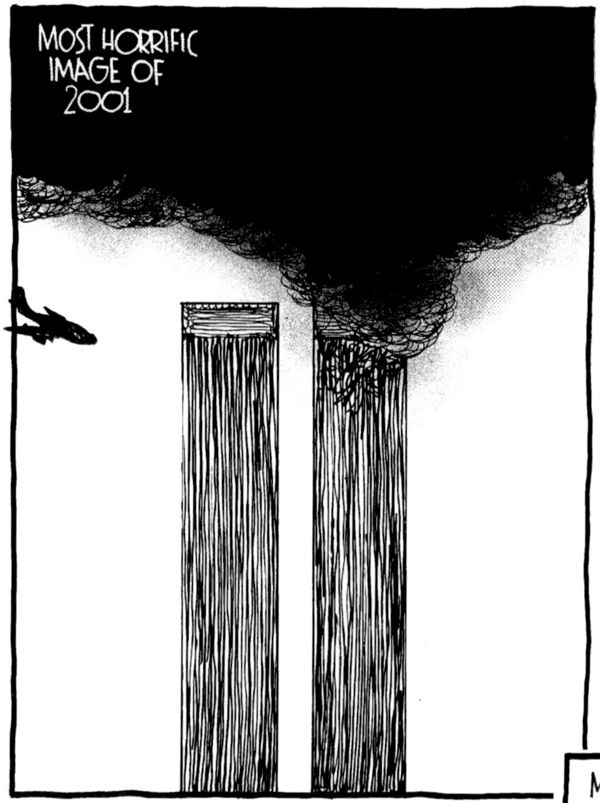
MOST HORRIFIC
IMAGE OF
2001

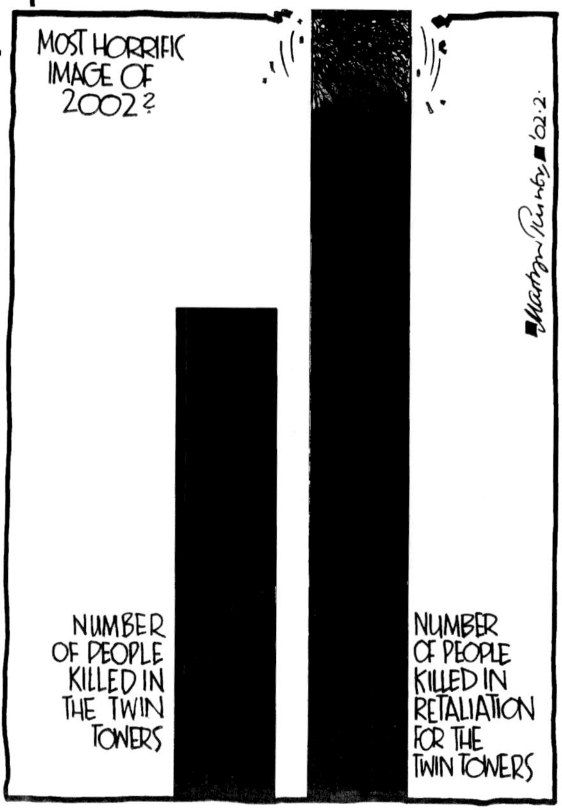
MOST HORRIFIC
IMAGE OF
2002?
NUMBER
OF PEOPLE
KILLED IN
THE TWIN
TOWERS
NUMBER
OF PEOPLE
KILLED IN
RETALIATION
FOR THE
TWIN TOWERS

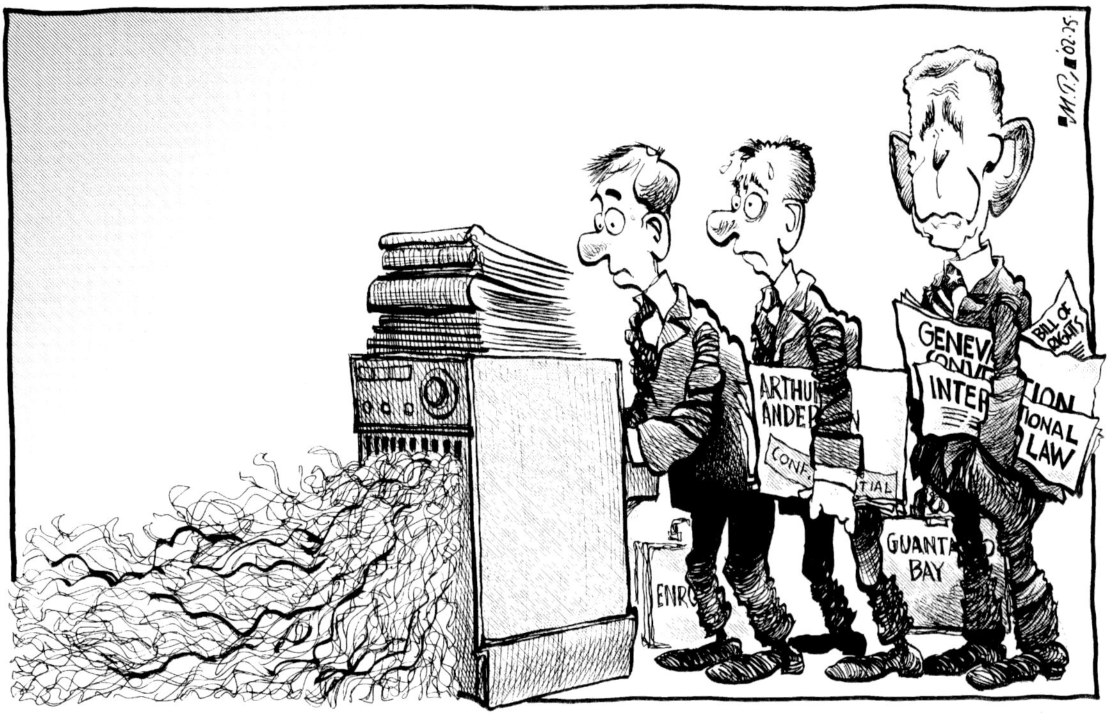
ARTHUR
ANDER
CONF
TIAL
GENEVA
CONVE
INTER
TION
IONAL
LAW
BILL OF RIGHTS
GUANTA
BAY
ENRO

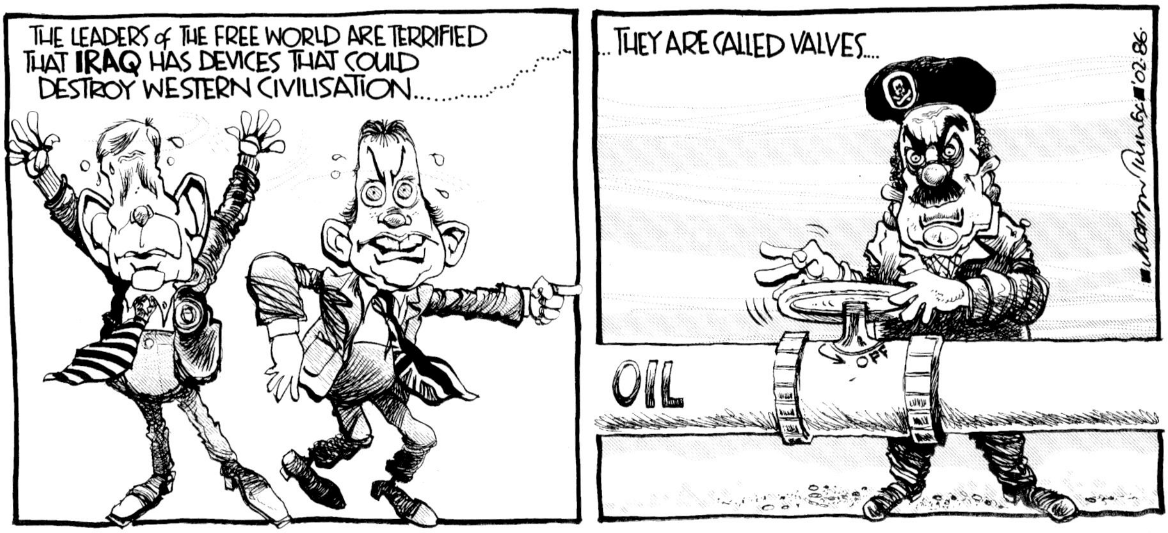
THE LEADERS of THE FREE WORLD ARE TERRIFIED THAT **IRAQ** HAS DEVICES THAT COULD DESTROY WESTERN CIVILISATION.........
...THEY ARE CALLED VALVES....
OIL
OFF

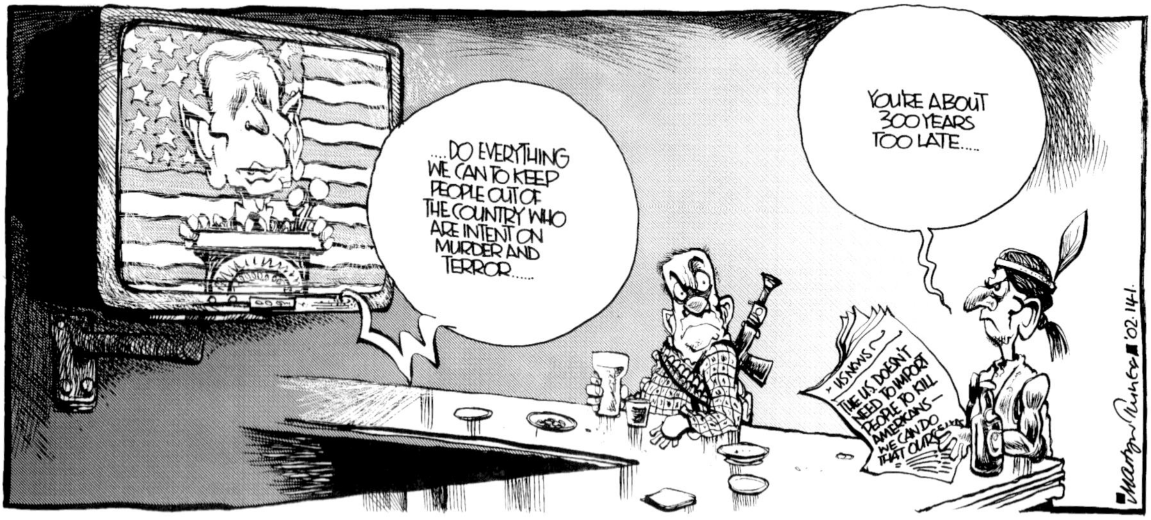
....DO EVERYTHING WE CAN TO KEEP PEOPLE OUT OF THE COUNTRY WHO ARE INTENT ON MURDER AND TERROR......
YOU'RE ABOUT 300 YEARS TOO LATE.....
US NEWS
THE U.S. DOESN'T NEED TO IMPORT PEOPLE TO KILL AMERICANS— WE CAN DO THAT OURSELVES

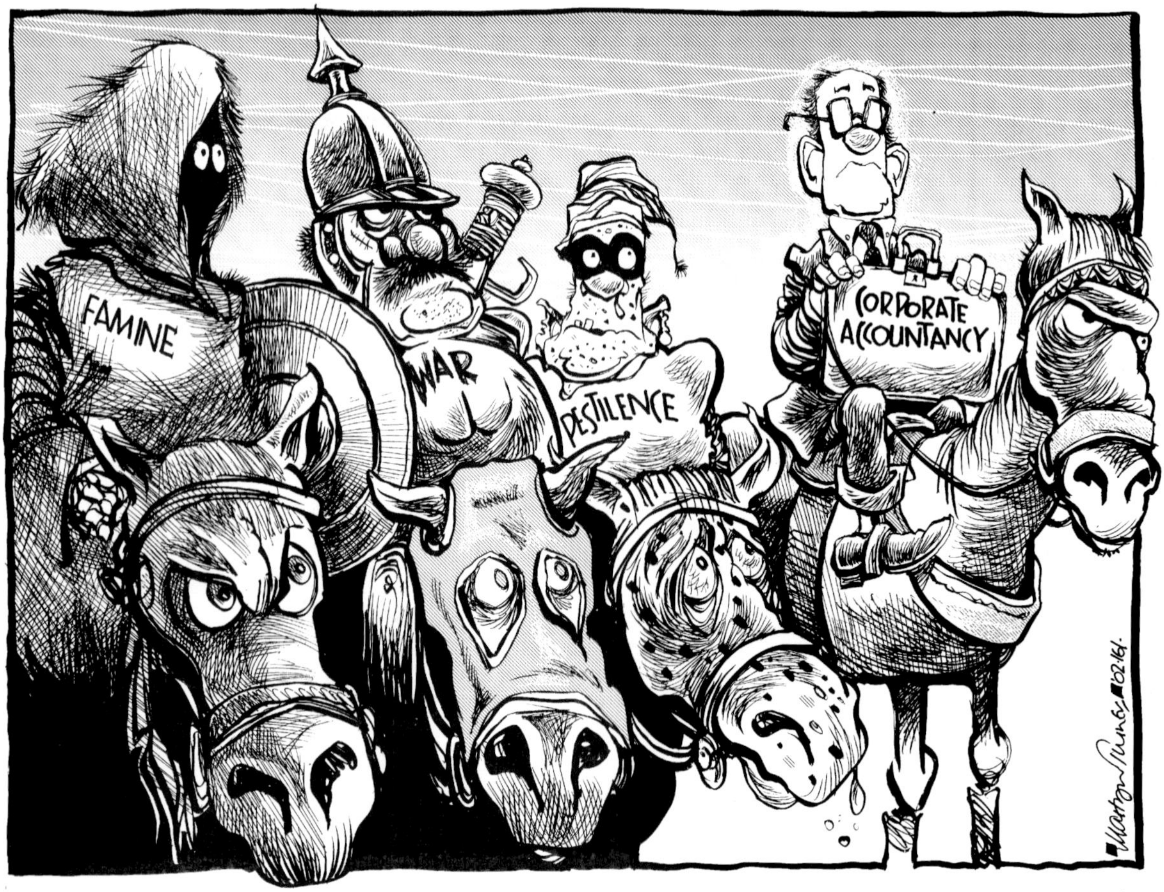
FAMINE
WAR
PESTILENCE
CORPORATE ACCOUNTANCY

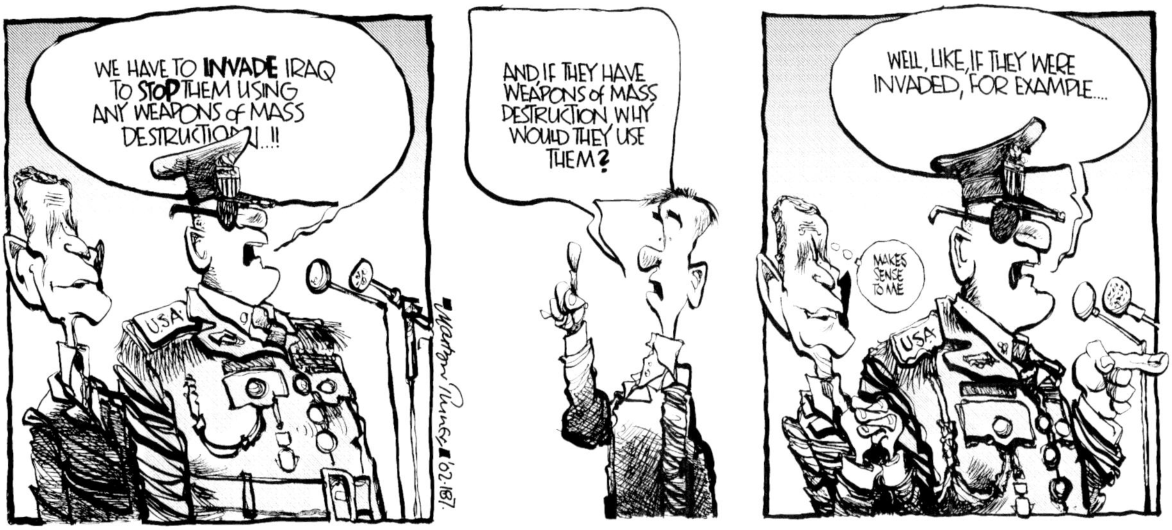
WE HAVE TO INVADE IRAQ TO STOP THEM USING ANY WEAPONS of MASS DESTRUCTION...!!
USA
AND, IF THEY HAVE WEAPONS of MASS DESTRUCTION, WHY WOULD THEY USE THEM?
WELL, LIKE, IF THEY WERE INVADED, FOR EXAMPLE....
MAKES SENSE TO ME
USA

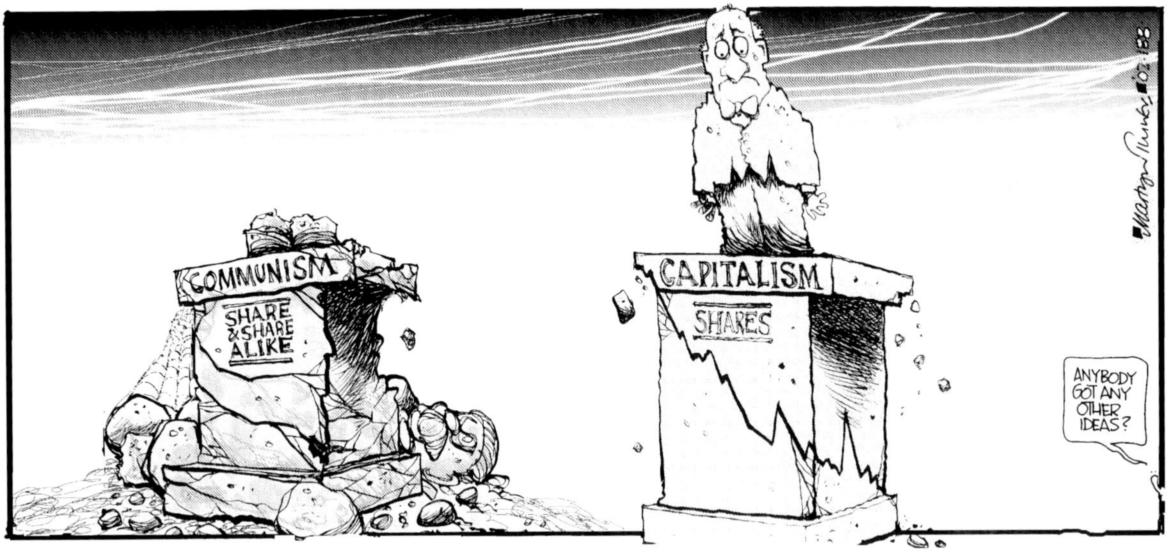
COMMUNISM
SHARE & SHARE ALIKE
CAPITALISM
SHARES
ANYBODY GOT ANY OTHER IDEAS?

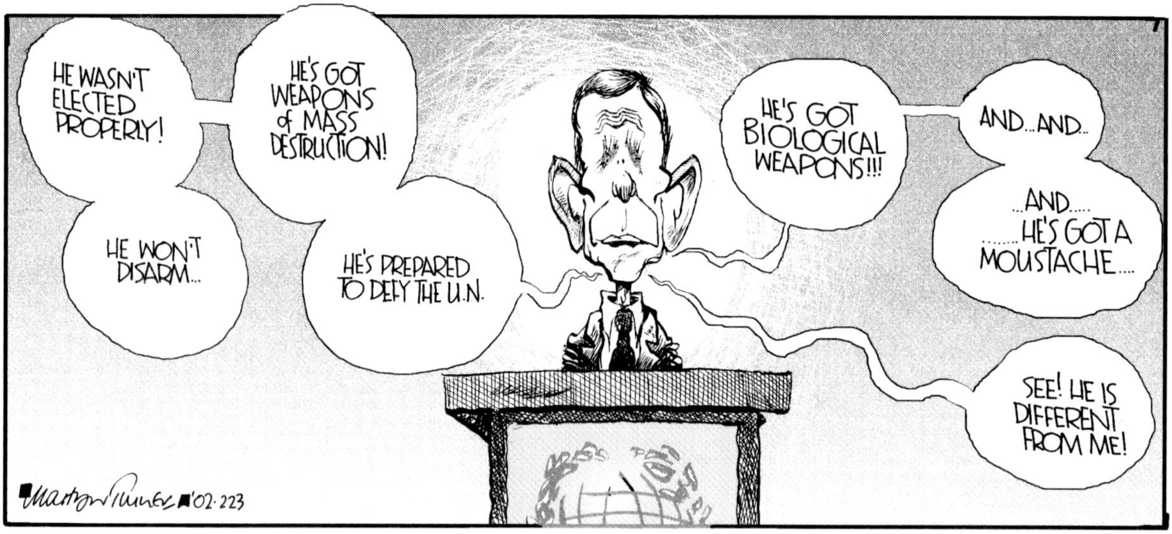
HE WASN'T ELECTED PROPERLY!
HE'S GOT WEAPONS of MASS DESTRUCTION!
HE WON'T DISARM...
HE'S PREPARED TO DEFY THE U.N.
HE'S GOT BIOLOGICAL WEAPONS!!!
AND...AND...
...AND..... ....HE'S GOT A MOUSTACHE....
SEE! HE IS DIFFERENT FROM ME!
Martyn Turner '02.223

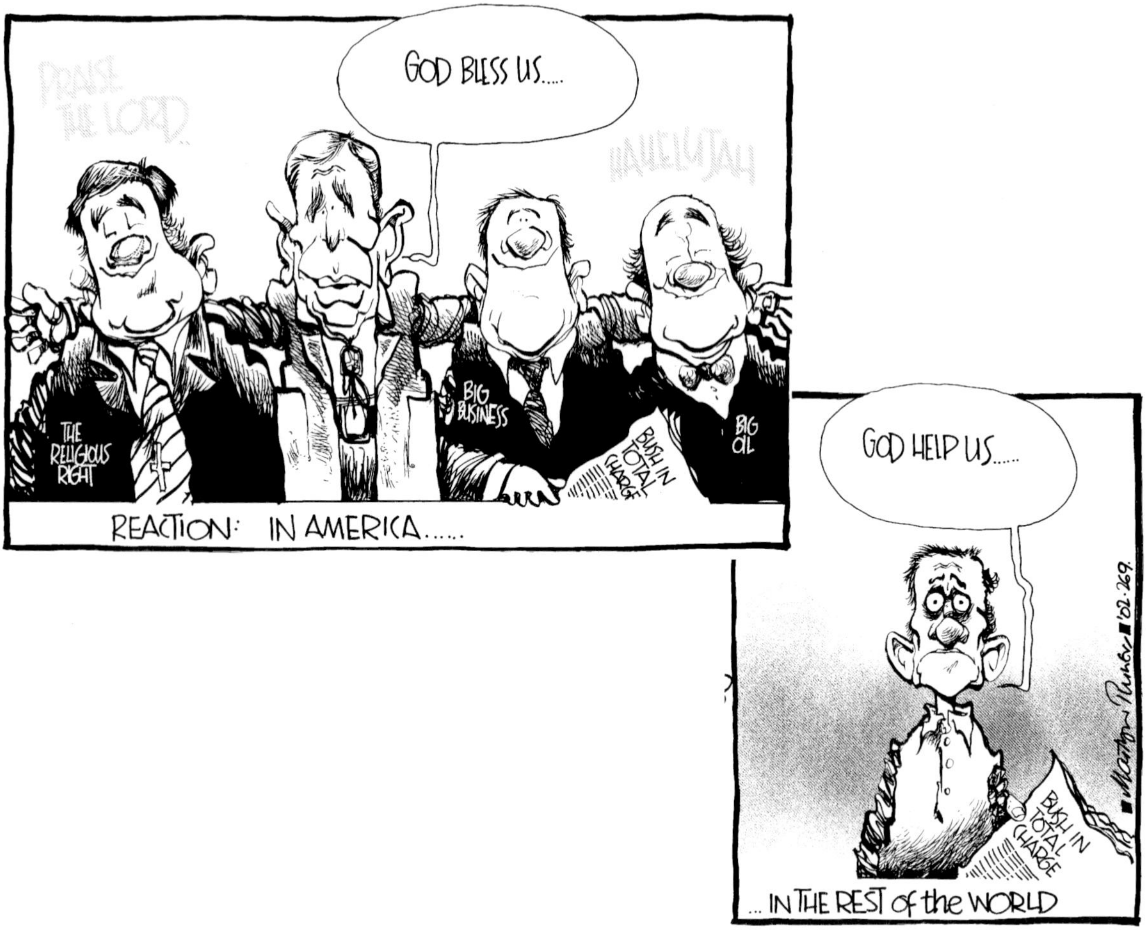
PRAISE THE LORD
GOD BLESS US.....
HALLELUJAH
THE RELIGIOUS RIGHT
BIG BUSINESS
BUSH IN TOTAL CHARGE
BIG OIL
REACTION: IN AMERICA.....
GOD HELP US......
BUSH IN TOTAL CHARGE
... IN THE REST of the WORLD
Martyn Turner '02.269.

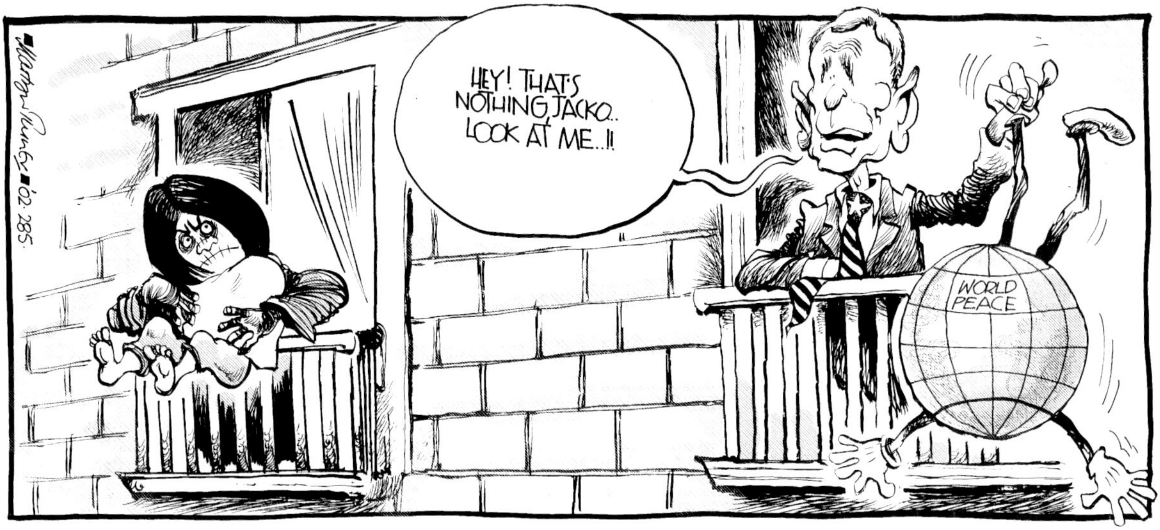
HEY! THAT'S NOTHING JACKO.. LOOK AT ME..!!
WORLD PEACE

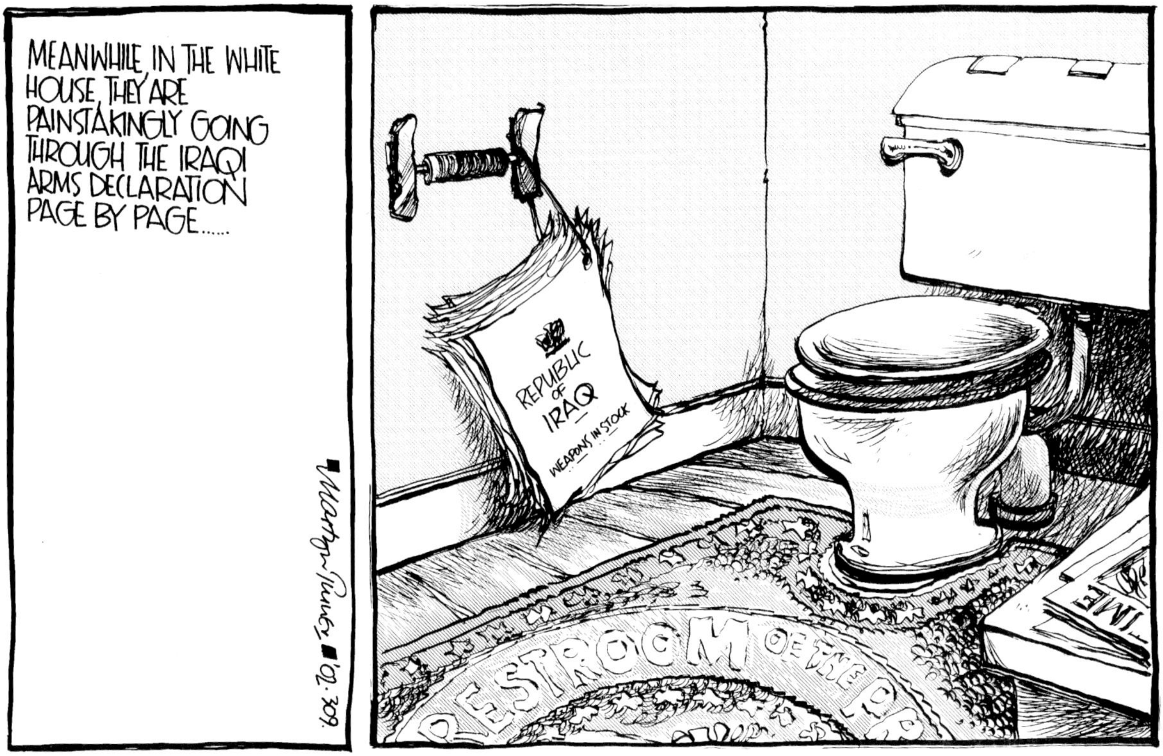
MEANWHILE, IN THE WHITE HOUSE, THEY ARE PAINSTAKINGLY GOING THROUGH THE IRAQI ARMS DECLARATION PAGE BY PAGE......
REPUBLIC OF IRAQ
WEAPONS IN STOCK
RESTROOM

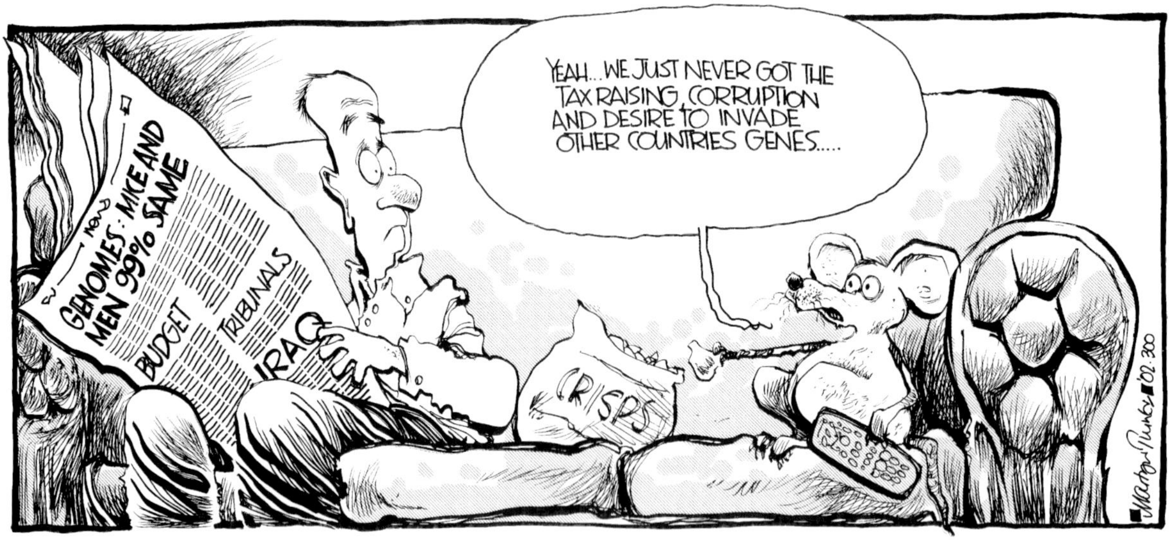
YEAH... WE JUST NEVER GOT THE TAX RAISING, CORRUPTION AND DESIRE TO INVADE OTHER COUNTRIES GENES.....
NEWS
GENOMES: MICE AND MEN 99% SAME
BUDGET
TRIBUNALS
IRAQ
CRISPS
Martyn Turner '02:300

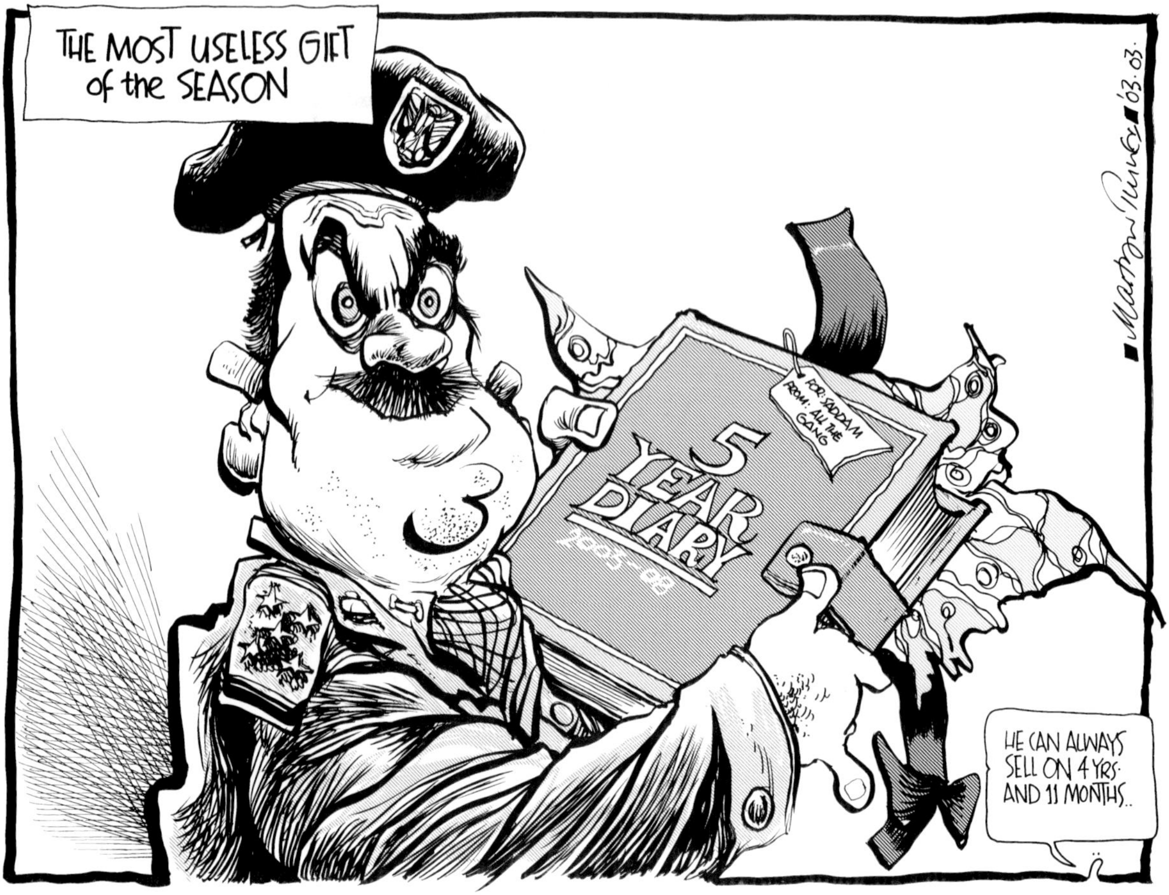
THE MOST USELESS GIFT of the SEASON
FOR: SADDAM FROM: ALL THE GANG
5 YEAR DIARY 2003-08
HE CAN ALWAYS SELL ON 4 YRS. AND 11 MONTHS..
Martyn Turner '03:03

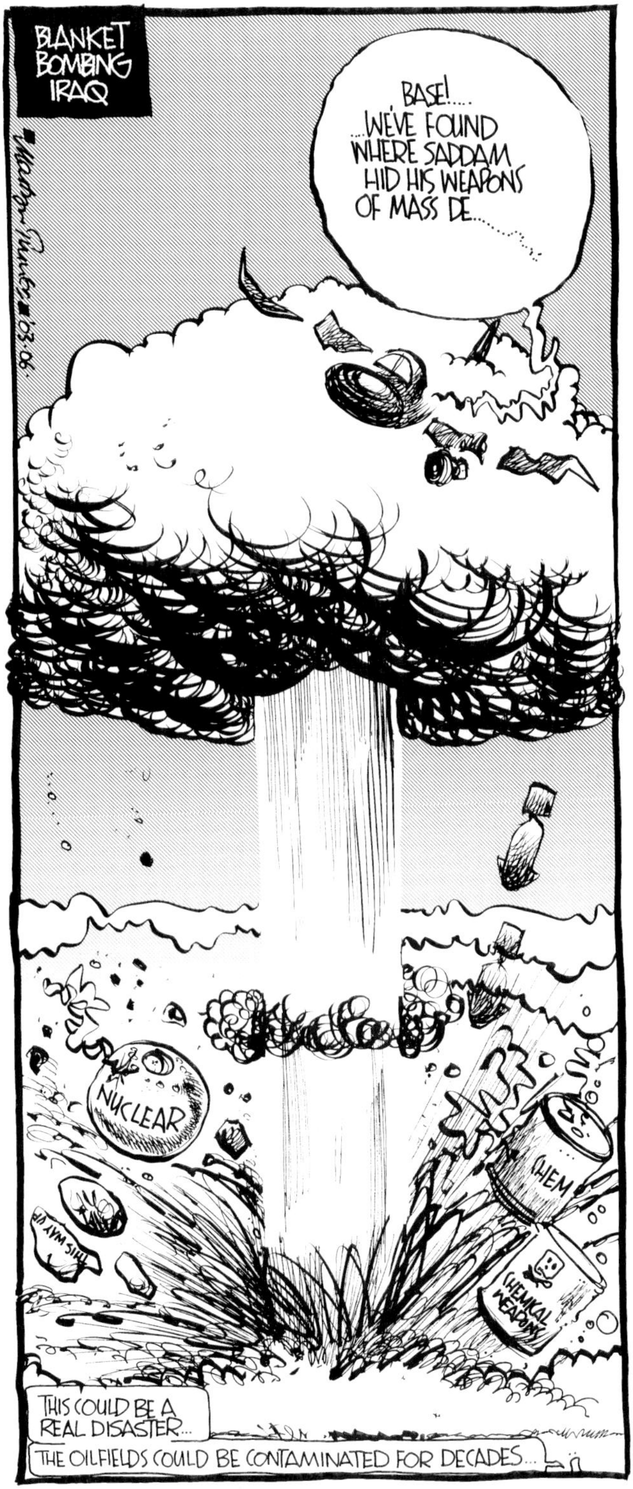
BLANKET BOMBING IRAQ
BASE!.... ...WE'VE FOUND WHERE SADDAM HID HIS WEAPONS OF MASS DE.........
NUCLEAR
CHEM
CHEMICAL WEAPONS
THIS WAY UP
THIS COULD BE A REAL DISASTER...
THE OILFIELDS COULD BE CONTAMINATED FOR DECADES...

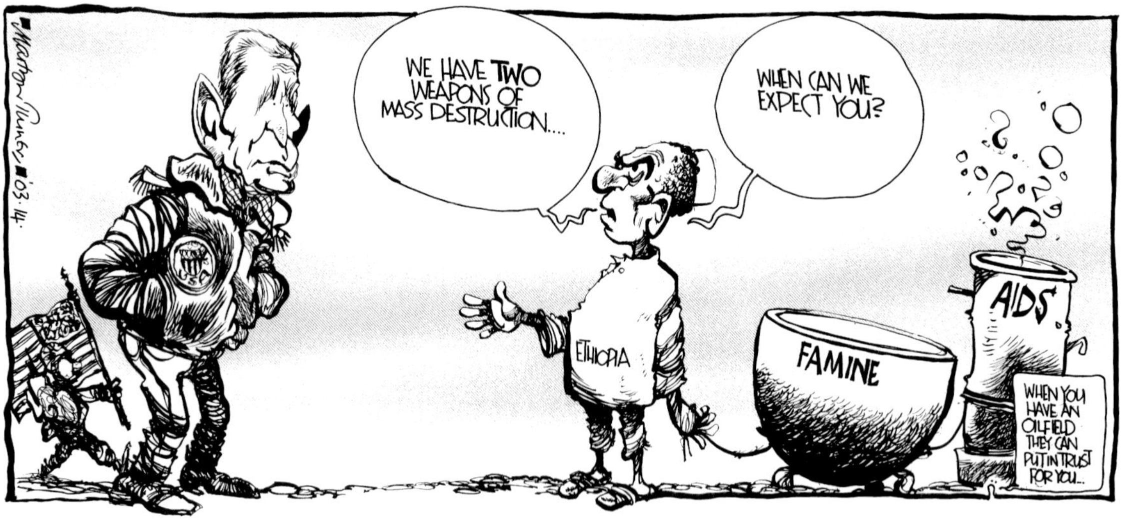

Martyn Turner '03.14.
WE HAVE TWO WEAPONS OF MASS DESTRUCTION....
WHEN CAN WE EXPECT YOU?
ETHIOPIA
FAMINE
AIDS
WHEN YOU HAVE AN OILFIELD THEY CAN PUT IN TRUST FOR YOU...

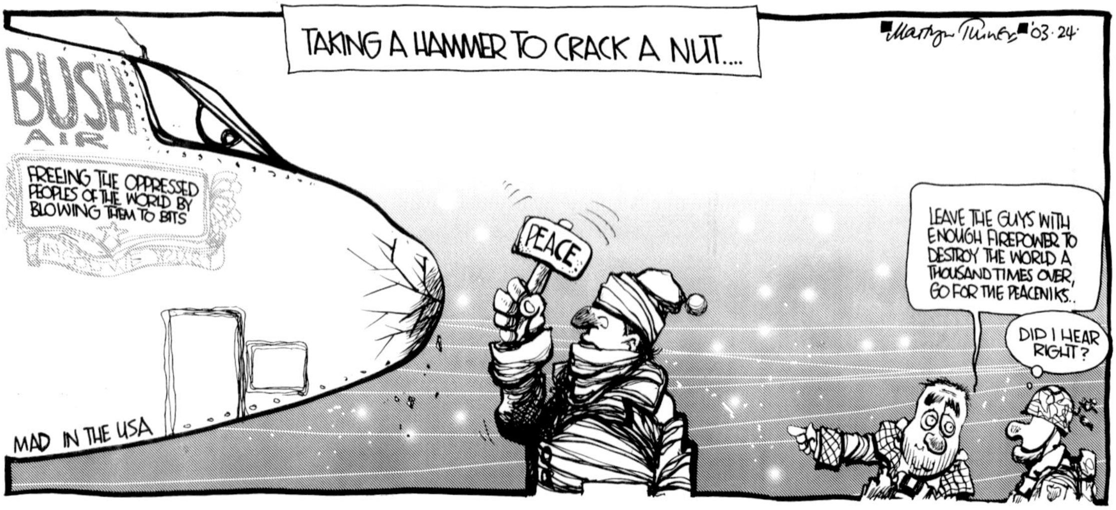

TAKING A HAMMER TO CRACK A NUT....
Martyn Turner '03.24.
BUSH AIR
FREEING THE OPPRESSED PEOPLES OF THE WORLD BY BLOWING THEM TO BITS
PEACE
LEAVE THE GUYS WITH ENOUGH FIREPOWER TO DESTROY THE WORLD A THOUSAND TIMES OVER, GO FOR THE PEACENIKS..
DID I HEAR RIGHT?
MAD IN THE USA

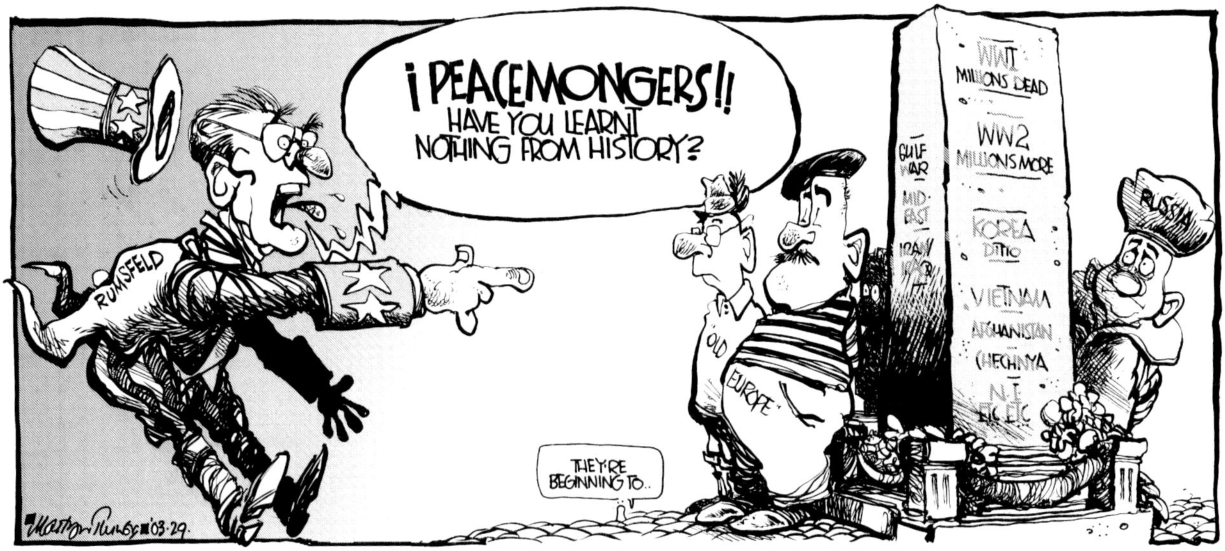

¡PEACEMONGERS!! HAVE YOU LEARNT NOTHING FROM HISTORY?
RUMSFELD
OLD EUROPE
RUSSIA
WW1 MILLIONS DEAD
WW2 MILLIONS MORE
KOREA DITTO
VIETNAM
AFGHANISTAN
CHECHNYA
N.I ETC ETC
GULF WAR
MID EAST
THEY'RE BEGINNING TO..

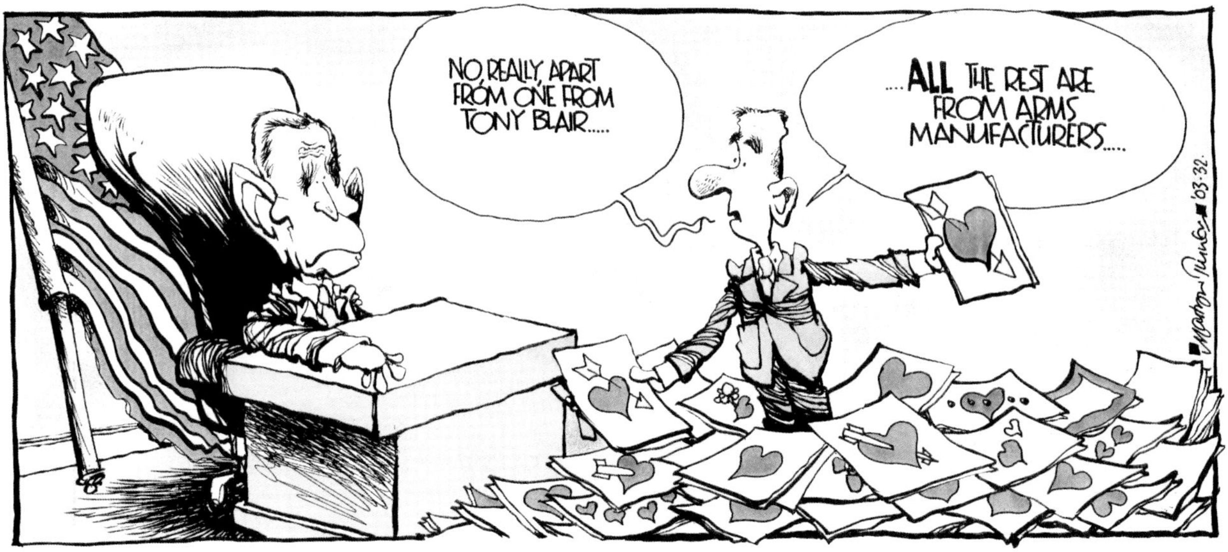

NO, REALLY, APART FROM ONE FROM TONY BLAIR.....
....ALL THE REST ARE FROM ARMS MANUFACTURERS.....

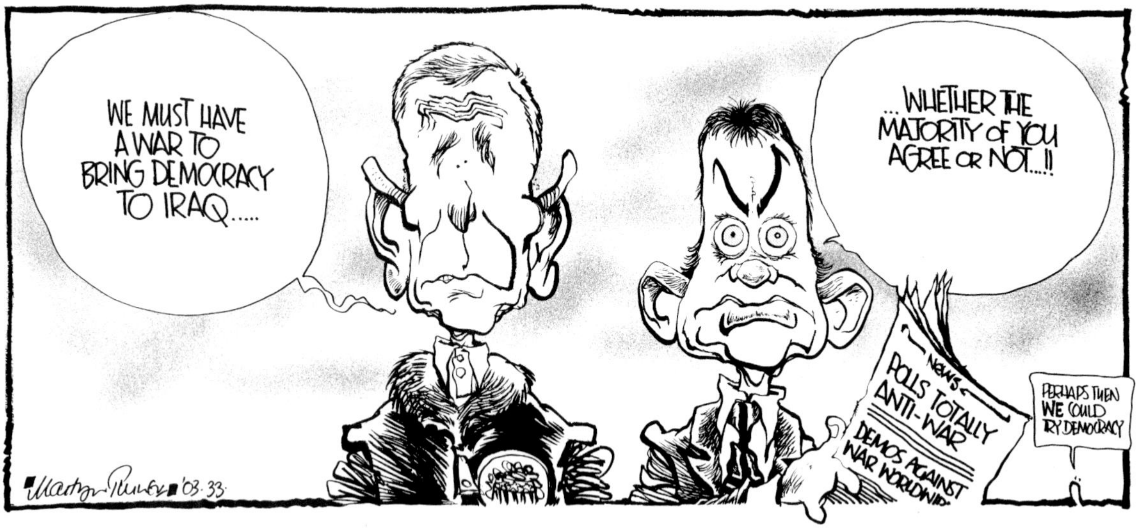
WE MUST HAVE A WAR TO BRING DEMOCRACY TO IRAQ.....
...WHETHER THE MAJORITY OF YOU AGREE OR NOT...!!
NEWS
POLLS TOTALLY ANTI-WAR
DEMOS AGAINST
PERHAPS THEN WE COULD TRY DEMOCRACY

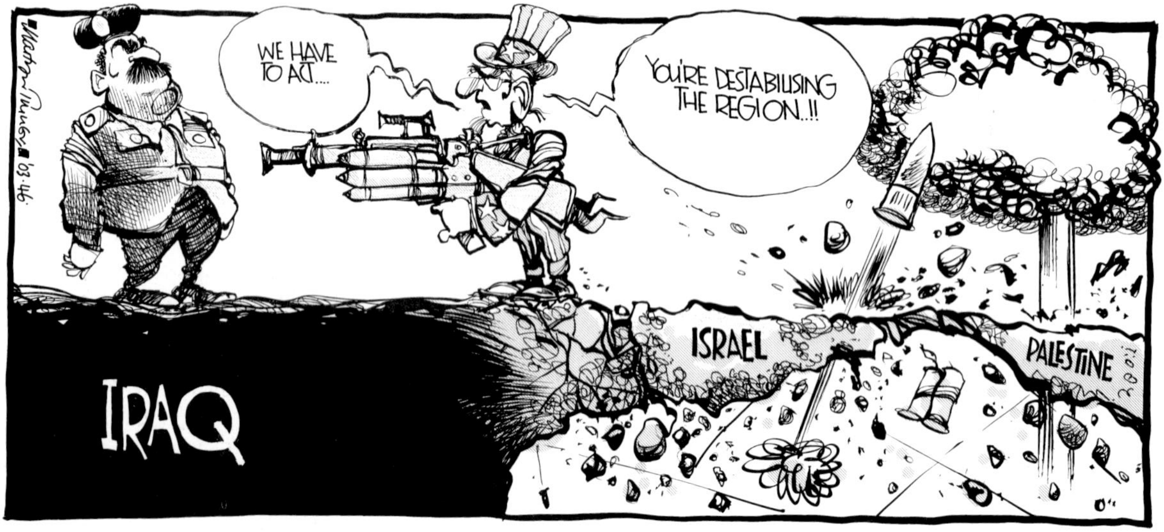
WE HAVE TO ACT....
YOU'RE DESTABILISING THE REGION..!!
ISRAEL
PALESTINE
IRAQ

...I CAN'T GIVE YOU THE NAMES OF THE PEOPLE WHO WILL DIE IN THE FORTHCOMING WAR...
TOMB OF THE UNKNOWN COLLATERAL DAMAGE
TOMB OF THE UNKNOWN IRAQI CONSCRIPT
TOMB OF THE KNOWN TYRANT
TOMB OF THE WESTERN SOLDIER
...BUT HERE IS A LIST OF NAMES OF THE PEOPLE WHO DEFINITELY WON'T DIE IN THE FORTHCOMING WAR.....
GEO. W. BUSH
DICK CHENEY
DONALD RUMSFELD
TONY BLAIR
COLIN POWELL
ETC ETC
WHATEVER HAPPENED TO LEADERS LEADING FROM THE FRONT..?
'03.52.

NATO: NEXT MOVES
USAF
IRAQ
FRANCE
'03.34.

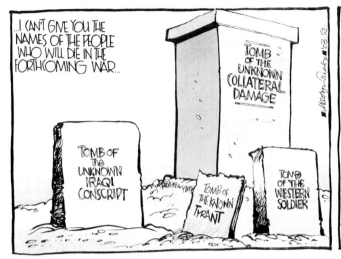

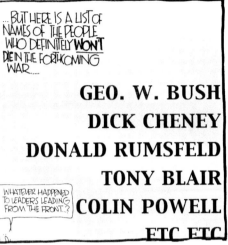

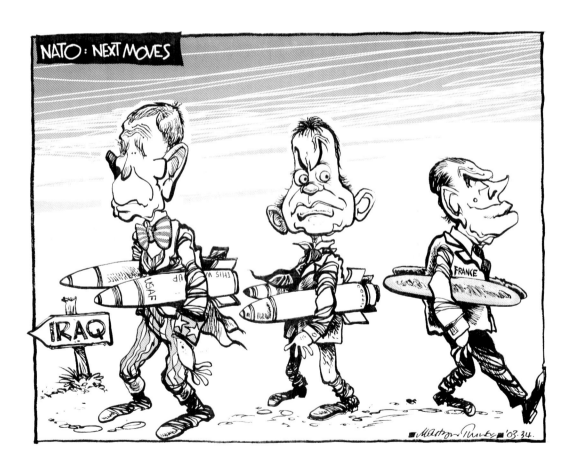

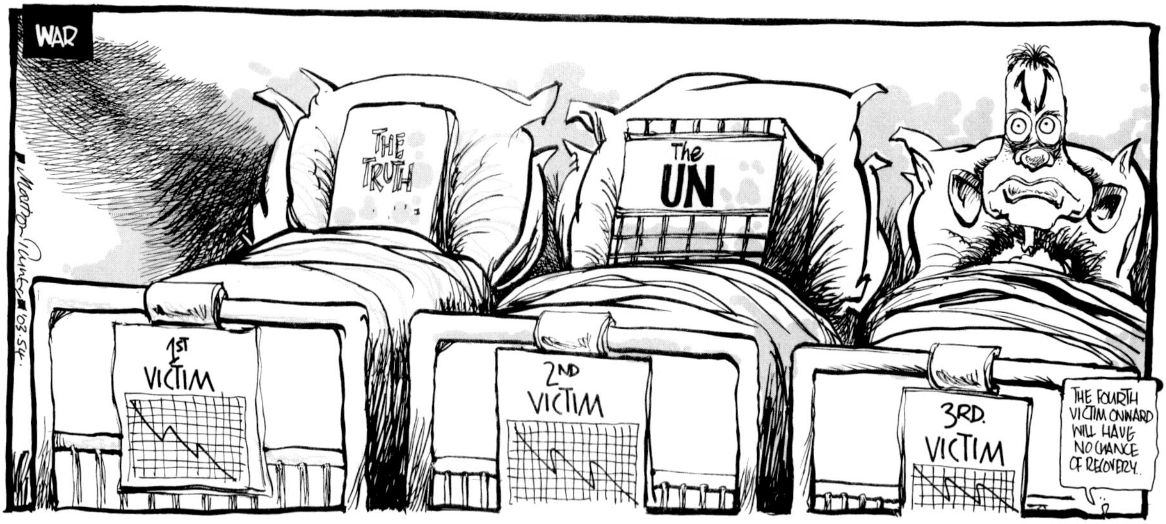
WAR
THE TRUTH
The UN
1ST VICTIM
2ND VICTIM
3RD. VICTIM
THE FOURTH VICTIM ONWARD WILL HAVE NO CHANCE OF RECOVERY...
Martyn Turner '03.54.

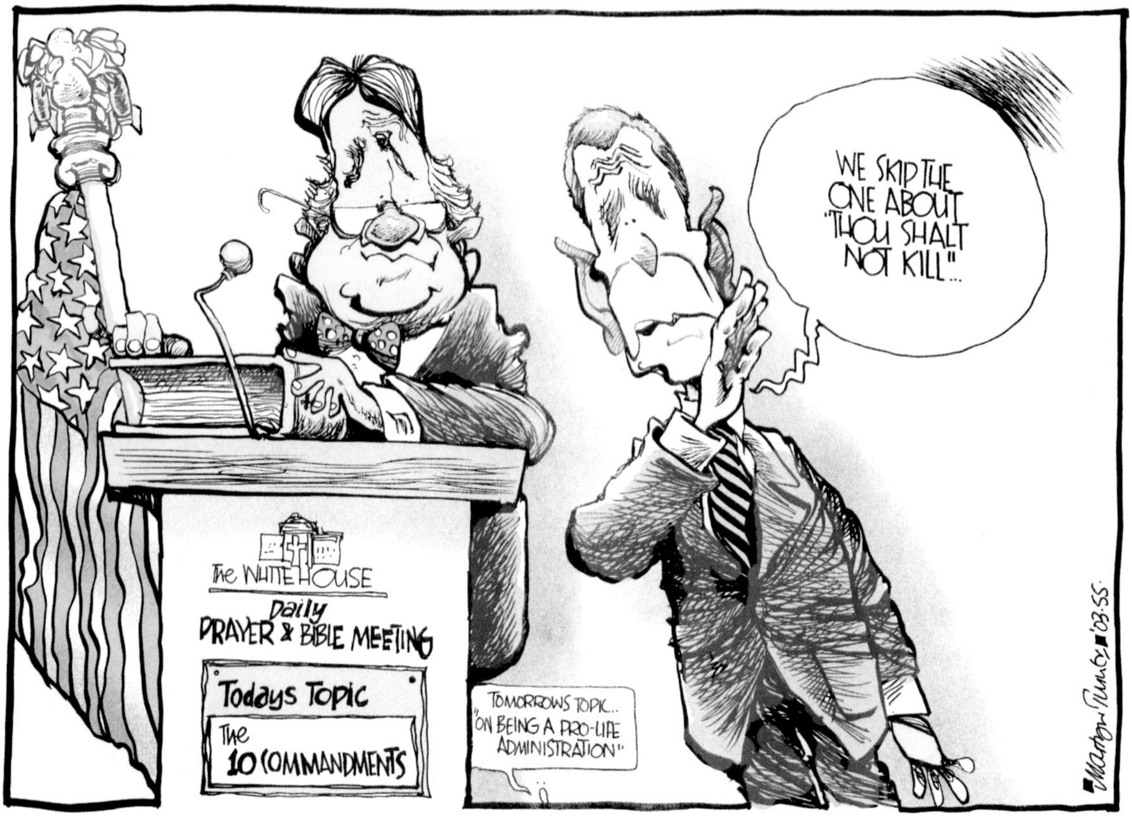
WE SKIP THE ONE ABOUT "THOU SHALT NOT KILL"...
The WHITE HOUSE
Daily PRAYER & BIBLE MEETING
Todays Topic
The 10 COMMANDMENTS
TOMORROWS TOPIC... "ON BEING A PRO-LIFE ADMINISTRATION"
Martyn Turner '03.55.

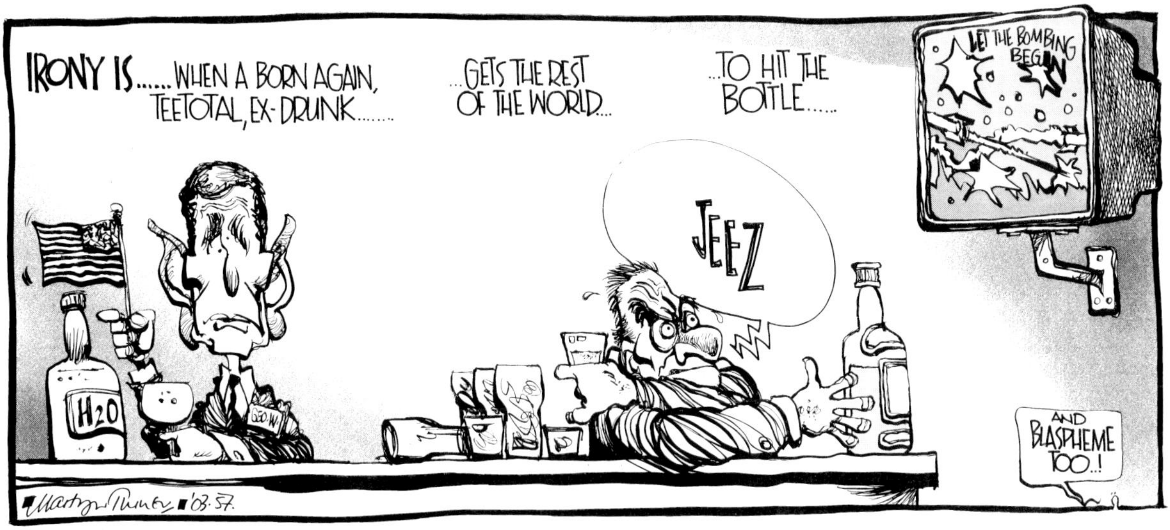
IRONY IS...... WHEN A BORN AGAIN, TEETOTAL, EX-DRUNK........
...GETS THE REST OF THE WORLD....
...TO HIT THE BOTTLE......
LET THE BOMBING BEGIN
H2O
JEEZ
AND BLASPHEME TOO..!
Martyn Turner '03.57.

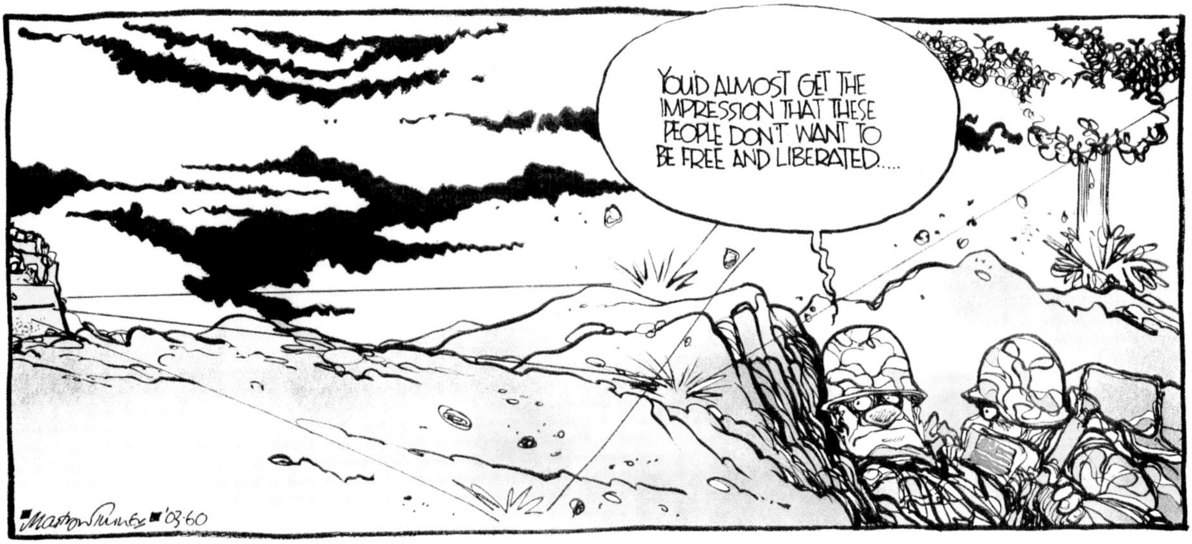
YOU'D ALMOST GET THE IMPRESSION THAT THESE PEOPLE DON'T WANT TO BE FREE AND LIBERATED.....
Martyn Turner '03.60

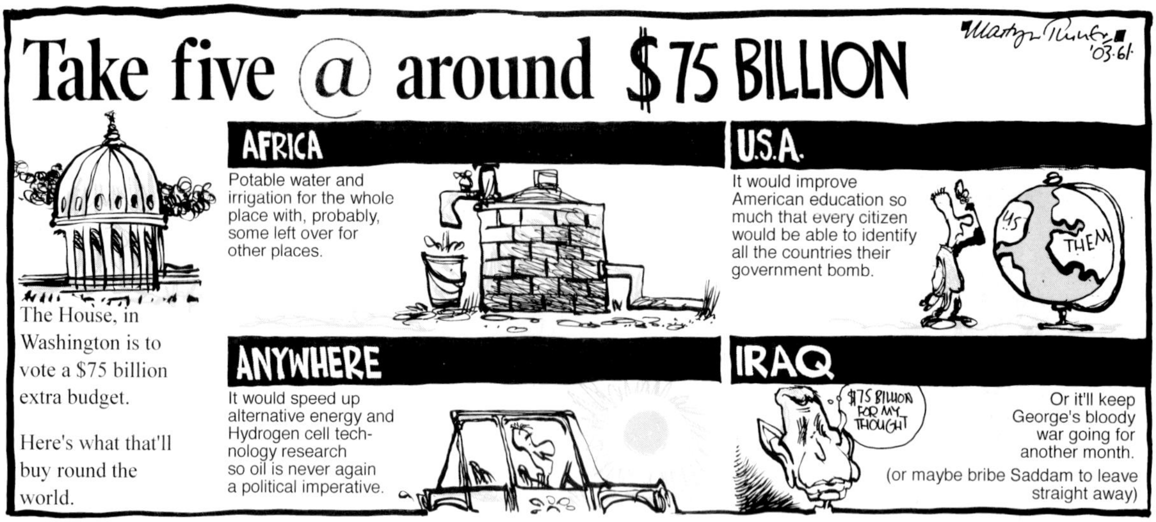
Take five @ around $75 BILLION
Martyn Turner '03.61.
AFRICA
Potable water and irrigation for the whole place with, probably, some left over for other places.
U.S.A.
It would improve American education so much that every citizen would be able to identify all the countries their government bomb.
US
THEM
The House, in Washington is to vote a $75 billion extra budget.
Here's what that'll buy round the world.
ANYWHERE
It would speed up alternative energy and Hydrogen cell technology research so oil is never again a political imperative.
IRAQ
$75 BILLION FOR MY THOUGHT
Or it'll keep George's bloody war going for another month.
(or maybe bribe Saddam to leave straight away)

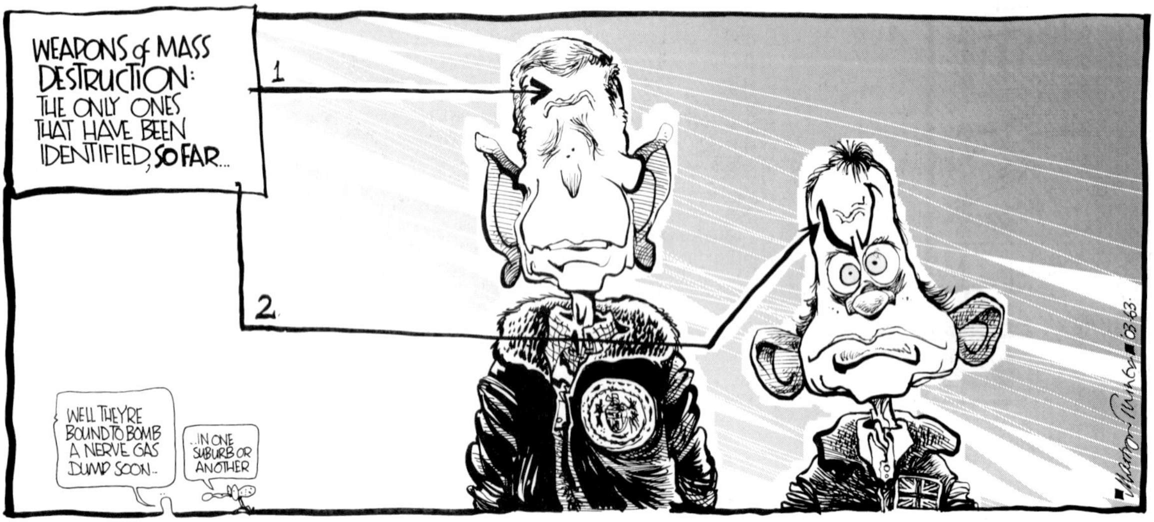
WEAPONS of MASS DESTRUCTION: THE ONLY ONES THAT HAVE BEEN IDENTIFIED, SO FAR...
1.
2.
WELL THEY'RE BOUND TO BOMB A NERVE GAS DUMP SOON..
..IN ONE SUBURB OR ANOTHER
Martyn Turner '03.63.

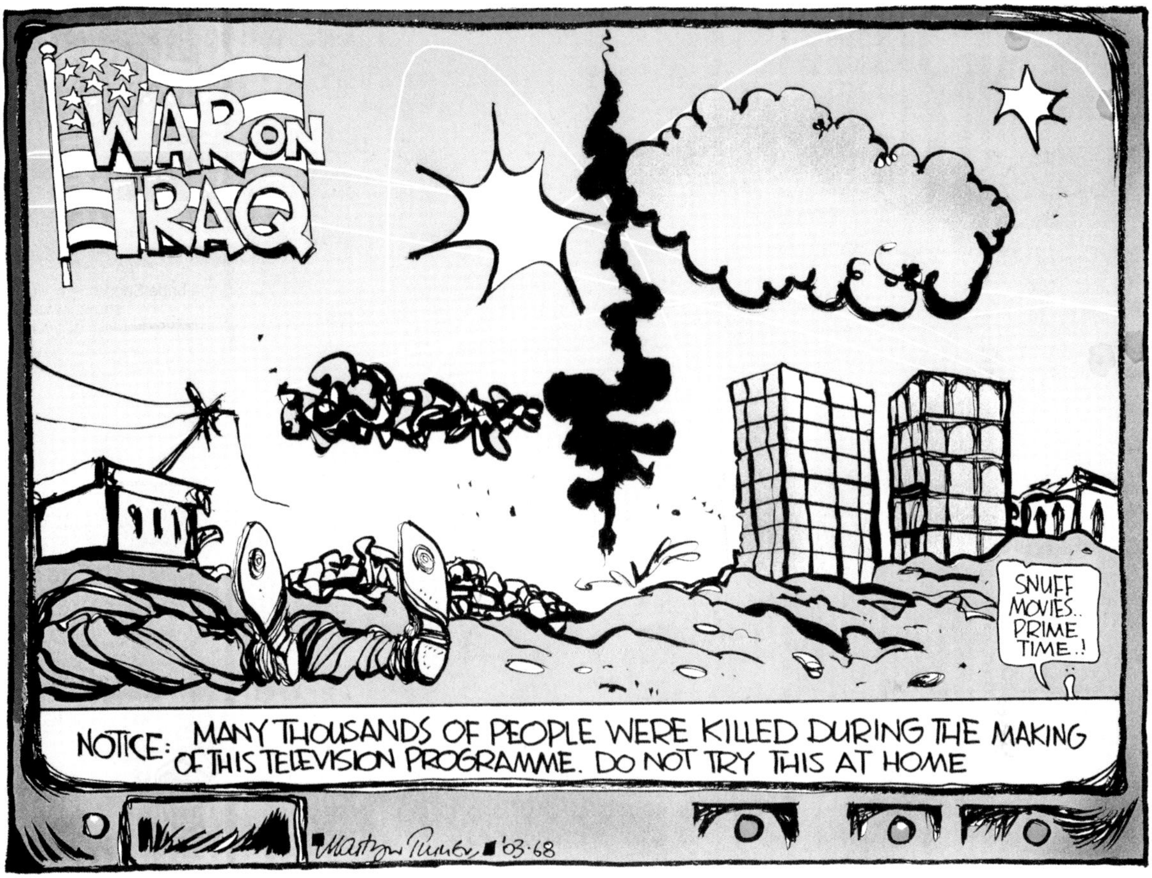
WAR ON IRAQ
SNUFF MOVIES.. PRIME TIME..!
NOTICE: MANY THOUSANDS OF PEOPLE WERE KILLED DURING THE MAKING OF THIS TELEVISION PROGRAMME. DO NOT TRY THIS AT HOME
Martyn Turner '03·68

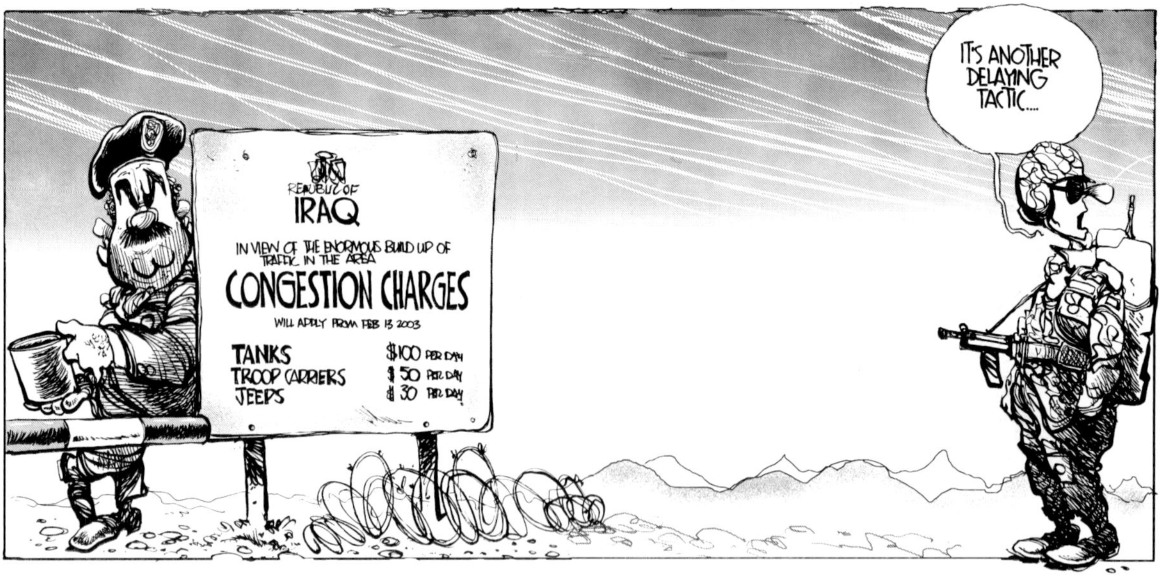
REPUBLIC OF
IRAQ
IN VIEW OF THE ENORMOUS BUILD UP OF TRAFFIC IN THE AREA
CONGESTION CHARGES
WILL APPLY FROM FEB 13 2003
TANKS $100 PER DAY
TROOP CARRIERS $50 PER DAY
JEEPS $30 PER DAY
IT'S ANOTHER DELAYING TACTIC....

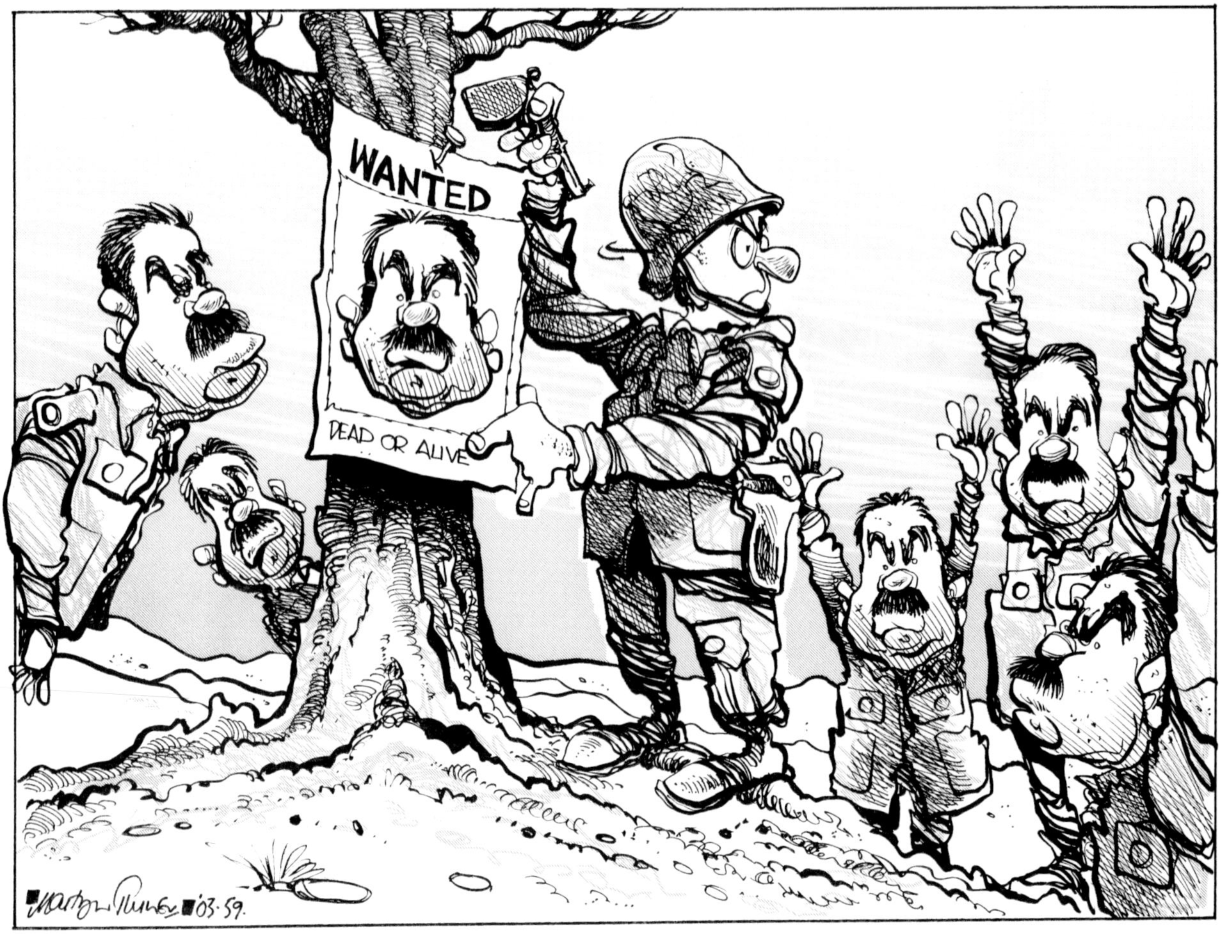
WANTED
DEAD OR ALIVE
Martyn Turner '03.59.

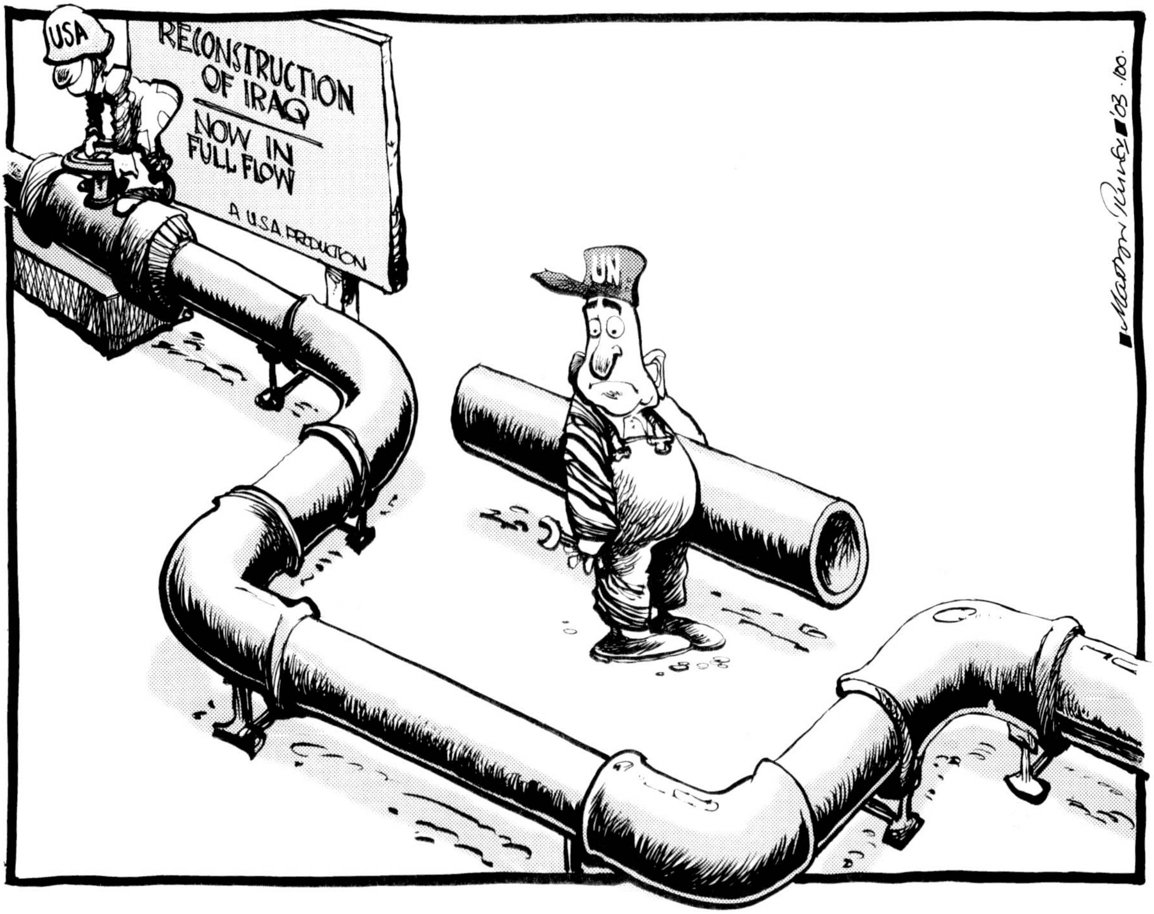
USA
RECONSTRUCTION OF IRAQ
NOW IN FULL FLOW
A U.S.A. PRODUCTION
UN

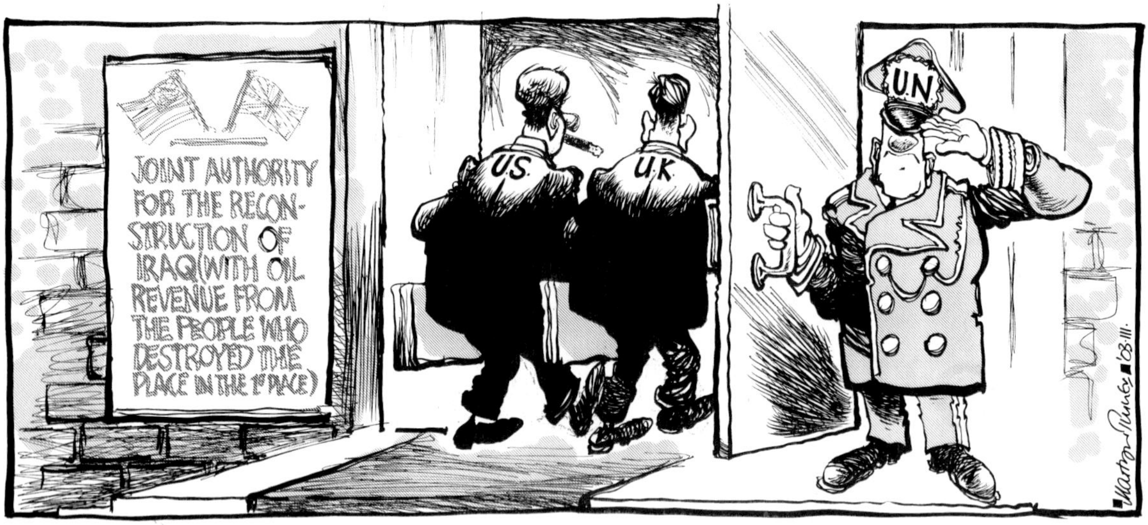
JOINT AUTHORITY FOR THE RECONSTRUCTION OF IRAQ (WITH OIL REVENUE FROM THE PEOPLE WHO DESTROYED THE PLACE IN THE 1st PLACE)
U.S.
U.K.
U.N
Martyn Turner '03.111.

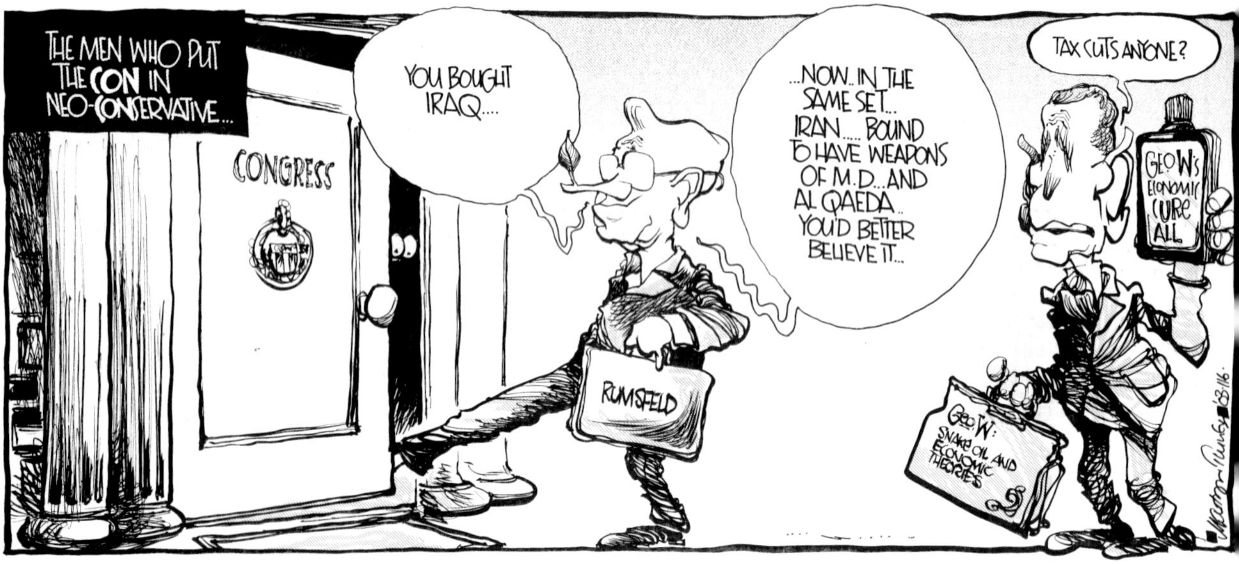
THE MEN WHO PUT THE CON IN NEO-CONSERVATIVE...
CONGRESS
YOU BOUGHT IRAQ....
...NOW.. IN THE SAME SET... IRAN..... BOUND TO HAVE WEAPONS OF M.D...AND AL QAEDA.. YOU'D BETTER BELIEVE IT...
TAX CUTS ANYONE?
GEO W's ECONOMIC CURE ALL
RUMSFELD
GEO W: SNAKE OIL AND ECONOMIC THEORIES
Martyn Turner '03.116.

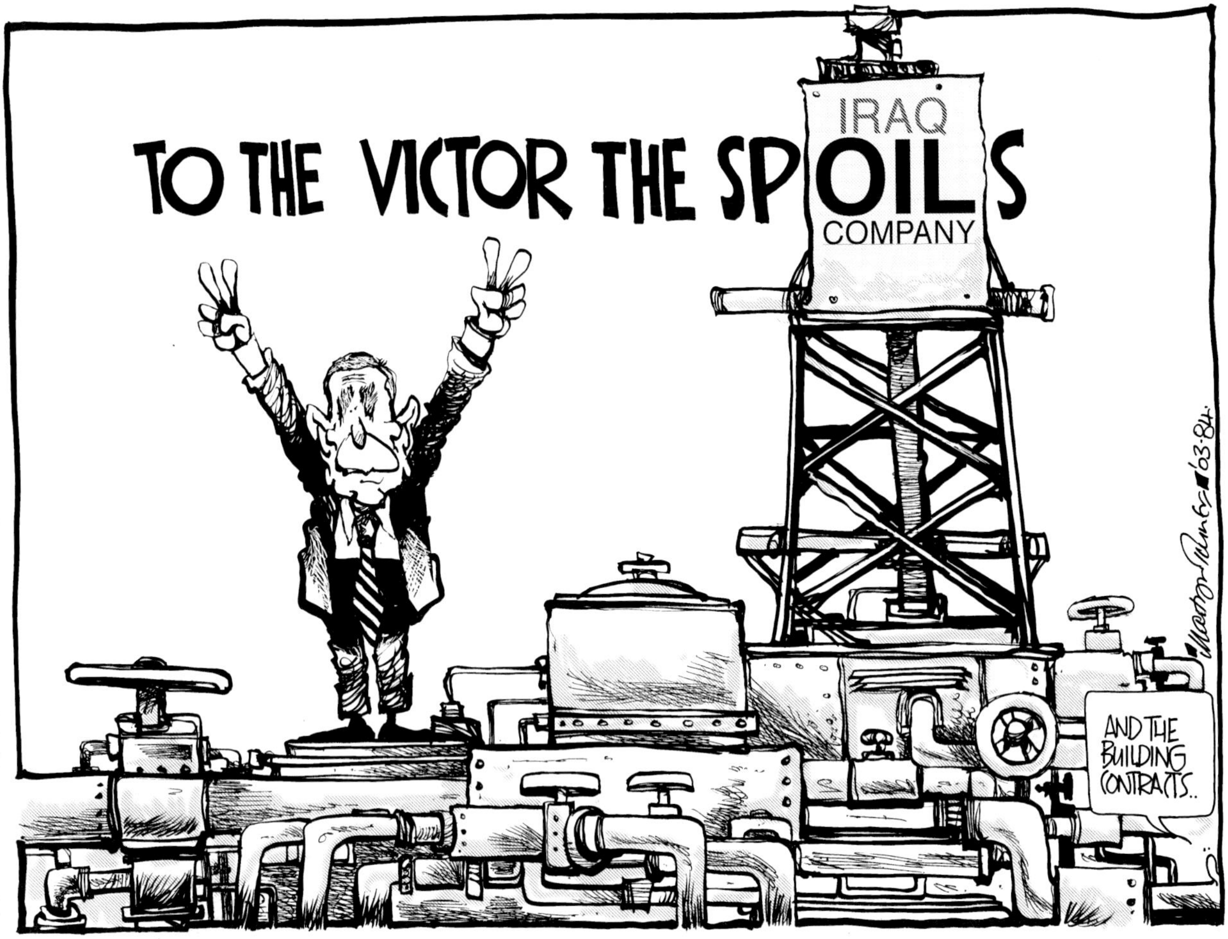
TO THE VICTOR THE SPOILS
IRAQ OIL COMPANY
AND THE BUILDING CONTRACTS..